KF 300 MOL

The American Legal Profession in Crisis

The American Legal Profession in Crisis

in Crisis

RESISTANCE AND RESPONSES TO CHANGE

James E. Moliterno

OXFORD
UNIVERSITY PRESS

OXFORD
UNIVERSITY PRESS

Oxford University Press is a department of the University of Oxford. It furthers the University's objective of excellence in research, scholarship, and education by publishing worldwide.

Oxford   New York
Auckland   Cape Town   Dar es Salaam   Hong Kong   Karachi   Kuala Lumpur   Madrid
Melbourne   Mexico City   Nairobi   New Delhi   Shanghai   Taipei   Toronto

With offices in
Argentina   Austria   Brazil   Chile   Czech Republic   France   Greece   Guatemala   Hungary
Italy   Japan   Poland   Portugal   Singapore   South Korea   Switzerland   Thailand
Turkey   Ukraine   Vietnam

Oxford is a registered trade mark of Oxford University Press in the UK and certain other countries.

Published in the United States of America by
Oxford University Press
198 Madison Avenue, New York, NY 10016

© Oxford University Press 2013

Library of Congress Cataloging-in-Publication Data
Moliterno, James E., 1953-
   The American legal profession in crisis : resistance and responses to change /
James E. Moliterno.
      pages cm
   Includes bibliographical references and index.
   ISBN 978-0-19-991763-1 (hardback)
      1. Practice of law—United States. 2. Practice of law—United States—History—
20th century. 3. Law—Social aspects—United States. 4. Social change—
United States. I. Title.
   KF300.M648 2013
   340.023'73—dc23
                                                                            2012043544

9 8 7 6 5 4 3 2 1
Printed in the United States of America on acid-free paper

Note to Readers
This publication is designed to provide accurate and authoritative information in regard to the subject matter covered. It is based upon sources believed to be accurate and reliable and is intended to be current as of the time it was written. It is sold with the understanding that the publisher is not engaged in rendering legal, accounting, or other professional services. If legal advice or other expert assistance is required, the services of a competent professional person should be sought. Also, to confirm that the information has not been affected or changed by recent developments, traditional legal research techniques should be used, including checking primary sources where appropriate.

*(Based on the Declaration of Principles jointly adopted by a Committee of the
American Bar Association and a Committee of Publishers and Associations.)*

> You may order this or any other Oxford University Press publication
> by visiting the Oxford University Press website at www.oup.com

To my parents, Nick and Mary Moliterno, for their wisdom and their gentle ways.
To Dick Aynes, without whose professional influence and inspiration,
I would not have embarked on an academic career.
To Valerie Moliterno, for her unending love and patience.

{ CONTENTS }

{ ACKNOWLEDGMENTS }

I am grateful for the generous research support of this project by Washington & Lee University in the form of summer grants and a semester leave. I am also grateful to my former school, The College of William & Mary, for its support.

Many Research Assistants contributed to this work. At Washington & Lee, John Eller, Andrew Atkins, Amelia Guckenberg, Leona Krasner, Greg Chakmakas, Matt Sorenson, Jillian Nyhoff, Nancy Anderson, Gina Lauterio, and Kelly Felgenhauer. At William & Mary, Chad Carder, John Pollom, and Anne Sommers.

I am also grateful for the business sensibilities of Valerie Moliterno—they made many important contributions to my thinking about certain aspects of this work.

{ PREFACE }

The message of the book is that the legal profession tends to look inward and backward when faced with crisis and uncertainty. I will recommend that greater advances could be made by looking outward to find in society and culture the causes of and connections with the legal profession's crisis. Doing so would allow the profession to grow with the society; solve problems with, rather than against, the flow of society; and be more attuned to the society the profession claims to serve.

The book examines, for example, how the legal profession reacted to the Watergate events and the attendant public loss of confidence in authority, how it reacted to the rush of immigrants into the country and into the legal profession at the start of the 20th century, and how it reacted to perceived threats of communist infiltration in the 1920s and 1950s. The book will end with a treatment of how the profession is reacting to the current economic crisis and then finally a chapter to tie the threads together.

The book does not attempt to solve any particular crisis, including the current one. Rather, the book's aim is to focus attention on the legal profession's mode of crisis management. Understanding how the profession deals with crisis is a productive step toward effectively resolving any particular crisis.

In each of the book's chapters, I isolate a time and source of crisis in the profession. Often there is a parallel crisis or development in society generally. Always there are societal influences that are a generalized form of the crisis being felt by the legal profession. In each chapter, I attempt to answer a series of questions:

What is the nature of the crisis?

What was the surrounding legal history of the time?

What, if any, relationship existed between the crisis and the surrounding general history?

What did the profession do about the crisis?

What were the results of the profession's actions?

Were the profession's actions inward or outward focused?

Perhaps the 21st century's legal profession can learn from, and improve upon, the 20th-century American legal profession's approach to change and crisis.

What Crisis? Who Speaks for a Profession?

> I am by no means blind to the failings of the legal profession....I know
> that we are often too conservative. We don't realize that the world is
> changing. We don't sufficiently look ahead. Instead of trying to help
> in so shaping changes that they accomplish benefits with a minimum
> of disturbance, we often stand stubbornly for the maintenance
> of methods that have been outworn.
>
> Henry P. Chandler, *What the Bar Does Today*,
> 7 AM. L. SCH. REV. 1017, 1022 (1930–34)

In 1930 as in 1900 as in 2013, this is the mode of crisis management and regulation of the American legal profession. The legal profession tends to look inward and backward when faced with crisis and uncertainty. Greater advances could be made by looking outward and forward to find in society and culture the causes of and connections with the legal profession's crises. Doing so would allow the profession to grow with society, solve problems *with* rather than *against* the flow of society, and be more attuned to the society the profession claims to serve.

I. What Is Crisis?

The law is a crisis-prone profession. It seems that every decade or so, events take hold that cause the profession to self-identify a professional crisis: the immigrant wave of the first two decades of the 1900s, the communist scares of the 1920s and late 1940s and 1950s, the civil rights movement and associated social activist lawyering of the 1960s and 1970s, Watergate, the litigation explosion crisis of the 1980s, the civility (and associated professionalism) crisis of the late 1980s and 1990s, and technology and globalization threats of the first decade of the 21st century. In each, the profession looked predominantly to maintain its status quo against the odds posed by a changing world. Occasionally the threat subsided for reasons entirely unassociated with the profession's efforts (e.g., the communist infiltration crisis). More often, the world changed to the profession's dismay, and the walls of resistance built by the profession were overrun.

In some ways, the American legal profession is always in crisis. By their very nature, American lawyers and courts find themselves at the center both of social movements and of more transient, private controversies alike. Being inside such events produces a feeling of crisis, an unsettled sense. That day-to-day placement of the legal profession in controversy's path creates a perpetual sense of crisis. But that perpetual sense of crisis is not the subject of this book. Instead, this book is about periods in the history of the American legal profession when it self-announced a state of professional crisis. In these special times, the crisis sense was different— more pronounced, to be sure, but even different in kind from the usual drama of courts and lawyers and deals. Outside these special times, the profession is confident in the midst of its daily regime of routine controversy, sees its place rightly there, and sees that the profession is a steadying influence amid crisis and controversy. Unlike the day-to-day sense of crisis, during these special crisis times that are the book's subject, the profession itself sees the crisis, feels and reacts to the crisis, and often even fears it. During these times, the profession is unsure of itself: less confident about its future and its place. This book is about some of those special times and about the profession's response. Does the profession see itself and its difficulties during such times as part of the larger society's problems and attributes? Does the profession respond to its crises by looking inward or outward?

II. Inward and Backward

My thesis is that the profession too often looks inward to diagnose and solve its crises. Doing so has caused the profession to be a late-arriving member of society during times of change. Doing so has caused the profession too often to fail in what could have been a leadership role in society. Rather, the profession has too often seen itself as a last bastion of a prior time, clinging too tightly to its past and failing to grow in step with world developments. This is not to say that the profession should dismiss its core attributes at the first signs of societal change; it is to say that a perceptive growing with change would be preferable to consistent, persistent resistance to change. We credit the greatest lawyers with being able to anticipate and predict the course of the law's change and the readiness of society for change. The legal profession has been a poor lawyer by this measure. The legal profession, as an institution, most often stays blind to change that is happening all around it.

One window on this long resistance to change can be seen in the apt remarks of Thomas Francis Howe, the 1922 chairman of the Professional Ethics and Grievances Committee:

> Ever increasing complexities of modern business, the rapid changes in its methods, and the relations of lawyers thereto, are constantly raising questions concerning proper professional conduct that were not contemplated—or even dreamed of—when the [1908] canons were prepared. As a consequence the

committees of local bar associations find that the canons are not only silent on many of the questions they are now called upon to answer, but do not even furnish any general principle applicable thereto.[1]

Already badly out of date in 1922, the American Bar Association's (ABA) 1908 Canons, the first effort at an official, national statement of lawyer ethics, lasted with only modest amendment until 1969.

This resistance to change could be characterized as careful, deliberate growth, resistant only to precipitous, rash change. The ABA founders' motives were summarized in this more positive light by a confidant of ABA founder Simeon Baldwin:

[W]hen innovation and change are demanded in every quarter, there ought to be found somewhere in our system a calm, conservative power which can expose fallacies, point out flaws, and suggest reforms without violence or shock to our government.[2]

Calm in the face of crisis is an attractive trait. But as will be seen in the coming chapters, the profession's reaction to crisis varied by the nature of the crisis but always served maintenance of the professional status quo. When outsiders threatened to invade the bar's homogeneity, the profession reacted rashly and often without much reflection (the influx of turn-of-the-20th-century immigrants or the communist infiltration threat, for example). By contrast, when social, economic, or technological change was occurring around the profession, the profession's calm became intractability and myopia (the civility crisis and the current technological, globalization, and economic developments, for example). In either event, the profession sought the status quo and resisted "innovation and change [that was being] demanded," even when change was inevitable or desirable.

One early ABA leader, James M. Beck, articulated well just how deep and sweeping was their wish for the past to be maintained:

In music, its fundamental canons have been thrown aside and discord has been established for harmony as its ideal. Its culmination—jazz—is a musical crime.

In the plastic arts, all the laws of form and the criteria of beauty have been swept aside by the futurists, cubists, vorticists, tactilists and other aesthetic Bolsheviki.

In poetry, where beauty of rhythm, melody of sound and nobility of thought were once regarded as the true tests, we now have the exaltation of the grotesque and brutal; and hundreds of poets are feebly echoing the barbaric yawp of Walt Whitman without the redeeming merit of his occasional sublimity of thought.

---

[1] Thomas Francis Howe, *The Proposed Amendments to the Bylaws*, 8 A.B.A. J. 436 (1922).
[2] Letter from Senator Charles Jones to Simeon Baldwin (August 10, 1878) in SIMEON BALDWIN, THE FOUNDING OF THE AMERICAN BAR ASSOCIATION 682 (1917).

In commerce, the revolt is one against the purity of standards and the integrity of business morals. Who can question that this is counterfeit? Science is prostituted to deceive the public by cloaking the increasing deterioration in quality. The blatant medium of advertising has become so mendacious as to defeat its own purpose.

In the greater sphere of social life, we find the same revolt against institutions which have the sanction of the past. Laws which mark the decent restraints of print, speech and dress have in recent decades been increasingly disregarded. The very foundations of the great and primitive institutions of mankind—like the family, the church and the state—have been shaken. Nature itself is defied. Thus, the fundamental difference in sex is disregarded by social and political movements which ignore the permanent differentiation of the social function ordained by God himself.[3]

It is possible to characterize the discrete crises described and analyzed in this book as a single, continuous crisis of professionalism. In *Lawyers' Ideals/Lawyers' Practices,* Trubek and Nelson[4] saw it this way. It is plainly true that the several responses to the several discrete crises have common elements. But while they may all be a part of the legal profession's effort to hold tight to the professionalism ideal and its benefits, each of the crises chronicled in this book presented a unique challenge and warrants individual treatment. Each period presented a unique mixture of sometimes overlapping elements.

The profession's focus, inward or outward, drives its understanding and its response to a looming crisis. By inward and outward focused, I mean a couple of things. First, were the profession's actions considerate of the outside world developments, or were they primarily focused on attributes of the profession? Second, did the profession attempt to adjust to world developments, or did it attempt to maintain the profession's status quo in the face of change? Looking inward regarding a crisis means defining the crisis as belonging to the profession rather than the society generally. So, for example, the civility crisis was defined as a crisis of lawyer behavior without reference to the simple fact that lawyers were members of a broader society that was becoming far more competitive. Looking inward means searching for solutions to problems within the profession's ethos, largely assuming that any problem may be solved without professional change or adjustment. Looking outward means locating a professional woe within the broader societal context—relating lawyers' troubles to corresponding trends and phenomena in the culture generally. In some instances, the more apt descriptors will be "backward" and "forward." These terms give a more temporal than spatial sense. The comparative exists

---

[3] James Beck, *The Spirit of Lawlessness*, 46 A.B.A. REP. 167, 171 (1921); *See also* MORTON KELLER, IN DEFENSE OF YESTERDAY: JAMES M. BECK AND THE POLITICS OF CONSERVATISM 1861–1936 197 (Coward-McCann, Inc., New York, 1958).

[4] ROBERT L. NELSON & DAVID M. TRUBEK, ARENAS OF PROFESSIONAL: THE PROFESSIONAL IDEOLOGIES OF LAWYERS IN CONTEXT 177–214 (1992).

on both spectra: from inward to outward and from backward to forward. Both sets help explain the profession's manner of seeing a crisis and framing a response. Whether characterized on one spectrum or the other, backward or inward vision produces the same result: service of the status quo.

The profession, it turns out, serves the status quo in multiple ways. At times, serving the status quo means making significant changes that will fend off outsiders or cultural change. At other times, serving the status quo means doing as little as possible in the vain hope that change will pass the profession by as if it were a bad dream rendered irrelevant by the morning light. In either event, the profession loses. Change comes and washes over the profession's walls.

III. Who Speaks for the Legal Profession?

In describing how the legal profession reacts to crisis, the first step is to determine who speaks for the legal profession. The profession has spoken through different voices and entities at different times in its history. The question is not susceptible of an absolutely clear answer, but there is value in providing as much of an answer as can be given. A broad approach to answering the "who speaks" question seems advantageous. I mean to include the views of the usual three branches of the American legal profession: the practicing bar, the judiciary, and the legal academy. I include in the practicing bar lawyers in service of government, many of whom have at various times been important spokespersons for the profession.

The first two branches, the practicing bar and the judiciary, have been important speakers for the profession since it was fair to claim that there *was* an American legal profession.

A. JUDGES

Important public statements by judges have marked developments in the legal profession. A few prominent judges were among the leaders of the early bar associations, including the ABA. Warren Burger arguably announced the profession's response to the "civility crisis" in the 1980s. Others critiqued the profession's response to crisis, such as Justice Douglas's warnings about the persecution of lawyers who deigned to represent those accused of communist ties.[5] Current Justices continue to chime in on issues affecting the legal profession. Justice Roberts challenged the relevance of the scholarly contribution of the academic branch in 2012, echoing words written for the *Michigan Law Review* 20 years earlier by former professor and Judge Harry Edwards.

---

[5] William O. Douglas, *The Black Silence of Fear*, N.Y. Times Mag., Jan. 13, 1952, at 7.

But more crucial than any statements by individual judges, or even the important organizational voice of the Conference of Chief Justices, the state judiciary
has spoken for the legal profession as its chief regulator. The judiciary has long
claimed the right to regulate the legal profession. In early times, when the practice
of law was primarily court practice, the notion that lawyers are officers of the court
strongly supported the claim. In the main, it is this court power to regulate that has
been delegated to state bar associations. In a real way, when a state bar association
speaks or acts, it does so on behalf of its state supreme court. (In a few states, the
legislature has claimed this power and delegated it to bar associations.) Thus, for
example, when state courts adopted the ABA's model ethics codes as their own, it
was the power of courts to regulate and supervise lawyers that allowed them to
speak for the legal profession. With few exceptions, mainly in low-status courts,
American judges have all been lawyers. This American phenomenon contrasts with
the norm in continental Europe, where most judges train to be judges and are never
lawyers; and with regimes such as those in China, where judges need not be and
usually are not law trained at all. Through this device, courts (and occasionally legislatures acting on the same power and often dominated by lawyer-members) speak
for the American legal profession.

B. LAWYERS AND THEIR ORGANIZATIONS

Charles Warren has amply demonstrated the influence of the early cadres of lawyers, especially those in Virginia, New York, Massachusetts, and Pennsylvania.[6]
Until the ABA began asserting itself as the proxy for the American legal profession around the turn of the 20th century, the profession was perhaps too loose to
be called an organized profession. Bar admission rules were almost nonexistent
during much of the 19th century, in part but not exclusively the result of generalized professional diminishment during Jacksonian times. Organizations of lawyers
in the United States did not follow the pattern of the British Inns. Instead, the
loose relationship among lawyers during the first three fourths of the 19th century
encouraged the shrewd and clever.[7]

> For most of the 19th century, no organization even pretended to speak for the
> bar as a whole, or any substantial part, or to govern the conduct of lawyers.
> Lawyers formed associations, mainly social, from time to time; but there was
> no general bar group until the last third of the century.[8]

---

[6] CHARLES WARREN, A HISTORY OF THE AMERICAN BAR; *see generally* (William S. Hein & Co.
1990) (1911).
[7] *See, e.g.,* JOSEPH G. BALDWIN, THE FLUSH TIMES OF ALABAMA AND MISSISSIPPI: A SERIES OF
SKETCHES (1854), *reprinted in* NOLAN, at 113–115. ("The older lawyers kept their experience 'as a
close monopoly,' forcing younger lawyers to 'run a gauntlet of technicalities' at a 'considerable
tuition fee to be paid by [the young lawyers'] clients.")
[8] LAWRENCE M. FRIEDMAN, HISTORY OF AMERICAN LAW 648 (2d ed. 1985).

The profession began to organize in earnest in the 1870s as state and local bar associations sprang up. The Bar of the City of New York, founded for the profession's "protect[ion], pur[ifaction] and preserv[ation],"[9] was easily the most prominent among a set of only marginally successful new enterprises. The ABA was founded at Sarasota Springs in 1878 by an exclusive group of mostly corporate lawyers. The earliest ABA leaders became lawyers at a time when university education for lawyers was unusual. Yet of the first 58 presidents of the ABA, 75 percent had some undergraduate education, and 59 percent had some university legal education.[10] The earliest among them had grown into prominence before the dawn of corporate power and their own places of influence were grown into rather than trained for. A second generation of ABA leadership, those who led it beginning in the early 20th century, formed their professional careers as corporate men.[11]

Early in its existence, the ABA's claims to represent the profession were hollow. By design, it represented a sliver of the profession, the so-called best men at the bar. Nonetheless, its assertions and actions did represent the actions of the most powerful segment of the profession, the segment that had the most influence. Its actions made things happen: higher educational standards, the spread of ethics codes, and changes in bar admission policies.[12] So although the early ABA had no formal power and in reality spoke for only a small segment of the bar, it effectively spoke for the profession.

1. Early Organizational Leaders and Speakers

Of those early speakers for the profession, a good bit is known. The earliest leaders of the ABA were learning how to be corporation lawyers because they had not trained to be so. Most of their professional lives had preceded the dawn of corporate power. But learn they did. A significant number of these early leaders represented railroad interests. Most had a core of their active practice representing corporations. Later in the ABA's still early years (the second 25 years of its existence), the leaders tended to have trained to be corporate lawyers.[13] While they were as much the gentlemen as the first leaders, they were far narrower in their interests. It has been said that while John W. Davis loved to read history, Simeon Baldwin loved to write it.[14] The second generation of early speakers for the profession were more narrowly focused on commerce than their predecessors had been.

---

[9] *Professional Organizations*, 6 ALBANY L. J. 233 (1873); Walter B. Hill, *Bar Associations*, 5 GA. B. ASS'N. REP. at 75 (1888).

[10] JAMES GRAFTON ROGERS, AMERICAN BAR LEADERS, 1878–1928 (1932); EDSON R. SUNDERLAND & WILLIAM J. JAMESON, HISTORY OF THE AMERICAN BAR ASSOCIATION AND ITS WORK (1953).

[11] *Id.*

[12] *See* chapter 2.

[13] John Austin Matzko, The Early Years of the American Bar Association, 1878–1928 at 507 (1984) (dissertation, University of Virginia) (on file with author).

[14] WILLIAM H. HARBAUGH, LAWYER'S LAWYER: THE LIFE OF JOHN W. DAVIS 378 (1973).

The first generation of presidents were almost Lincolnesque in their fond recollections of circuit-riding representation in the frontier. The first ABA president, James Overton Broadhead, produced diaries recalling the "exhilaration and adventure of [his] circuit-riding youth."[15] The romantic image of the young lawyer is enhanced by mentions of saddle bags packed with lunches and code books and Blackstone, "trying an action for forcible entry and detainer" for a fee of "ten Mexican dollars," arguing points of law with fellow lawyer-travelers, and "resting on the green grass with a saddle for a pillow."[16]

Charles Freeman Libby was perhaps the first example of the *second* generation of presidents, those who were born to corporate practice.[17] His remarks as president to his organization in 1910 followed those of the then-almost unknown president of Princeton, and later president of the United States, Woodrow Wilson. Wilson's remarks were not well received by the ABA members, as he provided them with an "onslaught" on all things corporate, which is to say, all things regarding the audience members' clients.[18] But Libby's remarks "on the Constitution, in the good old way lawyers love" were seen as "an adequate antidote to the disturbing gentleman from Princeton."[19] From Broadhead to Libby and on to the end of the 1930s, the tale of the ABA presidents' careers told the story of the changing exemplar of the leading lawyer from a country lawyer traveling from courtroom to courtroom, to a corporate man of office-practice fame.

Although all early ABA presidents represented railroads, utility companies, and other corporate interests, it would be an overstatement to say they *only* represented corporate interests. Occasionally they even represented unpopular clients. Stephen Strong Gregory, president in 1911–1912, for example, represented the highly unpopular assassin of the mayor of Chicago. He also represented Eugene Debs much before the celebrated espionage charges a few years later. In the Debs representation regarding labor union disruption of railroad terminals, Gregory's cocounsel were none other than Clarence Darrow and Senator Lyman Trumbull.[20]

The first 50 years of speakers for the profession were homogeneous. All the 50 presidents and 200-plus committee members were men. All were white (the ABA did not admit blacks in its early days, and great controversy ensued when it "accidentally" admitted two blacks to membership in 1912.)[21] Nearly all were born well

---

[15] Rogers, *supra* note 10 at 6.

[16] *Id.*

[17] *Id.*

[18] *Id.*

[19] *Id.*

[20] *Id.*

[21] A carefully orchestrated resolution-without-public-debate allowed the two mistakenly admitted to remain while demanding that applicants thereafter make their race known to the Executive Committee that considered membership. *See* 35 Ann. Rep. A.B.A. 12 (1912); Special Report Of The Executive Committee Concerning The Vote By The Committee To Elect Messrs. William H. Lewis, Butler R. Wilson, and William R. Morris to Membership in the Association, and the Rescission Thereof, 35 Ann. Rep. A.B.A. 93 (1912). "[T]he curtained solution to of the unhappy colored problem passed largely through [Francis Rawle's] sanctuary." Rogers, *supra* note 10 at 124.

and of means. Nearly all were Protestant.[22] Of the first 50 presidents, almost 25 percent were from New York; no more than 4 were from any other state.

Thomas Cooley and Frederick Lehmann are often cited as those who did not fit the mold of the hundreds of other ABA leaders during its first 50 years. Cooley was the son of a farmer and attended undistinguished country schools for a mere three years. He apprenticed into the profession and headed west to Michigan for a small-town practice. His great opportunity came when he was asked to codify the Michigan statutes. He achieved that task in brilliant fashion and was next asked to create reports for state supreme court decisions, a task at which he also excelled. When the University of Michigan launched a law faculty, he was one of its founding three members. Eventually he published a highly distinguished American edition of Blackstone's *Commentaries*. Cooley had indeed made his own way to leadership in the early American legal profession.[23] Lehmann was among the few leaders not born in the United States. He was born in Prussia and brought to Cincinnati by his father at age 3. Unhappy with life in his father's home, Lehmann ran away at age 11 and found his own way by doing a variety of farm work, sometimes in exchange for schooling. He continued to drift until he was hired by a doctor in Iowa. The doctor sponsored him to a seat at a local college, where Lehmann excelled. Eventually, after studying Blackstone, Kent, and Story, he was informally examined and admitted to practice. His practice had mixed success early on, but he made acquaintance with a fellow lawyer in Des Moines, whom he persuaded to run for governor. After some years of practice, he ventured to St. Louis where he won the business of the Wabash Railroad. He became president of the ABA when the Saratoga meetings began to exchange every other year with some prominent western cities. As part of the ABA effort to expand into the West, presidents were sometimes chosen from the places of a recent annual meeting.[24] He remained active in politics and eventually became solicitor general under President Taft, also a former ABA president.[25]

Both Lehmann and Cooley made their own careers and fortunes, unlike the rest of their fellow ABA presidents of the first 50 years. Lehmann, despite his foreign heritage, was early in life an American. The disadvantages of later foreign-born lawyers were not his. He and Cooley were both Horatio Alger stories, using their instincts and thirst for knowledge to drive their own success. Both stand in stark contrast to the standard-issue early ABA leader.

---

[22] Of the first 233 committee men, 227 were Protestant. Three of the 4 Catholics were "Baltimore-Catholics," descended from the Maryland founders. The fourth was from Louisiana, where Catholics were in great numbers among the elite. Of the two Jews, both were of early immigrant stock and had long roots in the United States. Neither was a recent immigrant.

[23] Rogers, *supra* note 10 at 77–79.

[24] Rogers, *supra* note 10, Forward at x. ("[The Association] tried to enlarge itself in the horizon of Western and Southern lawyers, and there are...selections for the presidency that are explainable chiefly on this ground.")

[25] Rogers, *supra* note 10 at 151–155.

2. A Structure Designed to Maintain the Status Quo

The early ABA procedures were meant to maintain the status quo among the leadership. Membership was by invitation only. A very small percentage of the membership, small as it was itself compared to the general lawyer population, attended meetings and held committee positions. In the crucial year 1908, when the ABA Canons of Ethics were adopted, a mere 312 members attended of the total membership of 3585.[26] In many years, fewer than 1 percent of the membership attended the annual meeting. Often, total membership fell below 1 percent of the licensed lawyers in the United States. Because of the ABA's organizational structure, power was concentrated in those who attended the annual meeting (and arguably among a much smaller group than that). So quite often, .001 percent of the U.S. lawyer population was speaking for the profession. But speak they did, in ways that the remaining 99.999 percent could not and did not.

At its 50th annual meeting, the last surviving founder, Francis Rawle, successfully opposed a constitutional amendment that would have placed term limits on key officers, urging the group to recognize that continuity and maintenance of ties to the past had been the foundation of the organization's success.[27] Rawle had served as the association's treasurer for its first 24 years before serving a term as president.[28] He bought the 17-cent carpenter's mallet that served as the gavel to open the first meeting in 1878; it remained the association's official gavel. During the year of Rawle's presidency, the gavel was decorated with the names of all the ABA presidents: first with silver, then with gold bands until there was room for no more. The mallet was stolen in 1946 and recovered, bands intact, at the Baltimore city dump by a long-time executive secretary.[29]

3. The ABA's Initial Structure

The ABA's initial structure, in place from 1878 to 1903, included a president, one vice president from each represented state, a secretary, a treasurer, and a council consisting of one member of each state. The vice president for each state and at least two members from each state were annually elected and constituted a local council for each state. These local councils were referred all applications for membership from each state.[30] All nominations for membership were made by the local council of the state to the bar of which the persons nominated belonged. All elections were done by ballot. Five negative votes sufficed to defeat an election to membership.

During the session of the association, the work was done by the association itself, but during the remaining days of the year, whatever work the association did

---

[26] Matzko, *supra* note 13 at appendix C.
[27] Matzko, *supra* note 13 at 495.
[28] Rogers, *supra* note 10 at 121.
[29] Walker Lewis, *The Birth of the American Bar Association*, 64 A.B.A. J. 996, 1002 (1978); Chester I. Long, 51 ABA Rep. 34–35 (1926).
[30] SUNDERLAND, *supra* note 10 at 6–7.

was done by its committees.[31] The five standing committees were (1) Jurisprudence and Law Reform, (2) Judicial Administration and Remedial Procedure, (3) Legal Education and Admission to the Bar, (4) Commercial Law, and (5) International Law. In 1895, the Committee on Law Reporting and Digesting was added; and in 1899, the Standing Committee on Patent, Trademark, and Copyright Law was created. The system of standing committees was supplemented by special committees appointed from time to time by vote of the association to deal with special matters. It was the practice to continue these special committees until they were discharged from further performance by a vote of the association.[32]

The members of the ABA spoke and voted in a purely individual capacity, representing no one but themselves. In the call for the organizational meeting, the proposed association was referred to as "a body of delegates, representing the profession in all parts of the country."[33] There was some sentiment that the organization should be a technically representative body, qualified to speak for local professional groups. However, no efforts were made to give the association a membership having a legally representative character in its first half century of existence. The one early effort in a representative direction was opposed vigorously.[34] Each state bar association annually appointed up to three delegates to the next meeting of the association. These delegates were entitled to all the privileges of membership at and during the meeting. In 1880, a further provision added that "in states in which no state bar association exists, any city or county bar association may appoint such delegates, not exceeding two in number." These provisions remained in effect until a general revision of the constitution and by-laws in 1919.[35]

4. Expansion Brings Change in the Structure

As the association increased its membership, carried its meetings into every section of the country, and asserted a more and more vigorous leadership of the entire American bar, questions began to arise regarding the adequacy of its organization and the efficiency of its procedure for meeting the enlarged demands it purported to shoulder. In 1916, Elihu Root, then-ABA president, took a major step to coordinate the state and local bar associations with the national association, by means of a subsidiary agency made up of bar association delegates. Root invited state and local delegates to meet with him at the annual meeting, that year in Chicago. He asked them "to consider what, if any, steps may be expediently taken to bring about a closer relationship, official or otherwise, between the ABA and such other organizations."[36] There were 84 delegates present from 54 bar associations.

---

[31] *Id.* at 19.

[32] *Id.* at 7, 21–23.

[33] *Id.* at 42 (quoting the original call letter).

[34] 11 ANN. REP. A.B.A. 13–15, 43 (1888); 12 ANN. REP. A.B.A. 5–6 (1889).

[35] 44 ANN. REP. A.B.A. 121–131 (1919).

[36] 41 ANN. REP. A.B.A. 94, 649 (1916).

5. The Major Changes in ABA Structure

The major changes in organization took place in 1936 and remain today the basic organizational structure of the ABA. Edson R Sunderland calls the post-1936 period of the ABA the "Era of Federation."[37] In 1936, the ABA underwent significant changes in its governing structure, going from a "fully autonomous association of individuals to an association of limited autonomy under almost complete control of a directing and supervising body called the House of Delegates, ..."[38]

"Under the new federalized plan the general control of the organization was lodged, not in the general membership of the Association, but in a body known as the House of Delegates, which was given all the powers necessary or incidental to the control and administration of the business of the Association and the determination of its policies and recommendations."[39] "[M]embership of the House of Delegates was carefully designed to give the House the broadest practicable representation of the groups and agencies actively interested in maintaining and developing high standards for the administration of justice in this country."[40] Fifteen classes or types of representatives were originally allowed to serve in the House of Delegates with two additional groups added later.[41]

Between sessions of the House of Delegates, a body known as the "Board of Governors," was given authority to perform all acts and functions that the House of Delegates might perform.[42] The Board of Governors is comprised of the president, the chairman of the House of Delegates, the last retiring president, the secretary, the treasurer, and the editor in chief of the *ABA Journal* together with one member chosen from each federal judicial circuit.[43] The positions are nominated by state delegates or by nominating petitions filed by members of the association and elected by the House of Delegates.[44]

The new ABA constitution, formulating the new organizational structure, was drafted and adopted at the 59th Annual Meeting of the ABA, held in 1936.[45] The purpose of the new constitution was to enable the association "to speak with an authoritative voice" and garner the "[c]ooperation of various organized units of the legal profession to increase efficiency and give a broader sense of professional solidarity and responsibility."[46]

---

[37] SUNDERLAND, *supra* note 10 at 14.
[38] *Id.* at 14.
[39] *Id.* at 175.
[40] *Id.* at 177.
[41] *Id.* at 177.
[42] *Id.* at 175.
[43] *Id.* at 179.
[44] *Id.* at 180.
[45] *Id.* at 173.
[46] *Id.* at 174.

6. Today's ABA

Today, the ABA, boasting membership of over 400,000 lawyers, can more credibly claim to speak for the profession. But even today's ABA does not truly and fully speak for the profession. Factions within the ABA vie for dominance, with one faction winning on one issue and losing on the next. ABA action itself has no formal effect on state law governing lawyers. In one area, the ABA accreditation of law schools (supported as it is by nearly all state bar licensure requirements that mandate graduation from ABA-accredited law schools), ABA action speaks unilaterally for the profession.[47] Barring the withdrawal of their accredited-school licensing requirements, the states have delegated to the ABA the authority to establish the educational requirements for new lawyers. In many other areas, ABA action is the expression of views by the dominant lawyer organization. On still other issues, including notably professional ethics issues, ABA pronouncements in the form of model rules or statutes, formally mean little unless the models are adopted by the various jurisdictions. Nonetheless, ABA action, especially when followed by consistent actions of numerous state bars, is the best evidence of the views of the late 20th and 21st century legal profession. Actions of courts and legislatures in their supervision of the legal profession continue to be a useful source of information about the views of the legal profession. Many such actions are taken at the behest of the profession itself and are adopted by lawyer-dominated institutions.

Although moderated over its existence, ABA leadership demographics have always been out of conformity with that of the lawyer population as a whole. In the early days, as an exclusive club, the ABA was meant to exclude the general population of lawyers, with only the "best men" being allowed membership, much less leadership. After the 1936 governance and membership reforms, the gap narrowed considerably but remained extremely wide. As of 1960, the leadership demographics were still dramatically different from those of lawyers at large. Of the 239 members of the House of Delegates, 21 practiced alone (8.7 percent), 73 were in small firms of 2–5 (30.5 percent), and 113 with larger firms (large for the time) (41 percent). Thirty-two were a mix of law professors, judges, bar officials, and business counselors. The median age was 55 and the youngest 36. At the same time, the population of lawyers looked far different. Sixty-eight percent practiced alone; only 23 percent practiced in a firm, all sizes from two lawyers up included. The median

---

[47] "In June 1995, the United States Department of Justice filed a civil antitrust suit against the ABA, alleging violations of antitrust laws in the accreditation program. The civil suit was concluded by a final Consent Decree that was approved in June 1996. It included a number of requirements concerning the Standards, many of which reflected revisions that the ABA had previously adopted. The Consent Decree was in force for a period of ten years and expired by its own terms on June 25, 2006. The Council has determined, however, that after the expiration of the Consent Decree, accreditation processes and procedures will continue to observe the substantive provisions of the Consent Decree." *available at* http://www.americanbar.org/content/dam/aba/publications/misc/legal_education/Standards/2012_2013_aba_standards_and_rules.authcheckdam.pdf.

age was 40.[48] The pattern of disproportionate large firm representation in the ABA House of Delegates has continued.

Rough estimates from later years suggest a continued trend.[49] In 1980, the proportion of House of Delegates members from small practices (five attorneys and under) was about one third that of the general lawyer population; the proportion of larger firm representation was about two and a half to one.[50] By 2005, the gap at the large firm end, though persistent, had lessened.[51] Should these gaps continue to lessen, the future House of Delegates might begin to better reflect the general lawyer population.

In another way, the ABA leadership was remarkably representative of the profession. The nearly all-white male profession was led by a predictably all-white male leadership. In 1960, there were a mere 7500 women lawyers in the United States, insignificantly more than existed in 1900. Numbers of minority lawyers were smaller still. By 1986, when the ABA's Stanley Commission issued its report on declining professionalism, significant advances in the diversity of the profession could be reported. The Report said that of the now 700,000 lawyers (1985), 110,000 (15.7 percent) were women, a dramatic increase from the 7500 of 1960. The report continued: though there were only 5600 minority students in 1971, the number had increased to 12,300 in 1985.[52] But the report then demonstrated the myopia and self-congratulatory nature of the profession's leadership: "We are as diverse as one could imagine." That statement said more about the association's imagination than about diversity success.

---

[48] Sylvester Smith, *The ABA House of Delegates*, 26 TENN. L. REV. 52 (1959); ALBERT P. BLAUSTEIN & CHARLES O. PORTER, THE AMERICAN LAWYER. A SUMMARY OF THE SURVEY OF THE LEGAL PROFESSION 2, 8 (1954).

[49] This data is an approximation, from a sampling of states. States included were Alabama, Alaska, Arizona, Arkansas, California, Colorado, Connecticut, Delaware, Ohio, Illinois, Missouri, and Oklahoma. The Lawyer Statistical Report indicated practice size for the general lawyer population (1980 and 2005). The ABA provided a listing of House of Delegates members by state. Martindale Hubble catalogued firm information by year, state, firm name, and practitioner. Martindale Hubble was the only available source for historical practice size data. A count of attorneys listed by firm (and across firm locations) provided the approximation of firm size. As Martindale Hubble is a catalogue only, the tabulation of attorneys listed is of limited accuracy. Compiled data was the count/tabulation of attorneys as indicated by the listing in Martindale Hubble in 1980, 2005.

[50] In 1980, about 26% of House of Delegates (HOD) members represented firms with 5 or fewer attorneys; 71% of the general lawyer population represented firms with 5 or few attorneys. About 31% of House of Delegates members represented firms with 21 or more lawyers; 13% of the general lawyer population represented firms with 21 or more lawyers. Fourteen percent of HOD members were unaccounted for in HOD data; outstanding groups were either not private practitioners or not identified in Martindale Hubbell.

[51] In 2005, about 38% of House of Delegates members represented firms with 21 or more lawyers; 26% of the general lawyer population represented firms with 21 or more lawyers. Data on gap at small firms, in 2005, is less reliable. Thirty-nine percent of House of Delegates members were unaccounted for in their data, with a likely concentration at small firms. Martindale Hubbell publishes less information on nonsubscribers in recent years.

[52] ABA Comm'n on Professionalism, "... In the Spirit of Public Service": A Blueprint for the Rekindling of Lawyer Professionalism, 112 F.R.D. 243, 253 (1986) [hereinafter Blueprint].

More recent leadership has become far more diverse. Of the presidents between 2001 and 2012, fully half have been women or members of minority groups. The size of law firms from which they are drawn, however, remains dramatically out of synch with that of American lawyers generally.

7. Law Firms

Law *firms* and their leaders do not speak for the profession in the sense meant in this book. Certainly leading lawyers, often partners at the major firms of their day, happen to be among leaders of prominent state bar associations and the ABA. In fact, as demonstrated earlier in this chapter, the ABA is dominated by law firm lawyers while the general lawyer population is more oriented toward solos and small firm practitioners. But the roles of law firm partner and bar leader are different, and the same person may occupy both roles at once. In the bar leadership role, the lawyer has the profession's interests at heart and speaks for them. But as law firm leader, the lawyer seeks the success of the particular firm. In no measure do law firms purport to speak for the profession. Their leaders speak for and seek the success of the firm, donning a different hat when they happen to become leaders of the organized bar.

C. LEGISLATURES

In some respects, American legislatures speak for the legal profession, usually by not speaking at all. One of the profession's most powerfully made claims is that of self-governance. This claimed difference from other of life's callings and occupations centers on the claim that lawyers govern themselves through their associations and disciplinary processes. A concession must be made in this claim that acknowledges the central role of courts, particularly state courts; but conveniently, courts are made up of judges and judges are, after all, lawyers. Legislatures, too, are dominated by lawyers. In the late 1950s, for example, a period straddling the communist infiltration crisis[53] and the civil rights movement,[54] fully two thirds of the U.S. Senate and 56 percent of the House were lawyers. Congress, however, and the state legislatures as well,[55] have remained largely silent on the lawyer regulation front.[56] By remaining quiet, legislatures have said something on behalf of the profession: they have supported the self-governance claim made by the organized bar. In the main, as lawyers, they have left the regulation of lawyers to the lawyers sitting as judges and those leading bar associations.

---

[53] *See* chapter 3.

[54] *See* chapter 4.

[55] Except for delegating power to bar associations in some states.

[56] A few counterexamples, such as Sarbanes-Oxley exist, but the level of legislative involvement in lawyer regulation has been very modest.

D. THE ACADEMIC LAWYERS

The legal academy spoke the least for the early legal profession and found its voice
amplified only when the ABA and state bar associations and supreme courts raised
the education standards for admission. The legal academy was born with the 1793
appointment of George Wythe as the first law professor in America, the chair of
Law and Police at the College of William & Mary in Virginia. Wythe and his successor St. George Tucker advanced the legal profession generally and the legal academy in significant ways. Two of their followers, David Hoffman of the University
of Maryland and George Sharswood of Penn, became the mid-19th century's chief
descriptors of the legal profession. Their early work in the 1830s and 1850s, respectively, largely framed the contours for more than a century's lawyer ethics law and
culture.[57]

Early ABA leaders, though not founders, did include some leading academics.[58]
The early creation of the Standing Committee on Legal Education and Admissions
to the Bar as one of the ABA's first committees (1879) and the 1893 creation of
the Section of Legal Education and Admissions to the bar as the association's first
section stated the ABA's case for its interest in legal education. But the founding of
the Association of American Law Schools (1900) and its subsequent split with the
ABA highlighted the tension between academic and practicing lawyers. Their one
common goal, higher education standards, united them despite deep differences.
The legal academy became far more prominent as a branch of the profession following ABA and state adoption of mandatory legal education requirements for
new lawyers. This action, more than any other, transferred the education of the
new members of the legal profession from the practicing branch of the profession
to the legal academy. This transition was most rapid during the first quarter of the
20th century. Until that time, with the exception of a few prominent voices, the legal
academy was a very modest source of expression on behalf of the legal profession.

Nonetheless, even the modern legal academy, which produces virtually all
the entrants to the profession, has spoken sparingly on behalf of the profession
because of a simple truth about the development of legal education: unlike medical
education's primary mission to prepare *doctors*, legal education's 1870s reform was
primarily aimed at preparing *law professors*. The decidedly academic and nonprofessional bent of the Harvard legal education reform has stayed with legal education despite all reality to the contrary. Of today's roughly 200 ABA-accredited law
schools, only about 10 or so routinely produce law professors. And even at those
10 or so, the vast majority of graduates practice law upon graduation or following
a judicial clerkship. Yet the model of education and the proving ground for legal
academics continues to express the nonprofessional model. Academic interest and

---

[57] George Sharswood, An Essay On Professional Ethics (1854); David Hoffman, A Course
of Legal Study 752–775 (1836).

[58] Examples include Henry St. George Tucker, dean and professor at Washington & Lee
School of Law and Henry Hitchcock, founder of Washington University School of Law.

scholarly production, not practice knowledge, remain the ticket to admission to the legal academy and the coin of the legal academic realm. If anything, knowledge of, or even interest in, law practice has been a negative qualification for the legal academy. As a result, the legal academy speaks little about the profession and speaks almost never *on behalf of* the profession.

IV. Conclusion

Knowing precisely what the legal profession thinks about an issue or how it has reacted to a crisis is sometimes impossible and rarely easy. Even when the evidence is fairly clear and unambiguous, no group as varied and complex and integrally involved in the system of government ever speaks with a single voice. Nonetheless, using varied sources of evidence, it is possible to say enough to be meaningful about the views and actions of the legal profession.

When the legal profession speaks and acts during a time of crisis, it speaks and acts in the service of its own status quo. At times, serving the status quo means significant change, as, for example, when the profession dramatically increased education requirements, increased enforcement of the character requirement, and established restrictions on advertising and contingent fees, all in the service of maintaining the profession's status quo of homogeneity. At other times, serving the status quo means doing as little as possible, as, for example, in the current crisis brought on by economic, technological, and globalization changes, during which the profession has done nothing more than modify existing lawyer regulation in ways that have already been dictated by the changes from outside the profession. Either way, when the profession speaks in service of its status quo, it fails. How it fails in different ways in different crises will be explored in the chapters that follow.

Immigration in the Early 20th Century

At the turn of the 20th century, the legal profession experienced a crisis brought on by a changing membership. The bar had already changed from a largely rural bar with the "country lawyer" as the prototype to a more urban bar with the corporate lawyer as the prototype. Now the urban segment of the bar was developing into a two-strata bar with corporate lawyers as the elite and urban, ethnic lawyers as an underclass.[1] The character of the bar was changing again.

This development was viewed askance for at least two reasons. First, the character of the bar as an elite, white male Protestant-dominated profession was threatened if not by the influence of the new lawyer underclass, then by the underclass's growing numbers. The professional elite felt that the influx of Jewish and Catholic lawyers besmirched the purity of the bar. Second, the work being done by this new lawyer underclass directly harmed the interests of the elite's clientele. The underclass represented workers and, to some extent, consumers of products with claims against their employers and the corporate producers of products. Injured railroad and factory workers now had counsel available to represent them. Low settlements of claims by insurance agents came less easily once workers had counsel.

The new lawyer underclass pressed claims scorned by the elite. Many of these claims were contingent fee claims. Further, many of the relationships between the underclass of lawyers and their clients were being forged through the lawyers' advertising and solicitation practices. Practices that had once been thought to be poor form, but not unethical or unlawful, were now actually having a deleterious effect on the bar elite and their clients. Previous experience with lawyer advertising had been little more than a mild annoyance. Nineteenth-century country lawyers had advertised; even founding father lawyers had placed newspaper notices addressed to prospective clients.[2] But now the practice of advertising mattered. Clients who

---

[1] James Moliterno, *Lawyer Creeds and Moral Seismography*, 32 WAKE FOREST L. REV. 781, 810 (1997).

[2] 1 ANTON-HERMONN CHROUST, THE RISE OF THE LEGAL PROFESSION IN AMERICA 41 n.109 (1965); *see also* ERWIN C. SURRENCY, THE LAWYER AND THE REVOLUTION (1964), *reprinted in* READINGS IN THE HISTORY OF THE AMERICAN LEGAL PROFESSION 74 (Dennis R. Nolan ed., 1980).

would not otherwise have representation had representation. Claims that would not otherwise be brought were being brought. And those claims were being brought against the elite lawyers' clients.

The profession remained in the control of the elite lawyers as newly formed bar associations asserted their claims to speak for the profession, and bar discipline committees made decisions about the application of new lawyer ethics codes. What did the profession do in response to this influx of urban, ethnic lawyers and the claims being filed by their formerly unrepresented clients? Through a variety of methods, the profession sought to exclude the new lawyers from the profession by raising entry barriers, it sought to control their activities by establishing the integrated (mandatory membership) bar and the code of ethics, and it sought to minimize the new lawyers' ability to communicate with prospective clients and to undertake matters on contingent fees (the only fee arrangement possible for many of their clients). By proposing and adopting these changes as bar association policy, by encouraging courts and law schools to adopt their proposed changes, the bar elite sought to maintain the status quo while the rest of society and culture changed. Every change was in service of the status quo of the corporate, white male Protestant domination of the profession and few worker claims, while the population diversified and industrialization altered corporate-worker relationships and interdependence.

The organized bar wielded its own newly forged weapons against the politically undesirable new segment of the bar. Indeed, beyond its being a mere social club, arguably the very purpose of the organized bar's foundation was the preservation of a white Anglo-Saxon Protestant elite, and the elimination or marginalization of the newer Southern and Eastern European lawyers who were increasingly populating American industrial centers.[3] The early bar had many goals, but all stemmed from the same motive: the desire to exclude undesirable groups from the practice of the law and to reduce the ability of underclass lawyers already licensed to reach and serve their clientele. Ostensibly, the bar had nobler goals in mind; it sought to restore the legal profession to the height of respect that it had enjoyed in Abraham Lincoln's time and also before the Jacksonian era. To be sure, the profession had suffered through the post-Revolutionary years, when lawyers became a hated class for enforcing Tory debt; and through the Jacksonian era, when all professions and elites were viewed with suspicion. Fundamentally, however, the turn of the 20th-century bar aimed to exclude the poor and immigrant lawyers who, with the help of part-time law schools in large urban centers, were entering the profession at an increasing rate.

Easy access to the bar was cited as the cause of the bar's inferior quality.[4] The obvious "remedy" was to restrict access to the bar, "to purify the stream at its

---

[3] *Id.*

[4] *Conference on Legal Education*, 8 A.B.A. J. 149 (1922).

source."[5] That urban immigrants, declared George W. Wickersham, attorney general to President Taft and senior partner in a prestigious New York law firm, "with their imperfect conception of our institutions, should have an influence upon the development of our constitution, and upon the growth of American institutions, is something that I shudder when I think of."[6] Eastern European immigrants were described by one lawyer as possessing little fairness, justice, and honor; the result, he continued, would threaten the Anglo-Saxon law of the land.[7] Interestingly, these attitudes so persisted that bar leaders during the 1950s and 1960s civil rights movement bemoaned the loss of character caused by Southern Europeans entry into the gene pool. "The heavy migration from South Europe has radically changed for the worse our racial stock. We are far more excitable than our Anglo-Saxon forebears, and it is a serious loss."[8]

A paramount objective of this elite was to structure the legal profession—its education, admissions, ethics, discipline, and services—to serve certain political preferences at a time when social change threatened the status and values of the groups to which elite lawyers belonged and whose interests they wished to protect.

Speaking at a bar function in Virginia, Thomas R. Marshall, the vice president of the United States under Woodrow Wilson and a member of the Indiana Bar, remarked that "we have permitted to drag their green trunks across and along the planks at Ellis Island thousands and hundreds of thousands of anarchists, revolutionists,... fellows who propose to take charge of this republic of ours."[9]

I. Demographics

The late 19th and early 20th century saw a wave of immigration. This wave, which lasted roughly from 1880 until 1924, was composed primarily of Eastern and Southern European immigrants.[10] These immigrants could not have been more different from the prior, traditional Northern European immigrants. The period of industrialization that followed the Civil War resulted in increased demand for unskilled labor to work in factories.[11] This need helped fuel a change in immigration

---

[5] *Proceedings of the Section of Legal Education and Admission to the Bar*, 44 ANN. REP. A.B.A. 681 (1921).

[6] George W. Wickersham, *The Moral Character of Candidates for the Bar*, 9 A.B.A. J. 617–621 (1923).

[7] Thomas Marshall, *Altruistic Evil*, 55 AM. L. REV. 349, 362–363 (1921); JEROLD S. AUERBACH, UNEQUAL JUSTICE: LAWYERS AND SOCIAL CHANGE IN MODERN AMERICA 107 (2d ed. 1977).

[8] JAMES R. SWEENEY, RACE, REASON, AND MASSIVE RESISTANCE: THE DIARY OF DAVID J. MAYS at 207 (2008) (MAYS).

[9] Auerbach, *supra* note 7 at 132; 55 AM. L. REV. 362 (1921).

[10] Charles Hirschman, *Immigration and the American Century*, DEMOGRAPHY, Nov. 2005, at 595–620.

[11] Ernest Rubin, *The Demography of Immigration to the United States*, ANNALS AM. ACAD. OF POL. & SOC. SCI., Sep. 1966, at 17.

patterns. Although the vast majority of immigrants to the United States were still European, the traditional immigrant sources of Northern Europe became displaced by a wave of immigrants from Russia, Italy, and Austria-Hungary as well as other areas of Southern and Eastern Europe.[12]

Immigrants in this period can therefore be divided into two different groups: old and new. Old immigrants are those from Northwestern Europe, particularly Great Britain; new immigrants included Italians, Slavs, Greeks, Poles, East European Jews and others from the south and east of the continent.[13] These new immigrants encountered prejudice and hostile reactions. Most often these groups settled in cities that were viewed as dangerous and radicalized.[14]

A general anti-immigrant mentality persisted despite the fact that the new immigrants had made rapid industrial growth possible. Congress adopted the Immigration Control Act of 1924, which effectively ended the wave of new immigrants by creating two classes of immigrants: quota and non-quota.[15] The act created an allocation system based on the "national origin" of prior immigrants.[16] The number of quota immigrants was limited to 2 percent "of the number of foreign-born individuals of such nationality resident in continental United States as determined by the United States census of 1890."[17] This quota system and the choice of the 1890 census severely limited entry to new immigrants, the vast majority of whose country fellows had come to America after 1890.

II. The Birth of Bar Associations

When the Civil War had come to a close, the American bar was overwhelmingly white, Anglo-Saxon, Protestant, and male. The prototype of the "country lawyer" dominated the American legal profession. Even as America industrialized and the country lawyer became more and more an anachronism, "images remained vivid of that child of the American frontier, self-taught in a Kentucky log cabin, the circuit-riding country lawyer in Illinois who became President to save the Union and died to make men free."[18] This image expressed everything that the American lawyer desired to be: both aristocrat and democrat, uniting the higher class and the lower class to achieve the perfect democracy.

However, as industrialization increased, immigration increased with it,[19] and the composition of the American bar slowly began to reflect that of the country as a

---

[12] *Id.*

[13] Hirschman, *supra* note 10 at 601.

[14] *Id.*

[15] Rubin, *supra* note 11 at 18.

[16] *Id.*

[17] 43 Stat. 153, 159.

[18] Auerbach, *supra* note 7 at 15.

[19] Hirschman, *supra* note 10 at 596; Rubin, *supra* note 11 at 17.

whole, immigrants included. Lawyers became alarmed that "[t]he proportion of white Anglo-Saxon Protestants within the legal profession and American society was diminishing as changing immigration and demographic patterns swelled cities and the profession with the foreign-born and their children."[20] One commentator, William Rowe, decried the fact that 15 percent of lawyers in New York City were foreign born, and fully 50 percent "were either foreign born or of foreign or mixed parentage."[21] As did others, Rowe decried the immigrants' lack of respect for authority and lack of moral judgment.

The aristocratic and democratic country lawyer was the product of a mostly homogenous society; but by 1900, that homogenous national and professional culture no longer existed. Recent Eastern and Southern European immigrants were considered "non-white," and were subjected to prejudice by Americans of longer standing.[22] Many lawyers saw a need to act to save this paradigm of the country lawyer, which itself no longer fit an industrialized and urbanized society; they saw these largely industrial and urban immigrants as a threat to that paradigm.[23]

This represented the first of several golden ages that the American legal profession would seek to preserve and restore unsullied, as if it existed under glass, immune from outside contaminants.

Elite lawyers' response to the stain on the ideal image was to organize themselves into bar associations, to which the lawyers from this new underclass could be denied admission and thus prestige. The first bar associations were established for the profession's "protect[ion], pur[ification] and preserv[ation]."[24] Bar associations were, in the first instance, simply a way of separating the elite from the recent immigrants. The first bar associations were voluntary, invitation-only organizations designed to resemble clubs more than today's more professional, more inclusive lawyer trade organizations. The exclusivity was by design, as lawyers created the voluntary associations "to insulate themselves from the rougher, unethical parts of the bar."[25] The composition of those "rougher, unethical parts" can be deduced from the location of the first bar association, the arrival point of the great part of the immigrants who began flooding into the country: New York City, the so-called dumping ground of the world.[26]

[20] Auerbach, *supra* note 7 at 5.

[21] William V. Rowe, *Legal Clinics and Better Trained Lawyers—A Necessity*, 11 Ill. L. Rev. 591, 601–602 (1917).

[22] Herschman, *supra* note 10 at 601.

[23] *Id.*

[24] *Professional Organizations*, 6 Albany L. J. 233 (1873); Walter B. Hill, *Bar Associations*, 5 Ga. B. Ass'n Rep. 75 (1888).

[25] Walter W. Steele, Jr., *Cleaning Up the Legal Profession: The Power to Discipline The Judiciary and the Legislature*, 20 Ariz. L. Rev. 413, 420 (1978).

[26] F. M. Danaher, *in* Section of Legal Education, American Bar Association, *Proceedings of the Section of Legal Education*, 34 Ann. Rep. A.B.A. 632, 646 (1911) [hereinafter *Proceedings of the SLE, 1911*].

The fact that the organized bar saw the new immigrants as undesirables who must be excluded is evident in the literature of the period. No less a figure than Roscoe Pound, dean of the Harvard Law School, referred to such people as "the defective, the degenerate of decadent stocks, and the ignorant or enfeebled victim of severe economic pressure."[27] In fairness, Pound was attempting to solve the legal problems that the presence of such "defectives" posed in his day; his work was not one of racist or anti-Semitic polemic. However, the fact that Pound was willing to refer to such people in this way, even if he was discussing ways of fulfilling their legal necessities, betrays the general attitude of the early 20th-century bar elites.

The purpose generally claimed for the organized bar, "to raise the standards of the profession and speak as a unified voice for the interests of attorneys as a class,"[28] was undoubtedly genuine. Lawyers truly bemoaned the decline in the reputation of the profession that accompanied its adherence to the corporate elites in America. However, the corporation lawyers who had become dominant still considered themselves to be the heirs of the country lawyer tradition and of all that was best in American legal life. They were not entirely unreasonable in that belief. The first wave of ABA leaders was raised prior to the dawn of corporate power, and they became leaders of the corporate bar and the profession by learning the ways of corporate representation. They spoke and wrote of the romanticized days of their circuit-riding youth.[29] The second generation of ABA leaders *trained* to become corporate lawyers as a career goal.[30] The corporation lawyers shared common ethnic origins both with the country lawyer and the men of industry whom they now served. For them, some other cause *must* have destroyed the esteem in which Americans once held the legal profession. In their own eyes, corporate lawyers were the same as the country lawyers that Americans once loved. The cause was the pollution of the bar by immigrants, who had no idea of ethical behavior, spoke broken English,[31] and belonged to strange religions that were either traditionally held in reprobation by English-descended Americans[32] or were

---

[27] Roscoe Pound, *The Administration of Justice in the Modern City*, 26 HARV. L. REV. 302, 311 (1913).

[28] Terry Radtke, *The Last Stage in Reprofessionalizing the Bar: The Wisconsin Bar Integration Movement, 1934–1956*, 81 MARQ. L. REV. 1001, 1002–1003 (1998).

[29] JAMES GRAFTON ROGERS, AMERICAN BAR LEADERS: BIOGRAPHIES OF THE PRESIDENTS OF THE AMERICAN BAR ASSOCIATION, 1878–1928 6, 7 (1932).

[30] John Matzko, The Early Years of the American Bar Association, 1878–1928, (1984) (dissertation, Univ. of Virginia) (on file with author).

[31] Isidore J. Kresel, *Ambulance Chasing, Its Evils and Remedies Therefor*, New York State Bar Association, *Proc.*, 52 (1929), 337–339 (citing an investigation in which the fact of attorneys who "could not speak the King's English correctly" was considered proof of their unfitness to practice law).

[32] Catholicism, of course, had been illegal in England, with short reliefs, since the 15th century, was only made legal in the 19th, and the prejudice that Protestant Englishmen had toward it was often carried over to America. *See, e.g.,* JOHN HIGHAM, STRANGERS IN THE LAND: PATTERNS OF AMERICAN NATIVISM, 1860–1925 5–7 (1988).

so alien that they denied Christianity altogether.[33] "Raising the standards of the profession," then, meant eliminating unethical conduct, and unethical conduct was whatever was not in accord with the country lawyer tradition that Americans had once so revered. Codes of ethics were therefore adopted to express this past legal tradition so perfectly that they immediately became an anachronism in their own time, a time dominated not by the country lawyer but by the urban, corporation lawyer.

The elite lawyers' influence was not limited to the ABA. State and local bar associations, faced with rapid social change as well, also defended stability, order, and control.[34] Before the move to the integrated bar, these bar associations often confined membership, as Simeon Baldwin, a major force in founding of the ABA, said, "to leading men or those of high promise." As the associations spoke more and more loudly on behalf of the entire profession, the profession's official view became that of the exclusive membership of the associations.

All of the profession's responses to increased immigration occurred in overlapping time frames, but the reactions to the immigrant wave all advanced three missions: keep the immigrants out of the profession, exert control over those already in, and cripple the practice and effectiveness of those who could not be kept out or thrown out.

III. Prevention of Entry to the Profession

The cleanest way to preserve the bar's homogeneity was to exclude immigrants from the profession in the first instance. Three strategies were engaged: discriminatory use of the good character requirement, a requirement of citizenship for entry to the bar, and increasing educational standards to prevent entry by immigrants of limited financial means.

---

[33] While wealthy Jews with long American roots generally enjoyed success in the American legal community, Jews of Eastern or Southern European background, who tended to be poor and without prominent connections, were discriminated against much as were all immigrants from that region. *See* Auerbach, *supra* note 7 at 185 (that a few German Jews from an earlier generation: Brandeis, Louis Marshall, Julian Mack, Samuel Untermeyer had securely established themselves), 186–187 (showing that even so, Jews often had a more difficult time securing employment than Anglo-Saxon Protestants), and 52 (citing Southern and Eastern European background as a factor in rendering a candidate's Jewishness too pervasive to be overlooked). Of the 233 committee-men from the first 50 years of ABA existence, 227 were Protestant. Three of the four Catholics were "Baltimore-Catholics," descendants of the Maryland founders and not recent immigrants. Of the two Jews, one was descendant of early-immigrating sephardic Jews. The remaining Catholic and Jew both graduated from Harvard. Matzko, *supra* note 30 at 512.

[34] LOWELL S. NICHOLSON, THE ORGANIZED BAR IN MASSACHUSETTS 17 (1952); GEORGE WASHINGTON GALE, THE ORGANIZED BAR IN CHICAGO 303, 310 (1950).

A. THE GOOD CHARACTER REQUIREMENT

While the requirement of good character has been in place for admission to the bar since time immemorial,[35] its potential for abuse was thoroughly exploited against recent immigrants and the poor in the late 19th and early 20th centuries. Other requirements have come and gone, but moral character requirements have been a fixed star in an otherwise unsettled regulatory universe.[36] Although the Supreme Court has stated that the qualities that have been compendiously described as "moral character"[37] are necessary for the legal profession,[38] [s]uch a vague qualification [as good character], . . . [so] easily adopted to fit personal views and predilections, can be a dangerous instrument for arbitrary and discriminatory denial of the right to practice law."[39] This statement identified the primary use of the standard in the late 19th and early 20th centuries in America.

Carelessly designed definitions of good character have been used to exclude or expel certain groups of "undesirables" from the legal profession. While good character requirements have existed throughout the history of the Anglo-American bar, the sudden interest in certification of good character at the turn of the 20th century was mostly the result of an effort to maintain the homogeneity of the profession's status quo demographics:

> Much of the initial impetus for more stringent character scrutiny arose in response to an influx of Eastern European immigrants, which threatened the profession's public standing. Nativist and ethnic prejudices during the 1920s, coupled with economic pressures during the Depression, fueled a renewed drive for entry barriers.[40]

The statements of the bar at the time make this conclusion unavoidable.

In a speech to the American Bar Association, Clarence Lightner[41] announced that the real problem with the bar's image was "the foreign element."[42] The idea "that there are in the profession lawyers whose services cannot be bought at any price for immoral use"[43] was unknown "in communities having a large foreign

---

[35] *See, e.g.*, Deborah L. Rhode, *Moral Character as a Professional Credential*, 94 YALE L.J. 491, 494 (1985) (explaining that a formal character requirements for practicing attorneys span almost two millennia).

[36] *Id.* at 496.

[37] Schware v. Board of Examiners, 353 U.S. 232, 247 (1957) (Frankfurter, J., concurring).

[38] *Id.*

[39] Konigsberg v. State Bar of California et al., 353 U.S. 252, 263 (1957).

[40] Rhode, *supra* note 35 at 499–500.

[41] Lightner was a long-time member of the Michigan Board of Law Examiners, and chairman of the Michigan and the Detroit Grievance Committees. *Restatement of Disbarred Attorney*, 20 MICH. L. REV. (1922). He was a frequent contributor to the *Michigan Law Review* and the *ABA Journal*.

[42] Clarence A. Lightner, *A More Complete Inquiry into the Moral Character of Applicants for Admission to the Bar*, 36 ANN. REP. A.B.A. 775, 779 (1913).

[43] *Id.*

population."[44] A career in law "is regarded by them as a desirable, because lucrative, business for their talented children"[45] Because of this apparently universal quest for money (seemingly, according to Lightner, unique to the foreign population),

> [a]n undue proportion of young men seeking admission to the Bar are of foreign birth or parentage, and they carry into the profession that point of view that they have acquired from their environment. The larger part of them have no character from a professional point of view, except, perhaps, the much-vaunted virtue of fidelity to the client.[46]

The bar at the time equated problems of character at the bar with the problem of foreigners entering the bar; since foreigners have no character, they must be the problem,[47] so the elite's reasoning went. Leading lawyers sounded their agreement with Lightner. George Wickersham, President Taft's attorney general, partner in a prominent New York firm, and frequent speaker at ABA meetings, explicitly sounded his approval of Lightner's paper, explaining why he quoted so extensively from it: "I find myself in such complete accord with what [Lightner] said."[48]

Lineage became a proxy for character. In 1929, a lengthy, publicized investigation in New York into the evils of ambulance chasing, resulted in recommendations of disciplinary proceedings against 74 lawyers. The chief counsel pointedly observed that some attorneys who had testified "'could not speak the King's English correctly...These men by character, by background, by environment, by education were unfitted to be lawyers.' The only remedy, he suggested, was a character examination, prior to law school admission, to eliminate those who lacked proper antecedents, home environment, education, and social contacts. If such an examination created a legal aristocracy, he told applauding members of the New York State Bar Association, so be it."[49]

The good character requirement operated as an excuse to preclude the admission of the socially outcast immigrants. In Pennsylvania, for example, the state that took its character certification process to the greatest extreme, the reasons given for rejecting good character certification were often neutral-sounding and principled, including such reasons as "[l]ittle regard for moral principles"[50] and "[n]o proper

---

[44] *Id.*

[45] *Id.*

[46] *Id.*

[47] This way of thinking is betrayed even in the report recommending the adoption of a code of ethics, in which the reasons for which a code is necessary are cited as "the shyster," the barratrously inclined, the ambulance chaser, the member of the Bar with a system of runners," all of which characteristics were applied primarily to foreigners. *Report on Professional Ethics*, at 601.

[48] George Wickersham, *The Moral Character of Candidates for the Bar*, 9 A.B.A. J. 617 (1923) (advocating for a pre-law training evaluation of moral character to "cleanse the bar").

[49] Isidore J. Kresel, *Ambulance Chasing, Its Evils and Remedies Therefor*, New York State Bar Association, *Proc.*, 52 (1929), 337–339.

[50] Walter C. Douglas, Jr., *The Pennsylvania System Governing Admission to the Bar*, 54 A.B.A. REP. 701, 703 (1929).

sense of right and wrong."[51] Often, however, reasons given were simply conclusions drawn from the applicant's lineage. Such labels as "dull," "colorless," and "stupid" were used as reasons for rejection.[52] Some applicants were rejected for crimes that their fathers, brothers, or even uncles committed, and the Board openly acknowledged the punishment of sons for the sins of their fathers without apology.[53] Two applicants were rejected because they had been employed as runners by law offices,[54] and one was rejected for seeing "no wrong in ambulance chasing, buying cases, employing runners, and advertising."[55] These rejections betray the same tired story: the lower and immigrant classes engaged in these practices; the established elite disapproved of the lower and immigrant classes. Therefore, these practices were unethical, and support of them proved a lack of good character.[56] This otherwise useful requirement was corrupted and used against qualified applicants for the bar, furthering the goals of nativism and the corporate legal elite.

Although not yet formally required for bar admission, applicants who had not graduated from college were four times as likely to be rejected on character grounds as those who had graduated. The results equate the lack of a college education, limited almost entirely to the poorer classes, with lack of character. The vast majority of existing bar members at the time, those presiding over the character decisions, had not themselves earned college degrees.

B. THE CITIZENSHIP REQUIREMENT

Statutes imposing a citizenship requirement for bar membership appeared during the last quarter of the 19th century. Prior to that time, the dominance of lawyers of British heritage would have made such statutes implausible without an exception for British, non-U.S. citizens. Most European immigrants, both old and new, were able to obtain U.S. citizenship; and as a result, these statutes had greater exclusionary effect on the West Coast, where the immigrant population was largely Asian.

The requirement of citizenship (or its medieval equivalent) for admission to the bar traces its roots to the very earliest days of English law.[57] In homogeneous societies, such a requirement does not serve as a significantly discriminatory weapon. In fact, during times of frequent warfare with neighboring countries, the citizenship requirement was a necessity to prevent attorneys with loyalties to nearby countries from infiltrating the bar.[58] However, this benign, even good, purpose for the

---

[51] *Id.*

[52] *Id.*

[53] *Id.* at 703–705.

[54] *Id.* at 703–704.

[55] *Id.* at 704.

[56] Douglas, *supra* note 50 at 705.

[57] *See* Kiyoko Kamio Knapp, *Disdain of Alien Lawyers: History of Exclusion*, 7 Seton Hall Const. L.J. 103, 122 (1996).

[58] Sanford Levinson, *National Loyalty, Communalism, and the Professional Identity of Lawyers*, 7 Yale J. L. & Human. 49, 64 (1995).

requirement did not long outlast the society for which it was formed. The use of this requirement as a weapon against foreigners—in this case, particularly those of Asian descent, began in the late 19th century.

During this period, more and more states prohibited noncitizens or nondeclarants from participating in a range of professions.[59] Law was no exception. At least by 1946, and possibly sooner, "[i]n every state alien attorneys are excluded from the practice of the law either by legislative act or by an administrative or court regulation."[60] In the state with the highest foreign population, for example, "[p]rior to 1974, nothing in the New York statutes or regulations allowed for the licensing of a foreign legal consultant."[61] Safeguarding the public from 'dishonest' or 'incompetent' attorneys,"[62] Americans "continued to rationalize the citizenship requirement"[63] by impugning the competency of the foreign born. One Oregon court, for example, explained why foreigners could rightfully be excluded from the professions:

> it is natural and reasonable to suppose that the foreign born, whose allegiance is first to their own country, and whose ideals of governmental environment and control have been engendered and formed under entirely different regimes and political systems, have not the same inspiration for the public weal, nor are they as well disposed toward the United States, as those who, by citizenship, are a part of the government itself.[64]

Aliens, by this reasoning, are presumed to be less loyal than citizens, even if the alien has already risked his life for America and declared his intention to become a citizen. Reliance on these justifications stereotyped aliens as a class.

Asians were particularly targeted by the citizenship requirement. Since Asians were ineligible for naturalization under federal statute, they were entirely powerless to remove this barrier. This, in effect, meant that Asian bar applicants were altogether denied the right to practice law in the United States, regardless of how willing they were to renounce their foreign citizenship.[65] Except for those who were native born, no Asian could practice law. American courts did not hesitate to affirm these restrictions, despite their overtly discriminatory effect.[66] Discrimination was pervasive, and the legal community was no exception.

---

[59] Konvitz, at 171–189.

[60] *Id.* at 188.

[61] Howard A. Levine, *The Regulation of Foreign-Educated Lawyers in New York: The Past, Present, and Future of New York's Role in the Regulation of the International Practice of Law*, 47 N.Y.L. Sch. L. Rev. 631, 637 (2003).

[62] Knapp, *supra* note 58 at 122.

[63] *Id.*

[64] Anton v. van Winkle, 297 F. 340, 342 (1924).

[65] Knapp, supra note 58 at 127.

[66] *See, e.g.,* in re Hong Yen Chang, 24 P. 156 (Cal. 1890) (stating that "[w]e have no doubt about the correctness" of the ruling forbidding persons of the Mongolian race from being naturalized) and in re Takuji Yamashita, 70 P. 482 (Wash. 1902)(stating that [i]t is clear that within the meaning of these words the applicant is ineligible because "a native of Japan [is] of the Mongolian race, and therefore not eligible to naturalization.").

Indeed, a California court was willing to announce that Asians were "a race of people whom nature has marked as inferior, and who are incapable of progress or intellectual development beyond a certain point."[67] More generally, said this court, the idea that "the Negro, fresh from the coast of Africa, or the Indian of Patagonia, the Kanaka, South Sea Islander, or New Hollander, would be admitted, upon their arrival, to testify against white citizens in our courts of law"[68] is "an insult to the good sense of the Legislature."[69] Such prejudices were not limited to those of Asian descent, but those directed at Asians were so explicit and violent that they serve as an excellent example of the attitudes prompting the citizenship requirement.

Some would argue that these statutes were not due to nativism, but rather of a simple desire to ensure the loyalty of attorneys to the legal system within which they work. However, whatever their cause, these nationality-based restrictions were upheld against challenge for many years.[70] Furthermore, the connection between restricting entry to the professions, particularly the legal profession, and nativism is not as tenuous as it may at first glance seem. Indeed, even the Supreme Court has recognized this characteristic of citizenship restrictions explicitly, albeit too late to relieve the situation. Justice Powell noted that such "wide-ranging restrictions for the first time began to impair significantly the efforts of aliens to earn a livelihood in their chosen occupations."[71] The legal profession used the citizenship requirement among its arsenal conceived to exclude the legal underclass.

C. THE EDUCATIONAL REQUIREMENTS

The Association of American Law Schools (AALS) and the ABA feuded for many years, torn apart by the dispute between the country lawyer and the legal scholar. The evolution of law teaching into a new profession distinct from that of practicing lawyers, as well as the "general apathy of the American Bar Association,"[72] led the AALS, originally simply a division of the ABA,[73] to separate and become its own structure. Only the values that the two still shared could bring them together again: the need to keep foreigners out of the practice of law as much as possible. Teachers and practitioners connected as their common interests pushed them together: higher educational standards would enhance the prestige and place of legal educators as

---

[67] People v. Hall, 4 Cal. 399, 405 (1854).

[68] *Id.* at 402.

[69] *Id.* at 403.

[70] Sanford Levinson, *National Loyalty, Communalism, and the Professional Identity of Lawyers*, 7 YALE J.L. & HUMAN. 49, 64 (1995).

[71] *In re* Griffiths, 413 U.S. 717, 719 (1973). Connecticut statute restricting the practice of law to citizens was struck down under strict scrutiny in *Griffiths*; strict scrutiny was only granted to nationality classifications in 1971. *See* Graham v. Richardson, 403 U.S. 365 (1971).

[72] Esther Lucile Brown, Lawyers and the Promotion of Justice 135 (1938).

[73] *See id.* at 136 (that the AALS was created "under the auspices" of a division of the ABA); Edson R. Sunderland & William J. Jameson, History of the American bar Association and Its Work 47 (1953).

it served the bar's effort to prevent the entry of immigrants. The ABA needed the
AALS to enforce stricter educational standards for entry into law schools for the
specific purpose of excluding immigrants and their children from the legal profession. Indeed, this mission was considered so important that legal education was
more thoroughly considered by the ABA than any other subject.[74]

Throughout the 19th century, standards for admission to law school were low
to nonexistent.

> [Harvard] was, until 1916, the only law school to require a college degree for
> admission. Among Frankfurter's American contemporaries, born between
> 1885 and 1889 and likely to enter law school between 1905 and 1910, fewer
> than 4 percent finished high school *and* college (while approximately 20 per-
> cent finished high school).[75]

The low standards and unlikelihood that lawyers had been formally educated highlights just how unusual the early ABA leaders were: of the first 58 presidents of the
ABA, 75 percent had some undergraduate education, and 59 percent had some legal
education.[76] The establishment of higher standards would prevent the influx of the
unfit immigrants into the profession and ensure the preservation of the profession's
ethnic homogeneity, even though the vast majority of current lawyers lacked the
educational credentials of the ABA leaders who pressed for the higher standards. It
could not be said that the educational standards would preserve an *existing educational* homogeneity. The educational standard of the lawyer population at the time
was remarkably low. The homogeneity that higher educational standards would
preserve was an ethnic and religious one.

The wealthy were far more likely to be able to go to college, both because of
tuition expenses and the loss of income that taking two to four years off of work
inflicted. The demand of the ABA that in order to become accredited, law schools
had to require at least two years of college prior to entry, operated as an effective
if not perfect exclusion of immigrants.[77] The ABA further demanded that all law
schools employ full-time faculty in "sufficient number . . . to insure actual personal
acquaintance and influence with the whole student body"[78] and withheld approval
from any commercial law school.[79] These measures crippled the efforts of the poor,
including almost all recent immigrants, to enter the legal profession.

---

[74] Edson R. Sunderland and William J. Jameson, History of the American Bar Association
and Its Work 72 (1953).

[75] Auerbach, *supra* note 7 at 28–29.

[76] Rogers, *supra* note 29; Edson R. Sunderland and William J. Jameson, History of the
American Bar Association and Its Work (1953).

[77] Special Committee, Section of Legal Education and Admissions to the Bar, American Bar
Association, *Report of the Special Committee to the Section of Legal Education and Admissions to
the Bar of the American Bar Association*, 46 ANN. REP. A.B.A. 679, 687 (1921) [hereinafter *Report
of the Special Committee*].

[78] *Id.* at 688.

[79] *See* Brown, *supra* note 72 at 46.

No inference is required to conclude that the heightened educational requirements were meant to exclude immigrants from the profession. The ABA's leaders
announced the purpose explicitly: in his famous speech supporting the requirement,
Elihu Root declared that any foreigners needed to be cleansed of their heritage
by the American influences.[80] Frederic R. Coudert, for example, in his speech to
the ABA, alluded to the foreigners who were crowding into the American bar and
connected their claimed incompetence with their lack of education. After blaming
"incompetency" for the general public's dislike of the law, he went on to condemn
most applicants to the bar, praising "the more intelligent and better-equipped young
men coming from one of the great university law schools of the country."[81] By
implication, then, the incompetency that was plaguing the American bar was due
to the poor and immigrant attendees of night and part-time schools, as opposed to
the "great university law schools." At the time of his remarks, the vast majority of
American-born lawyers had little or no formal education. But, he predicted, the foreign applicants, "unlearned, unlettered and utterly untrained young lawyers...will
continue to have a deleterious effect upon the administration of justice."[82] If admission to the bar was limited to graduates of the university law schools, most immigrants would be excluded with that step alone; and the ethnic composition of the
bar, itself mostly uneducated as well, could be preserved.

The debates of the Section on Legal Education of the ABA (the first section
established by the ABA,[83] indicating the importance which the ABA attached to
it) also establish that increasing educational requirements was designed to exclude
foreigners. F. M. Danaher, in describing the necessity of higher standards in New
York than elsewhere, specifically named the influx of immigrants as the motivation for the new, higher standards. Because New York was "the dumping ground
of the world,"[84] there were too many applicants for admission to the bar, he said.[85]
This influx of foreign applicants, he asserted, "has tended to lower the morals of
the profession and to foster unprofessional conduct."[86] He then explicitly affirmed
the goals of increasing educational requirements, declaring that it was necessary
"to adopt some of the requirements of time and cost and special training necessary for admission to the Bar in European countries,"[87] including a requirement
that applicants be "able to speak and write the English language correctly."[88] Even
those immigrants licensed to practice law in their own countries would be required

---

[80] Elihu Root, Address, New York State Bar Association, *Reports*, 39 (1916), 479.

[81] Frederic R. Coudert, *The Crisis of the Law and Professional Incompetency*, 36 A.B.A. Rep.
677, 682–683 (1911).

[82] *Id.* at 683.

[83] Sunderland, *supra* note 74 at 28.

[84] Danaher, *supra* note 26 at 646.

[85] *Id.* at 645–646.

[86] *Id.* at 645.

[87] *Id.*

[88] *Id.* at 648.

to meet the new educational requirements—unless, of course, they arrived from the Anglo-Saxon common law countries, in which case they could be admitted on motion without examination or formality.[89]

The difficulties that the poor experienced in fulfilling these educational requirements were often dismissed with scorn. Henry Bates stated that "there is no excuse for any man who is bright enough to get a high school education failing to get a legal education if he wants it."[90] Bates persisted in this opinion after hearing from one of the most reputable lawyers in Pennsylvania that he himself had been unable to afford more than a single year of law school.[91] In all, the debate in 1911 firmly establishes the goal of the increased educational requirements as the exclusion of the new immigrant class.

Some worry was expressed that heightened educational requirements would over-exclude and inadvertently keep out the American born. In Pennsylvania, a member of a special 1925 committee appointed to recommend appropriate changes in the state's bar admission requirements succinctly stated his view:

'What concerns us . . . is not keeping straight those who are already members of the Bar, but keeping out of the profession those whom we do not want.' Raising educational requirements could be problematic, because 'if we do that we keep our own possibly out.'

Pennsylvania pursued an alternate course for exclusion of immigrants: the preceptor system that required a prospective member of the bar to obtain the assistance of a current member as a sponsor in order to gain admission, with the obvious effect of limiting the admission of outsiders.[92]

Some men did oppose the new education measures, holding them to be useless. One questioned, "what office does this three years requirement perform aside from the patronage that it gives to the law school? For my part I am unable to see."[93] This lone objection voiced at the 1911 meeting was ignored; no response was ever given, nor was any further comment made. The speaker was isolated in his views.[94] Edward Lee, however, explicitly identified the true result of the measures at a later meeting, pointing out that

it would . . . deprive masses of people in our large cities, many of them of foreign extraction, from access to our courts and legal aid for want of lawyers familiar with their language and distinctive customs. To such people a lawyer is more than a mere lawyer; he is in addition an interpreter of the spirit of

---

[89] *Id*. at 647.

[90] Henry M. Bates, *in Proceedings of the SLE, 1911*, at 659.

[91] Russell Whitman, *in Proceedings of the SLE, 1911*, at 658.

[92] *See generally* Barry J. London et al., Comment, *Admission to the Pennsylvania Bar: The Need for Sweeping Change*, 118 U. PA. L. REV. 945, 945–947 (1970).

[93] James O. Crosby, *in Proceedings of the SLE, 1911*, at 636.

[94] *Proceedings of the SLE, 1911*, at 637. The next day someone mentioned Crosby's objection, but dismissed it as behind the times and let it be. *Id*. at 657.

our laws and of our institutions in his social and political contact with his kindred.[95]

Lee identified precisely the results of increasing the educational standards for admission to the bar: exclusion of the poor and the immigrant classes, with great detriment to both. He even gave a passionate argument for the rejection of the new standards, citing the many contributions of the foreign born and their value to law practice in America.[96] Lee provided the uncomfortable but obvious insight that made clear the true motivation for the higher standards: that "many . . . [of the bar's] noblest and most valued members never darkened the entrance of a college or law school, but [their] presence and learning have illuminated the highest courts in the land."[97] His pleas, however, if anything, provided further encouragement for adoption of the standards: the exclusion of these foreign born was precisely the goal of the new standards. George Price later alluded to the purpose of the standards, asking, as though the answer were obvious, "does the American Bar Association want to let down the tests simply to let in uneducated foreigners?"[98] He was dismissive of the contribution of the immigrants that Lee praised so highly, referring to them only briefly as "the young foreigners that he [Lee] talks about."[99] The overwhelming majority of the section sided with Price; when Lee made a motion to strike the requirement of college study and replace it with a more modest standard, it failed for lack of a second.[100] In the end, the committee "stood by the rule and stood by [its] record, and [was] not diverted by any of this lachrymose chatter about the poor boy."[101]

The report submitted to the section in 1921 could not have been more explicit about the desire of its members to keep out immigrants. It spoke of the need "to prevent the admission of the unfit and to eject the unworthy,"[102] and aimed to "purify the stream at its source by causing a proper system of training to be established and to be required."[103]

The report was entirely dismissive of the difficulties that the poor faced in attending school full time. "No man," it said, "who wants a college education need

---

[95] Edward T. Lee, *in* Section of Legal Education and Admissions to the Bar, American Bar Association, *Proceedings of the Section of Legal Education and Admissions to the Bar*, 44 ANN. REP. A.B.A. 656, 668 (1921) [*Proceedings of the SLE, 1921*].

[96] He even alluded to the opinion of most of the ABA by saying that was sorry to say that many Americans considered these immigrants "undesirables." The Section, however, was apparently unmoved, as it took a recess immediately thereafter, and no one spoke up in support of Lee's speech. *Proceedings of the SLE, 1921*, at 672.

[97] Lee, *in Proceedings of the SLE, 1921*, at 668.

[98] *Proceedings of the SLE, 1921*, at 676.

[99] *Id.* at 675.

[100] *Id.* at 677.

[101] Silas H. Strawn, *in Proceedings of the SLE, 1929*, at 639.

[102] American Bar Association, *Report of the Special Committee*, at 681. (Report of the Special Committee).

[103] *Id.*

go without."[104] It cited scholarships and work as ways the poor can attend college and law school,[105] despite the presentation to the committee by James Angell, president of Yale, who said that scholarships were "wholly inadequate to affect the situation."[106] Despite all evidence to the contrary, the report assumed that all was even in the world of opportunity to be educated: "[t]he man of slender means has now the advantages which once belonged only to the wealthy."[107] Further, the simultaneous moves against night law schools all but eliminated the opportunity to combine work and study, and only university law schools offered access to desirable professional positions. It was almost axiomatic among the elite that night schools were anathema; John Wigmore, at the first meeting of the Section of Legal Education, declared that "the principle that when a student enters upon his professional preparation in a law school, he must give to it his whole working time, and that no other and competing occupation is compatible with an adequate training...should...be fundamental in modern legal education."[108] Night schools were identified with immigrants. Night schools, observed the dean of the University of Wisconsin law school, enrolled "a very large portion of foreign names."[109] And with respect to scholarship support, the contemporary reality was that "[d]espite everything that full-time schools may do through scholarships and loans for students of restricted means...such [full-time] schools draw the great majority of their students only from the more favored classes in society."[110]

The committee was authorized "to publish from time to time the names of those law schools which comply with the above standards and of those which do not."[111] By 1936, only one part-time school had been approved by the ABA, while only eight full-time schools had failed to gain approval.[112] Furthermore, "[o]f the 94 institutions on the approved list for 1936, 90 were connected with colleges or universities."[113] Elihu Root, chairman of the special committee that submitted the report, had warned that "alien influences" must be "expelled by the spirit of American institutions."[114] Whether or not he succeeded in expelling alien influences from the legal profession, he certainly did a great deal to prevent aliens from entering it.

The more modest number of immigrants who could muster the resources and attend college and then law school would be made to conform. The requirements

---

[104] *Id.* at 684.

[105] *Id.*

[106] 8 A.B.A. J. 144–145 (1921).

[107] Report of the Special Committee at 682.

[108] John H. Wigmore, *A Principle of Orthodox Legal Education*, 17 Ann. Rep. A.B.A. 453, 452 (1894).

[109] William Draper Lewis, Legal Education and the failure of the Bar to do Its Public Duties, 6 AALS Proc. 42 (1906).

[110] Brown, *supra* note 72 at 43.

[111] Report of the Special Committee at 688.

[112] Brown, *supra* note 72 at 48–49.

[113] *Id.* at 50.

[114] Root, *supra* note 80 at 145.

were designed to ensure that those immigrants who did have the circumstances and ability to surmount the incredible obstacles placed in their paths and reach the bar would be thoroughly naturalized, and no longer belong to the culture with which they had begun.[115] Because so many of the unethical lawyers in the country "came right up out of the gutter into the Bar,"[116] they must be required to go to college so that they can "absorb the American boy's idea of fair play,"[117] which essentially meant to abandon "the methods [which] their fathers had been using in selling shoe strings and other merchandise."[118] Those who could not be excluded by the new requirements would "become Americanized,"[119] which could happen "whatever nationality a man is."[120] Once they had abandoned their culture's way of doing things, they would be safe members of the bar—not before. This approach formed a second line in defense of the status quo. If some of the "others" could not all be kept out, they could be made to fit in.

IV. Bar Integration

Bar integration, requiring every lawyer practicing in a state to belong in the bar association of that state, was another way of forcing immigrants who managed to enter the profession to fit it in. Bar integration had both proponents and opponents in the corporate elite, but all took their respective positions for the same reasons. Herbert Harley, the most prominent advocate of compulsory membership in the bar, thought that bar integration would "limit professional competition (thereby mitigating unethical behavior)."[121] In 1922, William D. Guthrie, then-president of the New York State Bar Association, opposed compulsory bar association membership. Such bar integration, he said, would democratize the bar at the expense of "the elite of the Bar, the best of the Bar." "Immigrants and their progeny," Guthrie stated, were responsible for "the difficult and grave problem and menace...arising from the admission to our bar in recent years of large numbers of undesirable members."[122] Some lawyers feared that if the bar was integrated, lower-level practitioners will seize control of the organization and debase it.[123]

---

[115] *See* Henry S. Drinker, Jr., *in* Section of Legal Education and Admissions to the Bar, American Bar Association, *Proceedings of the Section of Legal Education and Admissions to the Bar*, 54 A.B.A. Rep. 605, 621–624 (1929) [hereinafter *Proceedings of the SLE, 1929*].

[116] *Id.* at 624.

[117] *Id.*

[118] *Id.* at 622.

[119] George W. Wilson, *in Proceedings of the SLE, 1929*, at 628.

[120] *Id.* at 624.

[121] Auerbach, *supra* note 7 at 120.

[122] William Guthrie, *The Proposed Compulsory Incorporation of the Bar*, Part II, 4 N.Y. L. Rev. 223, 224–228 (1926).

[123] Glenn R. Winters, Bar Association Organization and Activities 9 (1954).

Under compulsory incorporation, . . . this outside and now wholly indifferent, callous and unwilling, if not hostile, mass would be given control by the mere power of numbers of the judicial district division of the new corporation and of the future of the bar in the city of New York, and would be vested with the right and power to speak officially for the profession in regard to professional ethics, improvement of the law, and standards of admission, discipline and disbarment![124]

Indeed, the *Journal of the American Judicature Society*, one of the vehicles of support for integration, stated that "[t]here has been justifiable fear on the part of existing state bar associations lest their membership be contaminated."[125] The final press for bar integration, however, was based upon the increased control it would give over the content and code of the bar.

The legal underclass was engaging in practices that the elite considered to be unethical, and "an adequately funded, integrated bar was considered the most effective method of curtailing these problems since an integrated state bar would control the miscreants through investigation and discipline." Furthermore, in its official capacity, the integrated bar would be capable of establishing binding ethics rules, disciplinary sanctions, and an infrastructure for adjudicating grievances. So while it was true that bar integration was opposed by many who felt it would give immigrants power in the bar associations,[126] it was supported by many for precisely the same reasons. One proponent of integration reassured his readers that "[s]hady practitioners are more easily controlled if they are in the bar organization and subject to its rules than if they are on the outside."[127] "Shady" practices are, of course, things like advertising and employing runners; immigrants could be prevented from these practices, and thereby either assimilated into the elite culture or pushed out of practice entirely[128] if they were required to be members of the state bar association. The American Judicature Society was fond of saying "that a lawyer not fit to associate with his colleagues is not fit to have clients or represent them in court."[129] The poor and immigrant lawyers were unfit to associate with the elite and therefore unfit to practice. Integrating the bar, then, would not only make it more difficult

---

[124] Guthrie, *supra* note 122 at190.

[125] *Redeeming a Profession: Introducing a Practical and Logical Plan for Bar Organization Which Will Enable the Bar to Realize Its Highest Ideals*, 2 J. Am. Jud. Soc. 105, 109 (No. 4, 1918).

[126] Auerbach, *supra* note 7 at 120–123.

[127] Winters, *supra* note 124 at 9.

[128] Winters's conclusion is that any lawyer worthy of being permitted to practice law belongs in the profession's organization, and any lawyer who is not worthy of membership in that organization ought not to be allowed to continue to practice his profession at all. *Id.* So those who advertise and employ runners *ought* to be forbidden to practice; that is that is the decision of the elite, and it must stand.

[129] *Study Bar Organization: Conference of Delegates at American Bar Association Meeting Creates a Committee to Bring This Subject to the Attention of the Organization Profession Throughout the Country*, 3 J. Am. Jud. Soc. 74, 74 (No. 3, 1919).

for them to practice, as the educational and ethical requirements did, but may well force them out of practice entirely.

Some feared the pollution that the unwashed would bring as a result of bar integration; however, these concerns were ultimately overridden by the control that integration would offer over those same unwashed. Both sides in the debate argued for different conclusions, it is true, but always for the same common goal, control, and marginalization of immigrant lawyers.

V. The Code of Ethics

The code of ethics that the early profession erected was designed principally to affect the immigrant lawyers. These lawyers were primarily urban solo practitioners, and their professional practices were about to be declared unethical because the established lawyers said they were. It is amply clear that the impetus behind the 1908 Canons was in large measure a subterfuge for class and ethnic hostility. The code was a subterfuge because it was not openly nativist. However, the reasons cited for requiring the code of ethics specifically target the practices of lower-class lawyers, who were in large part from poor and foreign backgrounds. Furthermore, the committee's report has an overtly nativist tone despite its lack of specific derogation.[130] Historians and lawyers alike have found that "[t]he ethical crusade that produced the Canons concealed class and ethnic hostility,"[131] and the content of "unethical" behavior therefore became the behavior of the disfavored ethnicities, regardless of its actual character. As one ethics scholar commented, the Canons "were motivated in major part by the large numbers of Catholic immigrants from Italy and Ireland and Jews from Eastern Europe beginning in about 1880,"[132] and "[d]eviance was less an attribute of an act than a judgment by one group of lawyers about the inferiority of another."[133]

Two pillars of this code were most prominent in their attack on lower-class lawyers; both of them, however, can be united under the single derogatory appellation of "commercialization of the profession," or, more specifically, "ambulance chasing."

A. ADVERTISEMENT

One of the most prominent objections to immigrant lawyers' practices was that they tended to advertise. The corporation lawyers who had become the elite in late

---

[130] *See* Committee on Code of Professional Ethics, American Bar Association, *Report of the Committee on Code of Professional Ethics*, 29 ANN. REP. A.B.A. 600, 601 (1906) [hereinafter *Report on Professional Ethics*].

[131] Auerbach, *supra* note 7 at 50.

[132] MONROE H. FREEDMAN, UNDERSTANDING LAWYERS' ETHICS 3 (1990).

[133] Auerbach, *supra* note 7 at 50.

19th and early 20th century America did not advertise; they had no need to do so. Elite lawyers already had connections enough to supply them with new clients, or they were retained by businesses as counsel and therefore had no need of new clients, particularly from among the lower classes who had little or nothing with which to pay them. The fact that the new lawyers, on the other hand, did advertise and aggressively seek new clients, particularly for tort cases taken on a contingent fee, made advertising ipso facto unethical.[134]

Here again the ideals of the country lawyer, as realized in the Industrial Revolution's big business firm, obfuscated the [then] current situation of the profession. The country lawyer and the corporation lawyer were both well-known in the community; they could rely on clients coming to them. In the lower-strata urban situation, however, relationships between lawyers and clients were entirely different. Lawyers were not well-known in the community simply by virtue of their profession; they were required to advertise in order to make the availability of their services known to potential clients, both for justice's sake and for their own economic necessity. The code of ethics prohibited nearly all advertising, a prohibition that would affect only the practices of the urban and largely immigrant underclass. Opposition to the "commercialization" of lawyers, the bugaboo that the established corporate society presented as the reason for their new prohibition on advertising, was the innocent front that sheltered the antagonism toward lawyers from ethnic minority groups who represented the formerly unrepresented in making claims against the elite lawyers' clients. Like the laws prohibiting sleeping under bridges, the advertising rules applied to lawyers for the rich and poor alike.[135]

Interestingly enough, this prohibition on advertising *was* new. Despite the fact that it is perfectly suited to the country lawyer ethos, those country lawyers themselves never saw a need to implement such a prohibition, and freely engaged in the limited advertising that the technology of their time allowed. Lincoln famously placed simple ads in local newspapers. Patrick Henry and Thomas Jefferson placed notices of their practice in the *Virginia Gazette*, though their notices warned clients that they would not undertake representation without up-front fee

---

[134] Nearly all advertising was prohibited under the Canons. All "solicitation of business by circulars or advertisements" was deemed unprofessional; it was "equally unprofessional to procure business by indirection through touters of any kind." Even "[i]ndirect advertisement . . . by furnishing or inspiring newspaper comments concerning causes in which the lawyer has been or is engaged, or concerning the manner of their conduct" was prohibited. Effectively all advertising was, then, forbidden, except, of course, for business cards. *Those* were used by the professional elite, and therefore could not possibly be unethical. American Bar Association, *Canons of Professional Ethics*, Canon 27 (1908), *reprinted in* Committee on Professional Ethics and Grievances, *American Bar Association, Opinions of the Committee on Professional Ethics and Grievances* 19 (Committee on Professional Ethics and Grievances ed., 1957) [hereinafter American Bar Association].

[135] ANATOLE FRANCE, THE RED LILY (1894) ("The law, in its majestic equality, forbids the rich as well as the poor to sleep under bridges, to beg in the streets, and to steal bread.").

payment.[136] The main ethical treatise on which the new code of ethics was based, Sharswood's in 1853, put no restrictions on advertising; and many ethical systems, including those of most of the states, permitted certain amounts of newspaper advertising, at least.[137] The new 1908 ABA Canons of Ethics, however, prohibited nearly all advertising; even business cards received only reluctant approval.[138] This sudden discovery of a legal norm against lawyer advertising, entirely baseless in the traditions of the profession, reenforces the conclusion that the corporate legal community imposed the rule as an ethnic and economic weapon, rather than as an attempt to restore the image of the profession in the public eye. To the extent it was a genuine effort to restore the public image of lawyers, it was an expression that the practices of the new underclass lawyers were the cause of any diminished public image of lawyers.

Included in the prohibition on advertising was any direct seeking of clients, including simply approaching them, telling them that they probably had a legal claim, and offering to represent them.[139] These acts of solicitation were considered the height of commercialism, and formed the substance of what was derisively called "ambulance chasing." To be sure, those lawyers engaged in these practices did so because the practices were an economic necessity to their livelihood. But they also doubtless considered themselves to be performing a needed service by informing those who might be ignorant of their claims and the legal recourse available to them. The ABA considered such education to be decidedly unethical. The hypocrisy of the elite in this matter is ironic. As one commentator noted, "my experience has been that it is the corporation agents who are the ones who rush to the hospital, or bedside of the dying, and try to get their releases from them."[140]

The early century move against advertising was so powerful that as late as 1955, one prominent bar leader and commentator stated that "[o]f all the forms of unethical conduct possible, it is doubtful that any embody more elements tending to weaken the force of the legal profession and hinder the administration of justice than does ambulance chasing."[141] The ABA leadership itself was hardly more

---

[136] 1 ANTON-HERMONN CHROUST, THE RISE OF THE LEGAL PROFESSION IN AMERICA 41 n.109 (1965); *see also* ERWIN C. SURRENCY, THE LAWYER AND THE REVOLUTION (1964), *reprinted in* READINGS IN THE HISTORY OF THE AMERICAN LEGAL PROFESSION 74 (Dennis R. Nolan ed., 1980).

[137] GEORGE SHARSWOOD, AN ESSAY ON PROFESSIONAL ETHICS (1854); *See* HENRY S. DRINKER, LEGAL ETHICS 213 (1953); James Moliterno, *Lawyer Creeds and Moral Seismography*, 32 WAKE FOREST L. REV., 781, 791–792 (1997).

[138] ABA Canons 27, 28.

[139] *Id.*

[140] Frank C. McGirr, *Sanitation of the Bar: Exposure at Bar Association Meeting of the Latest Methods for Employing Courts for Vicious Purposes by Ambulance Chasers*, 4 J. AM. JUD. SOC. 5, 6 (1920) [hereinafter *Sanitation of the Bar*].

[141] Note, *Legal Ethics: Ambulance Chasing*, 30 N.Y.U. L. REV. 182, 186 (1955).

subtle; indeed, it was ambulance chasing that inspired them to promulgate their code of ethics in the first place.[142] The Canons vehemently declared that "[i]t is unprofessional for a lawyer to volunteer advice to bring a lawsuit, except in rare cases where ties of blood, relationship or trust make it his duty to do so,"[143] which may be fairly translated as "except when corporate lawyers do it." The ABA also decided that employing others to seek out valid claims and recommend a lawyer's services is unethical.[144] No justification was given for its proclamation. Scholars, too, continually decried the supposed evils of ambulance chasing. The approbation has so deeply become the lore of the profession that a 21st-century bar association after dinner speech is highly likely to decry both lawyer advertising and the U.S. Supreme Court cases that have prevented the modern bar from its blanket prohibition.

Not only ethnic but also monetary considerations played a role in the prohibition on advertising. Most of the framers of the code represented business interests; most lawyers who advertised were serving the poor, often representing them in tort cases that arose as a result of injuries received in working for business, as well as some products liability claims. Such claims would be far less likely to be brought if urban, ethnic, underclass lawyers could be restrained from advertising about their services, soliciting the business of injured persons, and offering contingent fee arrangements to those unable to afford a pay-as-you-go lawyer fee, especially since most of those bringing the claims were ignorant of their claims' value until their lawyers' runners informed them of it. Since these advertising restrictions were virtually the only substantive changes from former state codes of ethics to the new ABA Canons, the inference is strong that the new restrictions masked ethnic and economic advantage taking. The prohibition on advertising had no other purpose than the suppression not only of the largely immigrant lawyers who relied on it for their livelihoods, but also of the largely immigrant blue-collar workers who made use of those lawyers to litigate their claims against the business interests that the elite lawyers who so despised the underclass almost universally represented.

B. THE CONTINGENT FEE

A contingent fee is simply an agreement by which payment to the attorney is subject to some contingency, generally either favorable settlement or favorable result at trial, the creation of a res from which the lawyer's fee can be drawn. Since ancient times, however, agreements between a litigant and a stranger to the claim to share

---

[142] ABA Committee on Code of Professional Ethics, American Bar Association, *Report of the Committee on Code of Professional Ethics*, 32 ANN. REP. A.B.A. 676, 682 (1907) [hereinafter Committee on Professional Ethics].

[143] American Bar Association Canon 28.

[144] *Id.*

the proceeds have been condemned as champerty.[145] In the case of a contingent fee, the attorney was considered a stranger to the lawsuit: that is, he was neither plaintiff nor defendant and he pursued the litigant's claim by paying for it (with his services) in exchange for part of the settlement. The rule made some degree of sense in the preindustrial society for which it was made; contingent fees were unnecessary, since the tort claims for which contingent fees primarily evolved were comparatively rare, and litigants were more likely to be on a level playing field financially. Allowing contingent fees in such a situation would have been nothing more than giving attorneys and clients an incentive to file dubious claims for their nuisance value.[146] It has been thought that the arrangement might even encourage perjury, since a lawyer, knowing that his fee rests upon his prevailing, may encourage his client or witnesses to stretch or invent the truth to achieve a favorable result.[147] The contingent fee offered little benefit and substantial cost. With the advent of industrialization, however, the balance of the benefits and costs of the prudential value of the contingent fee radically changed.

It was "the Industrial Revolution which brought into sharp contrast the group of lawyers who were willing to take cases on contingencies and those who were not."[148] The division was, of course, that between the hoi polloi and the elite:

> The latter [those who would not take a case on contingency] represented the defendant railroads, steamships, factories, power companies. They were the admitted leaders of the bar. The former [those who would take contingent fees] were the young lawyers struggling to make a living. They could scarcely help being an inferior class.[149]

The organized bar's continued opposition to contingent fees made this division perfectly obvious. Contingent fees, often the only way a poor person could afford any sort of legal service, were the heart of the immigrant lawyer's practice; without them, no one could afford his services, he could not afford to live, and his practice would necessarily fall to the wayside. Both the poor injured worker and the immigrant lawyer needed the contingent fee for their survival.

---

[145] James Moliterno, *Broad Prohibition, Thin Rationale*, 16 GEO. J. LEGAL ETHICS 223 (2002); Max Radin, *Maintenance by Champerty*, 24 CALIF. L. REV. 48 (1934).

[146] *See* Max Radin, *Contingent Fees in California*, 28 CALIF. L. REV. 587, 588 (1940) ("[t]he contingent fee certainly increases the possibility that vexatious and unfounded suits will be brought.").

[147] *See, e.g.,* Honorable George Sharswood, AN ESSAY ON PROFESSIONAL ETHICS, 32 ABA REP. 160–164 (1907) (suggesting that an attorney on a contingent fee would "be tempted to make success, at all hazards and by all means, the sole end of his exertions."). *See also* Lester Brickman, *Contingent Fees without Contingencies: Hamlet without the Prince of Denmark?*, 37 UCLA L. REV. 29, 40 (1989) (explaining that contingent fees are prohibited in criminal cases because of the risk of the attorney impeding justice, "presumably by suborning perjury").

[148] Radin, *supra* note 146 at 588.

[149] *Id.*

The lawyer needed the contingent fee because he was not part of the new elite that could rely upon being retained by the great industrial corporations for his livelihood. The lower-class lawyer required a certain degree of client turnover in order to survive, and offering a contingent fee to those otherwise unable to pay for legal services was the only way to ensure that turnover. The poor worker needed contingent fees even more. Auerbach eloquently described the necessity of such fees for the poor:

> An alarming proliferation of work and transportation accidents, most often borne by those least able to afford lawyers' fees, generated human tragedies which a profit economy and its legal doctrines exacerbated. Accident victims and the surviving members of their families were compelled to bear the full burden for the risks inherent in dangerous work. Corporate profit was the primary social value...legal services were available only to those who could afford to purchase them...[i]n more than half of all work-accident fatalities in Allegheny County [for example], widows and children bore the entire income loss. In fewer than one-third of these cases did an employer pay as much as five hundred dollars the equivalent of a single year's income for the lowest-paid workers. Similarly, more than half of all injured workers received *no* compensation; only 5 percent were fully compensated for their lost working time while disabled.[150]

Workers in such situations could hardly afford the out-of-pocket expense of retaining a lawyer at an hourly rate, particularly with the substantial risk of losing, thus suffering not only the expenses of their injuries but also the equally unrequited expenses of an unsuccessful legal venture. The contingent fee, however, provided a way for such workers to pursue their claims without worsening their situation. The arrangement was and is a necessary consequence of the desire to provide everyone with the capability of pursuing meritorious legal claims.

By the late 19th and early 20th centuries, when the new code of ethics was being formed and promulgated, the prudential value of the contingent fee already outweighed the risks beyond any serious question. In a rapidly growing and industrialized society, "[t]here were far too many persons who could pay no retainers and far too many lawyers who could not afford to insist on them."[151] At a time in which workers had precious little assistance, "the contingent fee arrangement did enable some workers to secure otherwise unattainable legal services."[152] The balance of the possibility of unmeritorious suits being brought and the certainty of the denial of any recourse for the wrongfully injured and others with legal claims can come down on only one side. Furthermore, one could argue whether the possibility of unmeritorious suits is a problem unique to, or even especially associated with, the

---

[150] Auerbach, *supra* note 7 at 44.
[151] Radin, *supra* note 146 at 588.
[152] Auerbach, *supra* note 7 at 45.

contingent fee agreement, since no one would deny "that vexatious and unfounded suits have been brought by men who could and did pay substantial attorneys' fees for that purpose."[153] If anything, the stake undertaken by a plaintiff's lawyer may reduce the likelihood of frivolous claims. The contingent fee lawyer is unlikely to contribute his services to what he regards as a claim unlikely of success. It was not the practice of defendants to pay significant sums to settle weak claims. The value of the contingent fee, then, outweighs any negative societal effect associated with such a fee arrangement.

However, elite corporate lawyers bemoaned the existence of the contingent fee as an attack upon legal professionalism. Nothing despaired the professional elite more than contingent fees and the lawyers whose practice depended upon them. All manner of the profession's woes were laid at the feet of the contingent fee. The reduced status and declining spirit of the entire profession were the claimed fruits of the contingent fee. Furthermore, corporate clients were losing money on the suits that contingent fees made possible, which gave the corporate legal elite no end of headaches. One lawyer present during the debates over the lawfulness of the contingent fee wrote "that every lawyer that got up here today in favor of this bill [which restricted contingent fees] was a corporation lawyer. Why they are so opposed to contingent fees I do not know."[154] Of course, he knew exactly why they were so opposed to contingent fees.

No objection to the contingent fee was too ridiculous or contrary to common sense to be forwarded as dispositive. One objection, for example, was that the client's interests are likely to suffer from the lawyer's urge to make as much money as possible.[155] Putting aside the assumption that a lawyer on a contingent fee will be greedier than one on an hourly fee (a questionable assumption at best), the more likely conclusion is that a lawyer would be *more* zealous for his client's interests because he is receiving part of the recovery. An hourly lawyer, on the other hand, receives his fee whether he wins or loses, and has significantly less monetary incentive to pursue his client's goals. Nevertheless, this objection was voiced often, as though questioning its obviously specious reasoning amounted to sympathizing with greed itself.

The disapproval of the contingent fee was pervasive among the elite. Therefore, when this same elite decided to draw up a code of ethics, it drew up a special canon intended to sharply limit the contingent fee.

The Canons could not, of course, eliminate the contingent fee entirely because the laws of the United States considered the validity of such fees "beyond legitimate controversy"[156] as early as 1877. Indeed, even many early state codes of ethics, based

---

[153] Radin, *supra* note 146 at 589.
[154] McGirr, *supra* note 140 at 11.
[155] *Ambulance Chasing, supra* note 141 at 185.
[156] Stanton et al. v. Embrey, 93 U.S. 548, 556 (1877).

largely upon the 1888 Alabama code,[157] acknowledged that the contingent fee was valid, including a statement that contingent fees may permissibly be higher than other fees because of the risk involved.[158] The most that ethical theorists could say was that contingent fees were "somewhat inconsistent"[159] with the prohibition on stirring up litigation. Contingent fees were therefore put under what was intended to be a severe stricture by the ABA: the Canons declared that contingent fee arrangements "should be under the supervision of the Court, in order that clients may be protected from unjust charges."[160] This Canon betrayed so much the prejudices of its authors that each point of it bears individual consideration.

The rationale for so restricting contingent fees, "that clients may be protected from unjust charges," is transparently specious. Presumably the writers of the Canon reasoned that contingent fees were often excessive. However, all fees were subject to the preceding Canon, which proposed no fewer than six factors for consideration in setting a neither exorbitant nor minimal fee.[161] One of those six factors was precisely whether the fee was contingent.[162] Why, then, were contingent fees subject to such additional scrutiny? Why insult the lawyer who worked for contingent fees with the presumption that he would charge extravagant fees for minimal service? Many of the contingent fee lawyers were foreign born; many were the children of foreign-born parents; almost all were from poor backgrounds; all were representing clients bringing claims against the Canon-drafters' clients. That, it seems, was reason enough.

The animus against the new lawyers is nowhere more evident than in the matters of ambulance chasing and the contingent fee, an animus that was enshrined in the code of ethics which governed the legal profession until 1969, and persisted thereafter until the Supreme Court trimmed the bar's sails based on First Amendment application. The two issues, ambulance chasing and the contingent fee, are commingled so thoroughly that even the contradictions of the hatred of them cannot be extricated. Indeed, often the elite's hatred of one contradicted its rationale for hatred of the other.

The standard condemnation of ambulance chasing, for example, including its system of runners who informed injured parties of their claims and recommended the services of a lawyer, was that it created litigation that would not otherwise have existed, fomenting disputes and otherwise disrupting society. The ABA condemned it on these grounds, declaring that it was "[s]tirring up strife

---

[157] *See* Committee on Professional Ethics at 678; *see also* Moliterno, *Lawyer Creeds and Moral Seismography*, 32 WAKE FOREST L. REV. 781, 789 (1997).

[158] *See* Committee on Profession Ethics at 709. While most of the codes did say that contingent fees "lead to many abuses," and that "certain compensation is to be preferred," no strictures were leveled against them that were not leveled against other forms of compensation. *Id.* at 710.

[159] HENRY S. DRINKER, LEGAL ETHICS 65 (1953).

[160] American Bar Association Canon 13, at 12.

[161] American Bar Association Canon 12, at 10.

[162] *Id.* at 11.

and litigation"[163] and that "to breed litigation by seeking out those with claims for personal injuries or those having any other grounds of action"[164] was an unethical practice. However, the contingent fee upon which these ambulance chasers rested their practices was condemned upon the exactly opposite grounds. The elite contended that, because it was more lucrative for the contingent fee lawyer to settle a case than to litigate it, that an ambulance chaser on a contingent fee was likely to settle rather than litigate, which might injure the interests of his client.[165] Their criticisms had come full circle: ambulance chasing was unethical because it stirred up litigation, whereas the contingent fee was unethical because it encouraged settlement rather than litigation. The new legal underclass simply could not win; but that was, after all, the idea.

VI. Conclusion

Waves of early 20th-century immigrants strained and blurred the legal profession's self-image. A crisis of identity ensued. The profession had choices. Look outward at a changing population to be served by lawyers and expand the vision of what lawyers do and for whom, or attempt to still the advances of time and culture and demographics to maintain the status quo in the profession. The legal profession chose the latter.

The legal profession's official response to changing demographics was to resist their reality. For at least 40 years while the face of America changed, the legal profession tried in vain to remain unchanged. The futility of such an effort is apparent. The cost in terms of lost opportunities to expand the understanding of what lawyers can do for society is immeasurable. The changes in advertising rules, heightening of educational standards, and enhanced resistance to contingent fees changed nothing about the lives of the elite lawyers who spearheaded the changes, except to protect them and their clients from the new class of plaintiffs' lawyers. Instead, each change protected and preserved the professional status quo.

According to idyllic folklore, the doors of access to the legal profession always swung open to anyone stung by ambition; lawyers might prefer a restricted guild, but democratic realties required them to settle for less. But this is a half-truth, which conceals the fact that doors to particular legal careers required keys that were distributed according to race, religion, sex, and ethnicity. In fact, what the profession settled for was much less than the folklore promised.

During the formative years of a new industrial power, the American bar used its authority to exclude the very people who had built that industrial power. The poor and the immigrants, upon whose backs the fortunes of the corporations were

---

[163] American Bar Association Canon 28, at 25.

[164] *Id.*

[165] *See Ambulance Chasing, supra* note 141 at 185.

created, were systematically excluded from the legal profession by the representatives of those corporations. Being called to defend the most helpless in society, the American bar did the exact opposite, harming them in ways that are with them still today.

The legacy of this program of discrimination is long and widespread. To this day, the poor have an exceedingly difficult task ahead of them if they desire to enter the legal profession. There are still relatively few reputable night schools because of the opprobrium that the bar heaped upon them; more affordable legal education would be a valued commodity in today's market conditions. There remains lingering disdain for the "ambulance chaser" and the personal injury lawyer, though the injured often decide that their own "ambulance chasers" might not be so bad, after all. The poor and immigrant lawyers of the early 20th century were the only representation available to the working classes, and the American legal profession did everything in its power to prevent them from being successful in that representation. This is, unfortunately, the legacy of the early organized American bar: a legacy that America and its legal profession would be better off without.

{ 3 }

Communist Infiltration

In two waves, America and its legal profession resisted the infiltration of a social and economic philosophy. Communism and communists, it seemed, were everywhere, under every rock and behind every tree. They were bent on warping American minds and subverting American values and principles. It lurked and threatened to undermine the American Constitution and way of life. The threat was mysterious and presented the danger of the unknown.

The legal profession swung at the threat in the dark, like a blindfolded child at a piñata. Central professional and legal values were turned on their heads to battle the menace. Assertion of First and Fifth Amendment rights, supported as necessities of a free society in other times, were equated with guilt in official ways. Unwillingness to swear loyalty meant disloyalty. Everyone was under suspicion.

This crisis eventually collapsed of its own weight. Purges, disbarment, and exclusion of the suspected did not alter the course of crisis. Time and economic implications did.

I. Some Background

A decade and a half after the Palmer Raids,[1] the federal government resumed its active pursuit of subversives, now more focused on the threat of domestic communism than the more generic and amorphous anarchists. With the formation of the House Committee on Un-American Activities ("HUAC") in 1938, the Hatch Act in 1939, the Civil Service Commission's War Service Regulations in 1942, and formation of the Attorney General's Interdepartmental Committee on Investigations in 1942, the fight was fully engaged.

---

[1] See A. MITCHELL PALMER, INVESTIGATION ACTIVITIES OF THE DEPARTMENT OF JUSTICE, S. DOC. No. 66-153, at 5 (1919), for Palmer's view of the Raids; see R.G. BROWN ET AL., NAT'L POPULAR GOV'T LEAGUE, TO THE AMERICAN PEOPLE: REPORT UPON THE ILLEGAL PRACTICES OF THE UNITED STATES DEPARTMENT OF JUSTICE (1920), for a critical view of the Raids by Zechariah Chafee Jr., Felix Frankfurter, Ernst Freund, and Roscoe Pound (among others).

In 1947, the President's Committee on Civil Rights reported that while "the government has the obligation to have in its employ only citizens of unquestioned loyalty...our whole civil liberties history provides us with clear warning against the possible misuse of loyalty checks to inhibit freedom of opinion and expression."[2] From 1945 to 1957, the HUAC conducted over 230 public hearings and examined over 3,000 witnesses, 135 of whom were cited for contempt. That same year, President Truman established the Federal Employee Loyalty Program, allowing the federal government to deny employment to "disloyal" individuals.[3] During 1947–48, the FBI examined over two million federal employees and conducted full investigations on over 6,300 of them.[4] The government's loyalty determination considered "[a]ctivities and associations of an applicant or employee," including "[m]embership in, affiliation with or sympathetic association with any foreign or domestic organization, association, movement, group or combination of persons, designated by "the Attorney General as totalitarian, fascist, communist, or subversive."[5] Attorney General Tom Clark generated a list of 123 "subversive" organizations.[6] He testified before a HUAC subcommittee that the government intended to "isolate subversive movements in this country from effective interference in the body politic." In a speech delivered shortly before his testimony, Clark declared that "[t]hose who do not believe in the ideology of the United States should not be allowed to stay in the United States."[7]

By 1951, the FBI had conducted full-scale investigations of 14,000 federal employees, leading to the resignation of 2,000 of them.[8] As the executive branch embarked on its loyalty investigations of government employees, the HUAC began to subpoena movie producers, screenwriters, and directors to examine alleged communist affiliations. In response, Hollywood personalities including Humphrey Bogart, Lauren Bacall, Groucho Marx, and Frank Sinatra, formed the Committee for the First Amendment and flew to Washington, DC, to support those called to testify. In October of 1947, 10 Hollywood witnesses refused, on First Amendment grounds, to answer questions from the HUAC. But after Congress cited the "Hollywood Ten" for contempt, the support from their colleagues fizzled. Within a month, top Hollywood executives agreed to blacklist the Ten.[9]

In their investigative hearings, the HUAC and the Senate Internal Security Subcommittee (SISS) routinely asked witnesses whether they were presently or had

---

[2] President's Comm. on Civil Rights, To Secure These Rights 49–50 (1947).

[3] Samuel Walker, In Defense of American Liberties: A History of the ACLU 177 (S. Ill. Univ. Press 2d ed. 1999) (1990).

[4] Thomas I. Emerson & David M. Helfield, *Loyalty among Government Employees*, 58 Yale L. J. 1, 14–17 (1948).

[5] *Id.* at 32.

[6] *See*, Robert Justin Goldstein, American Blacklist: The Attorney General's List of Subversive Organizations (2008).

[7] *Id.* at 64.

[8] Emerson & Helfield, *supra* note 4, at 32.

[9] Victor Navasky, Naming Names 77–88 (Hill & Wang rev. ed. 2003) (1980).

ever been a member of the Communist Party. There was no way to answer this question safely. Witnesses who denied any affiliation could be charged with perjury based on contradictory circumstantial evidence. Those who admitted a communist affiliation usually suffered adverse economic and social consequences.[10] As a result, a growing number of witnesses refused on constitutional grounds to answer questions, sometimes citing the First and sometimes the Fifth Amendments. But even these refusals had their consequences. Witnesses who invoked the Fifth Amendment right against self-incrimination were seen as admitting guilt and were labeled "Fifth Amendment Communists." Witnesses who asserted the First Amendment, as with the Hollywood Ten, usually received contempt of Congress citations.

Meanwhile, the Berlin blockade, the first Soviet test of an atomic bomb, and Mao Tse-tung's overthrow of Chiang Kai-Shek's government in China all contributed to the growing fear. The domestic threat was reenforced by Alger Hiss's 1950 perjury conviction and the espionage convictions of Julius and Ethel Rosenberg the following year.[11] In light of the unsettling domestic and global developments, citizens across the political spectrum viewed the Smith Act prosecutions as a necessary defense against the spread of communism.

The Supreme Court diminished associational protections in *Dennis v. United States*,[12] a decision that ACLU national chairman Roger Baldwin later called "the worst single blow to civil liberties in all our history."[13] The *Dennis* defendants' lawyers were abused for their lawyer associations.[14] *Dennis* came to the Court after FBI Director J. Edgar Hoover initiated Smith Act prosecutions of 12 senior leaders of the Communist Party of the United States of America (CPUSA). The government charged the defendants with violating the Act's membership clause, which made it unlawful to "organize[]...any society, group, or assembly of persons who teach, advocate, or encourage the overthrow or destruction of any such government [in the United States] by force or violence; or becomes or is a member of, or affiliates with, any such society, group, or assembly of persons, knowing the purposes thereof."[15] In arguing its case, the government construed the Act so broadly that it "made no effort to prove that this attempted overthrow was in any sense imminent, or even in the concrete planning stages."[16] Following a nine-month trial, the jury deliberated less than a day before convicting all 12 defendants.[17] The plurality opinion reinterpreted the clear and present danger standard, concluding that with respect to the CPUSA, the mere "existence of the conspiracy...creates the danger."[18] Justice

---

[10] Lucas A. Powe, Jr., The Warren Court and American Politics 77–82 (2000).

[11] *Id.*

[12] 341 U.S. 494 (1951).

[13] Walker, *supra* note 3, at 187.

[14] *See* later in this chapter.

[15] 18 U.S.C. §§ 10, 11 (1946) (current version at 18 U.S.C. § 2385 (2006)).

[16] Martin H. Redish, The Logic of Persecution 83 (2005).

[17] *Id.* at 81–87.

[18] *Dennis, supra* note 12, at 511 (Vinson, C.J., plurality opinion).

Black's dissent acknowledged the place that public fears were taking in the Court's decisions:

> Public opinion being what it now is, few will protest the conviction of these Communist petitioners. There is hope, however, that in calmer times, when present pressures, passions and fears subside, this or some later Court will restore the First Amendment liberties to the high preferred place where they belong in a free society.[19]

Dennis generated little public outcry, and even liberals like Norman Thomas and Arthur Schlesinger supported the decision. Despite criticism from no less than Eleanor Roosevelt, *Dennis* received widespread public support. Roosevelt spent the following two summers touring with Justice Douglas to criticize *Dennis* in public forums, an endeavor that at times met with hostility.[20]

With the Dennis authority in hand, investigations proceeded with no holds barred. Lower-level CPUSA officials were now targeted, and 126 lower-level officials were charged in the next few years. Albert Einstein emerged as a prominent figure in the communist investigations. When the SISS subpoenaed a high school English teacher named William Frauenglass to testify about possible communist affiliations in May of 1953, Frauenglass wrote Einstein requesting a letter of support. Einstein's response, which appeared as part of a front page story in the *New York Times*, counseled that despite the inevitable consequences, "[e]very intellectual who is called before the committees ought to refuse to testify."[21]

Six months later, electrical engineer Al Shadowitz drove to Princeton to see Einstein after receiving a subpoena from the SISS. Shadowitz informed Einstein that he intended to rely on the First Amendment rights of speech and association rather than the Fifth Amendment in refusing to answer the Committee's questions, a position that Einstein supported. At his public hearing, Shadowitz invoked the First Amendment and noted that "Professor Einstein advised me not to answer." Despite the efforts of Einstein and others, widespread public concern for those accused never materialized, and the government routinely won even its weakest cases.[22]

Following World War II, when the necessity of feigned alliance with Russia had largely passed, the nation's obsession and fear of communism escalated. Senator Joseph McCarthy took advantage of the mood and thrust himself into the national limelight by announcing his knowledge of the names of communists in the State Department. Eventually, his name became synonymous with narrow-minded, obsessive repression. Perhaps his greatest impact, and that of the House's

---

[19] *Id.* at 581 (Black, J., dissenting).
[20] ALLIDA M. BLACK, CASTING HER OWN SHADOW 155 (1996).
[21] Albert Einstein, *Open Letter to William Frauenglass*, N.Y. TIMES, June 12, 1953, *reprinted in* DAVID ROWE & ROBERT SCHULMAN, EINSTEIN ON POLITICS 494–495 (2007).
[22] FRED JEROME, THE EINSTEIN FILE: J. EDGAR HOOVER'S SECRET WAR AGAINST THE WORLD'S MOST FAMOUS SCIENTIST 238–248 (2002).

investigatory committee, HUAC, was felt in the entertainment industry and among lawyers. Among the lawyer targets, some had their own Left leanings, others merely dared to represent alleged communists, and a few were simply unwilling to submit to demands for disclosure of their political views.[23] In this hysterical time, the latter was taken as a certain sign of hidden fault.

The legal profession, especially at the national level, perceived a crisis of communist infiltration and fed the general population's madness. The ABA allowed its patriotic fervor to blind it to abuses of civil liberties without and within.

II. Red Scare Connection

The post-World War II heightened fear of communist infiltration in the profession was a rekindling of Red Scare fears of socialism—a generation and World War earlier. The profession had a crisis rehearsal of sorts in the times marked by the Palmer Raids and the generalized-but-intense fear of the socialist.[24] Successive ABA presidents from 1921–23 sounded Red Scare alarms.[25]

The Red Scare formed a thought bridge between the immigrant crisis and the post-World War II fear of communist infiltration. Talk in the period surrounding World War I was of lawyers' vigilance to curb the consequences of the disturbing fact "that we have permitted to drag their green trunks across and along the planks at Ellis Island thousands and hundreds of thousands of anarchists, revolutionists,...fellows who propose to take charge of this republic of ours."[26] The connection between the Red Scare and the professional crisis brought on by the immigrant wave was obvious. Many of the same Southern and Eastern European immigrants were seen as not only the source of falling moral standards of the profession but also the socialist ideas that threatened to infect America. The time of professional repose in between the Red Scare period and the post-World War II communist fear period began with the passage of the Immigration Control Act of 1924, stemming the tide of unwanted immigrants. The Act's passage prompted ABA Citizenship Committee Chair F. Dumont Smith's 1926 announcement, "The menace of Bolshevism is passed."[27] Not quite ready to let go of the menace and its

---

[23] *See, e.g., In re* Anastaplo, 121 N.E.2d 826 (Ill. 1954); *See also, In re* Anastaplo, 163 N.E.2d 429 (Ill. 1959), *aff'd*, 366 U.S. 82 (1961).

[24] *See, e.g.,* Rome G. Brown, *The Socialist Menace to Constitutional Government*, 4 A.B.A. J. 54 (1918).

[25] *See, e.g.,* W. A. Blount, *To the American Bar Association*, 7 A.B.A. J. 53 (1921); *see also* Cordenio A. Severance, *The Constitution and Individualism*, 8 A.B.A. J. 538, 541–42 (1922); *see also*, Severance, *The Attack on American Institutions*, 7 A.B.A. J. 633(1921); *see also*, R.E.L. Saner, *The Constitution and Nationality*, 9 A.B.A. J. 453 (1923); *see also*, 48 Ann. Rep. A.B.A. 445 (1923).

[26] Thomas Marshall, *Altruistic Evil*, 55 Am. L. Rev. 349, 362–363 (1921).

[27] F. Dumont Smith et al., *Report of the Committee on American Citizenship*, 49 Ann, Rep. A.B.A. 361, 364 (1926).

connection to the immigrant wave, in 1929, the ABA published a map of the United States illustrating the citizen-status of its inhabitants, with rural areas dominated by native-born Americans in white and urban areas dominated by recent immigrants in black.[28]

Anarchists Sacco and Vanzetti had been executed in 1927, and despite the enormous notoriety and extentively-debated fairness of the case and its professional implications, only two references to it may be found in the *ABA Journal* of the time. One was a comment on the case from the Canadian point of view.[29] The other, a one-line reference in the President's Address declaring that it was ABA policy to remain on the sidelines of controversial political matters.[30] The ABA policy of noninvolvement in controversial matters was selectively used or ignored when convenient. One decade before, the organization engaged major efforts against the influx of those anarchists with their "green trunks," and one decade later the ABA undertook a mission to undermine New Deal policies and programs. But later, in the 1950s and 60s, the policy was trotted out to justify the ABA remaining on the sidelines of the civil rights movement.[31]

III. A Calm, Conservative Power

The ABA had always been seen as a bastion of calm, conservative reaction to crisis, a by-product of resistance to change and innovation. In the main, this resolute calm allowed the legal profession to take the least possible action in response to crisis. Senator Charles Jones summarized the ABA founders' motives:

> [W]hen innovation and change are demanded in every quarter, there ought to be found somewhere in our system a calm, conservative power which can expose fallacies, point out flaws, and suggest reforms without violence or shock to our government.[32]

In the history of the profession, this "calm, conservative power" has usually meant little or no reaction to crisis and efforts to maintain the status quo. But here, in its exclusionary mode, a repeat from the immigrant-induced crisis, the conservative response to crisis was reversed and produced excessive response. The national arm of legal profession was, if anything, more vociferous in its denunciation of communists than local lawyers or the general public. But in this instance, as in the

---

[28] 54 ANN. REP. A.B.A. 302 (1929).

[29] William Renwick Riddell, *The Sacco-Vanzetti Case from a Canadian Viewpoint*, 13 A.B.A. J. 683, 694 (1927).

[30] Charles S. Whitman, Presidential Address at the Annual Meeting of the American Bar Association in Buffalo (Aug. 31, 1927), *in* 13 A.B.A. J. 491 (1927).

[31] *See* chapter 4.

[32] Letter from Senator Charles Jones to Simeon Baldwin (August 10, 1878) *in* SIMEON BALDWIN, THE FOUNDING OF THE AMERICAN BAR ASSOCIATION 682 (1917).

reaction to the immigrant crisis, excessive action was actually a means of maintaining the profession's status quo: if the feared others could be kept out by whatever drastic means were needed, the homogeneity of professional thought could be maintained.

One arm of the organized bar retained the general inclination against activity—the ABA Bill of Rights Committee. In its only report to the House of Delegates between 1950 and 1959, the report confessed, "Your committee has found little work to do."[33] This, at the height of attacks on the right against self-incrimination, the right to counsel for accused communists, and both forced speech (e.g., in the form of loyalty oaths) and suppressed speech. Until coming out of its shell to disagree with the House of Delegates' adoption of a series of resolutions criticizing the Supreme Court's security decisions as recommended by the Special Committee on Communist Tactics, Strategy and Objectives[34] in 1959,[35] the Bill of Rights Committee left the decade to the Special Committee on Communist Tactics.

IV. Purging Communists

The profession moved against lawyers and bar applicants in a variety of ways. The ABA demanded loyalty oaths of all members. Those who refused would be excluded from membership, and state bars were urged to exclude them from the profession entirely. The purported communist connections could not be too minor or too far in the past for exclusion to result.

The ABA could only authoritatively control its own membership. But to spread its influence, the ABA recommended that state bar leaders demand lawyers to take a loyalty oath.[36] The resolution demanded that every lawyer

file an affidavit stating whether he is or ever has been a member of the Communist party, or affiliated therewith, and stating also whether he is or ever has been a member or supporter of any organization that espouses the overthrow, by force or by any illegal or unconstitutional means, of the United States Government, or the government of any of the states or territories of the United States; and in the event such affidavit reveals that he is or ever has

---

[33] William A. Schnader et al., *Report of the Standing Committee on Bill of Rights*, 79 ANN. REP. A.B.A. 206 (1954).

[34] Roy M. Cohn & Thomas A. Bolan, *The Supreme Court and the A.B.A. Report and Resolutions*, 28 FORDHAM L. REV. 233, 236 (1959). For the full text of the resolutions and the debate preceding their adoption, *see* 45 A.B.A.J. 406–410 (1959).

[35] Norbert C. Brockman, The Politics of the American Bar Association (1963) (unpublished PhD dissertation, Catholic University of America, 1963) (on file with author).

[36] *See Proceedings of the House of Delegates*, 76 ANN. REP. A.B.A. 527, 531–532 (1951) (detailing the manner in which the ABA approved the loyalty oath resolution); *see also*, JEROLD S. AUERBACH, UNEQUAL JUSTICE 239 (1976) (further describing the circumstances surrounding the approval).

been a member of said Communist Party, or of any such organization, that the appropriate authority promptly and thoroughly investigate the activities and conduct of said member of the Bar to determine his fitness for continuance as an attorney.[37]

The oath was praised by national leaders as a means of ridding the profession of the disloyal. For example, Waldon B. White, Associate Justice of the Supreme Court of Tennessee and member of the ABA House of Delegates, suggested that "'our leaders' are dealing with the subversive threat to the U.S. [in the profession] in an appropriate manner."[38]

But others saw danger and alarming parallels underlying enforcement of such a loyalty requirement. When confronted with a case in which a bar applicant was denied membership because he failed to adequately respond to a question inquiring into "loyalty" of this kind, Justice Warren mailed to Justice Black a number of newspaper clippings detailing the Hungarian purging of the bar (disbarring 800, forcing 3,000 to testify as to their loyalty to the central communist government).[39] In the end, most state associations did not follow the ABA recommendation, and few commanded members to take the oath.

In Massachusetts, for example, pursuant to "An Act to Require Attorneys-At-Law to Take an Oath of Loyalty to the Principles of the Constitution of the United States and the Commonwealth," the following oath was proposed:

I, (insert name), do solemnly swear (or affirm) that I do not advocate, and have not advocated, nor am I a member of any political party or organization that advocates, the overthrow of the government of the United States or of this commonwealth by force or violence or by any other illegal or unconstitutional method; and that so long as I am an attorney, I will not advocate nor become a member of any political party or organization that advocates the overthrow of the government of the United States or of this commonwealth by force or violence or by any other illegal or unconstitutional method.[40]

Massachusetts Representative William E. Hays spoke out against what he called "hasty legislation." Referring to the Smith Act, he pointed out that there was "adequate Federal law to deal with any serious subversive activity."[41]

Despite the limited following of its oath resolution, the ABA continued its effort to purge communists from the profession by generating lists of those who had

---

[37] *Proceedings of the House of Delegates*, 75 ANN. REP. A.B.A. 102, 148–149 (1950)

[38] Waldon B. White, *Liberty under Law versus Communism*, 29 TENN. L. REV. 33, 33 (1961).

[39] Joshua E. Kastenberg, *Hugo Black's Vision of the Lawyer, the First Amendment, and the Duty of the Judiciary: the Bar Applicant Cases in a National Security State*, 20 WM. & MARY BILL RTS. J. 691, 754 (2012).

[40] Mary Elizabeth Basile, *Loyalty Testing for Attorneys*, 30 CARDOZO L. REV. 1844, 1858 (2009) (citing H.R. 2323, 157 Gen. Ct. (Mass. 1951)).

[41] *Id.* at 1859 (quoting *The Current American Swearing Epidemic: Supplementary Statement of Representative William E. Hays*, MASS. L. Q. 47, 50 (1951)).

exercised their Fifth Amendment rights at various committee inquiries and encouraging state and local bar associations to move against the licenses of these suspected communists.[42] In 1956, the ABA's Committee on Communist Tactics, Strategy, and Objectives issued a report applauding an amendment made by the Florida Bar to their Integration Rule, treating invocations of the Fifth Amendment as prima facie evidence of a lack of fitness to practice. And in 1951, referring to Michigan's affirmation of the ABA's position on cleansing the bar of communist influences, the president of the Michigan bar pointed out that the profession offers no refuge to those engaging in subversion under the guise of protecting individual liberties.

The attack on "Fifth Amendment Communists" received mixed success. The Civil Rights Committee of the Washington State Bar Association recommended against making an invocation of the Fifth Amendment in response to a question about communist affiliations or subversive activities sufficient grounds for disbarment. Instead, the Committee recommended a full investigation into the matter whenever an attorney pleads the Fifth in such circumstances.[43] But in Florida, Leo Sheiner was disbarred when he answered a question about his current affiliation with the communist party in the negative, but declined to answer whether he had *ever* been so affiliated.[44] The *Sheiner* decision drew praise from the ABA, and when he appealed, the ABA directed the Committee on Communist Tactics, Strategy and Objectives chairman Herbert R. O'Connor to file an amicus curiae brief opposing Sheiner's appeal to the Florida Supreme Court.[45]

George Anastaplo's fault was a refusal to answer the bar committee's questions about his affiliations and associations. By all accounts a man of excellent character, ability and intellect, Anastaplo was refused bar membership. Called the "Socrates of Chicago," he went on, despite his bar admission denial, to earn a PhD from Chicago and teach and write for many years. Abner Mikva wrote in the *Hyde Park Herald* that Anastaplo's refusal to answer the bar authorities' questions was a principled stance and not an ideological one. "The practice of law," Mikva wrote, "has been the poorer [for Anastaplo's exclusion]."[46]

Even long past activities with the communist party were enough to be disbarred or refused admission, such as in the following cases.[47]

Schware: Schware had been involved with the communist party for seven years, but in 1940 had repudiated all allegiance to communism, and since had on one occasion criticized 'anti-communist' sentiment as racist and

---

[42] *Proceedings of House of Delegates*, 37 A.B.A. J. 309, 312–313 (1951).

[43] *Civil Rights Committee Report*, 30 Wash. L. Rev. 318 (1955).

[44] Florida v. Sheiner, 112 So. 2d 571 (1959).

[45] Herbert U. Feibelman, *Can a Lawyer Invoke the Fifth Amendment? A Distinguished Florida Jurist Says "No!,"* 59 Com. L. J. 301 (1954).

[46] Abner Mikva, *Anastaplo: A Teacher Who Never Stopped Learning*, Hyde Park Herald, Nov. 12, 2003, at 4.

[47] *See* Note, *"Good Moral Character" as a Prerequisite to Admission to the Bar*, 65 Yale L. J. 873 (1956), for general information on Schware's refused application.

discriminatory. Thirteen years later, he was denied admission to the New Mexico Bar. Scholars have noted that none of the other grounds cited by the bar were evidence of moral shortcomings.[48] Unlike in most other disbarment actions, Schware was not accused of any present affirmative association, but rather of long-passed affiliations and alleged personally held beliefs. As both the dissent in *Schware* and a commentator noted, the denial of admission on the grounds of past affiliation is essentially permanent.[49]

Braverman:[50] Braverman was convicted for conspiracy to violate Section 2 of the Smith Act, for attending four meetings of the Maryland District of the Communist Party in 1948–49. The appellate court did not find error in giving the case to a jury with evidence of membership alone (without evidence of specific intent). "It found that there was legally sufficient evidence that Braverman, who had '. . . served as a member of the District Committee of the party, had been a candidate for chairman of one of its meetings, had served as its attorney, was a member of its 'white collar club' and had conducted classes for it in his home . . . ,' had joined that conspiracy with knowledge of its unlawful purposes."[51] Based on the conviction, he was disbarred in 1955.

Braverman had an otherwise spotless record as an attorney after admission to the bar in 1941. The court acknowledged that it felt compelled to disbar only because of the 'infamous' nature of the activity prosecuted under the Smith Act, leading to disbarment on the basis of moral turpitude.[52] He was reinstated over a vigorous dissent nearly twenty years later.[53]

Representing accused communists was hazardous as well. After representing Smith Act defendants,[54] five lawyers[55] were sentenced for contempt.[56] Dissenting from the Supreme Court's affirmance of the contempt judgment, Justice Black wrote, "[T]his summary blasting of legal careers . . . constitutes an overhanging

---

[48] Schware had a prior arrest for car theft (no indictment; car not in fact stolen); he had assumed a false identity for a short time (assumed an Italian name to avoid discrimination as a Jew); he had a prior arrest as one among thousands in a labor strike; he had a nol-prossed indictment for volunteering, and urging others to volunteer, for the Spanish Loyalist Army (in violation of the Neutrality Statute). *Id.* at 876.

[49] *Id.* at 877 (noting that the applicant's motion for a hearing on the permanency of his denied admission was not granted by New Mexico's high court); Schware v. Bd. of Bar Examiners, 291 P.2d 607, 635–36 (N.M. 1955) (Kiker, J., dissenting).

[50] Braverman v. Bar Ass'n of Balt., 209 Md. 328 (1955).

[51] *In re* Braverman, 271 Md. 196 (1974), *quoting* Frankfeld v. United States, 198 F.2d 679, 686 (4th Cir. Md. 1952).

[52] *Braverman, supra* note 50, at 344.

[53] *In re* Braverman, *supra* note 51.

[54] United States v. Dennis, 183 F.2d 201 (2d Cir. 1950).

[55] Three of the five were Jewish, one was Black, and one was Irish Catholic. AUERBACH, *supra* note 36, at 237.

[56] *Id.*; Fowler Harper & David Haber, *Lawyer Troubles in Political Trials*, 60 YALE L. J. 1 (1951); NAVASKY, *supra* note 9, at 37.

menace to every courtroom advocate in America. The menace is most ominous for lawyers who are obscure, unpopular, or defenders of unpopular persons or unorthodox causes."[57]

Two lawyers, Harry Sacher and Abraham Isserman, were especially affected by their representation of alleged Communist Party members. Prior to their representation of the *Dennis* defendants, each had many years of practice, some of which had been spent representing civil rights parties and labor.[58] Before his contempt conviction and later disbarment, Sacher had a "twenty-four year unblemished record."[59] The trial judge who cited Sacher for contempt received praise from then Attorney General Clark who had written that politically wayward lawyers should be punished.[60] After being jailed for contempt, the two were pursued by bar authorities. Sacher was disbarred by the Bar Association of the City of New York; Isserman by the New Jersey Bar.[61] Isserman's disbarment in New Jersey was followed by disbarment from the United States Supreme Court Bar.[62] Both were eventually reinstated after many years, during which the hysteria of the communist scare had subsided.[63]

Sacher and Isserman were not alone in being targets of bar punishment and harassment for their political views and associations. Many others who deigned to represent unpopular, feared clients followed in their steps.[64] The prospect of professional discipline from representation of communists became so likely that representation in these cases became almost impossible to find.[65] A lawyer willing to represent the government's mortal enemy risked near certain professional annihilation.[66] The raw number of reported cases of professional discipline can be found. But the number of lawyers silenced and the number of clients who went underrepresented can never be known. Justice Douglas described the professional phenomenon as a "black silence of fear."[67]

Although Isserman and Sacher were reinstated after a measure of the hysteria died down, for his simple refusal to answer bar application questions regarding

---

[57] Sacher v. United States, 343 U.S. 1, 37–38 (1952).

[58] AUERBACH, *supra* note 36, at 242.

[59] United States v. Sacher, 182 F.2d 416 (2d Cir. 1950).

[60] AUERBACH, *supra* note 36, at 241.

[61] *In re* Isserman, 9 N.J. 269 (1952).

[62] 348 U.S. 1 (1954).

[63] Ass'n of Bar of N.Y. v. Isserman, 271 F.2d 784 (2d Cir. 1959); *In re* Isserman, 35 N.J. 198, 204(1961).

[64] *In re* Sawyer, 360 U.S. 622, 626–627 (1959) (disciplining Smith Act defense counsel for criticism of trial judge).

[65] AUERBACH, *supra* note 36; NAVASKY, *supra* note 9.

[66] AUERBACH, *supra* note 36, at 246–258 (rendering numerous instances of professional discipline and harassment); Deborah L. Rhode, *Moral Character as a Professional Credential*, 94 YALE L. J. 481 (1985); NAVASKY, *supra* note 9; Note, *The Privilege to Practice Law versus the Fifth Amendment Privilege to Remain Silent*, 56 NW. U. L. REV. 644 (1961).

[67] William O. Douglas, *The Black Silence of Fear*, N.Y. TIMES, Jan. 13, 1952 (magazine), at 7, 37–38.

political views, George Anastaplo was refused twice, first at the height of the hysteria[68] and later when much of it had subsided.[69]

Repeated representation of accused communists carried its own strong inference of culpability. In the 1956 New Orleans SISS hearings, National Lawyers Guild lawyer Ben Smith was representing Winifred Friese, an assistant school librarian, officer of the Jefferson Parish PTA, and former CPUSA member. Senator Eastland asked Ben Smith and another lawyer representing those individuals before the subcommittee if they wanted to "clear" their names. One stated that he had never been a communist and that it was "the most ridiculous procedure [he] had ever heard of, a lawyer being called on to explain being a lawyer." Eastland expelled him from the proceedings. Ben Smith, by contrast, stated that he had never been a communist and did not believe in it. The SISS requested a copy of the transcript to support a possible perjury charge against Smith. The following year, when Smith represented two physics professors before the SISS in Memphis, Committee counsel J. G. Sourwine insinuated that Smith must be a communist lawyer because he regularly turned up at SISS hearings and suggestively asked the professors why they had employed a lawyer from New Orleans.[70]

Step by step, the ABA moved against communists. First, it announced that all communists should be required to register with government so that their activities could be closely monitored and publicized "mercilessly."[71] The House of Delegates took an early position on the related investigations of the film industry, stating that those who take the Fifth should be "compelled" to answer questions about their Communist Party membership. This stand was curiously accompanied by assertions that all civil rights and liberties of suspects should be protected. At its next annual meeting, it lent support to the Mundt-Nixon anti-subversion act, and it unanimously voted to expel all communists from ABA membership. Further, it voted to expel all who refused to answer questions from a bar committee, Congress, or other authorities.[72] Nearly six years later, the *ABA Journal* took the "rare" action of printing views in opposition to ABA-adopted policy, in this instance to ABA policy of drawing an inference of law breaking from the assertion of Fifth Amendment rights.[73]

When the next ABA act was a vote to support the investigatory activities of HUAC, Charles Curtis wrote a scathing dissent.[74] But the House of Delegates nonetheless voted to create what would be its chief communist-fighting body, the

---

[68] *In re* Anastaplo, 3 Ill. 2d 471, 121 N.E.2d 826 (1954).

[69] *In re* Anastaplo, 18 Ill. 2d. 182, 163 N.E.2d 429 (1959).

[70] Sarah Hart Brown, *Redressing Southern "Subversion": The Case of Senator Eastland and the Louisiana Lawyer*, 43 LA. HIST. 295 (Summer 2002).

[71] *Communists in U.S.: "Registration" Urged by House of Delegates*, 34 A.B.A. J. 281 (1948).

[72] *Communism and Communists: Association Votes Support of Mundt-Nixon Bill*, 34 A.B.A. J. 899 (1948).

[73] Ralph S. Brown, Jr., *Lawyers and the Fifth Amendment*, 40 A.B.A. J. 404 (1954).

[74] *Report of the Special Committee on Bill of Rights*, 74 ANN. REP. A.B.A. 264, 266 (1949).

Special Committee on Communist Tactics (SCCT). Its creation was accompanied by adoption of a resolution urging state bars to require loyalty oaths for all lawyers, a position that was in the main resisted by state and local bars.[75] For its part, the SCCT's first report urged expulsion and disbarment of all lawyers affiliated with the Communist Party. The SCCT expanded its activities while the Bill of Rights Committee slept. It filed amicus briefs arguing that no member of the Communist Party could be fit to be a lawyer,[76] and it brought lawyers asserting Fifth Amendment rights to the attention of state bar authorities, urging them to move against the lawyers' licenses.[77]

To the extent it had not been so before, membership in the National Lawyers Guild became synonymous with communist associations. At the ABA House of Delegates meeting on August 28, 1953, then-U.S. Attorney General Herbert Brownell announced that the NLG would henceforth be listed as a subversive organization, calling it the "'legal mouthpiece' of the Communist Party."[78]

That the announcement came to a cheering crowd at an ABA Annual Meeting was not lost on NLG leaders.[79] The NLG competition with the ABA was about ideas and social conscience. NLG never rivaled the ABA for professional prominence. But now, NLG leaders viewed the ABA as a conspirator with government, teaming for oppression of speech and ideas. The ABA had by this time taken action supporting the ouster of all communists from membership and supporting their disbarment. But it had not yet formally supported the disbarment of all NLG members. This had been seen as a refusal to fully equate NLG membership with Communist Party support. The attorney general's speech to the ABA stepped over that thin line.

Needless to say, it was even more likely that lawyers with communist or socialist ties or leanings would have difficulty gaining admission than they would be disbarred if already licensed. Several eventually prominent lawyers were initially denied admission by some bar based on various political associations or refusal to answer questions. George Anastaplo was not the only one.[80] Clyde Summers, who was excluded because his conscientious objector status restricted his ability to support the U.S. Constitution,[81] is a member in good standing of the New York

---

[75] *The Proposed Anti-Communist Oath: Opposition Expressed to Association's Policy*, 37 A.B.A. J. 123 (1951).

[76] *See, e.g., Scheiner v. Florida*, 82 So.2d 657 (Fla. 1955).

[77] *Report of the Special Committee on Communist Tactics, Strategy, and Objectives*, 80 ANN. REP. A.B.A. 461 (1955).

[78] Herbert Brownell, Jr., Address at the Diamond Jubilee Meeting of the American Bar Association in Boston (Aug. 27, 1953), *in* 78 ANN. REP. A.B.A. 334, 340 (1953); NAVASKY, *supra* note 9, at 37.

[79] Editorial, *The American Bar Association, Attorney General Brownell, and the National Lawyers Guild in Time of Crisis*, 13 NAT'L LAW. GUILD REV. 101 (1953).

[80] Rhode, *supra* note 66, at n. 226(quoting Andrew Patner, *The Quest of George Anastaplo*, CHICAGO, Dec. 1982, at 185, 189); *In re* Anastaplo, 366 U.S. 82 (1961).

[81] Rhode, *supra* note 66, at 567.

bar and the Jefferson B. Fordham Professor of Law, Emeritus, at the University of Pennsylvania. Robert Cover, one of the plaintiffs in *Law Students Research Council v. Wadmond*,[82] died at age 42 in 1986, having only two years before been at long last admitted to the New York Bar. At his death, he was the Chancellor Kent Professor of Law and Legal History at Yale Law School. At the time of their initial attempts at admission, each was regarded as unfit for membership in the legal profession. Lawyers must, after all, be guardians of liberty.

V. A Second Passing of the Crisis and a New Communist Threat: Civil Rights Activists

Although the 1926 announcement that "The menace of Bolshevism is passed,"[83] may have seemed premature in the early 1950s, the communist infiltration crisis did pass. It died of natural causes as the influence of communism itself waned. Unlike other crises to strike the legal profession (for example, the immigrant wave, the civil rights movement, technology and globalization), the communist infiltration crisis was not associated with a cultural change that overtook the legal profession and to which the legal profession had to eventually capitulate and adapt. Nothing the legal profession did affected the persistence of the crisis or its demise. The self-protective moves had no effect whatever except for the damage done to innocent lawyers' lives, and the associated loss to the community of their talents and courage during the time of their banishment.

　Instead, this crisis collapsed under its own weight. True, lawyers of today who happen to be as Left leaning as those of the 1950s have no trouble from the organized bar. The crisis and the profession's exaggerated demonization of Left lawyers diminished as the combination of Civil Rights era politics and sobering realities of the Cold War became everyday experiences rather than shocking news. By the mid-1960s, hysteria about communism had been replaced by nuclear face-offs and the space race. With one known and probably only few exceptions, the professional war against communists had ended by the late 1970s. The exception: the communist bar admissions issues persisted long after one might have thought they would pass. In one case, a legal aid lawyer fought for two years to be licensed because he answered the "communist question" by checking "decline to answer," which was among the three choices permitted on the application. The bar refused his admission and asked him to answer the question "yes" or "no." The applicant declined to do so. His admission to the bar was eventually ordered by the state supreme court.[84] By the time the Soviet Union and the Berlin Wall collapsed, and

---

[82] Law Students Civil Rights Research Cousel, Inc. v. Wadmond, 299 F.Supp. 117 (S.D.N.Y. 1969); *See also Tributes to Robert Cover*, 96 YALE L. J. 1699 (1987).

[83] SMITH, *supra* note 23.

[84] *See* Pushinsky v. W. Va. Bd. of Law Examiners, 266 S.E.2d 444 (W. Va. 1980).

China had opened its economic if not political system, communism had become a professional nonissue.

There was an explicit connection in the minds of many between the burgeoning civil rights movement and communist infiltration.[85] The connection in the South was encouraged in the 1930s when a Communist Party legal arm, the International Labor Defense, undertook the celebrated defenses of Angelo Herndon and the Scottsboro Boys.[86] J. Edgar Hoover and the FBI's wiretapping of Martin Luther King based on his alleged communist ties eventually became well known.

Among the injunctions entered against the operation of the NAACP in the South, one was obtained in part on the grounds that it was a subversive (that is, communist) organization.[87] Eventually that injunction was vacated as violative of association rights by the Supreme Court of the United States following *NAACP v. Alabama*.

The claimed connection between communism and civil rights activism was not an exclusively Southern phenomenon and extended beyond school desegregation and race issues and spread generally to the "New Left." At the 1968 Nebraska Bar Association Annual Meeting, the connection was described:

> Unfortunately, [following the *Dennis* convictions] something happened to breathe new life into what could have been a beautiful corpse. Out of the racial strife at home and the Vietnam War there evolved, developed, or came into being what is known as the 'New Left.'[88]

Now in a new form, the fading communist threat had been reborn in the form of antiwar protestors, draft resisters, school desegregation activists, and civil disobedients. The capacity for the communist to morph into new forms seemed unlimited, and the transition from attacks on communists to attacks on civil rights lawyers was smooth.

VI. Conclusion

The communist crisis simply passed. Unlike others, it left little mark beyond ruined careers. The early 20th-century immigrants washed into the profession and changed its demographic and its spirit, despite all efforts to keep them out. The entry of blacks and women during the civil rights era signaled dramatic changes in the profession. Incivility, battled feverishly but ineffectively in the 1990s and beyond, entered the profession's ethos. Technology and globalization, which the profession

---

[85] *See* chapter 4 for more on this connection.

[86] John D. Inazu, *The Strange Origins of the Constitutional Right of Association*, 77 TENN. L. REV. 485, 507 (2010).

[87] Louisiana *ex rel.* Grimillion v. NAACP, 366 U.S. 293 (1961).

[88] Hon. Donald E. Kelley, Address at the Annual Nebraska State Bar Association Dinner: The Lawyer's Response to the New Left (Nov. 7, 1968), *in* 48 NEB. L. REV. 774, 778 (1968–1969).

has tried to ignore away, have and will continue to make whatever change they wish. But the change in political balance that occurred in the 1960s and beyond had little to do with failed efforts to fight communist lawyers in the 1950s. The political shift had far more to do with civil rights era sensibilities, the demographic influence of blacks and women entrants, and eventually the mistrust of government spawned by Watergate. Efforts to prevent communist infiltration of the profession had but little effect on the long-term nature of the profession. As intense as the crisis was at its peak, it has had an almost imperceptible legacy.

The legal profession became as inflamed with fear of communism as had the HUAC and McCarthy-led committees. It was, if anything, more inflamed than the general public. Numerous dissenters within the profession were heard, but official action and pronouncements emanated from fearful leaders. So often, the legal profession has trumpeted its capacity to be a sobering force to calm fiery public alarm. In this crisis, the profession fueled the fires of passionate overreaction rather than dampen them, all in the service of preserving the professional status quo from the influence of feared outsiders.

4

A New Kind of Lawyering
THE CIVIL RIGHTS MOVEMENT

In a wide variety of contexts, civil rights lawyers and activists, and early federally supported legal aid lawyers disrupted the calm social professional serenity of the late 1950s. Their collective fault in the eyes of the organized, traditional strength center of the bar was the disruption to the legal, social, and cultural status quo that their work promised. The organized bar treated the civil rights movement itself as a crisis and targeted lawyers who disrupted the legal profession's settled norms. The profession saw the civil rights lawyers as introducing a new form of lawyering with social engineering as its goal. Thought inappropriate and unprofessional, the bar sought to dampen this reform-minded lawyering. When civil rights activist lawyers began stirring the pot, the profession was still reeling from its anticommunist fervor. Some saw the civil rights lawyer as no different from the communist. Eventually, Warren Burger decried the work of activist lawyers as a key element of the emerging "civility crisis," warning that "the jungle [was] closing in."[1] Curiously, the Charlotte School Board had only recently told Burger in a petition that it found itself in "a legal jungle" brought on by school desegregation litigation.[2]

Repeatedly during this period, courts rejected bar efforts to maintain the professional and social status quo. This period saw the most active involvement of courts, particularly the U.S. Supreme Court, trimming the profession's power over its members. The Court acted not in the traditional role of courts governing lawyers, but in the application of external legal norms that reined in the profession's regulatory excesses. Citizenship requirements for bar admission fell; minimum fee schedules were held unlawful; and perhaps most important, excessive regulation of lawyers' client-getting activities was held to violate the First Amendment, first on association grounds and later on speech grounds. The profession changed dramatically during this period but not of its own volition. Instead, change came as the result of court orders that upheld the acts of bold lawyers who violated the profession's

---

[1] Warren E. Burger, Address Before the American Law Institute: The Necessity for Civility (May 18, 1971), *in* 52 F.R.D. 211 (1971); *see* chapter 7.
[2] *Charlotte Board Tells Burger of "Legal Jungle,"* ROCK HILL HERALD, Aug. 21, 1970, at 4.

then-existing commands, and as a result of long-overdue changing demographics in the profession.

I. The ABA Passes on the Early Civil Rights Movement

In terms of its official policy arms, the ABA largely sat out the early stages of the civil rights movement. Still obsessed with communism, the 1950s ABA ignored the "whole area of Negro rights"[3] in the decade of *Brown v. Board*.

Lewis Powell, a Virginia moderate and mid-1960s ABA president, counseled the national profession to stay out of the fray and take no position. Powell had been a prominent lawyer in the Richmond firm of Hunton & Williams, and had been school board chair of both the city of Richmond and state of Virginia during the post-Brown time for action with "deliberate speed." The ABA, Powell wrote, should not take sides when new federal legislation comes out that involves controversial social questions. "[T]he prevailing view is that the Association must follow a policy of noninvolvement in political and emotionally controversial issues—however important they may be—unless they relate directly to the administration of justice."[4] Just how the civil rights legislation and school desegregation lacked a "direct relat[ionship] to the administration of justice" was left unexplained. Not everyone in positions of ABA authority believed the profession should take a pass.

> No doubt you will be confronted with critical public problems in which the bar will be called upon to take a stand. In the past on some occasions we have been prone to bypass thorny issues under the counterfeit argument that they are not within the purposes of the association. In my judgment that not only hurts the profession, but deprives the public of the views of the group most competent to speak.[5]

Powell acknowledged that the profession had been criticized at a Harvard Law School Forum for its noninvolvement in social issues but suggested that the profession can have nothing to do with civil rights because of its controversial nature. "The Association's responsibilities relate primarily to the legal profession, and these could not be discharged if our membership were lost, fractionalized or embittered by involvement in political controversy."[6] This position stands in contrast to the

---

[3] Norbert C. Brockman, The Politics of the American Bar Association at 194, 199 (1963) (unpublished PhD dissertation, Catholic University of America) (on file with author).

[4] Lewis F. Powell, Jr., *The President's Page*, 51 A.B.A. J. 101 (1965).

[5] Letter from J. Garner Anthony, former Board of Governors member, American Bar Association, to Lewis F. Powell, Jr., President, American Bar Association, (Aug. 31, 1964) (on file in Lewis F. Powell, Jr. Archives, Washington & Lee University School of Law Library, Series 5.1.6.4, Box 76).

[6] Powell, *supra* note 4.

activities of the ABA during the New Deal's social engineering project. In authorizing the study and report on New Deal legislation, the ABA adopted this resolution:

> Whereas the rapid development in recent months of novel legislation and governmental trends in the federal government, affecting the rights and liberties of American citizens and our constitutional form of government, have resulted in a great diversity of opinion throughout the United States as to the effect of these theories; and the questions involved hold a deep and peculiar interest for the bar of this country; And Whereas, The people of this country at all such times, look to the Bar for advice and guidance in such a crisis; Now, therefore, be it resolved, that the general council recommends that the executive committee create a special committee to study the effect of recent developments in national legislation and governmental policies, as affecting the rights and liberties of American citizens and the maintenance of the guarantees furnished by the United States Constitution. . . .[7]

Each set of events, changes in the law, and effects on the administration of justice were equally powerful and compelling. The ABA weighed in heavily to oppose the New Deal,[8] and sat quietly, allowing state bar associations to take the profession's lead in opposing civil rights progress. Even during the presidency of a prominent lawyer who had assisted in the abolition of Duke University's segregation policies, the ABA stayed away from the civil rights issues of the day.[9]

Although the ABA satisfied itself that it was simply staying out of a controversial fray, it was actually assisting in the evasion of law. Realization of the *Brown v. Board* mandate was in the balance, and the ABA's silence encouraged moves, many led by Southern lawyers and bar associations, to defy the application of law. Allowing the state bars to take the lead led to predictable results, especially in the South. State bars moved against the NAACP lawyers pursuing school desegregation cases with vigor. Their moves were among a range of measures taken to cripple the desegregation movement. But they were simultaneously attacking a new kind of lawyering on behalf of a profession bent on maintaining its status quo.

As was the "party line" when it explained its silence regarding the Sacco and Vanzetti trial, the ABA said that the civil rights movement was a "political" issue outside its scope of interest.[10]

---

[7] Ronen Shamir, *The Bar Association Hasn't Got the Guts to Speak: The Untold Story of the American Bar Association's Committee on the New Deal*, AM. BAR FOUND., Working Paper No. 9202, 1994 at 5–6.

[8] *Id.*

[9] The ABA President in 1957–1959 was Charles S. Rhyne. For two years prior, he was the president of the D.C. bar. He was a successful litigator in Baker v. Carr, establishing the "one man, one vote" principle, and he helped end Duke's segregation policies as a trustee.

[10] Charles S. Whitman, Presidential Address at the Annual Meeting of the American Bar Association at Buffalo (Aug. 31, 1927), *in* 13 A.B.A. J. 491 (1927).

II. Communism and Civil Rights Lawyers

The Sacco and Vanzetti noninvolvement coincidence highlights the connection
drawn by Southern politicians and leading lawyers between communism and the
civil rights movement. The connection in the South was encouraged in the 1930s
when a Communist Party legal arm, the International Labor Defense, undertook
the celebrated defenses of Angelo Herndon and the "Scottsboro Boys."[11] Leading
lawyers and politicians explicitly made the connection between communism and
civil rights activism. Mississippi Senator James Eastland, chair of both the Senate
Judiciary Committee and the SISS, claimed that the Court in *Brown* had "responded
to a radical, pro-Communist political movement in this country." Eastland, Senator
John McClellan of Arkansas, and Representative Edwin Willis of Louisiana used
their positions on the SISS, HUAC, and other investigative subcommittees to hold
public hearings on "Communist influence in civil rights protests."[12]

Chief Justice Warren inadvertently fueled the speculation about a connection
in his famous footnote 11 in *Brown*. In the footnote, he cited the Myrdal paper
and three other nonlegal sources, the authors of three of which had modest, but
at-the-time sufficient, communist ties to satisfy conspiracy mongers.[13] Reaction
of Southern politicians to *Brown* and the ensuing integration efforts linked integration with the nation's chief enemy in an effort to discredit the civil rights movement as subversive. The reaction to *Brown* was typified by the Georgia attorney
general who decried "[t]he meddlers, demagogues, race baiters and Communists
in the United States [who] are determined to destroy every vestige of states'
rights."[14]

The claims, while never verified, were far from unreasonable. The NAACP had
itself publicly worried about its effort to stave off communist influence in some
of its branches. "It is not amiss to recall that government evidence in Smith Act
prosecutions has shown that the sensitive area of race relations has long been a
prime target of Communist efforts at infiltration."[15] In 1950, the NAACP adopted
an "anticommunism" resolution, acknowledging that "certain branches of the
National Association for the Advancement of Colored People are being rocked by
internal conflicts between groups who follow the Communist line and those who
do not which threaten to destroy the confidence of the public in the Association
and which will inevitably result in its eventual disruption."[16] The resolution went

---

[11] John D. Inazu, *The Strange Origins of the Constitutional Right of Association*, 77 Tenn. L.
Rev. 485, 507 (2010).

[12] *Id.* at 507–508.

[13] Lucas A. Powe, Jr., The Warren Court and American Politics 42 (2000).

[14] *Id.* at 39.

[15] Gibson v. Fla. Legislative Investigation Comm., 372 U.S. 539, 580 (1963) (Harlan, J.,
dissenting).

[16] *Id.*

on acknowledge "a well-organized, nationwide conspiracy by Communists either to capture or split and wreck the NAACP."[17]

Some Southern lawyer-leaders who saw the claimed connection between communism and civil rights announced their efforts to use economic ruin to crush the civil rights movement. One such leader was Mississippi Circuit Court Judge Tom P. Brady, who "saw *Brown* as a virtual communist plot to mandate the amalgamation of the races."[18] In 1954, following *Brown*, Brady founded the Citizens' Councils as a nonviolent alternative to the Ku Klux Klan. Rather than use violence to achieve segregationist goals, the councils would impose financial and economic punishment on anyone supporting integration. The tie between the NAACP and the international communist movement was the central theme of hundreds of Council speeches and publications.[19]

In late 1954 and early 1955, Citizens' Councils sprang up across Alabama. In the last three months of 1955 alone, "membership in the Alabama Citizens' Councils grew from a few hundred to twenty thousand."[20] The Councils made clear their intentions to bury Alabama civil rights advocates under economic and social pressures:

The white population in this country controls the money, and this is an advantage that the Council will use in a fight to legally maintain complete segregation of the races. We intend to make it difficult, if not impossible, for any Negro who advocates desegregation to find and hold a job, get credit or renew a mortgage.[21]

That kind of economic threat underscores the danger inherent in many states' effort to force state filing of NAACP membership lists, finally held unconstitutional in *NAACP v. Alabama*.[22] Until the Alabama decision, however, with the Brady-like economic threats hanging in the air and being instituted, the NAACP was substantially weakened in the South. It may not have survived at all were it not for the Court's *Alabama* ruling. In a mere two years, from 1955 to 1957, NAACP membership in the South had fallen from 128,000 to 80,000, and almost 250 branches had closed. In states with the most active Citizens Councils and demands for membership lists, membership dropped by 75 percent and more. The litigation that led to *NAACP v. Alabama* effectively shut down the NAACP in that state from 1956 until 1964.[23]

---

[17] *Id.* at 581.

[18] POWE, *supra* note 13, at 68.

[19] NEIL R. MCMILLEN, THE CITIZENS' COUNCIL 198 (1971).

[20] DAN T. CARTER, THE POLITICS OF RAGE 84 (La. State Univ. Press 2d ed. 2000) (1995).

[21] S. SCH. NEWS, Jan. 6, 1955, at 2, *quoted in* Petition for Writ of Certiorari at 20, NAACP v. Ala. *ex rel.* Patterson, 357 U.S. 449 (1958) (No. 91).

[22] 357 U.S. 449 (1958).

[23] MICHAEL. J. KLARMAN, FROM JIM CROW TO CIVIL RIGHTS: THE SUPREME COURT AND THE STRUGGLE FOR RACIAL EQUALITY 383 (2004).

One result was the near absence of Southern lawyers willing to identify themselves with the civil rights cause by representing civil rights workers and activists. There were precious few Atticus Finches, and those few did not emerge unscathed.

III. Harassment of the Few Bold Lawyers in the South

Harassment of Southern lawyers who represented civil rights workers was fierce. A very few white Southern lawyers were willing to represent civil rights workers in the deep South. Among the few who did, at least one was disbarred in Mississippi.[24] A black lawyer representing school desegregation plaintiffs in Mississippi was harassed by a federal district judge regarding his professionalism, threatened with findings of professional misconduct, and interrogated long enough to fill 118 pages of transcript.[25] The harassment continued until the court of appeals said that the district judge was creating "humiliation, anxiety, and possible intimidation of a...reputable member of the bar."[26] The claims against the lawyer were entirely baseless. "All of the testimony taken in this matter...completely exonerates Brown from any improper conduct."[27]

In North Carolina, James Gilliland drew the ire of bar discipline authorities for publicly advocating compliance with the law; specifically, court ordered school desegregation pursuant to *Brown v. Board of Education.*[28] Gilliland was disbarred by the North Carolina Bar Association for alleged ethical violations in two domestic relations matters. The charges were brought against him by bar authorities following two related, public events. Gilliland, commander of his American Legion Post and secretary of the local Lions Club, was asked to speak about the recent school desegregation cases. In his talk, he asserted that he supported the Court's ruling and that the desegregation mandate should be followed locally. Not long after, while representing about a dozen individuals before the Charlotte session of the House Un-American Activities Committee, he asserted that the Committee's time would better be used pursuing school officials who were evading the school desegregation mandates. Gilliland had never before been the subject of bar complaints, but shortly after he made these public comments the bar instituted proceedings against his license and entered orders of disbarment.[29] His disbarment order was remanded

---

[24] JEROLD S. AUERBACH, UNEQUAL JUSTICE 264–265 (1976).

[25] *In re* Brown, 346 F.2d 903, 908 (5th Cir. 1965).

[26] *Id.*

[27] *Id.* at 909–910.

[28] *See,* Charles R. DiSalvo, *The Fracture of Good Order: An Argument for Allowing Lawyers to Counsel the Civilly Disobedient,* 17 GA. L. REV. 109, nn.127–130 (1982); *see also,* Daniel H. Pollitt, *Counsel for the Unpopular Cause,* 43 N.C. L. REV. 9, 10 (1964).

[29] Pollitt, *supra* note 28, at 10.

by the Supreme Court of North Carolina for failure of bar authorities to honor Gilliland's right to a jury trial.[30] Upon remand, Gilliland was acquitted.[31]

While the ABA sat out the remainder of the *Brown* decade, state bars, courts, and legislatures in the South moved into crisis-regulation mode. In numerous Southern states, moves against civil rights lawyers, particularly school desegregation ones, formed a component of the announced policy of "massive resistance" to *Brown*. The expansion of traditional prohibitions against solicitation, barratry, champerty and maintenance, though neutral sounding on its face, was targeted at NAACP lawyers.[32]

IV. William Kunstler: The Most Hated Lawyer in America[33]

Once Northern lawyers began to undertake representation and organization of Southern civil rights clients and causes, new forms of professional harassment emerged.

Among the lawyers whose work acted as a lightning rod for organized bar criticism was William Kunstler. Kunstler's identification with his activist clientele broke sharply with traditional lawyer norms of professional separation from clients and earned him a folk hero status among law students and young lawyers.[34] Kunstler went from representing civil rights workers including Mississippi Freedom Riders and other protesters in the South, to Black Panthers, to the Chicago Seven. Kunstler was not a large firm, New York lawyer who took up civil rights causes. His early practice in the 1950s was characterized by undistinguished representation in will, domestic relations, and real estate closing matters, with one ironic exception: referred by classmate Roy Cohn, Kunstler drafted a will for the soon-to-be-infamous Joseph McCarthy.

As a traveling civil rights activist lawyer, Kunstler needed pro hac vice admission in various courts to represent his clients, which was not always freely given.[35] Interestingly, Kuntsler regarded himself as a modern-day, "itinerant lawyer in the colonial tradition."[36] The image of Lincoln, riding circuit with his colleagues from rotating court day to court day is not one that traditional lawyers

---

[30] *In re* Gilliland, 248 N.C. 517, 103 S.E.2d 807 (1958).

[31] Pollitt, *supra* note 28, at 10.

[32] *See infra* nn. 84–88.

[33] DAVID J. LANGUM, WILLIAM KUNSTLER: THE MOST HATED LAWYER IN AMERICA (1999).

[34] Victor S. Navasky, *Right On! With Lawyer William Kunstler*, N.Y. TIMES, Apr. 21, 1970 (magazine), at 30.

[35] See John Kifner, *Kunstler Upheld by Appeals Court*, N.Y. TIMES, May 19, 1973, at 34, (for a description of a district court's refusal to admit Kunstler). Kunstler needed permission to represent a client in prison for refusing induction, having been transferred because of participation in a prison protest led by Rev. Daniel Berrigan. After excluding Kunstler, the district judge appointed the former Indiana state chairman of the Republican Party to represent the defendant.

[36] LANGUM, *supra* note 33, at 65.

would have attached to Kunstler. And to be sure, the political nature of their practices bears no comparison whatever. But in another sense, the comparison to a 18th- or 19th-century lawyer traveling from court to court to meet his clients and represent them, is apt. The mode of transportation and its speed and capacity had changed dramatically, but it was true that Kunstler seemed to be everywhere, especially throughout the South in the 1960s. Between the time of colonial lawyers and later Lincoln's circuit riding and Kunstler's traveling civil rights lawyer show, UPL (unauthorized practice of law) restrictions on cross-border law practice had become far more stringent.

The Chicago Seven representation won him national attention and, in some circles, derision. The circus nature of the Chicago trial, and especially Kunstler's openly hostile, two-way war with Judge Julius Hoffman, produced four years' worth of contempt citations that were later reversed by the Seventh Circuit.[37] The bar reaction to his ferocious representation in Chicago was strikingly swift. The Association of the Bar of the City of New York so anxiously awaited the opportunity to discipline Kunstler that it began proceedings before the Chicago Seven trial had ended, violating its own rules of procedure.[38]

In the end, confession came, as some elements within the organized bar realized that repressive mistakes had been made, especially in the context of efforts to chill zealous representation of the so-called new Left. The bar had "misconstrued...the dimensions and causes of courtroom disorders,...confus[ing] zeal in the defense of clients with revolution...[in its movement to] intimidate defense counsel."[39]

As they had to Kunstler, responding to outsiders with law practice restrictions was a key measure for Southern lawyer-dominated legislatures. Five Southern states enacted harsher restrictions on client getting, unauthorized practice, and community organizing activities, in an effort to prevent outside lawyers (especially NAACP lawyers) from organizing and recruiting plaintiffs for school desegregation cases that would force compliance with *Brown v. Board*. The Virginia bar's efforts to keep outside lawyers outside resulted in the Supreme Court's entry into the fray in *NAACP v. Button*.[40] The NAACP and its affiliate, the Legal Defense Fund (LDF) had chapters in Virginia. Through these chapters, Virginia residents were informed of the possibility of pursuing school desegregation suits by retaining NAACP and LDF lawyers. Lawyers affiliated with the NAACP were paid a per diem during such representation, but often without any other form of compensation. The Virginia State Bar proceeded against these lawyers and the NAACP on the ground that their

---

[37] *In re* Dellinger, 461 F.2d 381 (7th Cir. 1971) (reversing district court's imposition of 4 year, 13 day sentence for contempt).

[38] Tom Goldstein, *Bar Group Withdraws Charges Against Kunstler*, N.Y. Times, Feb. 21, 1974, at 34.

[39] NORMAN DORSEN & LEON FRIEDMAN, DISORDER IN THE COURT: REPORT OF THE ASSOCIATION OF THE BAR OF THE CITY OF NEW YORK, SPECIAL COMMITTEE ON COURTROOM DISORDER xiii–xvi (1973).

[40] NAACP v. Button, 371 U.S. 415 (1963).

conduct amounted to inappropriate solicitation of business and, in particular, that the NAACP, which was not a party to the various school desegregation litigation, had unlawfully interjected itself into litigated matters by soliciting plaintiffs and supplying lawyers. The Virginia courts held that the NAACP lawyers had acted unethically.[41] The Virginia courts asserted that the statutes' purpose was to uphold high standards of the legal profession by

> strengthen[ing] the existing statutes to further control the evils of solicitation of legal business.... Solicitation of legal business has been considered and declared from the very beginning of the legal profession to be unethical and unprofessional conduct.[42]

Eliminating the activities of the NAACP at that juncture would likely have spelled an end to school desegregation in Virginia for the foreseeable future. The Supreme Court reversed the Virginia courts' treatment of the issue, holding that such an application of the solicitation rules violated expression and association rights under the First and Fourteenth Amendments.[43]

V. A New Kind of Lawyering

Because states and local school districts had resisted compliance with *Brown*, it became necessary to pursue litigation community by community. To do so, the NAACP and LDF lawyers attended community meetings and informed potential plaintiffs that their school desegregation litigation could be supported by the NAACP and that lawyers from the organization would represent them. The state bars, courts and legislatures (dominated as they were by lawyers) sought to dampen NAACP efforts by pursuing the lawyers on ethics and criminal charges.

Meanwhile, labor unions endeavored to provide counsel to their members, and federally funded legal aid lawyers organized tenants and farm workers and represented entire classes of welfare recipients, institutional inmates, and others. Still other lawyers sought to represent middle class clients at lower cost, using office automation and high client volume generated by advertising.

In every instance the profession objected. In part, to be sure, the objections were motivated by opposition to the *causes* advanced by the new style of lawyer, but the objections were also to the new style of lawyering itself. To the traditional,

---

[41] The Virginia Supreme Court held that the actions of the NAACP constituted "fomenting and soliciting legal business in which they are not parties and have no pecuniary right or liability, and which they channel to the enrichment of certain lawyers employed by them, at no cost to the litigants and over which the litigants have no control." NAACP v. Harrison, 202 Va. 142, 155, 116 S.E.2d 55, 66 (1960).

[42] *Harrison*, 202 Va. at 154.

[43] Other "association" cases followed, arising largely from a new ethos of cause or issue lawyering that accompanied the first federally funded legal aid programs.

one-client-at-a-time lawyer, whose clients found the lawyer through word of mouth in clubs and churches and social organizations rather than through advertising, this aggressive new style of lawyering was unprofessional, distasteful, and demeaning to the profession generally. For these lawyers, cause lawyering was not proper lawyering at all, and it had to be stopped.

The profession accurately perceived that a new form of lawyering was emerging. Attorney General Nicholas deB. Katzenbach called for "new techniques, new services, and new forms of intra-professional cooperation . . . to analyze the rights of welfare recipients, of installment purchasers, of people affected by slum housing, crime and despair." "There are signs, too," he noted, "that a new breed of lawyers is emerging, dedicated to using the law as an instrument of orderly and constructive social change."[44] Charles Hamilton Houston viewed the mission of the Howard Law School, to which he brought respectability and accreditation, as the creation of "social engineers" capable of making real the teachings of sociological jurisprudence that emerged during the first half of the 20th century.[45] It was to be a cause-lawyer school. Neither Katzenbach's nor Houston's vision of lawyering meshed with the profession's status quo, and it met resistance from the organized bar as a result. Lawyers who were as fully committed to their clients' cause as were their clients threatened to disrupt the classical image of lawyers as being entirely independent and separate from their clients' goals.

The lack of any like criticism of segregationist lawyers, who believed just as deeply and fervently in their clients' causes as William Kunstler or Spottswood Robinson or Thurgood Marshall believed in theirs, is striking and telling. By all indications, for example, Collins Denny was a "cause" lawyer in service of his client, the Defenders of State Sovereignty and Individual Liberties.[46] The "Defenders" were a well-organized group of lawyers, local and state politicians, and interested citizens from "Southside" Virginia, the area of the state most defiantly opposed to the integration of public schools. In the wake of *Brown*, the Defenders organized for the purpose of defying the decision and maintaining segregated schools throughout Virginia. They took the position that if even one black child attended a white school, the result would be the destruction of Virginia's cultural heritage. Collins was the Defenders' lawyer but was also a founding member. He had the ear of the Gray Commission leaders who were formulating official government policy designed to enable Virginia's avoidance of the *Brown* mandate and maintain segregated schools. He was as fervent a believer in his clients' cause as were any of his clients. Lawyer William Old (later a judge in Chesterfield County, Virginia)

---

[44] *History of Civil Legal Aid*, NAT'L LEGAL AID & DEFENDER ASS'N, http://www.nlada.org/About/About_HistoryCivil (last visited Aug. 14, 2012).

[45] Susan D. Carle, *From Buchanan to* Button: *Legal Ethics and the NAACP (Part II)*, 8 U. CHI. L. SCH. ROUNDTABLE 281 (2001).

[46] DAVID J. MAYS, RACE, REASON, AND MASSIVE RESISTANCE: THE DIARY OF DAVID J. MAYS, 1954–1959, at 74, 38 (James R. Sweeney ed., 2008) (MAYS).

resurrected the "interposition doctrine" by writing a pamphlet and distributing it at his own expense.[47] The Defenders undertook a second printing and distribution.[48] Both Denny and Old were among leading lawyers advocating for their personal cause, which also happened to be their clients' cause. None received the opprobrium of the bar. Perhaps the explanation is to be found in the conservative nature of the cause and the matching nature of the profession of the time. More likely, the explanation is that these cause lawyers were advocating for the status quo rather than change. Yet it is fair to ask: how long and under what circumstances can the "status quo" be such after plain rulings of the Supreme Court mandate change?

The reaction of the bar in the 1960s and 1970s era civil rights movement stands in stark contrast to its attitude in the early years of NAACP activity.[49] In the 1910s and 1920s, the NAACP's legal strategy and representation were led by former ABA president Moorfield Storey, and claims of manufacturing litigation in violation of the ethics rules were largely ignored as irrelevant; In the 1950s and 1960s, state bar associations, with no remonstration from the ABA, led a charge to criminalize NAACP client solicitation activities.[50] Storey had been raised in a family active in the abolitionist cause. At the pre-Langdellian Harvard Law School, he spent his time in social events and regarded the mood as "study optional." His professional stature effectively immunized him from charges of ethics violations for barratry, solicitation, and the like. His story compared to that of Houston and Marshall is a telling example of the double standard that the organized bar has always applied.[51]

VI. Battle Lines in Virginia

By the post-Brown 1950s and 1960s, the profession's stance on NAACP activities had made a 180 degree turn from Storey's day. Now, in Virginia and other states, the organization's activities of holding town and church meetings to recruit possible school desegregation plaintiffs were made criminal, and lawyers involved were pursued relentlessly. Southern state bars took an active role in preserving the social status quo, despite clear Supreme Court precedents dictating that the time for change had come. The Virginia State Bar (VSB) filed a civil complaint against the NAACP and its lawyers in Richmond courts, alleging that they were engaged

---

[47] The doctrine posited that states had the power to "interpose" themselves between the federal government and state citizens. Though never effectively used, it was a rallying cry for adherents to the "massive resistance" movement. The Virginia Senate and House adopted an interposition resolution by near-unanimous margins. *See The State Responds: Massive Resistance*, Libr. Va. http://www.lva.virginia.gov/exhibits/brown/resistance.htm (last visited Aug. 14, 2012).

[48] Mays, *supra* note 46, at 80.

[49] Compare the experiences with bar authorities of Storey with that of Marshall and Houston in Carle, *supra* note 45.

[50] Mark V. Tushnet, Making Civil Rights Law 272–282 (1994).

[51] Carle, *supra* note 45, at 285–923.

in the unauthorized practice of law, simultaneously filing the same claim against the Brotherhood of Trainmen.[52] And the VSB repeatedly dogged Virginia lawyers who participated in representation with NAACP lawyers with charges of lawyer misconduct.[53]

In *Alabama v. NAACP* and *NAACP v. Button*,[54] the issue of resistance came to a legal crossroads. The moves against NAACP lawyers were part of a broader plan ("Massive Resistance" generally, and in Virginia, the "Stanley Plan") to hinder efforts to enforce *Brown v. Board*. Part of the Massive Resistance movement and the Southern Manifesto, proposed by Virginia Senator Harry F. Byrd and South Carolina Senator Strom Thurmond, the drive was to prevent even a single black child from attending a white school. More moderate segregationists, such as David Mays, a prominent Virginia lawyer and Pulitzer Prize winning author, were willing to allow that some token integration could occur in counties willing to tolerate it. The moderates' position was meant to stave off desegregation in all places where it was resisted by tolerating a de minimus measure of it to make the state's case for good faith compliance with *Brown*. In Virginia, for example, school districts in Arlington and Norfolk expressed a willingness to engage in modest amounts of desegregation. Hard-line segregationists sought to prevent tolerant districts from any desegregation; moderate segregationists viewed the Norfolk and Arlington willingness as a way of staving off more drastic amounts of desegregation in the rest of the state.

The Virginia legislature had significant lawyer representation, both among senior and junior members. A large number of young legislators was elected in 1954, most of whom were lawyers.[55] And the most influential senior legislators were lawyers.

The state senator and the state delegate who cosponsored the anti-NAACP lawyer legislation, Charles Fenwick and Harrison Mann, were both prominent Virginia lawyers with University of Virginia law degrees. Contemporary colleague David Mays said in his diary that "Fenwick presented a draft of a bill to harass the NAACP in Virginia."[56] Mann acknowledged at the time that one of the anti-NAACP bills was unconstitutional, but he would propose it anyway. Governor Stanley congratulated Mann, "saying he was delighted to find one lawyer who is willing to go forward with an unconstitutional bill."[57]

Other prominent Virginia lawyers were key players in the effort to punish and disable NAACP lawyers. William Munford Tuck from Halifax County, Virginia,

---

[52] *Virginia Bar Challenges NAACP Methods in School Cases*, THE FREE LANCE-STAR, June 30, 1959; *NAACP Methods Scored in Suit by Virginia Bar*, TUSCALOOSA NEWS, June 30, 1959.

[53] S. J. Ackerman, *The Trials of S. W. Tucker*, WASH. POST, June 11, 2000, at W14; MAYS, *supra* note 46, at 191.

[54] *Patterson, supra* note 21; *Button, supra* note 40.

[55] J. Douglas Smith, *"When Reason Collides with Prejudice": Armistead Lloyd Boothe and the Politics of Moderation*, 102 VA. MAG. HIST. & BIOGRAPHY 5, at 17 (Jan., 1994), *available at* http://www.jstor.org/stable/4249409.

[56] MAYS, *supra* note 46, at 158.

[57] *Id.* at 165.

a Washington & Lee law graduate and a prominent member of the state bar, practiced in Halifax and served as a state legislator, lieutenant governor, and governor before being elected to the U.S. Congress. He was a supporter of Senator Byrd's "massive resistance" initiative and helped draft the Stanley Plan.[58] Henry Taylor Wickham was the son of a state senator. Wickham served as an assistant to Attorney General Almond during important civil rights cases. Following *Brown v. Board*, Wickham began private practice with the prominent Richmond firm Mays and Valentine. Wickham would also assist in the drafting of the Stanley Plan.[59] John B. Boatwright served in the Virginia House of Delegates between 1922–23 and 1936–59. A staff member of the Gray Commission, Boatwright would assist in the drafting of the Stanley Plan.[60] Governor James Lindsay Almond, Jr. was a lawyer from the University of Virginia who served as a judge in Roanoke, as a U.S. congressman, and as the Virginia attorney general before becoming governor. As governor, Almond would shift the policy of Virginia away from Senator Byrd's "massive resistance" model, in favor of the passive resistance that followed court rejection of most provisions of the Stanley Plan.[61]

David Mays played a particularly significant role, having been legal advisor and chief drafter of the Gray Commission Report, and later chairman of the Virginia Commission on Constitutional Government.[62] There is no doubt that Mays played a moderating and stabilizing role on the Gray Commission, softening the views and demands of the most vociferous segregationists.

But some background is needed to understand what it meant to be called a "moderate segregationist" at the time. Mays was congratulated and thanked repeatedly for his Gray Commission role at a 1955 Virginia State Bar meeting, the same meeting at which the organization adopted a resolution condemning the Supreme Court for its invasion of states' rights in Brown.[63] At that meeting, Mays wondered whether everyone understood what he believed would be the consequence of following the strict segregationists' suggestion to close schools rather than allow some to be integrated by court mandate. Mays wrote the following:

[If we allow school closures to stave off integration], [o]ur Protestant Anglo-Saxons of the South (today the best strain of our American population and now a minority despised by Negroes and northern whites) will find themselves

---

[58] *TUCK, William Munford, (1896–1983)*, Biographical Directory U.S. Congress, http://bioguide.congress.gov/scripts/biodisplay.pl?index=T000395 (last visited Aug. 14, 2012).

[59] Jeremy Slayton, *Henry Taylor Wickham, Retired Lawyer, Dies at 88*, Richmond Times-Dispatch, Nov. 12, 2008, *available at* http://www2.timesdispatch.com/news/2008/nov/12/hwob12_20081111_212504-im-6590/.

[60] Lawrence Kestenbaum, *Index to Politicians*, Pol. Graveyard, http://politicalgraveyard.com/bio/boarman-bodziak.html (last updated June 18, 2012).

[61] Carl Tobias, *Essay: Public School Desegregation in Virginia during the Post-Brown Decade*, 37 Wm. & Mary L. Rev. 1261, 1277 (1996).

[62] Mays, *supra* note 46, at 215.

[63] Mays, *supra* note 46 at 62.

in the same position as the Catholics in their parochial schools—except for the fact that the Catholics are already integrating.[64]

Mays, the moderate, praised by his fellow lawyers for stabilizing the radical segregationists, referred to W. Hale Thompson of Newport News as that "unbelievably arrogant...nigger lawyer." Thompson had dared to suggest in a Gray Commission public hearing that "Thomas Jefferson, James Madison and Patrick Henry would be ashamed of some members of the General Assembly."[65]

When Mays described the pleasure of having two former FBI men play surreptitiously-made recordings of NAACP lawyer conversations with plaintiffs in the Prince Edward County case and the Charlottesville case, he made no mention of whether he was listening to an intrusion on the lawyer-client relationship. Instead he said, "These may prove very helpful in probable proceedings by the [Virginia State Bar] against Oliver Hill and possibly others." No evidence appears to exist that Hill was ever charged, but his colleague Samuel Tucker was repeatedly brought before bar authorities and charged with misconduct.[66] Mays openly favored the bills introduced by Charles Fenwick and Harrison Mann, which he thought were meant to "harass the NAACP."[67] As the Richmond Bar Association member attempting to field speakers for the annual meeting, he rejected the idea of inviting federal district judge Walter Hoffman, because Hoffman had recently ruled that blacks must be permitted equal access to Seashore State Park.[68] Mays also expressed ethnic prejudices that were reminiscent of the profession's views in the early part of the 20th century.[69] "The heavy migration from South Europe has radically changed for the worse our racial stock. We are far more excitable than our Anglo-Saxon forebears, and it is a serious loss."[70] This was a moderate segregationist.

As massive resistance crashed and burned under the weight of repeated losses in the courts, Mays lamented that he must stay on the sidelines and not say "I told you so." In his diary, though, he worried that he would at some point be drawn into the public discussion and "make both the niggers and the massive resistance boys mad." As a "moderate segregationist," he knew they could still

> lick this integration business (unless and until whites are willing to accept it) by letting in Negroes when we must, chasing them out afterward by one method or another short of violence, and forcing them to make each incident a separate lawsuit. That will give the NAACP lawyers indigestion,

---

[64] *Id.* at 63.

[65] *Id.* at 85–86.

[66] *Id.* at 191; S.J. Ackerman, *The Trials of S.W. Tucker*, WASH. POST, June 11, 2000, at W14.

[67] MAYS, *supra* note 46, at 158.

[68] *Id.* at 57.

[69] *See* discussion in chapter 2.

[70] MAYS, *supra* note 46, at 207.

assuming that we haven't succeeded in running them out of the courts beforehand.[71]

The moderates and strict segregationists simply saw the path to their common goal differently. The strict segregationists stood fast to a bright lined, zero-integration position. The moderates believed that less integration could be achieved by allowing for token integration, thereby staving off demands for full integration by the federal courts. And for both, an integral part of the strategy was to harass and punish civil rights lawyers for their new style of lawyering.

As a lawyer entity, the Virginia State Bar vigorously enforced the anti-NAACP restrictions.[72] In 1955, the Virginia State Bar adopted a resolution condemning the U.S. Supreme Court's decision in Brown:

"BE IT RESOLVED That The Virginia State Bar Association deplores the present apparent tendency of the United States Supreme Court, as reflected in Brown v. Board of Education, to invade by judicial decision the constitutionally reserved powers of the States of the Union."[73]

Two of the major speakers at the VSB Annual Convention that year, Virginia attorney general (later governor) Lindsey Almond and South Carolina Senator Strom Thurmond, cocreator of the Massive Resistance concept with Virginia Senator Harry Byrd, attacked the Supreme Court's invasion of state sovereignty in *Brown*. Then-president of the Virginia State Bar, Aubrey Bowles, Jr. expressed his confidence that with the cooperation of the voluntary bar association in Virginia (the VBA), greater success in this area would be achieved.[74] A few years later, Bowles was counsel for the VSB in its pursuit of disciplinary charges against NAACP lawyers.[75] One NAACP lawyer, in particular, was repeatedly the target of disciplinary proceedings, all of which were eventually dismissed by courts. Samuel Wilbert Tucker moved from county to county in efforts to enforce the *Brown* mandate. At every turn, he was charged with unethical conduct by the Virginia State Bar.[76] David Mays called him "Blue-Gum Tucker," "a racial slur referring to Tucker's very dark skin."[77]

---

[71] *Id.* at 261–262. Similarly, in his April 2, 1959, entry: "The only way is to let them in and 'bust' them out; make every Negro child a separate law case, not a class action. That will break the back o the NAACP's back and turn the federal courts into so many police courts, utterly swamped with litigation." *Id.* at 272.

[72] *Harrison, supra* note 41; THE FREE LANCE-STAR, *supra* note 52.

[73] Paul B. Dewitt, *Bar Activities*, 41 A.B.A. J. 1055–56 (1955).

[74] The original bar association in Virginia was called the Virginia State Bar Association, formed in 1888 as a voluntary organization. With the national wave of the integrated bar movement, the Association became the Virginia State Bar by legislative enactment in 1938, and the voluntary organization, the Virginia Bar Association was what was left behind.

[75] FREE LANCE-STAR, *supra* note 52.

[76] Ackerman, *supra* note 53; MAYS, *supra* note 46, at 191.

[77] MAYS, *supra* note 46, at 260.

Lewis Powell, partner at Hunton and Williams in Richmond, mid-1960s ABA president, and eventual United States Supreme Court Justice, was seen by most as a moderate, even-handed force. His compromise opinion in *Bakke v. Regents*[78] set the tone for race consideration in higher education admissions, charting its course between the positions of the other eight Justices, four each on opposite ends of the spectrum. As a result, Powell is a good gauge for the sentiments of the most even-handed, balanced Southern lawyers and bar leaders of the time.

As ABA president in the mid-1960s, Powell was a vocal condemner of civil disobedience, repeatedly decrying the actions of sit-in demonstrators' and Freedom Riders' testing of discriminatory laws that regulated racial treatment in the South.[79] He suggested that the only proper way to reform racially discriminatory practices was through the courts, believing that state courts in the South would give fair treatment to Blacks.[80]

In correspondence with Sidney Carleton, a former president of the Mississippi State Bar, Powell registered his views on Northern lawyers who represented Southern Blacks. Carleton, in an angry response to National Lawyers Guild representation in Mississippi, said the following:

> [T]here has never been a time when the lawyers of the state of Mississippi have not stood ready, willing, and able to represent those in need of legal representation. It has not, however, been the policy of either the Mississippi State Bar nor of its members to violate public policy or to engage in the unethical practices or to become accessories before the fact by agreeing in advance to represent persons in criminal proceedings arising from contemplated actions not then having occurred.[81]

Powell replied to Carleton with praise for the Mississippi Bar, in language that implies negative views of NAACP lawyers who had organized the school desegregation plaintiffs at issue in *Button*:

> My own view is that your bar took a fine step in its recent resolution on this subject. I think all of the southern bars should do the same thing, and follow them up with actual representation of Negroes—not to foment litigation but to defend those accused of crime. This is the best way I know to keep

---

[78] 438 U.S. 265 (1978).

[79] *See*, e.g., Lewis F. Powell, Jr., The President's Annual Address at the 88th Annual Assembly of the ABA in Miami Beach: *The State of the Legal Profession* (Aug. 9, 1965), *in* 51 A.B.A. J. 821 (1965) (calling civil disobedience "a dangerous trend"); *see also* JOHN C. JEFFRIES, JR., JUSTICE LEWIS F. POWELL, JR.: A BIOGRAPHY, 210–211(Fordham Univ. Press 2001) (1994).

[80] Lewis F. Powell, Jr., Speech at the Union Theological Seminary in Richmond 8 (Oct. 11, 1965) (on file in the Lewis F. Powell, Jr. Archives, Washington & Lee University School of Law Library, Powell Speeches, Box 80, Vol. 2).

[81] Letter from C. Sidney Carlton, Partner, Carlton & Henderson, to Ernest Goodman, President, National Lawyers Guild (Aug. 6, 1964) (on file in Lewis F. Powell, Jr. Archives, Washington & Lee University School of Law Library, General Correspondence during Presidency, Box 76).

northerners from 'invading' the southern states. I am afraid nothing can keep some of the radicals from defaming the South generally without the slightest recognition that lawlessness in the northern cities is on a larger scale.[82]

The Supreme Court result in *Button* was in serious doubt, and, as Mark Tushnet has discovered, an early draft opinion would have upheld Virginia's criminalization of the lawyer ethics rules regarding champerty, maintenance, barratry, and solicitation.[83] But after reargument occasioned by a change in Court members, a narrowly divided Court struck down the lawyer restrictions as violative of the First Amendment. Years of effort by the organized bar in the South to stave off social change had been dealt a serious blow. Time and time during this period, only the intercession of the courts stymied efforts of the organized bar to maintain the social status quo.

VII. And Elsewhere

Virginia was not the only state to pursue NAACP lawyers and activities, but the moves in Virginia are better documented than some others. In Virginia, House Bill 65, drafted by Senator James S. Thompson, created a legislative commission with the power to subpoena witnesses. This commission was used to investigate the NAACP under the newly passed anti-NAACP barratry laws. (This bill mirrored a Georgia bill that established a similar commission.) Senator Thomson testified that the set of bills would allow the committee to "bust that organization...wide open."[84]

In six other states (South Carolina, Georgia, Alabama, Texas, Arkansas, and Tennessee), anti-NAACP legislation was adopted, targeting the allegedly barratrous activity of the lawyers. But the traditional definition of "barratry" had to be altered in the legislation in hopes of reaching the organizing activity of the NAACP and its lawyers. The traditional definition of *frequently* stirring litigation had to be modified to reach one-time activities in some states and counties. In four states,[85] the definition of "person" was expanded to corporate entities so that the NAACP, as an organization, could be prosecuted along with its lawyers. But once so expanded, it was necessary to exempt banks and trust companies from the operation of new barratry statutes, lest they mistakenly be swept in with the prohibitions meant for the NAACP and other civil rights activist lawyers.

---

[82] Letter from Lewis J. Powell, Jr., President, American Bar Association, to C. Sidney Carlton, Partner, Carlton & Henderson (Aug. 17, 1964) (on file in Lewis F. Powell, Jr. Archives, Washington & Lee University School of Law Library, General Correspondence during Presidency Box 76).

[83] Mark V. Tushnet, *supra* note 50 at 272–300 (1994).

[84] Scull v. Va. *ex rel.* Comm. on Law Reform & Racial Activities, 351 U.S. 344, 346–47 (1959); Wayne Rhine, *Barratry—A Comparative Analysis of Recent Barratry Statutes*, 14 DePaul L. Rev. 148 (1965).

[85] Rhine, *supra* note 84, at 148 (*citing* Va. Code Ann. § 18.1-388 (1960)), Miss. Code Ann. § 2049 (1956), S.C. Code § 16-523 (1962), *and* Ark. Laws 1958, No. 16, § 1.

The Florida statute took a sweeping approach.[86] The statute provided that "whoever gives, promises, offers or conspires to give any...valuable thing...with the intent and purpose of stirring up strife and litigation; or with the intent and purpose of assisting...[or] influencing...the accused, sick, injured, uninformed, or others to sue or seek professional legal services or advice, shall be guilty of [barratry]." After all, one would not want to inform the uninformed of their opportunity to seek legal advice.

Meanwhile, Texas and its bar association made aggressive moves against the NAACP and its lawyers. Davis Grant (first assistant to the Texas attorney general) wrote to J. A. "Tiny" Gooch (the lawyer who defended the Mansfield School Board against the NAACP), informing him that John R. Grace (general counsel for the Texas Bar) had requested that there be an investigation into possible barratry by Clifford Davis and the NAACP, and that Grant suspected there were acts of barratry. Fellow Assistant Attorney General Elbert Morrow began to investigate the records of the NAACP that afternoon, particularly into the activities of J. Clifford Davis, who was the leading plaintiff's lawyer in the Mansfield Public Schools class action. The investigative report included no hard evidence against Davis, but was instead composed almost entirely of hearsay among residents (generally white) from the surrounding neighborhood. This became the report that led to the overarching investigation against the NAACP as an organization. An investigation into Ulysses Simpson Tate, a young attorney who was brought onto the Mansfield case once it had begun, was also commenced.[87] Separately, the State of Texas was investigating five potential violations of state corporate law by the NAACP.

The matters concerning Tate and Davis were brought to a court of inquiry by assistant Texas Attorney General Bill King, before Justice of the Peace B. T. Webb. Facts derived in this proceeding would be used in the main state proceeding against the NAACP, generally. The main proceeding was brought in the 7th Circuit Court of Tyler County, under Judge Otis Dunagan, and evidence of unlawful practice was presented. Ultimately the judge would deliberate for four hours before issuing a temporary restraining order, barring the NAACP from collecting contributions or filing lawsuits. The grounds for the decision were a mixture of corporate violations and lawyer ethics violations:

Foreign business practicing in TX without a permit;
Failure to file for or pay a franchise tax;
Barratry; and Illegal practice of law.

On May 28, 1956, the temporary injunction against the NAACP became permanent but was reduced to a ban on legal activities as opposed to educational and charitable programs within Texas borders.[88]

---

[86] FLA. STAT. § 877.01 (2012).

[87] ROBYN DUFF LADINO, DESEGREGATING TEXAS SCHOOLS: EISENHOWER, SHIVERS, AND THE CRISIS AT MANSFIELD HIGH 133 (1996).

[88] Id. at 134–137.

VIII. Beyond School Desegregation

Although school desegregation may have been the central core of the civil rights movement, many other aspects of the movement were pursued by aggressive lawyers of the new breed, and they also received the bar's ire and disapproval.

The favored strategy of the organized bar to resist this crisis was to attack the lawyers engaged in civil rights advocacy. Fewer lawyers representing civil rights plaintiffs would mean fewer advances for civil rights and fewer adjustments to the profession's status quo. The attacks on civil rights lawyers delayed progress but otherwise proved wildly ineffectual and served only to reenforce the profession's conservative reputation, in some ways setting the stage for the profession's embarrassment from the Watergate scandals. Nothing the profession did stemmed the tide of civil rights progress, and nearly all of the efforts to disbar or refuse admission of civil rights activists succeeded only in delaying the lawyers' membership in a profession that was rapidly changing along with the culture, all to the traditional core of the profession's dismay and consternation. In the civil rights crisis, the profession's efforts to stem the tide of change were largely frustrated by courts that sometimes reversed bar discipline and sometimes trimmed the power of state bars to regulate lawyer conduct that advanced civil rights causes.

Fierce criticism of poverty lawyers and civil rights activist lawyers came from the highest levels of judicial, government, and bar leadership. Ronald Reagan was openly hostile to legal services lawyers, first as governor of California and later as president of the United States.[89] Warren Burger, in his pleas for civility,[90] gave substantial blame for the impending downfall of the profession to lawyers in political trials, or as Burger called them, the "new litigation." He encouraged the legal profession to apply "rigorous powers of discipline" to the misbehaving lawyers by either the judicial or bar enforcement systems. Failure to do so, he warned, would allow "the jungle [to] clos[e] in on us."[91] Bar leaders and commentators followed the Chief Justice's lead.[92]

---

[89] Alan W. Houseman & Linda E. Perle, Securing Equal Justice for All: A Brief History of Civil Legal Assistance in the United States 29–33 (rev. ed. 2007).

[90] At the dedication of the Georgetown Law School building in 1971, a most striking contrast was framed by Chief Justice Burger's dedication speech and William Kunstler's "counterdedication" speech. Kunstler and others delivered their student-organized counterdedication speeches from the bed of a pick-up truck parked outside the building. *Burger Speaks and Kunstler "Counters,"* N.Y. Times, Sept. 18, 1971, at 25.

[91] Fred P. Graham, *Burger Assails Unruly Lawyers*, N.Y. Times, May 19, 1971, at 1 (quoting and excerpting from speech).

[92] Dorsen & Friedman, *supra* note 39; ABA Special Comm. on Evaluation of Disciplinary Enforcement, Problems and Recommendations in Disciplinary Enforcement xvii (1970); William A. Stanmeyer, *The New Left and the Old Law*, 55 A.B.A. J. 319 (1969).

A. CIVIL DISOBEDIENTS AND THEIR LAWYERS[93]

As ABA president, Powell was a vocal condemnor of civil disobedience, repeatedly decrying the actions of sit-in demonstrators' and Freedom Riders' testing of discriminatory laws regulating racial treatment in the South:[94]

> We have witnessed, over the past decade, the development of a heresy that could threaten the foundations of our system of government under law. This is the doctrine that each person may determine for himself what laws are 'just,' and that laws and court orders are to be obeyed only so long as this seems 'just' to the individuals or groups concerned.... In 1965 many people believed that civil disobedience of orders and laws deemed to be unjust is a legitimate means of asserting rights and attaining objectives. Indeed, it is not too much to say that this form of civil disobedience—and its own unique tactics of demonstrations, sit-ins, life-downs and mob pressure—has become the principal weapon of certain minority and dissident groups.... But our Constitution and tradition contemplate the orderly assertion of these rights.[95]

He did not mention states and state bar associations that were resisting the Brown mandate, ostensibly because they were of the view that it was unjust. While North Carolina's James Gilliland had been disciplined for advocating compliance with law, Terrance Hallinan found that *civil disobedience against* unjust laws would also draw the bar authorities' ire.

Civil rights worker and civil disobedient Terrence Hallinan was denied admission by the California Committee of Bar Examiners. Hallinan had graduated from Hastings Law School and passed the bar exam in 1965. He had for some time been engaged in various civil rights activities. His first arrest was in England at a 1960 peace march attended by about 100,000 people. Hallinan was in a group of about 300–400 who, led by Bertrand Russell, attempted to deliver a protest letter to the American Embassy. After the letter was refused, the group sat on a sidewalk blocking passage. Hallinan was convicted of "blocking a footpath." Once back in the United States, Hallinan joined the Student Non-Violent Coordinating Committee and worked on voter registration in Mississippi in 1963. There he was arrested on separate occasions for loitering and littering. No convictions resulted; he was released after the attorney general and the National Council of Churches intervened. Once back in San Francisco, he joined the Congress on Racial Equality, the NAACP, and the Ad Hoc Committee to End Racial Discrimination. With these organizations, Hallinan engaged in picketing and several sit-ins at businesses thought to engage in

---

[93] *See generally*, DiSalvo, *supra* note 28, at 443.

[94] *See, e.g.,* "The President's Annual Address: The State of the Legal Profession"; August 9, 1965; Miami Beach, FL; Annual Address; reprinted from ABA Journal, September 1965 (calling civil disobedience "a dangerous trend"); John C. Jeffries, Jr., Justice Lewis F. Powell, Jr. 210–211 (Charles Scribner's Sons, NY, 1994).

[95] *Id.* at 1–3.

racial discrimination in hiring practices. These activities resulted in six arrests, four of which were dismissed. The other two resulted in trials and convictions for unlawful assembly, disturbing the peace, remaining present at place of unlawful assembly, and trespass. Hallinan represented himself at these trials. Both the presiding judge and the prosecutor prepared documents for the bar examiners stating that Hallinan had "appli[ed] the standards of conduct required of members of the bar."[96] After a lengthy hearing, the Committee found Hallinan lacking good moral character. More than a year later, over a dissent, the California Supreme Court reversed the Committee and concluded the matter in Hallinan's favor.

One such reported case likely hides the rest of an iceberg's worth of prospective lawyers refused law school admission, denied bar admission without appeal, or deterred from the attempt to attend law school and gain admission.

From his earliest days leading the NAACP's legal team, Charles Hamilton Houston understood the threat of bar hostility to unpopular groups and causes. In one of his earliest cases, Houston, assisted by Thurgood Marshall, represented Bernard Ades against bar complaints.[97] Ades represented the Industrial Labor Defense, an organization with communist party leanings and a social reform agenda. Ades was charged with a variety of bar violations, including solicitation of clients, stirring up racial unrest, court criticism, and pressuring a capital defendant to bequeath his body to Ades for its later use in a death penalty protest. With Houston representing him, Ades was reprimanded for the inappropriate disposal of his client's body and his court criticism. Houston would be forever concerned about the use of bar discipline against NAACP lawyers.[98] In a variety of ways, Houston, and later Thurgood Marshall, sought to guard NAACP lawyers against anticipated bar discipline.[99]

Together, lawyers for various civil rights causes and the early government supported lawyers for the poor created a fresh ethos of lawyering, often producing friction with political and bar leaders, and sometimes attacks on their bar membership.

B. GOVERNMENT-FUNDED LAWYERS FOR THE POOR

When the National Lawyers Guild proposed government-funded legal services for the poor in the 1950s, the proposal was roundly criticized by leaders of the organized bar, perceiving it to be a step toward socialism and away from traditional lawyering. At the time proposing government-funded lawyers for the poor could only serve to further identify the Guild with the communist threat. The proposal was a

---

[96] Hallinan v. Comm. of Bar Exam'rs, 65 Cal. 2d 447, 449, 455–456 (1966).

[97] *In re* Ades, 6 F. Supp. 467 (D.Md. 1934); Carle, *supra* note 45, at 296.

[98] Carle, *supra* note 45, at 297–298; MARK V. TUSHNET, THE NAACP's LEGAL STRATEGY AGAINST SEGREGATED EDUCATION, 1925–1950 at 105 (1987).

[99] TUSHNET, *supra* note 30, at 272–300; CARLE, *supra* note 45, at 298–299.

component of the Guild resume that led to persecution of its members by the bar
in the years to follow. So certain was the persecution of identified Guild members
that when a Hale & Dorr lawyer was identified as a guild member during a 1954
HUAC hearing, the hearing witness, Joseph Welch, lamented that the lawyer would
"always bear a scar."[100]

At the earliest stages, leaders of the ABA were appalled at the prospect of
federally subsidized legal services. According to a member of the ABA Board of
Governors, federal legal services, like the "undermining influences of Communist
infiltration" with which he equated them, would inevitably substitute state regimentation for professional independence. For proposing federal subsidies, the Guild
earned the opprobrium otherwise reserved for Bolsheviks, another "organized
minority with ruthless methods."

> Pennsylvania Bar Association President Harold J. Gallagher warned that 'the
> entry of the government into the field of providing legal services is too dan-
> gerous to be permitted to come about in our free America.' It was absurd,
> these lawyers suggested, to believe that a needy client should obtain assis-
> tance anywhere but in the law office of an independent practitioner.[101]

The unavailability of services for the poor from the independent practitioner was
of no concern.

Eventually, ABA authorities softened and capitulated to the existence of federally funded lawyers for the poor. Problems with the bar's feeble efforts at providing
legal assistance to the poor were well known by ABA leaders.

> The principal deficiencies in [bar-organized] legal aid service generally have
> been: (i) incomplete geographic coverage—with some cities and sections of
> cities not served at all; (ii) indigency tests which are too low or too restric-
> tive; (iii) limitations on the scope of services rendered, which are also fre-
> quently much too restrictive and (iv) lack of funds with which to provide
> adequate personnel and services.[102] It is true that most lawyers would have
> preferred local rather than federal solutions. Certainty, this would have been
> my choice.[103]

Faults and gaps and failings notwithstanding, bar leaders would prefer not to have
federal resources provide additional service to the poor. Much later, in 1981, the

---

[100] AUERBACH, *supra* note 24, at 236–237

[101] AUERBACH, *supra* note 24, at 236–237, citing Robert G. Storey, Address before the State Bar
of California: The Legal Profession versus Regimentation (Oct. 1950), *in* 37 A.B.A. J. 100, 101,
103 (1951) and Harold J. Gallagher, *Annual Address*, 55 PA. B. ASS'N REP. 107 (1950).

[102] Memorandum from Lewis F. Powell, Jr. to Messrs. Pollak and Terris: Guidelines for Legal
Service Proposals 6 (Apr. 3, 1965) (on file in Lewis F. Powell, Jr. Archives, Washington & Lee
University School of Law Library, Memoranda and Reports Box 76).

[103] *Id.*

ABA became a steadfast supporter of the federal Legal Services Corporation in the face of Ronald Reagan's efforts to abolish it.

Professional opposition and harassment of legal aid lawyers proceeded on two fronts and with two different rationales: local bar associations expressed the concerns of solo and small firm lawyers who feared some of their marginal-but-paying clients would be served by legal aid lawyers;[104] state bars and powerful institutional interests saw their economic and political interests threatened by the lawsuits and legislative lobbying being done by legal aid lawyers on behalf of their clients.[105]

State and local bar associations in California, Texas, Florida, Pennsylvania, and Washington, DC, unsuccessfully sued the Office of Economic Opportunity (OEO), claiming it was violating ethical canons.[106] They claimed that legal services lawyers were engaged in unauthorized practice and were unlawfully soliciting clients.[107] In doing so, they were largely protecting local practitioners' turf.

Among the more dramatic statewide moves against legal services lawyers occurred in North Carolina. Spurred by complaints of local bar associations, the North Carolina Bar Association moved to block legal services lawyers' work entirely. The North Carolina Bar Association promulgated a rule that would disbar any lawyer working in a legal services office. Essentially, the new rule prohibited practicing with an organization whose directors included non-lawyers. OEO regulations required some representation on legal services boards by income-eligible non-lawyer community members. If successful, the move would have disbarred or run-off every legal services lawyer in the state. The miscalculation was in not accounting for a single program in Winston-Salem that had been founded by a few prominent state lawyers. Negotiations in the shadow of a federal lawsuit threat resolved the crisis, allowing legal services programs to continue operations.[108]

Perhaps the most vociferous fight between legal aid lawyers and a coalition of business and government interests was spawned by the California Rural Legal Assistance (CRLA) representation of farm workers.[109] CRLA moved in a variety of ways to increase wages for farm workers and demand government services for them. These lawsuits drew the ire and outrage of then-Governor Ronald Reagan and Senator George Murphy, speaking and acting on behalf of the California

---

[104] A. Kenneth Pye & Raymond F. Garraty, Jr., *The Involvement of the Bar in the War Against Poverty*, 41 Notre Dame Law. 860, 864–866 (1966); Fred J. Hiestand, *The Politics of Poverty Law*, *in* With Justice for Some 160, 160–189 (Bruce Wasserstein & Mark J. Green eds. 1970); Earl Johnson, Jr., Justice and Reform: The Formative Years of the American Legal Services Program, 84–86 (1978) (summarizing various conflict-producing combinations of political and bar interests).

[105] Harry P. Stumpf, *Law and Poverty: A Political Perspective*, 1968 Wis. L. Rev. 694.

[106] Johnson, *supra* note 104, at 91; Troutman v. Shriver, 471 F.2d 171 (5th Cir. 1969); Auerbach, *supra* note 24, at 273; Billie Bethel & Robert Kirk Walker, *Et Tu, Brute!*, 1965 Tenn. B. J. 11, *quoted in* Pye & Garraty, *supra* note 104, at 866–869.

[107] Johnson, *supra* note 104, at 91.

[108] *Id.*

[109] Houseman & Perle, *supra* note 89, at 15–16.

agribusiness industry.[110] At the time, state governors had the power to veto funding for their state's federally funded legal aid programs, but that veto could be overridden by the OEO director. Only once was a California governor's veto sustained: in 1970, Governor Ronald Reagan vetoed the funding, and the veto was sustained by then-OEO Director Donald Rumsfeld.[111] Unsuccessful efforts by Murphy would have placed full control of legal services programs in the hands of governors, localizing control to suppress locally unpopular legal aid activities, and would have prohibited legal aid suits against the government.[112] The latter effort was a part of a national affront to the successes of legal aid lawyers in various government-defendant matters, especially in the arena of welfare reform.[113]

In some instances, courts refused to certify legal aid organizations whose community organizing went beyond traditional law service bounds. A New York Appellate Division objected to certifying more than one legal services provider for a particular county, for fear of their "unseemly competition" for representation of nonpaying clients, and out of worry that the court could not maintain minimum standards of conduct. The court also expressed concern about the applicants' mixing of community action goals and legal service.[114]

Along with labor union lawyers, federally funded legal aid lawyers were a significant part of the new style of lawyering, cause, or group lawyering, that did not go unchallenged by the organized bar and, acting through the bar, powerful economic interests. The standard one-client- at-a-time model of lawyering did not suit the goals of legal aid lawyers and union lawyers. Their strength lay in collective action that allowed a marshaling of modest resources in pursuit of a cause. The standard bar obstruction first took the form of unauthorized practice restrictions and later advertising and solicitation rules.

Having failed in its efforts to restrict the activities of school desegregation lawyers,[115] the Virginia Bar worked to stifle opportunities for labor unions to provide counsel to their members.[116] And the Illinois Bar initially prevented the United Mine Workers from hiring inside, house counsel.[117] Each of these efforts was rejected by a Court whose decisions fostered the accumulation of power through collective legal action. "Collective activity undertaken to obtain meaningful access to the courts is

---

[110] Hiestand, *supra* note 104; John D. Robb, *Controversial Cases and the Legal Services Program*, 56 A.B.A. J. 329 (1970); Auerbach, *supra* note 24, at 274–275.

[111] Hiestand, *supra* note 104, at 182.

[112] Robb, *supra* note 110, at 329–330.

[113] *See, e.g.,* King v. Smith, 392 U.S. 309 (1968); *see also*, Shapiro v. Thompson, 394 U.S. 618 (1969).

[114] Application of Cmty. Action for Legal Servs., Inc., 26 App. Div. 2d 354, 63 (N.Y. App. Div. 1966).

[115] *Button*, *supra* note 40.

[116] Bhd. of Trainmen v. Virginia, 377 U.S. 1 (1964).

[117] UMW v. Ill. Bar Ass'n, 389 U.S. 217 (1967) (The Bar had claimed this to amount to the unauthorized practice of law).

a fundamental right within the protection of the First Amendment."[118] The Court's rejection of the bar's insistence on the traditional one lawyer-one client notion of lawyering laid the legal groundwork for legal aid lawyers' representation of causes, groups, and social issues, rather than individual clients. This sort of representation presented the shocking circumstance for powerful economic interests and government agencies, not used to having to deal with poor people on so nearly an equal footing.[119] As the lawyer in charge of OEO programs in California put it, "What we have created [in CRLA] is an economic leverage equal to that of large corporations. Clearly that should not be."[120] The mere concept of such power residing in poor people and their lawyers seemed foreign to the legal profession.

Lawyers representing causes could not simply wait in their offices for the causes to arrive in the personage of an eligible client. While Attorney General, Nicholas Katzenbach tried to deter bar application of advertising and solicitation restrictions against poverty lawyers when he announced that lawyers should "go out to the poor rather than wait.... To be reduced to inaction by ethical prohibitions is to let the canons...serve the cause of injustice."[121]

An uneasy measure of conditional cooperation regarding federally funded legal aid eventually emerged from the organized bar at the national level.[122] Even as the ABA began to cooperate with federally funded legal services, its best and most able spokespersons continued to put an unduly positive face on the organization's prior record of opposing meaningful legal services for the poor. William McCalpin, who was truly instrumental in shaping the ABA's more enlightened position on legal services, prefaced his strong advocacy for support of legal services by imagining an ABA previously unaware of the legal needs of the poor: "Recently we have begun to be aware of the possible legal needs of 40,000,000 disadvantaged citizens."[123] The prior month's issue of the same *ABA Journal* featured an article by Marvin Frankel that began with a statement more reflective of reality outside the walls erected by the ABA: "It is no new discovery that the promise of equal justice is a hollow one for people too poor to retain counsel."[124]

---

[118] United Transp. Union v. State Bar of Mich., 401 U.S. 576, 585 (1971).

[119] Robb, *supra* note 110 at 330–331; HOUSEMAN & PERLE, *supra* note 89, at 10.

[120] AUERBACH, *supra* note 24, at 274.

[121] National Conference on Law and Poverty, Proceedings at v, 64–65 (Washington DC 1965).

[122] In later years and controversies, the ABA grew to be almost unerringly supportive of legal services programs, fighting against, for example, President Reagan's proposal to zero-fund the Legal Services Corporation in 1980. HOUSEMAN & PERLE, *supra* note 89.

[123] F. William McCalpin, *The Bar Faces Forward*, 51 A.B.A. J. 548, 550 (1965).

[124] Marvin E. Frankel, *Experiments in Serving the Indigent*, 51 A.B.A. J. 460 (1965)(hoping against some of the early evidence that the ABA would allow new, OEO funded legal services offices to be established rather than merely pressing for additional funding for the traditional legal aids under the supervision of NLADA). Ironically, some years later in an oral history of his ABA involvement, McCalpin himself described the unfortunate, introspection practiced by the ABA in dealing with difficult issues. Interview by Olavi Maru with F. William McCalpin (Aug. 22, 1975). Visited March 10, 2004 http://www.abf-sociolegal.org/oralhistory/mccalpin. html. Tape MCA-1-B.

The ABA adopted a resolution of support for the new federal legal services program as long as its lawyers would operate within the ethical standards of the legal profession.[125] The announced constraint was no constraint at all; legal aid lawyers, like any lawyers, would of course be expected to comply with lawyer ethics rules relating to confidentiality, conflicts, and the like. But the rules regarding solicitation, not yet reformed by later court decisions,[126] would dampen the envisioned activism and would subject legal aid and other cause lawyers engaged in community organizing to continued harassment by bar authorities for direct solicitation of clients.

That is precisely what happened to ACLU-affiliated lawyer Edna Primus.[127] In South Carolina, Medicaid assistance to pregnant mothers on public assistance was being conditioned on the mother's sterilization. At the invitation of a local businessperson, Edna Smith Primus, one of three lawyers practicing with what they called the "Carolina Community Law Firm," spoke at a meeting of mothers affected by this practice. Among those at the meeting was Mary Etta Williams, who had been sterilized by Dr. Clovis H. Pierce after the birth of her third child. At the meeting, Primus advised those present of their legal rights and suggested the possibility of a lawsuit. Primus and her office mates had a relationship with the ACLU.

Subsequently, the ACLU informed Primus that it was willing to provide representation for the mothers who had been sterilized. By letter, Primus then informed Williams of the ACLU's offer of free legal representation. When Williams visited Dr. Pierce to discuss the progress of her third child who was ill, she was met by Dr. Pierce's lawyer. There with her sick child, the lawyer asked Williams to sign a release of liability in favor of Dr. Pierce. Williams showed Primus's letter to the doctor and his lawyer, and they made a copy. In the intimidating setting with her children's health care in the balance, Williams never pursued the matter against Dr. Pierce.

Shortly thereafter, however, the South Carolina Bar moved against Primus's license, imposing discipline that was later reversed on First Amendment grounds in the Supreme Court.[128] Stymied by the Court in its efforts to restrain poor people's lawyers from directly offering their pro bono services, the organized bar eventually adopted rules that acknowledged the First Amendment constraints on bar power.[129]

---

[125] McCalpin, *supra* note 122, at 551; Richard Pious, *Congress, the Organized Bar, and the Legal Services Program*, 1972 WIS. L. REV. 418, 420–421 (discussing the political background for the ABA resolution).

[126] *In re* Primus, 436 U.S. 412 (1978). In later adopting the Model Rules, the ABA accounted for its inability to propose enforceable rules on soliciting lawyers who lacked financial gain incentives. *See* MODEL RULES OF PROF'L CONDUCT, R. 7.2.

[127] *Primus, supra* note 126; *see also* ACLU v Bozardt, 539 F.2d 340 (4th Cir. 1976). Compare *Primus* with Ohralik v. Ohio State Bar Ass'n, 436 U.S. 447 (1978), a politically neutral case decided on the same day.

[128] *Primus, supra* note 126, at 423–424 (1978).

[129] *Compare* MODEL RULES OF PROF'L CONDUCT, R. 7.1–7.5 (2009), *with* MODEL CODE OF PROF'L RESPONSIBILITY, DR 2-101 to 2-105 (1980) (ABA treatment of advertising and solicitation pre and post Bates v. Arizona State Bar, 433 U.S. 350 (1977)).

IX. Courts Restrict the Profession's Power

The stage had been set for the *Primus* case not only by *Button*, but also by a series of opinions in which the U.S. Supreme Court trimmed the regulatory power of the state bars. Closely connected to the new kind of lawyering, some aggressive lawyers dared to advertise and price compete, both in violation of the organized bar's ethics rules.

The first crack came when consumers asked why lawyers are required to charge a fixed, minimum fee and cannot price compete.[130] The Goldfarbs had contracted to buy a home in Fairfax County, Virginia, and the lender who financed the purchase required them to obtain title insurance, which necessitated a title examination. By state statute, the examination could be performed legally only by a member of the Virginia State Bar. The Goldfarbs unsuccessfully tried to find a lawyer who would examine the title for less than the fee prescribed in a minimum fee schedule published by the Fairfax County Bar Association and enforced by the Virginia State Bar. They then brought a class action, seeking injunctive relief and damages, and alleging that the minimum fee schedule and its enforcement mechanism constituted price fixing in violation of § 1 of the Sherman Act. Although holding that the State Bar was exempt from the Sherman Act, the district court granted judgment against the Fairfax County Bar Association and enjoined the publication of the fee schedule. The court of appeals reversed, holding not only that the State Bar's actions were immune from antitrust liability as "state action," but also that the county bar association was immune because the practice of law, as a "learned profession," is not "trade or commerce" under the Sherman Act. The Supreme Court held that the minimum fee schedule, as published by the county bar association and enforced by the State Bar, violated § 1 of the Sherman Act. For the Court, the schedule and its enforcement mechanism constituted price fixing since the record showed that the schedule, rather than being purely advisory, operated as a fixed, rigid price floor. The fee schedule was enforced through the prospect of professional discipline by the Virginia State Bar, by reason of attorneys' desire to comply with announced professional norms, and by the assurance that other lawyers would not compete by underbidding.

Now that lawyers had the right to price compete, some did. But with the stringent advertising rules of the time, carryovers from the early century's effort to cripple the practices of the immigrant lawyers, how could a willingness to price compete be communicated to prospective clients?

As late as 1975, the ABA Model Code adopted in nearly every state, retained all the strictures that had ever regulated lawyer advertising and more. The ABA Model Code of Professional Responsibility advertisement regulations began with a general catch-all, requiring ads to be done in a "dignified manner"[131] and not

---

[130] Goldfarb v. Virginia State Bar, 421 U.S. 773 (1973).
[131] Model Code of Prof'l Responsibility, DR 2–101 (1980).

be "false, fraudulent, misleading, or deceptive,"[132] but they quickly turned into an exhaustive list of permissible and prohibited actions. For example, advertisements on television, radio, and in print media were limited to 25 specific categories of information. Permissible information included names, fields of practice, date and place of birth, date and place of admission to the bar, schools attended, dates of graduation, degrees, other scholastic distinctions, public offices, military service, legal authorship, legal teaching positions, memberships, offices, committee assignments, legal fraternities, licenses, professional societies, foreign language ability, bank references, the names of clients represented (with written consent), whether credit cards are accepted, and office and telephone answering service hours.[133] If the information sought to be advertised was not in the list authorized for disclosure, an attorney was required to apply to the agency having jurisdiction under state law to receive approval before advertising the desired information.[134]

Adding to the regulations on print, radio, and television advertising, the Model Code drafted additional restrictions for what lawyers may place on professional notices, letterheads, and offices. Again the guidelines start with a catch-all requirement mandating the information appear in a "dignified form."[135] The Code went on to limit letterhead material to names, address, telephone number, names of firm associates, and names and dates relating to deceased or retired members.[136] The designation "OF COUNSEL" was limited to those attorneys having a continuing relationship with a lawyer or firm other than being a partner or associate. Moreover, the designation "GENERAL COUNSEL" was reserved for the attorney who "devotes a substantial amount of professional time in the representation of that client."[137]

Further detailed restrictions on lawyer advertising included those on "Personal Notices," which may contain professional announcements declaring a new or changed association. These notices may only be mailed only to lawyers, clients, former clients, personal friends, and relatives.[138]

Last, the Model Code prohibited an attorney from holding himself out publicly as a specialist unless the advertisement mirrored one of the permitted designations dictated by the Model Code.[139] Permissible specialties were limited to a lawyer admitted to practice before the United States Patent and Trademark Office who may use the designation "Patent," "Patent Attorney," "Patent Lawyer," "Registered Patent Attorney," or any combination of those terms on letterhead and office signs.[140] If lawyers wanted to include other distinctions or certifications

---

[132] *Id.*
[133] *Id.*
[134] *Id.*
[135] MODEL CODE OF PROF'L RESPONSIBILITY, DR 2-102 (1980).
[136] *Id.*
[137] *Id.*
[138] *Id.*
[139] MODEL CODE OF PROF'L RESPONSIBILITY, DR 2-105 (1980).
[140] *Id.*

they could only do so by gaining the approval of the authority having jurisdiction under state law.[141]

The test case came when lawyers in Arizona set up a legal clinic law firm, the business model of which was to use technological tools of the time to routinize basic legal work, lower prices, and attract volume business from middle class clients.[142] (Think forward by 30 years to LegalZoom and other online providers of routine legal services.) These lawyers' activities mainly transgressed bar ethics rules because their lawyer advertisements stated prices. When the State Bar of Arizona found the lawyers involved to be subject to discipline, the issue was framed for Supreme Court resolution.

The profession's effort to justify the blanket ban on price advertising sounded a 1970s professionalism harangue in the era of Ralph Nader and Truth-in-Lending consumerism. The profession argued that permission of advertising would have an "Adverse Effect on Professionalism."

> [P]rice advertising will bring about commercialization, which will undermine the attorney's sense of dignity and self-worth.
>
> The hustle of the marketplace will adversely affect the profession's service orientation, and irreparably damage the delicate balance between the lawyer's need to earn and his obligation selflessly to serve.
>
> Advertising is also said to erode the client's trust in his attorney: Once the client perceives that the lawyer is motivated by profit, his confidence that the attorney is acting out of a commitment to the client's welfare is jeopardized.
>
> And advertising is said to tarnish the dignified public image of the profession.[143]

Despite its recent arguments that lawyers could and should set fixed minimum prices, the profession claimed that the "Inherently Misleading Nature of Attorney Advertising" should permit its prohibition:

> (a) [B]ecause such services are so individualized with regard to content and quality as to prevent informed comparison on the basis of advertisement,
>
> (b) because the consumer of legal services is unable to determine in advance just what services he needs, and
>
> (c) because advertising by attorneys will highlight irrelevant factors and fail to show the relevant factor of skill.[144]

Consistent with its efforts to suppress the activities of the NAACP with the application of barratry statutes, the profession suggested that advertising had the undesirable effect of stirring up litigation. The profession further claimed that advertising

---

[141] *Id.*
[142] Bates v. State Bar of Ariz., 433 U.S. 350 (1977).
[143] *Id.* at 368.
[144] *Id.* at 372.

would adversely affect the quality of lawyer service by encouraging lawyers to sell "packaged services" rather than individually designed, bespoke services. Finally, despite all evidence to the contrary, the profession argued that competition would drive up fees. Knowing that the profession only recently failed to protect its scheme of enforceable, minimum fees, this claim approached the ridiculous.

> [A]dvertising will increase the overhead costs of the profession, and these costs then will be passed along to consumers in the form of increased fees.
>
> [T]he additional cost of practice will create a substantial entry barrier deterring or preventing young attorneys from penetrating the market and entrenching the position of the bar's established members.[145]

The Court would have none of it, and struck down the blanket ban on advertising by lawyers in favor of permitting state bars to regulate advertising that is "false or misleading," language that smacked to the profession as consumer protection, false advertising language that would now apply to lawyers and used car salesmen alike.

X. Demographics Change the Profession

In greater numbers than ever before, blacks and women entered a grudgingly accepting profession during this time frame. Certainly there were earlier exceptions, but they were few and far between. Very few women practiced law in the 19th century. Most state bars explicitly excluded them, and the Supreme Court upheld the prohibition in the name of the claimed fundamental incompatibility of women for rigors of law practice. A justice of the Wisconsin Supreme Court captured the 19th-century attitude:

> Nature has tempered women as little for the judicial conflicts of the courtroom, as for the physical conflicts of the battle field.... [O]ur profession...has essentially...to do with all that is selfish and malicious, knavish and criminal, coarse and brutal, repulsive and obscene, in human life. It would be revolting to all female sense of innocence and the sanctity of their sex.[146]

His description gives pause about those men who choose to practice law.

The "girl applicants" were said to present a "vexing problem" in the 1920s. Some were admitted, but with trepidation.

> The girl applicants have presented a vexing problem. There are now a good many of them. There is no intrinsic reason that I know of why girls should

---

[145] *Id.* at 377.
[146] *In re* Goodell, 39 Wis. 232, 245 (1895) (Ryan, C. J., dissenting) (opposing the admission of Lavinia Goodell to the bar).

not make competent lawyers, but those who have applied for admission this year have been with few exceptions of very inferior quality. Most of them have been stenographers from the small law offices who have taken night law courses with the idea that if they can be admitted they may be able to increase their salaries by doing part typewriting and part law. Most of them clearly can never become competent lawyers, but after they have worked for years to get a law degree, we hesitate to say to them that they give us a general impression of poor quality and that we will not pass them.[147]

The U.S. Supreme Court used somewhat more restrained words to convey the same attitude in the course of upholding states' exclusion of women from law practice. Rejecting Myra Bradwell's claim that she was denied her constitutional rights when Illinois denied her a law license for the sole reason of her gender, one concurring member of the Court said:

> [T]he civil law, as well as nature herself, has always recognized a wide difference in the respective spheres and destinies of man and woman. Man is, or should be, woman's protector and defender. The natural and proper timidity and delicacy which belongs to the female sex evidently unfits it for many of the occupations of civil life.... The paramount destiny and mission of woman are to fulfill the noble and benign offices of wife and mother. This is the law of the Creator.[148]

In 1886, Alice R. Jordon Blake, using only her initials, was accepted at Yale Law School. Her gender was soon discovered, and she was allowed to continue but told she would be attending on a nondegree basis. When she completed the studies, the faculty met and awarded her degree with full honors because of her stellar performance.[149] That year, Yale added this message to its application: "It is to be understood that the courses of instruction are open to the male sex only." No other woman would graduate Yale Law School for 74 years.[150]

Very little changed during the first half of the 20th century. It was not until 1920 that women were permitted to practice law before the courts in every state.[151] Women were excluded from membership in the ABA until 1918[152] and from the Association of the Bar of the City of New York until 1937.[153]

In 1938, Pauli Murray's rejection letter from the University of North Carolina Law School read, "Members of your race are not admitted to the University."

---

[147] Alan Fox, *Higher Education Standards Urged for Admission to Law Study in N. Y.*, 13 A.B.A. J. 121, 123 (1927).

[148] Bradwell v. Illinois, 83 U.S. 130, 141 (1872) (Bradley, J., concurring).

[149] WILLIAM C. KING, THE WORLD'S PROGRESS 160 (1896).

[150] Barbara Joan Zeitz, *The Lady & The Law School*, COUNTHERHISTORY (AM. ASS'N OF UNIV. WOMEN, ILL.), Oct. 2009, *available at* http://aauw-il.org/information/herstory/Oct2009.pdf.

[151] CLARICE FEINMAN, WOMEN IN THE CRIMINAL JUSTICE SYSTEM 134 (3rd ed. 1994).

[152] RICHARD L. ABEL, AMERICAN LAWYERS 107 (1989).

[153] CYNTHIA FUCHS EPSTEIN, WOMEN IN LAW 248 (Illini Books 2d ed. 1993).

Eventually, she finished first in her class at Howard University Law School, where she was the only female in her class. In 1944, Murray's rejection letter for an advanced degree program at Harvard Law School read: "Your picture and the salutation on your college transcript indicate that you are not of the sex entitled to be admitted to Harvard Law School."[154]

The percentage of women in law classes barely topped 3 percent by 1965, a year after the landmark Civil Rights Act. Academics claimed that the low numbers were due to women's disinterest, but statistics suggest a pattern of discrimination. Despite increasing numbers of women applicants, women constituted about 3 percent in each class between 1951 and 1965.[155] Women remained less than five percent of the enrollment at ABA-approved law schools until the 1970s.[156] Both faculty (nearly 100 percent male at the time) and male students found innumerable ways to make the educational environment inhospitable to women.

The market for women lawyers was comparable to their acceptance into the law school environment. When Sandra Day O'Connor graduated third in her class at Stanford Law School in 1953, the only job that she was offered was as a legal secretary.[157] She declined the offer.

The change in admissions to law schools expanded more quickly than did the job market. In 1960, women comprised only 3.5 percent of the enrollees at ABA-approved law schools; in 1970, they comprised 8.5 percent; in 1980, they comprised 33.6 percent; and in 1986, they comprised 40.2 percent.[158] In 2002, 50 percent of all law school entrants in the United States were women.[159] Of the new entrants to the bar in 2003, 46 percent were women.[160]

Nothing but the social mood change of the civil rights movement and the antidiscrimination laws that flowed from it could have produced this dramatic increase. Law and culture changed much faster than the profession and its culture.

Although law changed just as quickly for minorities as for women, the legal culture has not. It is true that much progress has been made since the ABA accidentally admitted two black lawyers to membership in 1912 and had to fashion a scrambling retreat to save face while ensuring such a mistake could never occur again, entry into the profession since the civil rights era has been slow. In 2000, while the U.S. population was 25 percent nonwhite, the lawyer population was less than 10 percent nonwhite. At the same moment, while the black population in America was close to 13 percent, blacks accounted for barely over 4 percent of lawyers. Membership

---

[154] Zeitz, *supra* note 150; *see also*, STATES' LAWS ON RACE AND COLOR (2d ed. 1997 Pauli Murray ed.) (Introduction, Davison Douglas).

[155] Harvard Law Record (Dec. 9, 1965) at 7, *cited in* EPSTEIN, *supra* note 153 at 53.

[156] ABEL, *supra* note 152, at 90.

[157] Ed Magnuson et al., *The Brethren's First Sister: Sandra Day O'Connor*, TIME, July 20, 1981, at 12.

[158] ABEL, *supra* note 152, at 285.

[159] ABA COMM'N ON WOMEN IN THE PROFESSION, CHARTING OUR PROGRESS 4 (2006).

[160] RONIT DINOVITZER ET AL., AFTER THE JD 19 (2004).

in the ABA reflected that same proportion, with just over 90 percent of members being white. In 2005, the House of Delegates had an overall minority population of about 14 percent, higher than the percentage of lawyers in the ABA and in the general lawyer population, but 24 states had no minority members in the House of Delegates.

XI. Conclusion

The bar's overall strategy of exclusion to stave off change was not new. The activities of this period remind of the efforts during the immigrant-wave crisis. There, as here, the bar remained blind to changes in demographics, social conditions, and culture. As the United States became richer for the influx of new cultures in the early 20th century, the profession endeavored to stay "pure;"[161] as U.S. society became more aware of the needs and interests of its less powerful members, the profession sought to prevent them from securing legal representation and access to the justice system. Just as the profession sought to dampen the impact of a new and more aggressive form of personal injury plaintiff's lawyer at the turn of the century, here it sought to stave off the development of a new and more aggressive lawyer, the "cause" lawyer.

The profession's effort to resist change failed for a variety of reasons, not least of which was the slowly changing, but changing indeed, demographics of the profession itself. As the increase in law students during the 1960s and 1970s poured new lawyers onto the legal market, more and more of those new lawyers were committed to social justice and the aggressive lawyering that it demanded. Though still growing too slowly to approach anything like proportionate shares, more of the new lawyers were women and minorities as well. The profession, trying to preserve social norms of the 1950s was itself at the beginning stages of its own transformation, a transformation driven by a changing membership.

As well, courts, not acting as traditional regulators of the legal profession, but as appliers of external limits on the profession's power to police its members, for the first time entered the fray and forced significant change on an unreceptive legal profession.

---

[161] Elihu Root et al., *Report of the Special Committee to the Section of Legal Education and Admissions to the Bar of the American Bar Association*, 44 ANN. REP. A.B.A. 679, 681 (1921).

5

The Deepest Embarrassment: Watergate

"American Lawyers—A Sick Profession?"[1]

I. The President's Men Embarrass Their Profession

A sense of crisis overwhelmed the legal profession in the wake of the Watergate revelations. The prominent role of lawyers in the scandals presented an unprecedented public relations crisis for the profession.

> And now, once again, with the advent of new scandals in Washington in which a number of lawyers have been accused of unethical conduct, our profession is once more faced with a crisis and our stock has dropped to what is, perhaps, its lowest point in the past twenty years.[2]
>
> Watergate has sent a pall over the country and a shadow over our profession. While it is patently unfair to blame our profession for Watergate just because many participants happen to be lawyers, I do think that the blame that has been cast upon us ultimately will have a healthy effect on the profession and a positive influence on the country. We...must move deliberately but more quickly to provide additional protection for the public and to discipline those among us who are not following the highest principles of the profession.[3]

In 1975, the ABA's Standing Committee on Professional Discipline reported on the progress of state bar discipline of those involved in Watergate, but emphasized that "Watergate is regarded as a national problem, and the profession's efforts to cope with it will be assessed on a national basis."[4]

---

[1] US News and World Report, March 25, 1974 at 23.

[2] The Bar Examiner Vol. 42, pp. 156, 157—Burton B. Laub, Dean, Dickinson School of Law, Address at Joint Luncheon "Law—A Bad Trade but a Noble Profession."

[3] Chesterfield Smith, *1973–1974: Activity on Many Fronts for the Association*, 1041; *see also* Robert Meserve, 59 A.B.A.J. 985 (suggesting in 1973 that the national profession must respond to the national crisis created by Watergate).

[4] ABA Reports, Standing Committee on Professional Discipline 1975.

The legal profession was enormously embarrassed by the Watergate scandals. Lawyer after lawyer, many high government officials, were shown to be involved in various politically motivated crimes and shenanigans. Checks were doctored; files stolen; financial and other records destroyed; letters forged. Lawyers were deeply involved[5]—and many of them.

> During the Senate Watergate hearings, Senator Herman Talmadge happened to notice a list I had prepared, while still at the White House, of all the people I thought were criminally involved in Watergate. The Senator asked me why there were [asterisks] beside some names and not others. I responded: 'After I did the list—just my first reaction was there certainly are an awful lot of lawyers involved here. So I put a little asterisk beside each lawyer (because I thought) how in God's name could so many lawyers get involved in something like this?'[6]

The turnaround from pride to shame that Richard Nixon and his key men were lawyers was swift. In 1969, ABA President William Gossett proudly connected the legal profession to Nixon and his men:

> Let me record in passing that not only is President Nixon a lawyer; twelve members of his cabinet and subcabinet also are members of the profession. And no fewer than fifteen of the President's appointments to key positions in federal agencies have been lawyers who have been active as officers or as Section or Committee chairmen of the Association.[7]

By 1972, the ABA was racing to distance itself from any connection with the president and his men.

Watergate occurred in the midst of a period marked by a massive shift in social thinking about those in authority. Watergate was the capper and not the onset of society's mistrust of authority and public officials. Throughout the preceding decade, Timothy Leary and others popularized slogans such as, "Think for Yourself and Question Authority."[8] The civil rights movement, the antiwar movement, and the early stages of the women's movement all partook in a strong measure of mistrust of officialdom. By the time the Watergate dust settled, the nation had had its

---

[5] *See Robert W.* Meserve, *Lessons and Challenges for the Legal Profession,* 59 A.B.A. J. 681 (1973) (stating that "[t]he WATERGATE scandal, its ramifications still unfolding, is certain to rank as a dark episode in our political history. It has posed serious challenges to the legal profession because lawyers in high places are among those linked with it and because the faith of the American people in the justice system, and in the governmental structure itself, are at stake.").

[6] JOHN W. DEAN III, LOST HONOR, 254 (Stratford Press 1982).

[7] William T. Gossett, *President's Page,* 55 A.B.A. J. 699 (1969).

[8] The term was later attributed to Leary, but all who lived through the time recall the familiar bumper sticker. *See, e.g.,* Phillip E. Johnson, *The Creationist and the Sociobiologist: Two Stories about Illiberal Education,* CAL. L. REV. (1992)("The student revolt of the 1960s opened with a "Free Speech Movement," and the bumper sticker that directs us to "Question Authority"...").

fill with those in authority. Watergate expanded those categorically mistrusted to include lawyers in a new and powerful way.

II. A Single-Event Crisis

The Watergate crisis for the legal profession occurred in the context of the changed national mood about authority and government. But it would not have been an embarrassment for the *legal* profession except for the event series of Watergate. The trigger was Watergate's lawyer-dominated wrongdoers. As a single-event-triggered crisis, the Watergate crisis was far less complex than other crises dealing with social change, massive technological change, or immigration patterns. Once in the open, the series of events in the Watergate scenario were what they were, and the profession's task was more associated with public relations recovery than with fending off outsiders or meddling technology or 1960s social change.

Perhaps no single event had ever created such an enormous crisis for the legal profession as did the Watergate break-in and cover-up. In one stroke, the legal profession found itself in the crosshairs of the public and potential public regulators. And in that same stroke, the nation found a focal point for the building skepticism of leaders and government and authority that had been growing during the preceding decade. As much as the embarrassment of so many lawyers being involved in the scandal, the legal profession's responsibility for the justice system and leadership in the government brought the profession under public scrutiny.

III. The Profession's Public Relations Response

The measure of embarrassment was so great that the word "Watergate" could barely be uttered in official ABA writings.[9] The ABA even managed to adopt a resolution reaffirming its ethics code and condemning those involved in the Watergate crimes without mentioning the word "Watergate":

WHEREAS, The Code of Professional Responsibility, promulgated by the American Bar Association and adopted by the various jurisdictions, recognizes the vital role of the lawyer in the preservation of society and is predicated upon the obligation of lawyers to maintain the highest standards of ethical conduct; and

---

[9] *See Watergate, Sex, and Marijuana Dominate Debate at Washington August Meeting*, 59 A.B.A. J. 1131 (1973) (stating that "[t]he action on Watergate consisted of a resolution, which declared that the Association "condemns and denounces any action on the part of members of the legal profession which might cast aspersions upon the integrity of the profession" and calls for prompt disciplinary action against lawyers whose conduct violates the Code of Professional Responsibility. The resolution as adopted omits any direct reference to the Watergate affair.").

WHEREAS, The code specifically enjoins lawyers from all illegal and morally reprehensible conduct; and

WHEREAS, Congressional and judicial proceedings and reports of the news media have disclosed alleged instances of professional misconduct by members of the legal profession; and

WHEREAS, The American Bar Association recognizes that a primary objective of the organized bar is the preservation of the integrity of our system of ordered liberty under law; and

WHEREAS, It is in the interest of the profession, the public, and any individuals involved that appropriate proceedings be instituted properly;

BE IT RESOLVED, That the American Bar Association reaffirms its dedication to the ethical standards as set forth in the Code of Professional Responsibility; and

FURTHER RESOLVED, That the Association condemns and denounces any action on the part of members of the legal profession which might cast aspersions upon the integrity of the profession; and

FURTHER RESOLVED That those lawyers whose conduct contravenes the Code of Professional Responsibility should be subjected to prompt and vigorous disciplinary investigation and appropriate action should be taken forthwith and

FURTHER RESOLVED, That a certified copy of this resolution be sent to the Bar Associations of all states.[10]

The ABA moved swiftly to quell the disastrous public reaction to the legal profession's perceived ethical lapse, and with some measure of cover. During the next few years, the ABA pushed through approval and advancement of the Multistate Professional Responsibility Exam, an accreditation-based ethics course requirement for law schools, and set the Kutak Commission to its work of making the lawyer ethics code more law-like.[11] A 2012 article in the *ABA Journal*, subtitled "How a 'third-rate burglary' provoked new standards for lawyer ethics," attributed all three developments to Watergate, acknowledging that the change from Model Code to Model Rules took longest of the three.[12] Looking back on the 40th anniversary of Watergate, the article said,

After Watergate, schools began to make legal ethics courses a required class. Bar examiners added an extra section on ethics... Changes in ethics rules were more gradual, but just as profound.

---

[10] *Id.*

[11] *See House Disapproves UMVARA, Supports the Exclusionary Rule, and Adopts New Law School Standards*, 59 A.B.A. J. 384 (1973). (Finding that, "[t]he actions that prompted the most debate were: []Law school standards. The house approved a complete revision of the Association's standards for the approval of law schools, but only after amending the standards to require instruction in the duties and responsibilities of the legal profession.")

[12] Mark Curriden, *The Lawyers of Watergate*, June 2012 A.B.A. J. 36, 64 (2012).

The positive changes made by the profession were reactive and not proactive.[13] They were what the profession needed to do to dampen the fire of negative public opinion. The need for such changes could easily enough have been foreseen by a profession better in tune with the 1960s rising distrust of public officials, government, and authority generally. Society had for a decade begun to question authority and demand more openness and accountability. The good that could have been done by a profession able to make proactive changes to enhance ethics training for lawyers and modification of its code to a more law-like format was lost. Instead, the profession regulated itself only in response to embarrassment and scandal. It engaged in regulation-by-crisis. The society's sense of the profession's genuineness in enhancing its ethics training was predictably dubious. The end of the Watergate period blended almost seamlessly into the lawyer bashing of the litigation boom.[14]

What did the profession do? In the weeks, months, and years following Watergate's major revelations, the American legal profession moved to require all freshly minted lawyers take a course in lawyer ethics and pass a lawyer ethics exam.[15] Even more fundamentally, it charged a commission with the responsibility of revamping its own model ethics code, adopted only two years prior to the onset of the Watergate defalcations. Almost none of the changes had the slightest effect on current members of the bar.

A. LAWYER ETHICS IN LAW SCHOOLS

In the days and months following the major Watergate revelations, the ABA moved to spearhead the addition of lawyer ethics courses in law schools, first proposing that law schools *offer* such courses and then as Watergate fever intensified, mandating that law schools *require* all students to take such courses. In the end, no one could earn a degree from an ABA-accredited law school without first taking a course on lawyer ethics, which was required to cover the then-dominant ABA Model Code of Professional Responsibility. Only a handful of states permit a person to take the bar exam without a degree from an ABA-accredited law school. In effect, the ABA required that nearly every future lawyer would study its model code of ethics. What better way to demonstrate to the public that the dominant lawyer organization cares about lawyer ethics?

---

[13] *See Robert W.* Meserve, *The Legal Profession and Watergate*, 59 A.B.A. J. 985 (1973) (stating that "[w]e must act in the present era of anxiety to sustain and serve the moral and tolerant tradition that has taken generations of patient effort to create.").

[14] *See* chapter 6.

[15] Joe E. Covington, *The Bar Examiner*, N.C.B.E. 50 (1981). Finding that ("[f]ollowing Watergate, public attention was strongly focused on the ethical standards of the legal profession... The purpose of MPRE is not to exclude persons from he practice of law, but it is to ensure that persons admitted to the bar are prepared to cope with ethical problems in the practice of law.").

It is true that a proposed accreditation standard regarding (but not requiring) law school teaching of lawyer ethics (section 302) existed in draft form prior to the Watergate scandal, and the scholarly attribution of section 302's adoption to Watergate has been mixed. Paul Hayden suggested there was no connection between Watergate and the new accreditation standard 302 that required law schools to make the ethics course mandatory for all students.[16] But even Hayden acknowledged that "[s]cholars are certainly not wrong to connect Watergate to the rapid creation of required ethics courses in law schools—that did generally occur after the full lawyer involvement in the scandal had become clear…"[17]

Others scholars found the connection to be clearer and closer. Kathleen Clark wrote:

The profession apparently felt that it had to do something to repair the image of lawyers, and in 1974 the ABA did indeed take action. What kind of reforms did the ABA adopt in order to prevent future Watergates? The ABA adopted an accreditation requirement that law schools ensure that each graduate receive instruction in legal ethics.[18]

Philip C. Kissam registered his views:

[T]he Watergate affair aroused public and professional concerns about the ethical behavior of lawyers, and the profession responded by establishing a professional ethics part to state bar examinations and by requiring law schools to teach 'legal ethics.'[19]

Likewise, Roger Carmton and Susan Koniak saw a connection:

[Discussion of the ABA requirement of accredited law schools to teach professional responsibility]…[was] [f]irst adopted in August, 1973, in the midst of the Watergate disclosures."[20]

Perhaps most telling, the ABA's own Robert MacCrate, architect of the early 1990s MacCrate Report on reforming legal education, suggested a connection:

The 1973 [accreditation standards] recognized developments in clinical skills instruction as well as the growing attention to professional responsibility in law school curricula…but in August 1974, in the wake of Watergate, the following specification was added to the Standard, 'Such required instruction

---

[16] Paul T. Hayden, *Putting Ethics to the (National Standardized) Test: Tracing the Origins of the Empire*, 71 Fordham L. Rev. 1299 (2003).

[17] *Id.* at 1332.

[18] Kathleen Clark, *The Legacy of Watergate for Legal Ethics Instruction*, 51 Hastings L. J. 673 (2000).

[19] Phillip Kissam, *Lurching Towards the Millennium: The Law School, the Research University, and the Professional Reforms of Legal Education*, 60 Ohio State L. J. 1965, 1984 (1999).

[20] Cramton, Roger C. and Susan P. Koniak. *Rule, Story, and Commitment in the Teaching of Legal Ethics*, 38 William and Mary L. Rev. 145, 148 (1996).

need not be limited to any pedagogical method as long as the history, goals, structure and responsibilities of the legal profession and its members, including [the ABA Code of Professional Responsibility] are all covered.'[21]

Prior to any Watergate revelations, there was a watered-down draft of section 302 in existence. And some claimed that the existence of the draft prior to Watergate makes Watergate a watered-down cause of the resolution's adoption.[22] But the draft that existed before the full Watergate affair came to light did not mandate that law schools *require* a course in lawyer ethics. It merely required that law schools *offer* such a course, along with several others required to be offered by the same provision.[23] The amendment to the draft resolution came during the February 1973 floor debate,[24] when a motion brought by the State Bar of Arizona was passed in the House of Delegates. So the weak draft that existed before Watergate became a much stronger mandate by floor action in 1973, by which time there were new Watergate revelations emerging almost daily. Although it did not begin hearings until May, the Senate Select Committee (chaired by Sam Ervin) was formed on February 7, 1973. A month earlier still, when Judge Sirica opened the Watergate burglars' trial on January 7, federal investigators already knew of the CREEP (Committee to Re-Elect the President) slush fund used to finance illegal activities against Democrats.[25] The convictions of McCord and Liddy were entered on January 30. As far back as August 1, 1972, *The Washington Post* reported that funds meant for CREEP had been deposited in a Watergate burglar's account.[26] Regarding the floor amendment adoption in 1973, ABA President Robert Meserve said that this amendment evidenced the ABA's "desire that there be greater law school emphasis on the teaching of professional responsibility."[27] Although it is fair to say that the major revelations were yet to come when the ethics course requirement was adopted in February 1973, the lawyer involvement in Watergate writing was on the wall.

The difference between offering a course and requiring the course for graduation is enormous. Little or no public relations benefit would have come to the profession by adopting a standard that required law schools to merely offer lawyer

---

[21] MacCrate, Robert, *Educating a Changing Profession: From Clinic to Continuum* 64 TENN. L. REV. 1099, 1123 (1997).

[22] Hayden, *supra* n. 16 at 1332.

[23] 302(a) The law school shall offer:
(i) Instruction in those subjects generally regarded as the core of the law school curriculum,
(ii) Training in professional skills, such as counseling, the drafting of legal documents and materials, and trial and appellate advocacy,
(iii) Instruction in the duties and responsibilities of the legal profession.
98 ANN. REP. A.B.A. 351, 353.

[24] 59 A.B.A. J. 384, 388–390 (1973).

[25] *The Watergate Trial: Overview; available at* http://www.fordlibrarymuseum.gov/museum/exhibits/watergate_files/content.php?section=1&page=a

[26] *Brief Timeline of Events, available at* http://watergate.info/chronology/brief.shtml

[27] Robert W. Meserve, *President's Page*, 59 A.B.A. J. 327 (1973).

ethics. Nothing short of a mandate, an assurance, that every subsequent law graduate would have taken and passed the lawyer ethics course would do to show the profession's serious commitment to ethics.

The difference between offering and requiring a course can be seen in the developments that followed the adoption of section 302. Young, beginning law faculty like Thomas Morgan and Ronald Rotunda were asked by their law schools to teach this new, required course on lawyer ethics. Neither would likely have done so without the request of his school, and the school would not have made the request without the mandate of section 302. They developed the course and their materials,[28] which remain among the most popular texts for the course almost 40 years later. The same story with less well-known faculty occurred across the spectrum of law schools. Faculty energy went into the development of the course and materials, and soon there was an excellent array of texts to rival that of any other typically required law school course. Before the mid-1970s, there had been almost no available texts at all.

Furthermore, ABA consideration of other preexisting lawyer ethics proposals changed in Watergate's wake. To be adopted after Watergate, even preexisting proposals had to meet the standard of aiding the recuperation of an ailing profession in public eyes. For example, in 1975, the ABA held a conference in Chicago to discuss a draft of new rules that would reform and modestly relax its highly restrictive advertising rules. The conferees concluded, however, that profession permission of advertising would only serve to fortify the public's qualms with the profession.[29] The fear of added public displeasure caused the bar to maintain out-of-date advertising regulations that would be stricken as unconstitutional only two years later by the Supreme Court.[30] In doing so, the Court cited societal change and sounded the strong consumerist notes that had emerged in the prior decade.

The preexistence of section 302 as one provision in a package of accreditation changes does not disconnect its amendment and adoption from Watergate. Its adoption would be touted as a way for the profession to enhance public perception of its efforts to instill ethical norms in lawyers.[31]

B. THE MULTISTATE PROFESSIONAL RESPONSIBILITY EXAM

Post-Watergate, the profession moved to show its concern about lawyer ethics by adding a national lawyer ethics exam to the bar admission process.[32] The Multistate

---

[28] MORGAN, ROTUNDA AND DZIENKOWSKI, PROBLEMS IN LEGAL ETHICS (Foundation Press 11th ed. 2011).

[29] JETHRO K. LIEBERMAN, CRISIS AT THE BAR at 91 (W. W. Norton & Company, Inc. 1978).

[30] Bates v. Arizona State Bar, 433 U.S. 350 (1977).

[31] Robert W. Meserve, *President's Page*, 59 A.B.A. J. 327 (1973) (highlighting this change as evidence of the ABA's "desire that there be greater law school emphasis on the teaching of professional responsibility").

[32] Leslie C. Levin, *The MPRE Reconsidered*, 86 KENTUCKY L. J. 395, n. 14 (1997).

Professional Responsibility Exam came into being and flourished in the latter half of the 1970s.

The creation of a national lawyer ethics exam to the bar admission process is credited to the National Conference of Bar Examiners (NCBE). The NCBE came into existence in 1931 as the states were establishing formal bar exams as entry gates to the profession. The establishment of bar exams was one of many entry barriers established as an outgrowth of the profession's reaction to the wave of immigrants in the first quarter of the century.[33]

The NCBE is a nonprofit organization that developed the standardized tests for admission to the bar exam in individual states.[34] Its most significant product, the Multistate Bar Exam (MBE) resulted from a "universal concern among bar examiners regarding the mounting burden of preparing and grading papers in the light of the...increase in law school enrollment during the 1960s."[35] The present, standard-issue bar exam format, a 200-question, multiple-choice, multistate exam (the MBE), combined with a set of essay questions on state law, dates from only the 1970s.[36] The MBE was added to the bar exam in February 1972 as a way to both increase efficiency of grading and to aid in ensuring as much fairness as possible.[37]

NCBE's mission, according to its website is

- to work with other institutions to develop, maintain, and apply reasonable and uniform standards of education and character for eligibility for admission to the practice of law; and
- to assist bar admission authorities by
  — providing standardized examinations of uniform and high quality for the testing of applicants for admission to the practice of law,
  — disseminating relevant information concerning admission standards and practices,
  — conducting educational programs for the members and staffs of such authorities, and
  — providing other services such as character and fitness investigations and research.[38]

Although some have discounted the MPRE success story's connection to Watergate, the profession's consistent efforts in the 1970s to upgrade its public image as ethics sensitive is too much to ignore.[39] Even those who discount the connection

---

[33] *See* chapter 2.
[34] About Us NCBE Mission (2011), http://www.ncbex.org/.
[35] *Id.*
[36] Society of American Law Teachers Statement on the Bar Exam July 2002, 52 J. Legal Educ. 446 (2002).
[37] *About Us NCBE Mission* (2011), http://www.ncbex.org/.
[38] *Id.*
[39] Hayden, *supra* note 16 at 1301.

acknowledge "that several strong historical forces coalesced in the late 1970's to propel the MPRE's initial development . . ."[40]

Watergate was not merely among those strong historical forces: it played a major role in generating them. The MPRE Committee drafters themselves made the Watergate connection, even if they sometimes referred to Watergate cryptically as "[t]he involvement of prominent lawyers in widely publicized political scandals."[41] Other Committee members were more open in attributing credit for the increased attention on ethical testing to Watergate.[42]

C. QUICK MOVE TO A NEW CODE:
THE KUTAK COMMISSION AND THE MODEL RULES

The existing lawyer code at the time of Watergate was the nearly new, unanimously adopted[43] Model Code of Professional Responsibility, said by Lewis Powell, the ABA president who launched the Model Code drafting committee to "truly reflect the essential spirit and ideals of our profession."[44] The ink was barely dry on the new ABA Model Code when CREEP and its so-called plumbers began their political crimes and shenanigans, including the dismantling of Edmund Muskie's campaign by means of forged correspondence.[45] The 1908 ABA Canons of Legal Ethics had lasted for more than 60 years; but in Watergate's wake, the ABA would set the Kutak Commission to work on revamping the 1969 Model Code a mere 7 years after its much-ballyhooed adoption.

The social climate mandating improvements in ethical standards arose in the wake of the Watergate scandal... Because of the problems with the Code and *public perception of the profession*, the ABA formed another commission to reconsider the established standards." (emphasis added)[46]

The transformation of legal ethical standards from internal fraternal norms to public code of law, though met with considerable resistance in the legal community, was a necessary response to the diminishing public faith in lawyers... The result was a new era of intensified internal regulation, and external scrutiny by courts and legislatures.[47]

---

[40] *Id.*

[41] Eugene Scoler, *A Decade in the Development and Drafting of the Multistate Professional Responsibility Exam*, 59 The Bar Examiner 20, 21 (1990).

[42] Joe Covington, 50 The Bar Examiner 12.

[43] Bernard Segal, *President's Page*, 55 A.B.A.J. 893 (1969).

[44] ABA House of Delegates Meets in Dallas, 55 A.B.A.J. 971 (1969).

[45] Bernstein, Carl & Woodward, Bob, *FBI Finds Nixon Aides Sabotaged Democrats*, WASHINGTON POST A01 (Oct. 10, 1972).

[46] Flowers, Roberta K., *What You See Is What You Get: Applying the Appearance of Impropriety Standard to Prosecutors*, 63 MISSOURI LAW REVIEW 699, 710 (1998).

[47] Benison, Audrey I., *The Sophisticated Client: A Proposal for the Reconciliation of Conflicts of Interest Standards for Attorneys and Accountants*, 13 GEORGETOWN JOURNAL OF LEGAL ETHICS 699, 708 (2000).

Despite the claim that the new code would repair Watergate-related problems of the 1969 Code, the ABA chose not to adopt provisions that might actually have done so. Kutak Commission-proposed rules included a confidentiality exception that would allow an attorney to disclose information if the head of an organization insisted on committing illegal activities that were detrimental to the organization.[48] However, the ABA decided to approve a rule that only allowed the attorney to withdraw from representation, which is in essence what the CREEP attorneys did.[49] The ABA also refused to adopt a proposed confidentiality provision that would allow attorneys to disclose a client's fraud in order to rectify the consequences of that fraud. The best the new ABA code did was to allow for a "noisy withdrawal," meaning that an attorney could disclose the fact that he or she was withdrawing, and possibly alert the public about a potential problem. And even this provision was slipped in past an unsuspecting House of Delegates by placing it in the less closely monitored Comments section. The Reporter for the Kutak Commission said shortly after the noisy withdrawal adoption, "some fools may not understand that Rule 1.6 does not mean what it seems to mean."[50] The "fools" were the House of Delegates members who voted to adopt the noisy withdrawal measure without knowing what they had voted for. Major reform was defeated; minor reform was slipped in under dark of night by a wily reporter while the House of Delegates slept.

Many critics were disappointed by the ABA's decisions on new code provisions, and some states did not adopt the proposed amendments. Eighteen years after the ABA's adoption of the Model Rules, a mere four states had approved codes based on the Model Rules.[51] States had only recently made the move to the 1969 Model Code and were slow to abandon it, particularly when the Model Rules made so few substantive changes. A change in style to a more law-like format was not enough to motivate state bars to move quickly to adoption. The public relations gains were made by the ABA's adoption of a substantively barely-different code. The less-visible adoption by the states was of less consequence to repairing the profession's image.

IV. Conclusion

Again, as had been the case in the early part of the century, reforms and changes were adopted that imposed no burden on the lawyers who created the changes. Increased ethics teaching in law schools, an additional hurdle in the bar admission

---

[48] CENTER FOR PROFESSIONAL RESPONSIBILITY, AMERICAN BAR ASSOCIATION, A LEGISLATIVE HISTORY: THE DEVELOPMENT OF THE ABA MODEL RULES OF PROFESSIONAL CONDUCT, 1982–2005 291–292 (Chicago 2006).

[49] *Id.* at 293–294.

[50] Geoffrey C. Hazard, *Rectification of Client Fraud: Death and Revival of a Professional Norm*, 33 EMORY L. J. 271, 306 (1984).

[51] http://www.americanbar.org/groups/professional_responsibility/publications/model_rules_of_professional_conduct/chrono_list_state_adopting_model_rules.html

process, and the modest changes to the substance of the ethics code would have no effect on established lawyers. In essence, change was no change for them.

This time, unlike the immigrant crisis and the communist infiltration, the moves were not made to prevent admission or promote expulsion of an unwanted group. Nor was the Watergate crisis like the civil rights crisis in which a new style of lawyering was resisted by the bar's leadership. Instead, the Watergate crisis was a genuine PR (*public relations* as opposed to *professional responsibility*) disaster. It was brought on by acts of establishment lawyers, including the president himself, a president so recently claimed proudly as a member of the profession that now distanced itself from him and his top aides.

This different-natured crisis called for different responsive measures, ones that had more public relations impact than substantive impact. While measures to remove communists by virtue of loyalty oaths and disbarment for Fifth Amendment taking were aimed at removing their targets; and instituting higher educational standards, invigorated character examinations, and restrictions on advertising were meant to prevent the admission of or cripple the effectiveness of the new immigrant class of plaintiffs' lawyers, no one seriously thought that a law school ethics course or the MPRE would prevent the admission of future Nixons and Deans and Bud Kroghs. Krogh has said his own course on lawyer ethics had no effect on his decisions.[52] Both Dean and Krogh say that the simple fact is that what they did was wrong, and they never stopped to ask that basic question.[53] The post-Watergate moves, while they did create new entry barriers related to ethics, created entry barriers wholly unrelated to the Watergate misconduct. Neither did the new ethics code address issues that would have changed the Watergate conduct.

There was nothing in the Model Code that encouraged the Watergate miscreants' behavior. Their original bar admission was not the result of ineffective gatekeeping at the law school or bar exam levels. The combination of post-Watergate measures, while having some desirable side effects in the form of emphasis on ethics teaching, were public relations measures, pure and simple. They were not intended to and did not solve any professional problems that led to the Watergate conduct.

---

[52] *The Lawyers of Watergate*, June 2012 A.B.A. J. 36, 64 (2012).
[53] *Id.*

6

The Litigation Boom

During the latter half of the 1970s and continuing through the 1980s, a wide range of phenomena were swept under the rubric of the "litigation boom," or, sometimes, "litigation explosion." Either term implied dramatic, powerful forces that were changing the American litigation landscape. Increased court filings (especially in federal court); astronomical jury verdicts; and excessive pretrial, discovery and trial maneuvering were all decried as symptomatic of America's litigation crisis. The air was full of talk about the justice system and lawyer failures. Some of it was about so-called preposterous claims against fast food giants for spilled coffee and obesity. Some of it was about two-year-long trials.

The wide range of phenomena gathered under the litigation boom umbrella was matched by the range of causes to blame for it. Too many lawyers, too many greedy lawyers, too many new "rights laws," judges who failed to use their powers of remitittur, an American culture of blame and expectation of a legal remedy for every wrong, lawyer advertising, an uptick of frivolous claims, and civil discovery abuses—all were said to be to blame for the destructive forces of excessive litigation.

The negative results attributed to this boom were also quite diverse: a breakdown in social responsibility, escalating malpractice and products liability insurance premiums, increases in court costs and lessening of court efficiency, advantage taking by contingent fee lawyers, and professional embarrassment in the public eye. Doctors were being driven from their practices by the cost of insurance and the misery of defending malpractice claims. Drug companies said they would stop making critical vaccination drugs because of lawsuits over side effects. The economy was being dampened by the cost of law.

The profession responded on two fronts. First, the profession proposed changes in law and procedure, especially in the areas of tort reform and civil procedure. Second, the profession identified the crisis as a major public relations problem; so close on the heels of Watergate, the profession could ill afford another public relations calamity.

In terms of bar action, the period began with the 1976 Pound Conference, significant for its birthing of modern alternative dispute resolution (ADR) usage. The middle period saw the work of the Action Commission to Reduce Court Costs and Delay, whose task was to address substantive ills in the civil justice system.[1] In the mid-1980s, Warren Burger's complaints about tort liability and contingent fees inspired the Stanley Commission. The Commission's product, *In the Spirit of Public Service: A Blueprint on the Rekindling of Lawyer Professionalism* (The Stanley Report),[2] challenged lawyers to comply with higher standards than the minimum required by ethics codes. The Stanley Report forms a bridge between the litigation boom and the civility crisis.[3] Finally, the ABA issued its most outward-looking, most forward-thinking report of the century: *The Report of the Task Force on Outreach to the Public*,[4] The Task Force's job was to formulate a plan for reaching beyond the walls of the legal profession to inform the public about the justice system and its challenges; its report represents the best available model for the way in which the legal profession should do its work.[5]

I. Did It Happen?

The increase in court filings, especially federal ones, during the 1970s is undisputed. Whether this increase should be characterized a "boom" or an "explosion," however, remains a matter of hot dispute in the second decade of the new millennium. It is beyond dispute, though, that the terms "boom" and "explosion" were in regular use to describe the litigation status of America throughout the 1970s, 1980s, and 1990s.

Walter Olson captured much of the sentiment from the late 1970s and 1980s in his 1991 book, *The Litigation Explosion*.[6] He focused on law and culture to claim that there was now "an industry devoted to stirring up lawsuits for profit,"[7] and that movement from formalism to legal realism sent a society prone to disputing into the courts to find refuge in the law. Olson was far from alone in his proclamation that the courts were clogged with unnecessary disputes. Law professors, sociology professors, and university presidents announced a new disease in American life: the "craving" or "fever" to sue over anything. They were joined by the popular press and stand-up comedians. *Businessweek, U.S. News and World Report*, and many others reported on the phenomenon that everyone was suing everyone. Brothers sued brothers, students sued teachers, patients sued doctors, and on and on.

---

[1] *See* Leonard F. Janofsky, *A.B.A. Attacks Delay and the High Cost of Litigation*, 65 A.B.A. J. 1323 (1979).

[2] *See* A.B.A. Commission on Professionalism, *In the Spirit of Public Service: A Blueprint for the Rekindling of Lawyer Professionalism* (1986).

[3] *See id; see also* chapter 7.

[4] *Report of the Task Force on Outreach to the Public*, 114 No. 2 ANN. REP. A.B.A. 87 (1989).

[5] *See id.*

[6] *See* WALTER K. OLSON, THE LITIGATION EXPLOSION: WHAT HAPPENED WHEN AMERICA UNLEASHED THE LAWSUIT (1992).

[7] *See id.* at 52.

John Barton, extrapolating from then-current trends, said in 1975 that "implausible as it may appear," the federal appellate courts would decide about one million cases per year by the first part of the 21st century.[8] In fact, the number of federal appellate filings fell to 55,126 in 2011, a 10-year low.[9] Extrapolations can be dangerous and yes, may produce implausible results that never occur. But nonetheless, Barton's bold statements, in no less serious a place than the *Stanford Law Review*, were repeated and repeated by the doomsday predictors of the civil justice system's impending collapse. Barton's article was a special favorite of Warren Burger.[10]

Marc Galanter, the Rand Corporation, and many others were dubious. Galanter and Rand suggested the federal filings increase was mostly due to large increases in very low-effort cases such as Social Security claims and government efforts to collect on defaulted student loans and overpaid veteran's benefits. None of these kinds of cases require much, if any, district judge time. The vast majority are resolved without any activity on the part of a district judge. None reflect a litigation-hungry society or money-grubbing lawyers. Galanter, in particular, sought to debunk the claims about the overloaded justice system:

> A persistent and well-funded campaign depicts American civil justice as a pathological system, presided over by arrogant activist judges and driven by greedy trial lawyers, biased juries, and claimants imbued with victim ideology who bring frivolous lawsuits with devastating effects on the nation's health care system and economic well-being. Although the available evidence overwhelmingly refutes these assertions, this set of beliefs, supported by folklore and powerfully reinforced by media coverage, has become the reigning common sense.[11]

The official data from a given year, 1979, show a dramatic increase in federal court filings, but not of the type to cause alarm:

> The 162,469 civil cases filed in the district courts during the twelve month period ended December 31, 1979, represents the largest influx of cases during any comparable twelve month period. A number of districts showed tremendous increases in civil filings over the same period a year ago....The most substantial increase in filings in the district courts was in U.S. plaintiff cases, which increased 46.7 percent over 1978. This is directly related to the increased activity on the part of the federal government in filing cases for recovery of overpayments and enforcement of judgments. This increased

---

[8] John H. Barton, *Behind the Legal Explosion*, 27 STAN. L. REV. 567, 567 (1975).

[9] Admin. Office of the U.S. Courts, *2011 Annual Rep. of the Dir.: Judicial Bus. of the Fed. Courts* (2012).

[10] *See* Warren E. Burger, *Isn't There a Better Way?*, 68 A.B.A. J. 274, 274 (1982); Speech of Warren E. Burger, 63 A.L.I. PROC. 32, 34–35 (1986).

[11] Marc Galanter, *The Hundred-Year Decline of Trials and the Thirty Years War*, 57 STAN. L. REV. 1255, 1269–1270 (2005) (citing WILLIAM HALTOM & MICHAEL MCCANN, DISTORTING THE LAW: POLITICS, MEDIA, AND THE LITIGATION CRISIS (2004)).

activity, related mostly to delinquent or defaulted student loans, caused the number of such cases to jump from 4,666 in 1978 to 13,223 in 1979, a rise of 183.4 percent.[12]

The huge increase in filings was substantially attributable to filings by the United States to recover debts and overpayments. There were also less significant increases in some other types of filings, giving something for each side of the debate to highlight.

Other case types with significant increases over 1978 were cases related to medical malpractice (up 60.0 percent), negotiable instruments (up 30.8 percent), banks and banking (up 25.7 percent) and the Freedom of Information Act of 1974 (up 24.5 percent).[13]

Statistics on the number of court filings can mislead, but they mislead in both directions. First, a massive increase in low-engagement civil actions occurred, driving the number of filings up, but without a commensurate workload consequence. Prisoner petitions in federal court increased rapidly, but they require far less judicial time than ordinary civil actions. Most are dismissed early, involve little or no discovery, and proceed to trial at a miniscule rate.[14] It is also true, however, that there was an increase in complex cases. Rights cases and class actions increased significantly and require significant measures of discovery and judicial resources. These are not simply contract disputes or basic tort cases.

Individual courts and federal judges took matters into their own hands and succeeded at reforms within their particular fiefdoms. In Cleveland, Federal District Judge Thomas Lambros brought techniques to resolve disputes without significant litigation from his state court judge experience. In state court, his claim to fame was a domestic relations reconciliation program that produced fewer final orders of divorce and reduced the measure of litigation in those that proceeded to final judgment. In federal court, it was a wide range of innovative ADR techniques, including use of mock juries to inform parties and hasten their willingness to settle.[15] In the mid-1960s in the Eastern District of Virginia, Judge Alvin Bryan created the now-famed "rocket docket." The court has consistently been the fastest to judgment in civil matters of all federal district courts and high in the criminal pace rankings. The solution in the EDVA is simple: the schedule for the case's development is managed by a judge from the outset; no continuance is a good continuance. The joke

---

[12] Admin. Office of the U.S. Courts, Statistics Division 5–9 (1979).

[13] *Id.*

[14] *See* Lewis F. Powell, Jr., *Are the Federal Courts Becoming Bureaucracies?*, 68 A.B.A. J. 1370, 1372 (1982) ("To be sure, as is true of Section 1983 suits, most of the Section 2254 cases are not burdensome and can be disposed of on order.").

[15] *See* Carl E. Feather, *Bar Association Honors Retired Judge Tom Lambros,* STAR BEACON (Oct. 10, 2010), http://starbeacon.com/local/x921681626/Bar-Association-honors-retired-Judge-Tom-Lambros.

among lawyers practicing in the court is that the only successful excuse for gaining a continuance is a death in the family. But it has to be the *lawyer's* death.[16]

Whether it happened or not, for present purposes the question is: what did the legal profession do about it? The profession saw it as a public relations problem; the public was upset at lawyers and the profession needed to ameliorate that, especially on the heels of Watergate.

II. If It Happened, or Not, What Were the Causes Seen by the Public?

The causes of the boom were seen everywhere, but three received the main thrust of public blame: lawyers who were too numerous, too greedy and lacked professionalism; too much law that was creating too many new rights; and the development of American culture into a valueless society that needed law to resolve even the most mundane dispute.

A. LAWYERS

Not long before the enormous bulge of new lawyers was admitted in the 1970s, the fear was that there were too few lawyers.[17] That brief flash of fear passed quickly as hordes of students crowded the law school halls in the 1970s.[18] The "too many lawyers" concern and its connection to litigiousness was not new. In 1902, the supply of new lawyers was feared to have outstripped demand: "Year by year the various law schools send increasing armies of new recruits, far beyond the requirements of even this litigious community."[19]

The lawyers being added in the 1970s were special in at least two ways. First, they were far more diverse than their predecessors. By the end of the 1970s, women were a significant presence in law schools and were becoming lawyers at close to the same rate as men. Minorities were also more represented than in the past, but their growth was more modest.[20] Second, in addition to bringing demographic change, the new entries brought a new mindset. Having grown up during the 1960s and 1970s, these 20-somethings bore the marks of the civil rights era. To them, the new, more aggressive kind of lawyering born in the civil rights era was normal. Enforcing

---

[16] *See* Jerry Markon, *A Double Dose of Molasses for the Rocket Docket*, WASH. POST, Oct. 3, 2004 at C04, *available at* http://www.washingtonpost.com/wp-dyn/articles/A3007-2004Oct2.html (recounting two celebrated criminal matters that have slowed even the rocket docket).

[17] *See* 1959 A.B.A. SPECIAL COMM. ON ECON. OF LAW PRACTICE, LAWYERS' ECON. PROBLEMS AND SOME BAR ASS'N SOLUTIONS REP. 2 (1959).

[18] *See* Richard L. Abel, *The Transformation of the American Legal Profession*, 20 LAW & SOC'Y REV. 7 (1986); Barbara A. Curran, *American Lawyers in the 1980s: A Profession in Transition*, 20 LAW & SOC'Y REV. 19 (1986).

[19] 10 THE LAW STUDENT'S HELPER 35 (Feb. 1902) (on file with the author).

[20] *See supra* chapter 4 (elaborating on this demographic change).

new rights statutes came naturally and comfortably. Using the courts, especially federal courts, to remedy wrongs was part of their being.

Until the Reagan cutbacks in legal aid in the early 1980s, more of these new lawyers entered a legal aid practice than ever before. On the criminal side, *Gideon v. Wainwright* created an enormous new market for indigent criminal defense work.[21] Lawyers being paid, even if quite modestly, filed more motions and prosecuted more appeals than did unpaid lawyers or, as was often the case before *Gideon*, no lawyer at all. Legal aid lawyers, even with the heavy caseloads they shouldered, undoubtedly made more work for courts to do in a wide variety of ways. They resisted eviction or foreclosure petitions by lenders and landlords when unrepresented tenants and debtors previously just walked away. They pursued a wide variety of actions under the new rights statutes, such as Truth-in-Lending claims, that would otherwise not have been filed. And most offensively to some, they organized tenants and farmworkers and welfare recipients to pursue their clients' causes. Law school clinics expanded dramatically during this time as well, providing a small army of free and enthusiastic student-lawyers for the poor. Beyond the standard-issue clinic that emulated a legal aid office, clinics of all kinds sprang up: environmental law clinics, domestic violence clinics, and criminal appeals (habeas) clinics, to name a few. These clinics performed significant amounts of public legal service, and with that service came court filings that might otherwise not have existed. Combined, by 1980, there were far more lawyers in absolute terms, and the newly added lawyers differed in their client relationships and inclination to ask courts to solve the problems of their clients, many of whom lacked power on election days. By the end of this period, and in announcing the civility crisis that followed, Warren Burger worried about "political trials" and "the jungle [that was] closing in on us."[22]

William Reece Smith was among the profession's officials worried about the influx of lawyers in numbers never before seen. In his 1981 ABA President's Page, he pondered the litigation boom problems and suggested that the law schools may be producing too many lawyers for the system to absorb.[23] But he was careful to say that if lawyers were spread in places and practices that were underserved, even the then-35,000 new lawyers per year might not be too many. His concern with the rapid increase in the number of lawyers was widely shared. Others simply saw the profession in some transition phase as a result of the rapid growth in lawyer admissions. In particular, because women and, to a lesser extent, minorities were entering the profession for the first time, some simply saw the time as a period seeking balance.[24] If anything, this marked the

---

[21] *See* Gideon v. Wainwright, 372 U.S. 335 (1963).

[22] Warren E. Burger, *Address Before the American Law Institute: The Necessity for Civility* (May 18, 1971), *in* 52 F.R.D. 211 (1971).

[23] *See* William Reece Smith, Jr., *How Many Lawyers Are Enough?* 67 A.B.A. J. 244, 244 (1981).

[24] *See* Richard L. Abel, *The Transformation of the American Legal Profession*, 20 Law & Soc'y Rev. 7 (1986); Barbara A. Curran, *American Lawyers in the 1980s: A Profession in Transition*, 20 Law & Soc'y Rev. 19 (1986).

beginning of a long-overdue change in law profession demographics. The 1986 Stanley Commission Report, celebrating the changing demographics, found itself expressing a moment of myopia and over-self-congratulation. By that time, about 16 percent of lawyers were women, and close to 10 percent of current law students were members of minority groups. The Stanley Report declared demographic victory: "We are now as diverse a profession as one could possibly imagine." The statement revealed much about the imagination of the bar elite.

At least as common as the worry about too many lawyers—and connected to it to be sure—was the worry that lawyers had become greedier and had lost the ability to rein in client excesses. The profession, popular literature, and the public alike wondered how a lawyer could go forward to file a lawsuit on a client's behalf over a bad date or a missed call by a sports official or "mal-parenting." Had lawyers become so hungry for a buck that they would accept a fee to do anything? Had they lost their sense of professionalism?

One indication for many that lawyers had lost their sense of professionalism was the sudden burst of lawyer advertisements. Lawyers were suddenly everywhere, hawking their wares on late night and daytime television, on billboards and public bus sideboards. Everyone had his or her favorite lawyer advertisement to make fun of around the water cooler. Maybe the one in which the lawyer goes into a boxing ring to fight for his clients. Maybe the one with soft background music and a lawyer in diving gear who comes up from the bottom with jewels and pearl necklaces, riches miraculously found for his clients. The lid came off lawyer advertising in 1978. Suddenly, from no ads emerged many. Nothing had (at least yet) changed about the number of lawsuits being filed as a result of advertising by lawyers. But plainly, the illusion of litigiousness was created by the dramatic uptick in advertising after *Bates*. Surely, it appeared, everyone was suing everyone. At least two reactions were possible and common: "why don't I join the parade and make some money?"; and "what is wrong with my society and country?"

B. TOO MUCH LAW

Some suggested the litigation boom was the direct result of changes in law that provided both more rights and less certainty. The former would make claims available that were not so before; the latter would encourage litigation over issues that were previously clear enough that disputing parties would settle and not resort to litigation.

Once a right was created, they suggested, someone would be more likely to feel wronged. Some of the increased filings were also due to new regulatory laws surrounding the environment, occupational health and safety, and Medicare. Congress also toughened drug laws during this same period, and the number of federal drug cases increased significantly during the 1980s.[25] All contributed to the boom. The

---

[25] *See* TERENCE DUNGWORTH AND NICHOLAS M. PACE, STATISTICAL OVERVIEW OF CIVIL LITIGATION IN THE FEDERAL COURTS 7–8 (1990).

fact that lawyers represented clients in these new areas could have come as a surprise to no one, especially the Congress that had created the claims in the first place.

Not only did Congress create many new "rights statutes" during the 1960s and 1970s, it expanded the means by which existing claims could be brought. The chief expansion came in the 1966 amendments to Federal Rule of Civil Procedure 23, the federal class action rule.[26] Two features of these amendments invigorated the use of class actions. First, the rule was explicitly made a vehicle for damage claims. No longer was the rule confined to claims for injunctive or declaratory relief. This change made class actions the go-to vehicle for consumer class actions. Second, the presumption changed from opt-in to opt-out. This change meant that those who were determined to be members of a class would be bound by the results of the case, and their claims would be at issue unless they took an affirmative step to opt out of the class. Combined, these changes fueled a dramatic increase in the use of federal class actions for consumer, securities, and product-injury claims. Cases against banks, lenders, the tobacco industry, asbestos manufacturers, automakers, and innumerable others consumed significant judicial resources.

It was difficult to simultaneously blame too much law *and* too many lawyers. Understood in "too much law" terms, the real dispute was between an overprotective legislative branch and understaffed courts; misbehavior, greed or other traits of the now-too-many lawyers had nothing to do with this dispute.

Justice Powell's concerns reflected this "too much law" attitude. Powell worried about the number of cases in federal court from three sources: federal habeas actions under § 2254, civil rights actions under § 1983, and diversity jurisdiction matters. In 1981, these three combined produced 40 percent of the federal court case filings.[27] All had dramatically increased during the 1970s. Powell emphasized the need to limit these areas, and undoubtedly this "too much law" mood played some role in the receptivity to Ronald Reagan's deregulation themes in the 1980s.

C. CULTURE

Some commentators characterized the time as one in which litigation arose over the "disappointments of everyday life."[28] Many lawsuits were born from attempts to bring areas of life once regulated by informal understandings within the scope of the courts' jurisdiction.[29] As the diversity of the nation and concepts of personal freedom increased, commentators suggested, informal

---

[26] *See* 383 U.S. 1029; 112 Cong. Rec. 4229; Exec. Comm. 2094; H. Doc 391, 89th Cong. (adopting amendments to the Federal Rules of Civil Procedure effective July 1, 1966); FED. R. CIV. P. 23.

[27] *See* Lewis F. Powell, Jr., *Are the Federal Courts Becoming Bureaucracies?*, 68 A.B.A. J. 1370, 1371 (1982)

[28] MARY ANN GLENDON, A NATION UNDER LAWYERS 264 (1996).

[29] *See id.* at 266.

understandings decreased, leading to a surge in litigation as people took to law-suits as their only alternative.[30]

American culture, it was said, lost its way and its values. Religious beliefs no longer held the connective force they once did. Communities were less engaged. This phenomenon helps explain the enormous popularity of the *Book of Virtue* by William Bennett. People yearned for social connectedness and common sets of values and virtues. In the absence of informal means of solving problems through commonly accepted values, the law stood as the next best thing.

Commentators were fond of comparing the U.S. level of litigation per capita with those of other industrialized countries. They came to wildly different conclu-sions about comparisons between the United States and other common law coun-tries, and to some extent the same was true of Western Europe. But as between the United States and Japan, all seemed to agree that there was a stark difference, with the Japanese being far less litigious than Americans. In general, this was explained by the far fewer number of lawyers per capita in Japan, and the more trusting cul-ture.[31] Few paid attention to the nature of the legal profession in Japan in which a very small number of legal professionals are licensed to practice in court (bengoshi) while many more are licensed only to do document preparation, business arrange-ments and the like. In the United States, all these are lawyers. So the raw numbers comparison of U.S. lawyers to Japanese bengoshi was highly misleading. They sug-gested that the Japanese seemed to live in a far more rigid society and engaged in far less litigation than Americans. This was the trade-off, some said, personal rigidity versus an individualistic, independent spirit. The price the United States paid for not being molded into the same size and shape by schools and workplaces might be more lawsuits.

To the extent this change happened in the culture, the federal government unquestionably supported it in the form of the rights statutes. Before 1967, a man over 55 who was terminated in favor of a younger worker had no recognized claim, and he could only brood over his loss of income. After 1967, and with additional protections added in 1975, he could file a claim under the Age Discrimination in Employment Act.[32] A woman harassed by a male work supervisor before 1980 had almost no chance of success in resolving her dispute in either formal or informal processes. But now, with Catherine MacKinnon's work in place in the form of EEOC regulations, she could make a claim, or at least stand taller in an informal challenge within the workplace with law standing nearer to her position.[33] Before lawyer advertising, a woman harmed using a Dalkon Shield may or may not have

---

[30] *See id.*

[31] PATRICK M. GARRY, A NATION OF ADVERSARIES: HOW THE LITIGATION EXPLOSION IS RESHAPING AMERICA 46–48 (1997).

[32] *See* Age Discrimination in Employment Act of 1967, 29 U.S.C. § 621 *et seq.* (2012).

[33] *See* 29 C.F.R. §§ 1625–1627 (2012) (implementing the Age Discrimination in Employment Act).

pursued a remedy. After lawyer advertising, it was more likely that such a claim would be made.

People were empowered to act within legal avenues, and through a variety of devices they acquired knowledge of the law's place in resolving their dispute. They pursued legal remedies more frequently, they had more power when negotiation was pursued, and they consumed judicial resources.

D. AN EXAMPLE

The confluence of causes may be seen in the following nearly true story. Consider the following microcosm of the boom in the person of Darnell C. Turner,[34] a Black Nationalist leader in Cleveland, Ohio. Turner was not a Black Panther, or Malcolm X or Dr. King, so he was hardly a person of fame and notice in America. There were many Darnell C. Turners in a hundred cities across America. But in Cleveland, he was an important figure leading an organization that was actively pursuing local community control of law enforcement and other normally government-provided functions. His community was dissatisfied with city police and sought control. Turner was charged with and convicted of various crimes in the late 1960s and early 1970s and spent considerable time in Ohio penitentiaries. Now it was the later 1970s, the midst of the litigation boom.

In 1967, a new law came into effect: the federal Freedom of Information Act (FOIA).[35] The Act gave citizens the right to ask for information from federal agencies, and gave agencies a defined set of reasons why revelation could be refused. If the citizen-requestor remained unsatisfied, an administrative appeal process was outlined. If still unsatisfied, the Act authorized a claim available in federal court. In its first 7 years of existence, the law had resulted in approximately 200 federal court complaints filed.[36] Ten years later, in 1984, more than 400 cases were filed in that year alone.[37] Congress endeavored to amend the Act to clarify agency obligations in the hope of avoiding such a volume of district court complaints, but to no avail.

Between 1974 and 1976, Senate investigations revealed atrocious violations of civil rights by the FBI in its investigation of and tactics used against citizens in the COINTELPRO program. The Church Committee chronicled outrageous story after outrageous story of criminal violations engaged in by the FBI. The American public learned there was a "Rabble Rouser Index" and a "Key Black Extremist

---

[34] This case is based loosely but accurately on a case I worked on as a clinical law student in 1979. For conflict disclosure purposes, I suppose that makes me part of the litigation boom problem.

[35] *See* Freedom of Information Act, 5 U.S.C. § 552 (1966).

[36] *See* STAFF OF SUBCOMM. ON ADMIN. PRACTICE AND PROCEDURE OF THE S. COMM. ON THE JUDICIARY, 93RD CONG., FREEDOM OF INFORMATION ACT SOURCE BOOK: LEGISLATIVE MATERIALS, CASES, ARTICLES III (Comm. Print 1974).

[37] *See* U.S. Dep't of Justice, *New FOIA Lawsuits Remain at High Level*, 7 FOIA UPDATE 1 (1985), *available at* http://www.justice.gov/oip/foia_updates/Vol_VI_3/page2.htm.

Index," whose "members" were to be "neutralized." The public learned that these indexes included some extraordinarily benign people and organizations, including the Southern Christian Leadership Conference and most black university student groups. The public learned of dirty tricks meant to discredit and ruin prominent black leaders, such as Martin Luther King. Some of the activities sounded much like the Watergate plumbers' dirty tricks on behalf of the Committee to Re-Elect President Nixon. "Tricks" was a somewhat misleading word to describe the activities, sounding like antics such as 12-year-olds' prank telephone calls and minor acts of vandalism. In fact, the acts done by the FBI's agents were far graver. As William C. Sullivan, former assistant to the director, put it,

> This is a rough, tough, dirty business, and dangerous. It was dangerous at times. No holds were barred....We have used [these techniques] against Soviet agents. They have used [them] against us....[The same methods were] brought home against any organization against which we were targeted. We did not differentiate. This is a rough, tough business.[38]

Darnell C. Turner thought back on some strange events that undermined his organization in the same time frame as the acts investigated by the Church Committee. He turned to a lawyer he had once known in Cleveland who was now a clinical professor at a state law school. With the professor-lawyer's help, Turner filed a FOIA request for information about himself and his organization from the FBI. In part, he hoped to learn of information about his investigation by federal authorities that might aid him in his criminal appeals. In part, he hoped to find information that might lend itself to a civil rights claim against state authorities under 42 U.S.C. § 1983 or against federal authorities in a *Bivens* action, a new claim available against federal agents who violate civil rights.[39] In part, he just wanted to know when and why and by whom he had been investigated and targeted.

Turner learned that he was indeed on both the Rabble Rouser and the Key Black Extremist Indexes, and therefore highly likely to be a target of investigation and wrongful tactics. The FBI and other agencies produced tens of thousands of pages in response to his request. But they also notified him of thousands more that they would refuse to reveal under the various statutory provisions. The pages that were released included hundreds of thousands of redactions: words, phrases, and paragraphs that the agencies claimed were exempt from disclosure.

Review of the released documents was illuminating; Turner learned about a wide variety of investigative techniques used against him. He learned that members of his organization were actually FBI plants, but the redactions prevented him from

---

[38] *See* STAFF OF SUBCOMM. ON ADMIN. PRACTICE AND PROCEDURE OF THE S. COMM. ON THE JUDICIARY, 93D CONG., FREEDOM OF INFORMATION ACT SOURCE BOOK: LEGISLATIVE MATERIALS, CASES, ARTICLES 23 (Comm. Print 1974).

[39] *See* Bivens v. Six Unknown Named Agents of Fed. Bureau of Narcotics, 403 U.S. 388 (1971).

learning their identities. He wanted to learn more and pursued the administrative appeals process. Still unsatisfied with the results, Turner filed a FOIA complaint in federal district court. His lawyers were the clinical professor and the professor's eager students.

Turner's and many other FOIA cases were not only increasing in number, they were burdensome and time consuming for judges. As a result of precedent in the DC Circuit,[40] district judges often found themselves in the position of having to review the contested documents and redactions in camera. In Turner's case, that meant tens of thousands of difficult-to-read photocopies of FBI reports and the tedious task of evaluating each and every redaction for its lawfulness. Turner's FOIA case was hardly unusual as FOIA cases go. He was not Bobby Seale or Martin Luther King. There were many hundreds of "Turners" in the Black Nationalist movement across the United States. And that says nothing of the members of the Communist Party, the New Left, and the hordes of ordinary citizens who were also requesting documents from the government. The new cases, whether they were FOIA cases, workplace discrimination cases, or drug-harm litigation, were not ordinary tort and contract claims.

A convergence of multiple factors led to Turner's civil action. These factors combined to make his claim part of the "boom."

1. *First, availability of claims.* Turner's claim did not exist before July 1, 1967, the date on which FOIA became effective. FOIA was one of many new rights statutes adopted in the 1960s and 1970s. The general provisions of the 1964 Civil Rights Act. The employment provisions of Title VII, age discrimination, disability discrimination, voting rights, housing rights, workplace harassment.[41] FOIA was a drop in the bucket, but there were many sources of new drops. Without FOIA, there was no claim for Turner to file.

2. *Second, knowledge.* Turner learned of his possible claim from a government investigation. Watergate spawned the age of the congressional investigation. The Church Committee was one of many that looked into government and business defalcations, drug company failures and frauds, and so on. Media took up the investigative reporter cause. Still flush from the Watergate investigative triumphs, reporters searched and revealed all civil rights abuses, workplace discrimination, judicial corruption, corporate abuses of consumers, and more. People learned from government and media that they had been wronged. On the ordinary tort and class action front, lawyer advertisements played an important knowledge role as well. A person might reasonably conclude, watching the flood of post-*Bates* lawyer advertisements,

---

[40] *See* Vaughn v. Rosen, 484 F.2d 820 (D.C. Cir. 1973), *cert. denied,* 415 U.S. 977 (1974). A Vaughn Index is a document that agencies prepare in FOIA litigation to justify each withholding of information under a FOIA exemption. In *Vaughn,* the court required such an index to determine the validity of the agency's withholdings in the case.

[41] *See* Civil Rights Act of 1964, 42 U.S.C. § 2000 *et seq.* (2012).

that everyone was suing everyone. A wide range of people learned that they, too, might have a legitimate claim. Without knowledge, Turner's claim would never have been filed.

   3.*Third, counsel.* Turner found willing counsel to bring his claim in a law school clinic. There was dramatic growth of law school clinical programs in the late 1960s and throughout the 1970s. Turner could not have found counsel there in an earlier time. Turner's lawyer and his lawyer's eager students were available at no cost to Turner. This period not only saw dramatic expansion of law school clinic counsel availability, but more important, plaintiffs' lawyers were making the public far more aware of their eagerness to serve, and to serve at no cost absent recovery. As long as the claim could produce damages, counsel could be found. The claim might be an ordinary tort claim, a medical or drug malpractice or damage claim, a workplace wrong, and more. Counsel was available to Turner when it would not have been available 10 years earlier.

A claim—with knowledge of it—and counsel to litigate it. Each aspect was necessary to enable Turner to become part of the boom. Turner's story was repeated untold times with slightly different substitutions from the menus of claim availability, knowledge, and counsel access. And at least in Turner's case, some credit for his claim being brought must be given to the outrageously unlawful conduct of the FBI. Without it, there would have been nothing for the Church Committee to publicize, and Turner's interest in learning what happened to him and his organization would have been substantially dampened.

One option to have fewer court filings would be to have fewer laws giving individuals the right to see government documents about them, to dampen knowledge about government and corporate abuses, or to ensure that there are no lawyers willing to represent clients who have claims other than business versus business disputes.

E. PARTICULAR NON-RIGHTS CASES

There was plenty of attention paid to non-rights cases as well. No new statute created ordinary tort claims, although the movement of the mass-tort variety into class action form was triggered by the 1966 amendments to the civil procedure rules. Class actions aside, everyone seemed to have their favorite story of civil justice gone mad, lawsuits over the smallest of slights producing whopping jury awards. Three million dollars for spilled coffee. The actual stories were most often of little interest: just the catch line of the amount awarded for the miniscule harm was enough.

The McDonald's coffee burn case was held up as the prime example of abusive, frivolous lawsuits that were embarrassing the legal profession and the judiciary and were crippling American business. ABC News called it "the poster child of excessive lawsuits."[42] It was the butt of jokes on *Seinfeld* and *Late Night with David Letterman*.[43] It was water cooler talk.

The background story is worth recounting. In the McDonald's coffee case,[44] a 79-year-old woman in a car driven by her son ordered coffee at a McDonald's drive-through window. The son stopped the car so that his mother could open the lid and put in sugar and creamer. In the process of opening the lid to do so, she spilled the coffee on her lap and was scalded by the 185-degree liquid. At the hospital, she was treated for a week with skin grafts to recover from third-degree burns. Her medical bills were $10,500, and she anticipated additional medical needs during her recovery period. She asked McDonald's to settle the matter for $11,000. McDonald's refused. Before filing her lawsuit, now with counsel employed, she offered to settle the matter for $90,000; McDonald's made a counteroffer of $800. Once the lawsuit was filed, a mediator recommended a settlement of $225,000. Again, McDonald's was not willing to settle.

The jury heard evidence that McDonald's employee instructions were to brew the coffee at approximately 200 degrees and maintain it between 180 and 190 until served. Other vendors of coffee kept their coffee at a lower, safer temperature, the evidence showed. Third-degree burns would result much faster from skin contact with 185-degree coffee than with 160-degree coffee. The jury also heard that McDonald's had received at least 700 complaints of significant coffee spill burns, but that it preferred to keep the coffee at the higher temperature for taste and customer satisfaction reasons. One of McDonald's assertions regarding this plaintiff was that as an old person, her skin was more susceptible to burns from hot liquid than the skin of a younger person. Of course, McDonald's sold coffee to old people at the high temperature nonetheless.

The jury awarded $160,000 in actual damages and $2.7 million in punitive damages. One can only infer that these 12 people were outraged at McDonald's' callousness in maintaining the dangerous situation of excessively high coffee temperatures in the face of the many injured customers. The trial judge reduced the $2.7 million to $480,000 (three times the actual damages). And the parties settled for an undisclosed sum (surely less than $600,000) to avoid the appellate process and delay. The case was labeled as the poster child for frivolous lawsuits and was held up to ridicule and scorn of the judicial system and plaintiffs' lawyers, in particular.

---

[42] Lauren Pearle, *I'm Being Sued for What?* ABC News (May 2, 2007), http://abcnews.go.com/TheLaw/Story?id=3121086&page=1.

[43] *See* Boyle v. Christensen, 251 P.3d 810, 812 (Utah 2011) (recounting the enormous and misleading comedy and news treatment of the McDonald's coffee case and holding that the mention of the case in a 2010 closing argument required a new trial).

[44] *See* Liebeck v. McDonald's Restaurants, No. CV-93-02419, 1994 Extra LEXIS 23 (2d Judicial Dist., Bernadillo Cnty., N.M., Aug. 18, 1994).

Even as he was reducing the punitive award from $2.7 million to $480,000, the judge made clear that this was a case about outrageous corporate callousness.

> [T]he written transcript is not going to reveal the attitudes of corporate indifference presented by the demeanor of the witnesses for the Defendant McDonald's as well as their employees, but the jury was exposed to it and I think that they properly considered it in their deliberations. And let me say that with knowing the risk of harm, the evidence and testimony would indicate that McDonald's consciously made no serious effort to warn its consumers by placing just the most simple, adequate warning on the lid of the cup in which the coffee was served....This is all evidence of culpable corporate mental state and I conclude that the award of punitive damages is and was appropriate to punish and deter the Defendant for their wanton conduct and to send a clear message to this Defendant that corrective measures are appropriate.[45]

Neither ABC News, nor David Letterman, nor Warren Burger heard the evidence at trial. The judge and jury who did hear the evidence found that punitive damages were appropriate.

Had McDonald's served coffee at ordinary temperatures and not risked serious injuries to customers to maintain the salability of each pot of coffee well past its normal shelf life, there would have been no $2.7 million punitive damage verdict to outrage Warren Burger and others. The case might just as easily have been spun as an instance of outrageously callous corporate conduct. Or considering the judge's reduction of the award, it might easily have been cast as an example of the success of the American justice system, showing the checks that are available on occasional jury excess. But in the mood of these times, it was a story whose details were rarely recounted and whose import was about a justice system gone haywire.

IV. Warren Burger's War

Warren Burger led the professional charge during the boom years. He encouraged the Pound Conference in 1976 and the Stanley Report in 1986. He spoke on the subject repeatedly, year after year at ABA and ALI (American Law Institute) meetings and elsewhere. He decried a widely divergent set of problems, all under the aegis of the litigation boom; and by the end of the period, he was announcing the onset of the civility crisis. He complained about large tort verdicts, increased contentiousness, the caseload in federal courts, delays in court, and lack of use of ADR. Sometimes he seemed to blame the American people. But always he spoke of these matters as the fault of some unidentified group of lawyers, as if he expected

---

[45] RALPH NADER & WESLEY J. SMITH, NO CONTEST: CORPORATE LAWYERS AND THE PERVERSION OF JUSTICE IN AMERICA 272 (1998) (quoting the *Liebeck* transcript).

there was no need to identify them because the group was well-known enough to his audience. His references to contingent fees abuses and high damage awards may have made the target lawyers clear enough.

He referred to the "litigation explosion during this generation," suggesting that one reason our courts have become overburdened is that Americans are increasingly turning to the courts for relief from a range of personal distresses and anxieties. Remedies for personal wrongs that once were considered the responsibility of institutions other than the courts are now boldly asserted as legal "entitlements." The courts have been expected to fill the void created by the decline of church, family, and neighborhood unity.[46] Chief Justice Burger spoke of the "inherently litigious nature of Americans" and deplored "a notion abroad in our times—especially since the 60's and early 70's which I hope will pass—that traditional litigation—because it has been successful in some public areas—is the cure-all for every problem that besets us or annoys us."[47]

He spoke repeatedly at ALI and ABA meetings of the explosion and what should be done about it. In 1976, he congratulated the ABA on its cosponsorship of the Pound Conference and speaking of the explosion, he suggested that the following measures would assist in solving the problems: (1) legislation to curtail federal diversity jurisdiction; (2) congressional action to add badly-needed additional federal judges; and (3) a requirement by the Congress for an impact statement for each bill introduced, detailing what effect it would have on the work of the courts if it were adopted.[48] By contrast, at the 1986 ALI meeting, he focused mainly on "extraordinary changes that have recently been occurring in the litigation process." He offered a "few examples" of these changes: a jury award of $1 million compensatory and $10 million punitive damages in a personal injury case; another personal injury case in which the jury awarded $125 million, including $110 million in punitive damages; a $39 million punitive damage award; and case in which the jury awarded $1,600 in compensatory and $3.5 million in punitive damages. He gave no account of the facts of any of these examples. Only the amounts of the jury awards were of interest. "[I]t would serve no useful purpose to undertake to try to analyze these cases in full."[49] Like the general public, Burger cared little about the actual facts of the cases.

It was curious to complain about large verdicts as if they were the fault of lawyers. To be sure, a plaintiff's lawyer had asked for the damages to be awarded, and a defense lawyer had asked that there be no damages awarded. But always it was 12 citizens writing the award number on a verdict form. McDonald's coffee and similar cases were all instances of juror outrage at corporate conduct, conduct that was proven to be true to the jury's satisfaction. Some credit for the enormous verdicts and increase in claims must be given to the corporate conduct that produced the verdicts.

---

[46] *See* Warren E. Burger, *Isn't There a Better Way?*, 68 A.B.A. J. 274, 274 (1982).

[47] Warren E. Burger, Remarks at the American Bar Association Minor Disputes Resolution Conference (May 27, 1977), *in State of the Judiciary and Access to Justice Before the Subcomm. on Courts, Civil Liberties, and the Admin. of Justice of the H. Comm. on the Judiciary*, 95th Cong. 287 (1977).

[48] *See* 101 ANN. REP. A.B.A. 603 (1976).

[49] Speech of Warren E. Burger, 63 A.L.I. PROC. 32, 35 (1986).

It was also curious to be concerned with federal caseloads when the lawsuits of which Burger complained were nearly all state court matters. Further, if the concern was with court overloads generally, it was curious to suggest reduction in diversity jurisdiction. Every diversity case not permitted in federal court has another courthouse available.

V. What Change Occurred?

Change took the form of civil procedure reforms of essentially two types: toughened sanctions devices and increased court management of litigation.

In 1983, to combat the perception that more frivolous claims were being filed, Congress amended Federal Rule of Civil Procedure 11 to make judges more likely to impose sanctions on lawyers who file frivolous claims or motions. The goal was to "discourage dilatory or abusive tactics and to streamline the litigation process by lessening the amount of frivolous matters brought before the federal courts."[50] Most states followed with their own versions of the same. The trouble with the new Rule 11 was that it was used. Now, with its encouragement for judges to impose sanctions, more and more lawyers filed motions under the newly amended rule asking judges to sanction opposing counsel.

Called the most controversial civil procedure amendment ever,[51] the 1983 version became a lightning rod, with many claiming that it chilled the civil rights and employment law plaintiff and the plaintiff with a novel claim.[52] The pre-1983 version of Rule 11 was ineffective because it was largely ignored, but the 1983 rule generated a tremendous amount of satellite litigation, defeating its own purpose. Because determinations under Rule 11 are largely fact based, judges found themselves engaged in ancillary litigation over the application of Rule 11 itself.[53] So great was the added burden imposed by the 1983 amendment that by 1993, Congress

---

[50] FED. R. CIV. P. 11 advisory committee's note (1983).

[51] Carl Tobias, *Reconsidering Rule 11*, 46 U. MIAMI L. REV. 855, 856–857 (1992).

[52] *See* Stephen B. Burbank, *The Transformation of American Civil Procedure: The Example of Rule 11*, 137 U. PA. L. REV. 1925, 1925 (1989); Carl Tobias, *Rule 11 and Civil Rights Litigation*, 37 BUFF. L. REV. 485, 485 (1988–89); Georgene M. Vairo, *Rule 11: A Critical Analysis*, 118 F.R.D. 189, 197 (1988).

[53] *See* Georgene M. Vairo, *Rule 11: A Critical Analysis*, 118 F.R.D. 189, 197 (1988). In 1991, Professor Vairo reported that over 3,000 cases dealing with Rule 11 had been reported, which one can assume are just a fraction of the number of cases in which sanctions were imposed (or refused) under the rule. *See* Georgene M. Vairo, *Rule 11: Where We Are and Where We Are Going*, 60 FORDHAM L. REV. 475, 480 (1991); *see also* Lawrence C. Marshall et al., *The Use and Impact of Rule 11*, 86 NW. U. L. REV. 943, 952 (1992) (finding that in the 12 months before a survey conducted by the authors, 24.3 percent of attorneys surveyed reported involvement in a case in which formal Rule 11 motions were made but no sanctions imposed; 7.6 percent were involved in cases in which Rule 11 sanctions were imposed; 24.5 percent of attorneys surveyed had experience with in-court reference to Rule 11, with no formal motion or request for sanctions; and 30.3 percent had experienced references to Rule 11 out of court).

amended the rule once again, this time to encourage private settlement of Rule 11 disputes by adding a "safe-harbor" provision. Under the 1993 version, a party seeking Rule 11 sanctions must first give notice to the alleged Rule 11 transgressor, allowing 21 days to correct statements or allegations in a pleading to conform to Rule 11 before a court would get involved.

Pursuing the themes of the litigation boom worriers, Congress adopted the Civil Justice Reform Act of 1990[54] and the Judicial Improvements and Access to Justice Act of 1988.[55] The former introduced greater judicial control over pretrial procedures including discovery and tracking into ADR and the latter raised the diversity of citizenship amount in controversy requirement from 10 to 50 thousand dollars.

Cutbacks in class actions came in waves.[56] In the early 1990s, federal courts adopted stricter standards for certifying classes, substantially reducing the federal court availability for class actions. The result was a move of class action litigation into state courts. Some particular counties became known as plaintiff friendly in their class certification and damage award tendencies. Not to be outdone by the courts, Congress first trimmed federal class actions in 1995 legislation, making it more difficult for securities claims to be brought as class actions. Then, in 2005, the enactment of the Class Action Fairness Act (CAFA)[57] was meant to funnel more class actions back into the federal courts by loosening the diversity of citizenship requirements. This move allows many defendants to remove state class actions to federal court. Once in federal court, the stricter class-certification requirements of the 1990s apply and result in far fewer viable class actions going forward. The jury is still out on whether the strategy has worked. There was the predicted initial uptick of state class action removals to federal court in 2006, but removals have since fallen back to pre-CAFA levels. Nonetheless, as of 2008, there was an increase in class action activity in federal courts of 72 percent, as would be predicted by the CAFA supporters. But the increase is not attributable to removals from state court. Instead, the increase had more to do with class actions filed initially in federal court in labor and consumer protection act cases, both presenting federal questions.[58] Whether CAFA will in the end reduce the number of successfully certified class actions remains to be seen.

---

[54] *See* Civil Justice Reform Act of 1990.

[55] *See* Judicial Improvements and Access to Justice Act of 1988, Pub. L. No. 100-702, 102 Stat. 4642 (codified as amended in scattered sections of 28 U.S.C.).

[56] In 1975, 3,061 class actions were begun in federal courts. By 1980, the number plunged to 1,568. Experts attribute this to limitations on the use of class actions; "judges are more stringent about certifying plaintiffs as a class, and use of the courts as a vehicle of social change has subsided." Douglas Martin, *The Rise and Fall of the Class-Action Lawsuit*, N.Y. TIMES, Jan 8, 1988.

[57] *See* Class Action Fairness Act of 2005, Pub. L. No. 109-2, 119 Stat. 4-14 (codified as amended in scattered sections of 28 U.S.C.).

[58] *See* Emery G. Lee III & Thomas E, Willging, *The Impact of the Class Action Fairness Act of 2005 on the Federal Courts, Fourth Interim Report to the Judicial Conference Advisory Committee on Civil Rules* 1–3 (Apr. 2008).

VII. What Did the Profession Do?

The profession's response can be seen as bracketed by the Pound Conference in 1976 and the Stanley Report in 1986, with the Action Commission activities in between. It closed the period with the Task Force on Outreach to the Public in 1988–89.

The Pound Conference in 1976 was held to commemorate the 70th anniversary of Roscoe Pound's paper "The Causes of Popular Dissatisfaction with the Administration of Justice." The emulation was down to the last detail as the talks were presented in the very room where Pound had delivered his talk in 1906. The theme of the conference served as a reminder that the problems facing the profession were not new ones.

The central and most lasting event of the conference proved to be the delivery of a paper by Harvard professor and ADR advocate Frank Sander. "Varieties of Dispute Resolution" jump started a move to teach and use mediation, arbitration, and a variety of other dispute resolution processes. Of course, lawyers had always negotiated, and arbitration had made some progress before the boom. But the massive increase in the use of arbitration and mediation, especially as annexed to court proceedings, can be traced to the Pound Conference. Unlike the paucity of such offerings in 1975, in 2012, every law school offers courses in negotiation, mediation, and arbitration. Some include it in aspects of their mandatory skills curriculum, and thus every student receives some instruction in the ADR arts. The ABA did not then and has never added such a requirement to the accreditation standards. Nonetheless, the course books in these areas have multiplied, and it is the rare student who has not at least had exposure to negotiation instruction in law school.

The Action Commission was formed to "reduce court costs and delay." It was announced by 1979–80 ABA President Leonard Janofsky in an *ABA Journal* article, "ABA Attacks Delay and High Costs of Litigation."[59] In his charge to the Commission, he urged a move from study to action. He did so with some level of exaggeration, at least according to a Rand study. Janofsky suggested that "civil cases...are often not reached for three or more years." There were such lengthy cases, to be sure, but their proportion in the federal system stayed a near constant 7 or 8 percent from 1971–86. The incidence of lengthy litigation had not "boomed." The vast majority of matters were resolved in under one year, and the median time to resolution for that same period was about nine months.[60]

Janofsky made clear that there was both a substantive set of problems to be solved and a public relations problem to be addressed. "The infamous twin evils—cost and delay—contribute substantially to a climate of cynicism and mistrust of the legal profession, the judiciary and the legal system."[61]

---

[59] *See* Leonard F. Janofsky, *A.B.A. Attacks Delay and the High Cost of Litigation*, 65 A.B.A. J 1323 (1979).

[60] *See* TERENCE DUNGWORTH AND NICHOLAS M. PACE, STATISTICAL OVERVIEW OF CIVIL LITIGATION IN THE FEDERAL COURTS 21–22 (1990).

[61] Janofsky, *supra* note 59.

In its work, the Action Commission experimented in various discrete locations on three fronts. First, in Kentucky, it instituted a system with both simplified procedures and intense court control. The level of court control was similar to that of the "rocket docket" Eastern District of Virginia. In the Kentucky location, the combination of procedural simplification and court control reduced average time from filing to termination from 16 to 5months. In a state court of appeal in California, the experiment was at the appellate level. Time for and length of briefs was substantially shortened while time for oral argument was expanded. This experiment also shaved time off the litigation process, reducing time for appeals from 14 to 8 months. Third, the Commission experimented with technology: the telephone. It used increased teleconferencing for motions in a few New Jersey and Colorado trial courts. In each instance, the telephone reduced costs for litigants considerably.

The Stanley Commission's charge was to focus on the professionalism failings of lawyers, also a contributing factor in the litigation boom. The Commission focused on the "practices of some lawyers" that "cry out for correction."[62] Who these lawyers were was never explicit, but the Report's references to contingent fees, advertising, and discovery abuse afford valuable clues.

Reenforcing the identity of "some lawyers," the Report bemoans the "legal status of lawyers as businesspeople." Blame was laid at the feet of the Supreme Court for the de-professionalizing influence of *Bates, Button, Trainmen,* and *Goldfarb.* Lawyers can now advertise, organize for representation of labor or a group of civil rights plaintiffs, and can no longer fix minimum prices. All of these cases, the Report views, robbed the profession of its claim to professional status and distinction from business.

Substantively, the Report encouraged ADR, continuing legal education, pro bono, reporting of false advertising, policing of fees, and "adherence to higher standards than the minimum enforceable ones." Although the Commission had been inspired by Warren Burger's speeches, there was only modest attention paid to the substantive topic of tort reform as such.

The "higher standards" pitch is a curious charge and one often repeated at bar association luncheons. In some respects, it may be sensible to suggest, for example, higher-than-required levels of care in safeguarding client property or more-restrained-than-required advertising themes and claims. But more often, the ethics rules represent a balance between or among competing responsibilities. The confidentiality rules and their exceptions are such an instance, among many. A lawyer advances a client's interests to maintain confidences. But other interests compete. The justice system wants to know when a witness or client perjures himself; the public wants to know when a client is committing a serious fraud; a targeted individual wants to know when the client is about to inflict serious bodily harm. The exceptions allowing revelation of confidences define a balance point where the value

---

[62] A.B.A. Commission on Professionalism, *In the Spirit of Public Service: A Blueprint for the Rekindling of Lawyer Professionalism* 10 (1986).

pointing toward revelation wins. Suggesting that lawyers follow "higher" standards really means they should follow different standards, ones that favor the particular after-dinner speaker's or report writer's preferences among the competing duties.

The "perception of others" was a recurrent theme of the Report:

> [L]awyers as a group are blamed for some serious public problems. Many individuals blame lawyers for the huge increase in medical malpractice litigation, with a concomitant sharp increase in the costs of insurance protection, for example. Many blame lawyers when public playgrounds and sports programs are threatened with a loss of liability insurance and may be forced to discontinue use of facilities for recreational activities.[63]

At all points in its action, the ABA treated the litigation boom in part as a public relations problem: the public fails to understand how the court process works, why it takes time, and why it is expensive. Each report written, each President's Page, spoke of the disconnect between reality and public perception as well as the serious damage to the profession and the justice system that results from public misperception.

Finally, the ABA issued its most outward-looking, most forward-thinking report of the century: The Report of the Task Force on Outreach to the Public,[64] whose job it was to formulate a plan for reaching beyond the walls of the legal profession to inform the public about the justice system and its challenges. This report represents the best available model for the way in which the legal profession should do its work.

Some saw the Task Force as a mere public relations body whose job would be to fashion advertising slogans favoring the profession. This task was little more dignified than the advertising that was claimed to bring the profession into disrepute and shame.

But in fact, the Task Force did what the profession should always do. First, it engaged the talents of non-lawyers in more than a for-show role. A significant part of its report was written by David L. Protess, a non-lawyer Consultant to the Task Force and Associate Professor and Co-director of the Urban Journalism Center, Northwestern University's Medill School of Journalism. Second, it proposed serious efforts to engage those outside the profession, not merely for the purpose of educating the public about the justice system, but also for the genuine cross-learning and cooperation that could be developed. The report speaks of lawyers engaged with community groups to solve problems relating to community affairs and the litigation that could be avoided by such cooperative solutions. "The legal profession alone cannot solve its own problems, the problems of the justice system or those

---

[63] *Id.* at 2.
[64] *See Report of the Task Force on Outreach to the Public*, 114 No. 2 ANN. REP. A.B.A. 87 (1989).

of the communities it serves."[65] Read that again. Truer and rarer words were never spoken by the profession.

The Task Force recognized the significant benefits of reaching out past the professional usual suspects for problem solving in a way that has been otherwise totally foreign to the legal profession:

> Greater public participation in the effort to improve the system will not only yield continued improvement but also should result in more accurate perceptions and more realistic expectations. . . .The joint effort is vital because other groups within society can bring ideas and resources to the solution of these problems which are simply unavailable to the legal profession operating in isolation.[66]

The follow-through was less than the promise of outward thinking promised by the Task Force's plan. Although the Board of Governors adopted most of the Task Force's recommendations,[67] the focus changed from forming genuine partnerships with non-lawyers and co-problem solving to very modest public and lawyer education efforts.

In 1990, a National Conference on Outreach to the Public followed the adoption of the recommendations. Held at the ABA midyear meeting in Los Angeles, some 400 "bar leaders" attended and set two goals for the outreach effort: first, to exchange ideas about how to show the public the good that is done by lawyers; and second, to help lawyers understand the profession's problems and improve their client relation skills.[68] There was no mention of partnering with non-lawyers to solve problems in the legal profession.

A Commission of Partnership Programs was formed. It produced a summary report regarding the National Outreach Conference. Its mission was "to serve as a catalyst and resource for an ongoing, comprehensive national effort addressing public and attorney perception of the legal profession and the justice system." Where the Task Force had seen partnerships for co-solving of problems in the legal profession, the resulting Commission on Partnerships saw an "effort to address . . . perceptions." Three programmatic efforts were emphasized by the Commission on Partnerships: (1) "the National Model Partnership Program 'Meet Your Judges,' (2) the bar response to the drug crisis, and (3) exploration and development of initiatives aimed at improving lawyer's client relations skills."[69] Nowhere to be found was the public role in solving problems of the legal profession that had been envisioned by the Task Force.

---

[65] *See id.* at 88.
[66] *Id.* at 90.
[67] *See* 114 ANN. REP. A.B.A. 79, 943 (1989).
[68] *See* 115 ANN. REP. A.B.A. 934–935 (1990).
[69] *See* 116 ANN. REP. A.B.A. 877 (1991).

The Task Force was dissolved and replaced by standing committees who managed and implemented the results of the Los Angeles conference,[70] results that bore little resemblance to the recommendations of the Task Force. The promising moment and opportunity for genuine work with non-lawyers to solve the legal profession's problems passed quietly with empty results.

So did the ABA actually sponsor a public awareness program, or did it simply educate fellow lawyers about the public image problem? Mainly it did the latter, with precious few new initiatives for public awareness approved as a result of the Task Force on Outreach Recommendations. This is the ultimate in inward-looking thinking: the profession recognized that a problem is a public awareness and misunderstanding problem but did not bother to tell the public.

VIII. Conclusion

The debate over whether the litigation boom occurred or was conjured from large but insignificant increases in court filings continues. But in either event, the legal profession's litigation boom crisis was largely of the public relations nature. The public declared war on the legal profession for a wide range of public woes from increasing insurance rates to closed public playgrounds to high cost of the justice system sapping otherwise productive corporations of their ability to grow. The profession responded with conferences and committees that addressed both the substantive issues of the justice system and perception problems. For once, but briefly, the profession acknowledged that it cannot solve its problems alone. But just as quickly, that moment of insight passed, and the profession engaged the effort to reenforce the status quo image of an honorable and distant profession, fully committed to the "spirit of public service."

---

[70] *See* 115 ANN.REP. A.B.A. 1590 (1990).

{ 7 }

The Loss of Civility

Unquestionably, "popular respect for the legal profession is steadily falling"; there is "much cause for discouragement and some cause for alarm."[1] "Lawyers...are blamed for some serious public problems," including the enormous costs of increased litigation.[2] "Year by year the various law schools send increasing armies of new recruits, far beyond the requirements of even this litigious community."[3] Lawyers act with "exaggerated contentiousness,"[4] as if they were "gladiators" in a war, making every effort to "wipe out the other side."[5] Among the causes of this crisis is the attitude that the law is no longer a profession, but a mere competitive business in which its members face increased "economic pressures."[6] Better legal education may not even help because "the evil...is not so much a professional as an American fault. It has its source in our inordinate love for the almighty dollar."[7]

Without the footnotes, it takes some care to distinguish the previous paragraph's early 20th-century quotations from its end-of-the 20th-century quotations.[8] "[D]issatisfaction with the administration of justice is as old as the law," raising cries of professional decline with some regularity.[9] Once again in the 1980s, as it had before, the profession expressed its worry that it had become too business-like. Individual lawyers and law firms understood that they were in the business of providing legal services to paying clients. The profession persisted in denying that any such thing was true. The professional party line was that this is a profession in pursuit of the public good.

---

[1] Morris Gisnet, A Lawyer Tells the Truth 11–12 (1931).

[2] ABA Comm'n on Professionalism, *"...In the Spirit of Public Service": A Blueprint for the Rekindling of Lawyer Professionalism*, 112 F.R.D. 243, 253 (1986) [hereinafter *Blueprint*].

[3] 10 The Law Student's Helper 35 (Sprague 1902) (on file with the author).

[4] Roscoe Pound, *The Causes of Popular Dissatisfaction with the Administration of Justice*, reprinted in 29 Ann. Rep. A.B.A. 395, 406 (1906).

[5] Robert L. Haig & Robert S. Getman, *Does "Hardball" Litigation Produce the Best Result for Your Client?*, N.Y. St. B.J., Jan. 1993, at 24, 26 (quoting a local bar president).

[6] *Blueprint*, *supra* note 2, at 261

[7] *Proceedings of the Association of American Law Schools* 11 (1906) [hereinafter *1906 AALS Proceedings*].

[8] Facts are always perceived within the context of their times; today's perceived problems are not always tomorrow's. For example, in 1959, an ABA Special Committee on the Economics of Law Practice concluded that the major problem facing the profession was that too few people were entering the law schools.

[9] Pound, *supra* note 4, at 395.

In the mid-1980s and into the 1990s (some would say still to present date), the legal profession experienced what came to be called a "civility crisis." Others referred to the same phenomenon as a professionalism crisis. Lawyers simply were not as nice to one another as they had once been. Competitive zeal had taken hold and driven some members of the profession to be foul, mean-spirited, unduly competitive, and overly client-interest driven. In this crisis, the American legal profession sought an unprecedented result: not only to maintain a status quo, but rather to restore an era lost 100 years before. So thoroughly was the profession caught up in nostalgia, it created an image of a former, much-sought time that never actually existed.

The theme of the crisis—a loss of civility for some, a more general loss of professionalism for others—became a catch-all for a wide range of professional woes. Many of the acts complained of were already prohibited by the existing ethics code. Some were more breaches of etiquette than violations of codes. A wide range of slights to colleagues, courts, opponents, and clients folded into the professional malaise of the day. The affronts covered a wide range from physical violence to failure to consult with opposing counsel before filing a motion.

Encouragement for lawyers to recapture a lost brotherhood (yes, "brotherhood") of civility came in multiple forms, supported by both moral and pragmatic reasons. Some urged lawyers to believe that civility was more effective lawyering, advancing the interests of the lawyer's client. Others urged a "rekindled" spirit of professionalism from older times, defining the "good" lawyer as one who possessed the civility trait. These commentators said that client favoring or not, uncivil conduct toward professional colleagues should never be part of the lawyer's role. One plain theme of the manners critique was the targeting of civil rights and other "cause lawyers," who turned their attention to affecting social causes with unacceptable zeal rather than merely resolving private disputes, as good lawyers should. In this way, the civility crisis was an extension of the professional response to both the civil rights era and the litigation boom. Another suggested sign of the lack of civility was the move by lawyers into common business practices such as advertising. Even the use of advanced business technologies, such as IBM Selectric typewriters and other efficient document generation equipment, were seen as a sign that lawyers were breaking with their professional past.

I. A Civility Dream Team

An all-star cast—a civility dream team—chimed in to condemn the loss of professional demeanor.[10]

---

[10] Robert L. Nelson & David M. Trubek, *Arenas of Professionalism: The Professional Ideologies of Lawyers in Context*, in LAWYERS' IDEALS/LAWYERS' PRACTICES: TRANSFORMATIONS IN THE AMERICAN LEGAL PROFESSION 177, 178 (Robert L. Nelson et al. eds., 1992) ("The spokespersons in the professionalism campaign are not marginal: they are a wealthy and accomplished group of lawyers. Many belong to firms that have grown and prospered in recent years.").

A. WARREN E. BURGER[11]

As far back as 1971, Warren Burger decried the "new litigation" and, in his view, the incivility it begat. He warned that this new kind of aggressive lawyering must be avoided "if we are to keep the jungle from closing in on us."[12] When he warned of the jungle that was closing in, Burger was bemoaning cause lawyering, which he considered unacceptably aggressive.

> The professional standards and traditions of the bar in the past served to restrain members of the profession from practices and customs common and acceptable in the rough-and-tumble of the marketplace. Historically, honorable lawyers complied with traditions of the bar and refrained from doing all that the laws or the Constitution allowed them to do.[13]

> 'Bar association bashing' would be a more accurate description of what I have engaged in, because I have previously and will again tonight explain how the organized Bar's failure to set and maintain high ethical standards for the legal profession has caused much of the decline in professionalism among lawyers and the corresponding decline in the public esteem of lawyers.[14]

> It is not merely the right but the duty of members of the Bar to challenge the failure of the leadership of the organized bar to set high standards and the failure of the local bar associations to enforce the same high standards. You, as Students of the Law, have an especially heavy burden in this regard. This is a heavy legacy that we pass on to you. We hope that you will live up to it.[15]

B. CLARENCE THOMAS[16]

Thomas, unlike most others, recognized the connection between lawyer behavior and the broader society.

> There have been studies done (and task forces formed) to discover what is to be done to forestall this slide into a legal 'state of nature.' These efforts have not been successful, I believe, because—while I think that there are surely some special reasons to explain why common decency is disappearing from law practice—the decline in good manners in law practice is only one manifestation of the general erosion of common standards to decency throughout society.

---

[11] Warren E. Burger, *The State of Justice*, 70 A.B.A. J. 62 (Apr. 1984); Warren E. Burger, *The Decline of Professionalism*, 63 FORDHAM L. REV. 949 (1995).

[12] Warren E. Burger, The Necessity for Civility, Address to the American Law Institute (May 18, 1971), *in* 52 F.R.D. 211, 212 (1971).

[13] Burger, *The State of Justice, supra* note 11 at 63.

[14] Burger, *The Decline of Professionalism, supra* note 11, at 950.

[15] *Id.* at 958.

[16] Clarence Thomas, *Civility*, 39 S. TEX. L. REV. 655 (1998).

Unlike others, I would not be so quick to attach this change to an increase in the financial pressures that have occurred in the legal profession. To be sure, one cannot deny that the demand for ever higher billable hours by larger and larger firms may force some to ignore the common standards of professional decency, that must guide our conduct toward one another as lawyers, judges, professors, or students. But at its core, I believe that the decline in civility among lawyers is due to a broader, more intellectual change in our vision of the law's role in our society.

Thomas went on, specifically blaming the incivility on the social changes of the 1960s and 1970s.

The law was no longer a process to settle private controversies; it was no longer simply our democracy's way of funneling certain conflicts and disputes into a neutral forum for adjudication. As I have described elsewhere, the generation of the 1960s envisioned the law and the legal system as a tool to achieve social change, not as a process for state-sponsored dispute resolution.... If that is the case, then deliberation and consensus-building become unnecessary. If you believe that you know the right answer, and that is the *only* right answer possible, then you will have little interest in participating in the deliberation and compromise made possible by civility.[17]

C. WILLIAM H. REHNQUIST[18]

Rehnquist sounded a somewhat more realistic note, acknowledging that nostalgia played a role in cries of incivility.

There is nothing intrinsically good or bad about change, and generalized complaints that the profession is 'losing its professionalism' may represent only a nostalgic yearning for the 'good old days' that people in my age range always seem to have. But it does not appear that the organization of the profession is moving in a particular direction, and that academic institutions concerned with the profession—that is, law schools—should pay attention to and examine what is happening.... It is only natural, I suppose, that as the practice of law in large law firms has become organized on more and more of a business basis, geared to the maximization of income, this practice should on occasion push towards the margins of ethical propriety.[19]

---

[17] *Id.* at 656, 658–659 (emphasis added).

[18] William H. Rehnquist, *Dedicatory Address: The Legal Profession Today*, 62 IND. L.J. 151 (1987).

[19] *Id.* at 152, 154.

D. RUTH BADER GINSBURG[20]

Commenting on the worries about loss of civility among judges, Ginsburg commented:

I question...resort to expressions in separate opinions that generate more heat than light...Yet one has only to thumb through the pages of current volumes of United States Reports and Federal Reporter Second to come upon condemnations by the score of a court or colleague's opinion as, for example, 'folly,' 'ludicrous,' 'outrageous,' one that 'cannot be taken seriously,' 'inexplicable,' 'the quintessence of inequity,' a 'blow against the people,' 'naked analytical bootstrapping,' 'reminiscent of Sherman's march through Georgia,' and 'Orwellian'.... The most effective dissent, I am convinced, 'stands on its own legal footing'; it spells out differences without jeopardizing collegiality or public respect for and confidence in the judiciary.[21]

E. SANDRA DAY O'CONNOR[22]

As she bemoaned the rise of the business-oriented practice of law, O'Connor and others blended moral reasons with a more pragmatic one: courteous lawyers are more effective for their clients.

It has been said that a nation and its laws are an expression of the highest ideals of its people. Unfortunately, the conduct of our nation's lawyers has sometimes been an expression of the lowest. Clients increasingly view lawyers as mere vendors of services, and law firms perceive themselves as businesses in a competitive marketplace....When the lawyers themselves generate conflict, rather than focusing on the dispute between the parties they represent, it distorts our adversarial system. More civility and greater professionalism can only enhance the pleasure lawyers find in practice, increase the effectiveness of our system of justice, and improve the public's perception of lawyers.... The common objection to civility is that it will somehow diminish zealous advocacy for the client. I see it differently. In my view, incivility disserves the client because it wastes time and energy—time that is billed to the client at hundreds of dollars an hour, and energy that is better spent working on the case than working over the opponent.... Codes of ethics and professional conduct are good starting points and no doubt necessary. But they focus on what a lawyer should not do rather than teaching lawyers what they affirmatively ought to do.[23]

---

[20] Ruth Bader Ginsburg, *Speaking in a Judicial Voice*, 67 N.Y.U. L. Rev. 1185 (1992).
[21] *Id.* at 1194–1196.
[22] Sandra Day O'Connor, *Professionalism*, 76 Wash. U. L. Q. 5 (1998).
[23] *Id.* at 6–10 (emphasis removed).

F. JOHN PAUL STEVENS[24]

Virtually everything you do in your professional capacity becomes an indelible part of your reputation. An advocate who does not command the confidence of the judge bears a much heavier burden of persuasion than one who never misstates either the facts or the law. Moreover, litigation is far more difficult and time-consuming when opposing counsel do not trust one another.... Second, let me remind you of the importance of civility. A polite rejection of a settlement proposal can be just as firm as a show of indignation, and a succinct objection as telling as an unnecessary harangue.... I can assure you that most judges regard the incivility of counsel as a confession that they would rather not discuss the relevant facts or the controlling law. Courtesy is an essential element of effective advocacy.[25]

G. ANTHONY M. KENNEDY[26]

Like Burger and Thomas, there were others who likened the loss of civility in the legal profession to a loss of some of the basic aspects of humanity.

Civility is not some casual idea, some little word to which we make a brief bow. It is not a one-hour continuing legal education course we take before rushing off to fractious debate. It is not a bumper sticker slogan: 'Have You Hugged Your Adversary Today?' Civility is the mark of an accomplished and superb professional, but it is more even than this. Civility is an end in itself.

Civility stands for the proposition that we owe respect to our fellow citizen because of the humanity we share in common. Civility underscores the idea of individual worth and dignity, the idea which is the first premise of democratic theory. Civility has deep roots in the idea of respect for the individual. We are civil to each other because we respect one another's aspirations and equal standing in a democratic society. We must restore civility to every part of our legal system and public discourse. Civility must always characterize the deliberations of this profession.

Civility defines our common cause in advancing the rule of law. Our honest and decent citizens must be persuaded to devote themselves to public life, but they will be reluctant to do so if our discourse is not marked by civility. If our own best people do not admire our discourse, neither will the people of other nations, the people who seek those principles that are the basis for common beliefs, principles vindicating the rule of law in their own societies.[27]

---

[24] John Paul Stevens, Opening Assembly Address, American Bar Association Annual Meeting (Aug. 3, 1996) *in* 12 St. John's J.L. Comm. 21 (1996).

[25] *Id.* at 29–30.

[26] Anthony M. Kennedy, *Law and Belief*, *in* Trial 23 (July 1998).

[27] *Id.* at 25–26.

Collectively, in their praise of civility and their worry about its loss, the Justices sounded themes that were common in the literature of the time. Thomas, O'Connor, and Burger all tied the civility crisis in the profession to the general loss of professionalism and rise of a business orientation. Curiously, the ABA blamed the same phenomenon on the Court, resulting, the bar said, from its decisions in *Bates, Button, Trainmen, and Goldfarb*.[28] Some did tie the loss of civility to broader social ills. Burger and Thomas connected the loss of civility to the more aggressive lawyering style of civil rights lawyers and the general rise in "rights statutes." O'Connor sounded a note that would become a popular one among lower courts and bar associations: incivility harms the uncivil lawyer's client interests. Lawyers, especially aggressive ones, never bought this connection.

II. And the Lower Courts Followed

Cries of civility "foul" were not confined to Supreme Court Justices. In published opinion after published opinion, courts at every level conveyed their dissatisfaction with the state of professionalism exhibited in their courtrooms. In doing so, judges expressed their view that the "client-favoring" reason offered by lawyers for contentious behavior was unacceptable, some going as far as to articulate that the duty of civility to court and colleagues surpassed the duty to clients. Harsh disapproval of lawyers was the order of the decade. A few of many examples follow.

> *In re* First City Bancorporation of Tex., Inc: 'His attitude and remarks toward opposing attorneys, opposing parties, and the bankruptcy court were—to understate his conduct—obnoxious. Although incivility in and of itself is call for concern, what is most disconcerting here is the rationale [the lawyer] gives for his behavior. [He] asserts that his deplorable and wholly unprofessional conduct helps him recover more money for his clients. Unremorsefully and brazenly, [he] contends that his egregious behavior serves him well in settlement negotiations and is therefore appropriate.'[29]

> Dahl v. City of Huntington Beach: 'This case illuminates the growing incivility among contending lawyers which mars our justice system and harms clients and the public interest.'[30]

> Pesaplastic, C. A. v. Cincinnati Milacron Co.: '[T]he attorneys of the Law Firm have conducted themselves in a manner not befitting officers of the court.... [T]hey represent yet another case of attorneys having "sold out to the client." In so doing, the attorneys of the Law Firm lost sight of the fact that, as members of the bar, and officers of the court, our primary responsibility is

---

[28] *Blueprint*, supra note 2 at 10.

[29] *In re* First City Bancorporation of Tex., Inc., 282 F.3d 864, 865 (5th Cir. 2002) (per curiam) (emphasis added).

[30] Dahl v. City of Huntington Beach, 84 F.3d 363, 364 (9th Cir. 1996).

not to the client, but to the legal system. Our judicial machinery is dependent upon the full support of all members of the bench and bar. Advocacy does not include "game playing." Conduct such as that engaged in here must not, can not, and will not be tolerated.'[31]

Paramount Communications, Inc. v. QVC Network Inc: 'The issue of discovery abuse, including lack of civility and professional misconduct during depositions, is a matter of considerable concern to Delaware courts and courts around the nation. One particular instance of [Mr. Jamil's] misconduct during a deposition in this case demonstrates such an astonishing lack of professionalism and civility that it is worthy of special note here as a lesson for the future—a lesson of conduct not to be tolerated or repeated....

Staunch advocacy on behalf of a client is proper and fully consistent with the finest effectuation of skill and professionalism. Indeed, it is a mark of professionalism, not weakness, for a lawyer zealously and firmly to protect and pursue a client's legitimate interests by a professional, courteous, and civil attitude toward all persons involved in the litigation process. A lawyer who engages in the type of behavior exemplified by Mr. Jamail on the record of the Liedtke deposition is not properly representing his client, and the client's course is not advanced by a lawyer who engages in unprofessional conduct of this nature.'[32]

Miller v. Bittner: "The most troublesome aspect of this lawsuit is the lack of professionalism and civility displayed by the lawyers.... This case serves as an example of the unfortunate lack of civility in the practice of law which is receiving considerable attention at this time.... The adversary process in the judicial arena does not require attorneys to be clothed in a suit of armor and fight to the bitter end. The parties, the profession, and the public all lose when the attorneys fail to treat each other with common courtesy."[33]

In possibly the most vociferous and curious judicial exposition on civility, one court announced new standards and threatened their application against a plaintiff's lawyer who had filed a motion clearly proper under the rules of civil procedure, but which the court thought was uncivil to opposing counsel because the motion had been filed without first consulting opposing counsel who had himself been late filing a pleading without permission of the court.[34]

We address today a problem that, though of relatively recent origin, is so pernicious that it threatens to delay the administration of justice and to place litigation beyond the financial reach of litigants. With alarming frequency,

---

[31] Pesaplastic, C.A. v. Cincinnati Milacron Co., 799 F.2d 1510, 1522–1523 (11th Cir.1986) (per curiam) (emphasis added).

[32] Paramount Communications, Inc. v. QVC Network Inc., 637 A.2d 34, 52–54 (Del. 1994). Mr. Jamail's exploits became infamous examples of incivility.

[33] Miller v. Bittner, 985 F.2d 935, 941 (8th Cir.1993) (emphasis added).

[34] Dondi Props. Corp. v. Commerce Savs. And Loan Ass'n, 121 F.R.D. 284 (N.D. Tex, 1998).

we find that valuable judicial and attorney time is consumed in resolving unnecessary contention and sharp practices between lawyers. Judges and magistrates of this court are required to devote substantial attention to refereeing abusive litigation tactics that range from benign incivility to outright obstruction. Our system of justice can ill-afford to devote scarce resources to supervising matters that do not advance the resolution of the merits of a case; nor can justice long remain available to deserving litigants if the costs of litigation are fueled unnecessarily to the point of being prohibitive.

As judges and former practitioners from various backgrounds and levels of experience, we judicially know that litigation is conducted today in a manner far different from years past. Whether the increased size of the bar has decreased collegiality, or the legal profession has become only a business, or experienced lawyers have ceased to teach new lawyers the standards to be observed, or because of other factors not readily categorized, we observe patterns of behavior that forebode ill for our system of justice. We now adopt standards designed to end such conduct.[35]

Among the announced courtesy standards were these two:

(I) Lawyers will be punctual in communications with others and in honoring scheduled appearances, and will recognize that neglect and tardiness are demeaning to the lawyer and to the judicial system.

(J) If a fellow member of the Bar makes a just request for cooperation, or seeks scheduling accommodation, a lawyer will not arbitrarily or unreasonably withhold consent.

In *Dondi*, the defendant insurance company lawyer had filed a pleading beyond the deadline set by the civil procedure rules. He had not asked the court's permission for the late filing, nor had he communicated with plaintiff's counsel about the lateness. When the plaintiff's lawyer filed a motion to strike the late pleading, as was authorized by the civil procedure rules, the court admonished the plaintiff for failing to consult with defendant's counsel before filing the motion, something about which the civil procedure rules were silent. Plaintiff's counsel had complied with the adopted rules of civil procedure, but failed to meet the district judge's sense of courtesy; the defendant's lawyer had violated the adopted rules of civil procedure, but had not offended the judge's sense of courtesy. Civility had "run amok."[36]

The Seventh Circuit led the way in pursuing new civility rules among federal courts of appeal.[37] The court commissioned a survey of judges and lawyers in the circuit to gauge the level of the civility problem. Somewhat curiously, the court did

---

[35] *Id.* at 286.

[36] *See* Monroe Freedman, *Civility Runs Amok*, LEGAL TIMES, Aug. 14, 1995, at 54.

[37] INTERIM REPORT OF THE COMMITTEE ON CIVILITY OF THE SEVENTH FEDERAL JUDICIAL CIRCUIT, 143 F.R.D. 371 (1992) [hereinafter INTERIM REPORT]; FINAL REPORT OF THE COMMITTEE ON CIVILITY OF THE SEVENTH FEDERAL JUDICIAL CIRCUIT, 143 F.R.D. 441 (1992) [hereinafter FINAL REPORT].

not seem to entertain the possibility that there was no civility crisis, because when the data returned a dubious-at-best crisis finding, it went on to issue guidelines to solve the problem. The lack of civility had so clearly become engrained in the common wisdom, that no other conclusion from the data seemed plausible.

According to the commissioned lawyer survey on professionalism: "More than 41%,... of the responding judges and lawyers believe that lack of civility is a problem...Among responding judges, 45% find civility lacking, but 39% do not. Among responding lawyers, 42% find civility lacking, but 50% do not."[38] So, less than half of both lawyers and judges believed there was a problem. Nonetheless, drastic action was needed. Preliminary and then final recommendations were made and then pursued:

- Copies of the Interim Report were to be "circulated, read, and discussed by interested administrators and faculty members in all law schools...to facilitate a discussion of the possibility of including civility training in law school curricula."[39]
- "Both public law offices and private law firms should immediately consider the development of civility training as part of the training provided for newly hired attorneys.... [P]ublic law offices and law firms should circulate this Interim Report to stimulate discussion of civility questions and encourage attorneys to develop recommendations to improve civility standards."[40]
- "All lawyers and judges in the Seventh Federal Judicial Circuit should consider participation in one of the Inns of Court; public offices and private law firms should encourage participation in the Inns of Court; and if an Inn of Court does not exist in a particular area, lawyers and judges in that area should consider establishing one."[41]
- Standards for Professional Conduct within the Seventh Federal Judicial Circuit should be adopted.[42]

"Law school training programs [were] the most frequently selected recommendation by responding lawyers and jurists as a possible solution to civility problems," something none of the respondents would have to attend, of course.[43] "The second preference of survey respondents was law firm training programs. Both public offices and law firms can develop civility codes or standards for all their attorneys."[44] Although most of the survey respondents did not rank a civility code at the

---

[38] INTERIM REPORT at 378.
[39] *Id.* at 412.
[40] *Id.* at 377.
[41] *Id.*
[42] *Id.*
[43] *Id.* at 411.
[44] *Id.* at 412.

top of their recommended solutions, the Committee determined that such a code was needed.[45]

In its Final Recommendations, the Committee recommended that the Proposed Standards for Professional Conduct within the Seventh Federal Judicial Circuit be adopted, and that each lawyer practicing in the circuit's courts be required to certify, as a precondition to admission and to filing an appearance in any court within the circuit, that he or she has read and will abide by the Standards.[46]

The Committee proposed that civility training, including education regarding the Standards for Professional Conduct, be implemented by law schools, public law offices, private law firms, and corporations with in-house counsel. Additionally, it recommended that all lawyers and judges consider participation in civility, professionalism, or mentoring programs in professional legal associations and bar associations, as well as participation in one of the American Inns of Court.[47] This adopted civility creed created 30 duties that lawyers owe to other counsel, 8 duties lawyers owe to the court, 12 duties the court owes to lawyers, and 3 duties judges owe to each other.[48]

III. Not Just the Legal Profession

The culture was generally experiencing a similar enhancement of competitive juices. Business, government, and individuals experienced heightened competition, often from unexpected sources. Each responded in kind.

The emerging global economy meant that the United States was no longer an economic island on which foreign goods were no real threat to domestic manufacturers. In 1984, Toyota embarked on a joint venture with GM and made its first serious inroads into American domestic market shares, traditionally held by Ford, Chrysler, and GM.[49] At around the same time, Sony developed the first CD player and began its march to replace Magnavox and Zenith in the home entertainment marketplace.[50] Sony's corporate expansion into the United States was launched with its acquisition of CBS Records, Inc. in 1988 and Columbia Pictures Entertainment, Inc. in 1989, turning them into Sony Music Entertainment and Sony Pictures Entertainment, respectively.[51] The business mood at the time required fighting for market share against competitors never before imagined. U.S. industries of long

---

[45] *Id.* at 415.

[46] FINAL REPORT at 447.

[47] *Id.*

[48] *Id.* at 448–452.

[49] *History of Toyota*, TOYOTA, http://www.toyota-global.com/company/history_of_toyota/ (last visited July 20, 2012).

[50] *Corporate History*, SONY, http://www.sony.net/SonyInfo/CorporateInfo/History/history.html (last visited July 20, 2012).

[51] *Id.*

standing faltered in the face of foreign competition. Steel and rubber, for example, closed and left behind empty, hulking plants and mills that served as bold, daily reminders that competitions lost brought harsh consequences.

Cities, counties, and states stepped up their competition with one another with an ever-escalating tax incentives race to entice businesses to forsake a neighboring political division and relocate.[52] Beginning in the 1980s, these tax incentive programs heightened competition among political subdivisions, as they engaged veritable bidding wars for business relocation, often into "enterprise zones."[53] It was county versus neighboring county and Ohio versus Pennsylvania versus Michigan. A war to protect and attract local jobs was on. State policymakers competed for votes based on their aggressive campaigns to out-duel the competition and attract jobs.[54] Economists were not so sure about the competition's overall effectiveness for enhancing economic activity, but the competition was fierce.[55]

The general population was not immune from the increasingly competitive climate. Road rage showed its head, changing the formerly placid act of driving in some locales into an exercise in self-preservation. It emerged as an identifiable condition and captured significant media attention. In *Bowling Alone,* Robert Putnam included a description of the condition among his list of symptoms of emerging incivility and social disconnection in the 1990s. The term was popularized during the late 1980s, specifically by newscasters at KTLA, a local television station in Los Angeles, California. Between 1987 and 1988, a rash of freeway shootings occurred on the 405, 110, and 10 freeways in Los Angeles. The AAA Motor Club went so far as to instruct its millions of members on how to respond to drivers with road rage or aggressive maneuvers and gestures.[56]

A decade of road rage later, the condition was recognized by therapists as a "disease," listed in the Diagnostic and Statistical Manual of Mental Disorders.[57] According to an article published by the Associated Press in June 2006, the behaviors typically associated with road rage are the result of "intermittent explosive disorder." This conclusion was drawn from surveys of some 9,200 adults in the United States between 2001 and 2003 and was funded by the National Institute of Mental Health.[58]

---

[52] Veena Iyer, Cuno v. DaimlerChrysler, Inc. *Dormant Commerce Clause Limits State Location Tax Incentives*, 40 HARV. C.R.-C.L. L. REV. 523, 523 (2005).

[53] *See, e.g.,* OHIO REV. CODE ANN. §§ 5709.62(A), 5709.93(A) (LexisNexis 2012).

[54] George Voinovich, *Court Wrong To Threaten States' Tax Incentives*, CRAIN'S CLEVELAND BUS., Oct. 11, 2004, at 10. http://www.crainscleveland.com/article/20041011/SUB/410110722/0/ SEARCH

[55] ALAN PETERS & PETER FISH, ENTERPRISE ZONE INCENTIVES: HOW EFFECTIVE ARE THEY, IN FINANCING ECONOMIC DEVELOPMENT IN THE 21ST CENTURY 113, 116 (Sammis B. White et al. eds., 2003).

[56] Daniel B. Rathbone & Jorg C. Huckabee, *Controlling Road Rage*, AAA, http://www. aaafoundation.org/resources/index.cfm?button=roadrage (last visited July 20, 2012).

[57] *Intermittent Explosive Disorder*, MAYO CLINIC, (June 10, 2010), http://www.mayoclinic.com/ health/intermittent-explosive-disorder/DS00730.

[58] *Study Says Millions Have "Rage" Disorder,* USA TODAY (June 5, 2010), http://www.usatoday. com/news/health/2006-06-05-rage-disorder_x.htm.

Others sought to debunk the road rage phenomenon.[59] But stories of severe road rage offenders[60] and celebrity road ragers[61] kept the conversation lively about this new, aggressive, uncivil behavior.

The language used to decry road rage was strikingly similar to the language used to decry lawyers' "new" unprofessional behavior patterns. Lawyers were simply behaving as the culture had begun to behave. Competition was fiercer for shares of the economic pie, for space on the freeways, and for representation of clients. To the extent that lawyers were more aggressive not only in their efforts to please and attract clients, but in their advocacy, they were largely reflecting the increase in competition that their clients were feeling in everyday business life.

IV. Law Practice Had Changed with the Culture

Both the practice of law and the world in which it lived became more competitive. The profession noticed that lawyers behaved in a more competitive manner under these conditions. The 1990s saw the beginning phases of dramatic changes in law firms that would come to fruition 15 years later.[62] No longer were clients a stable income source. No longer could large firms maintain the formerly pure-pyramid structure. Corporate law departments were replacing much of the work formerly done by associates, work that generated steady and certain profit shares to partners.

Commentators agreed that law practice was changing, becoming more competitive. Scathing critiques of the legal profession's lost way were many, as was this typical remark from Sol Linowitz:

From the 1940's to 1990, the large law firms grew rapidly and steadily, feeding on the ever-increasing intervention of the government in what had once been private business—complicated tax codes, aggressive antitrust enforcement, anti-discrimination laws, environmental requirements, questions of corporate governance, and securities issues.[63] Together with the sheer size, [reworked] compensation arrangements tolled heavily against collegiality.[64]

---

[59] Read Mercer Schuchardt, *Understanding Road Rage*, COUNTERBLAST: THE e-JOURNAL OF CULTURE & COMMC'N (Nov. 2001), http://www.nyu.edu/pubs/counterblast/issue1_nov01/articles/schuchardt.html (discussing the August 1998 *Atlantic Monthly* article written by Michael Fumento and his attempt to discredit road rage).

[60] *Motorist Sentenced in Road Rage Assault*, L.A. TIMES (Sept. 18, 1999), http://articles.latimes.com/1999/sep/18/local/me-11557.

[61] *This Day in History: Jack Nicholson Smashes Windshield in Episode of Road Rage*, HISTORY.com, http://www.history.com/this-day-in-history/jack-nicholson-smashes-windshield-in-episode-of-road-rage (last visited Aug. 24, 2012).

[62] *See* chapter 9.

[63] SOL M. LINOWITZ, THE BETRAYED PROFESSION: LAWYERING AT THE END OF THE TWENTIETH CENTURY 100–101 (1994).

[64] *Id.* at 104.

V. Enter the Remedy: Creeds

While the practice of law was changing, the organized profession sought to turn back the clock. The remedy pursued by the organized bar to soften competitive excess was a patently ineffectual wholesale adoption of lawyer creeds, asking lawyers to aspire to be more considerate of one another. Ignoring the world outside the profession, the profession behaved as if civility had suddenly become a uniquely lawyer-behavior problem. If only lawyers would promise to behave as did 19th-century lawyers, the problem would be solved. The challenge the profession undertook was to extract this promise from the lips of every American lawyer.

Chief Justice Warren Burger addressed the ABA in 1984 and again decried a decline in professionalism.[65] Burger enunciated a widespread perception that the Bar only lived up to the minimum standards as articulated in the Model Rules of Professional Conduct.[66] The ABA's prompt response in the form of the Blueprint for the Rekindling of Lawyer Professionalism[67] validated this perception[68] and asserted that the strictures of the Model Rules, in and of themselves, did not create an acceptable level of professionalism.[69]

The Model Rules had only recently supplanted the Model Code. The Model Rules, made *more* law-like to save the profession from the public relations disaster of Watergate, were *too* law-like and included too little aspiration and inspiration, according to the Blueprint. Consequently, the report advocated the adoption of nonenforceable ethical creeds that would exhort the lawyer to conform to standards above the minimum standards of the Rules.[70] In 1988, the ABA House of Delegates recommended that state and local bar associations adopt creeds of professional conduct.[71] Subsequently, the ABA Torts and Insurance Practice Section adopted such a creed.[72] The ABA House of Delegates also approved a creed created by

---

[65] Chief Justice Warren W. Burger, Remarks at the Midyear Meeting of the American Bar Association (Feb. 13–14, 1984), *reprinted in* 52 U.S.L.W. 2471 (Feb. 28, 1984).

[66] *Id.* In 1984, Justice Burger was speaking at a time when few states had actually adopted the Model Rules of Professional Conduct, which were adopted by the ABA's House of Delegates in 1983. *See* CHARLES W. WOLFRAM, MODERN LEGAL ETHICS 2.6.2, at 62–63 (practitioner's ed. 1986).

[67] *Blueprint*, supra note 2.

[68] *See id.* at 265 ("All segments of the Bar should:...resolve to abide by higher standards of conduct than the minimum required by the Code of Professional Responsibility and the Model Rules of Professional Conduct.").

[69] The ABA Blueprint for Professionalism attributed some of the shortcomings to external economic pressure, and thus stopped short of totally internalizing the blame. *Id.* at 257 ("Rhetoric about the 'special' character of the profession remains, but the reality is that, as a matter of law, lawyers must now face tough economic competition with respect to almost everything they do.").

[70] *See id.* at 296–297.

[71] 113 No. 2 Ann. Rep. A.B.A. 25 (1988).

[72] http://www.americanbar.org/content/dam/aba/administrative/tips/lawyers_creed_of_professionalism.authcheckdam.pdf

the Young Lawyers' Section called a Lawyer's Pledge of Professionalism.[73] Other ABA entities followed. The ABA creed was similar to the 1989 "Texas Lawyer's Creed—A Mandate for Professionalism."[74] State and local bar associations quickly seized the bait and began to draft nonbinding creeds.[75]

Further invigorated by the Seventh Circuit's adoption of standards in 1992, the ABA renewed its call for creeds:

> RESOLVED, That the American Bar Association encourages federal, state, territorial and local bar associations and courts to adopt standards of civility, courtesy, and conduct as aspirational goals to promote professionalism of lawyers and judges.[76]

In the report (but not in the Resolution), the committee says that the "common principles of such standards" should be the following:

> A lawyer's duty to represent each client zealously within the bounds of the law is a duty to be honored consistent with the lawyer's responsibility to a justice system;
>
> In addition to the duties of candor, honesty and diligence that a lawyer owes to the judiciary under rules of professional conduct, a lawyer owes to the judiciary a duty of respect;
>
> A judge owes to the practicing bar a duty of attentiveness, courtesy, respect and a dedication to the proper administration of courts;
>
> A lawyer owes opposing counsel, parties and the courts a duty of courtesy, fairness and cooperation;
>
> A lawyer owes to the profession adherence to a higher level of conduct than observance of rules of professional conduct.[77]

This resolution was approved by voice vote.[78]

Professionalism creeds swept the nation in the 1990s. At a time when Rule 11 sanctions abounded, when the definition of "hardball litigation" was debated, and when the bar conducted seminars on dealing with the S.O.B. lawyer, bar associations across the nation were racing to adopt good manners oaths.[79] But, although

---

[73] http://www.americanbar.org/content/dam/aba/migrated/cpr/pledgeofprofessionalism.auth-checkdam.pdf

[74] *See generally* Eugene A. Cook et al., *A Guide to the Texas Lawyer's Creed: A Mandate for Professionalism*, 10 Rev. Litig. 673 (1991) (discussing and analyzing the Texas Lawyer's Creed—A Mandate for Professionalism).

[75] As of late 1995, 26 states and 62 local bar associations had adopted creeds. *See* Rob Atkinson, *A Dissenter's Commentary on the Professionalism Crusade,* 74 Tex. L. Rev. 259, 278 n.74 (1995).

[76] 120 Ann. Rep. A.B.A. v. 2 at 231 (1995).

[77] *Id.* at 232.

[78] *Id.* at 41.

[79] *See, e.g.,* Texas Lawyer's Creed—A Mandate for Professionalism (1989).

the claim was that these developments were the result of a decaying moral fabric among lawyers, a more complex set of truths was at play.

To be sure, law practice and the bar had changed dramatically, in some ways undoubtedly for the worse but in other ways for the better, since the days of David Hoffman's aspirational resolutions,[80] elitist bar admission policies, and client and self-interested drafting and adoption of legal ethics rules. Indeed, among the first reasons to have bar associations was the fear that the children of Southern and Eastern European immigrants and other undesirables were going to infiltrate the profession.[81] By the 1980s and 1990s, the organized bar, happily, could no longer rely on the homogeneity of its membership and its membership's virtually common, elitist upbringing to ensure maintenance of its definition of civility among the group's members. Much to the better for the profession and society, there no longer was an exclusive club for anyone to infiltrate. To the extent the new creeds were merely a hoped-for return to the moral force of formerly common values in the membership's actions toward each other, toward the court, and toward its clients, the creeds were bound to fail because that former profession no longer existed. The creeds not only failed, but they also briefly retarded the progress toward pluralism of the profession in the process.

The reality is that lawyers in the imagined golden age[82] were not civil to fellow lawyers who were outside of their own socioeconomic group and practice orientation. To the extent that lawyers *were* more civil in some golden age than they are today, that former civility only existed within a commonly interested group of lawyers who had essentially agreed not to compete with one another for clients,[83] and who together formed a profession-ruling class that recognized the enemy, to whom they were anything but civil, as all lawyers who looked or spoke or thought differently from them. Not coincidentally, at some of these historical junctures, the outsider's clients were largely people who had claims against the clients of the profession's ruling class.[84] Civility has, at various times in the history of the American legal profession, been what members of particular practice cohorts gave to one another, but not to those members of the profession who were outside the cohort. During such times, outsiders of one description or another have been the object of uncivil conduct by the most well-established members of the profession.[85]

---

[80] David Hoffman, A Course of Legal Study, Fifty Resolutions on Professional Deportment 752–775 (Arno Press 1972) (1836).

[81] *See* chapter 2.

[82] A "golden age" is a moving target, probably corresponding to the 50 years preceding the professional memory of the current senior members in the practice.

[83] *See* Henry S. Drinker, Legal Ethics 5, 190–191 (Greenwood Press 1980) (1953); George W. Warvelle, Essays in Legal Ethics § 324, at 205–206 (1902).

[84] Jerald S. Auerbach, Unequal Justice 44–48.

[85] *See id.*

The perceived need by both the public and the profession[86] for enhanced civility in the legal profession was the basis for acceptance by both lawyers and non-lawyers of a need for professionalism creeds. What was far less clear is whether a return to the civility of the past actually represented the higher ethical standard that its proponents would have the profession and public believe it to be.[87]

What are the "higher" standards urged by Burger and the Blueprint after all? Occasionally, a lawyer duty points in a singular direction, as, for example, in the care of client property. Measures to take even greater care of client property than is required might be regarded as a truly higher standard. But more often, and in all the controversial areas of lawyer ethics, lawyer standards are really a balance between or among competing responsibilities and goals. The goal of maintaining client confidences is balanced with the grave consequences to the public of maintaining client information that implicates serious future harm, for example. The adopted bar ethics rules articulate the balance by creating an exception to the duty of confidentiality. The general and most prominent lawyer duty—to further clients' lawful and legitimate interests—is balanced against various responsibilities to courts and third parties in the form of all manner of ethics rules that prohibit making material false statements[88] or uttering a lawyer's personal opinions to a lay fact finder[89] or failing to inform a careless sender of a misdirected e-mail.[90] Breaching any of those duties would further client interests in ways that have been determined to be unacceptable because of the serious harm the actions do to other, competing interests. These rules and many more act as fences beyond which legitimate client-favoring activities may not pass. They express the point at which the ethics rule adopters have balanced client-favoring duties with other duties. In any of these more common areas of lawyer ethics, an advocate of a "higher" standard simply favors one of the competing duties more than the rule drafters did. As a result, such an exhortation, either in a creed or an after dinner speech, is not a call for the familiar "higher standard than the minimum imposed by the rules."[91] Rather, it is a call for a different balance of competing duties than is currently mandated by the governing, enforceable rule. In particular, civility creeds tend to favor duties to other lawyers or courts more than the drafters of the ethics rules did. Higher standards in this context are merely different standards from the lawfully adopted ones. The only legitimately higher standard is a solemn commitment to balance carefully the competing interests.

---

[86] For an analysis of the differences between the public's view and the profession's view of the current problems, see Deborah Rhode, *The Professionalism Problem*, 39 Wm. & Mary L. Rev. 283 (1998).

[87] *See* Burger, *supra* note 11, at 62; *Blueprint*, *supra* note 2, at 251.

[88] Model Rules of Prof'l Conduct R. 4.1 & 3.3 (2010).

[89] *Id.* at R. 3.5.

[90] *Id.* at R. 4.4b.

[91] *Blueprint*, *supra* note 2, at 265.

Lawyers, as well as the public, recognized the need for more integrity and civility in the legal profession. Some lawyers blamed the decline in lawyer civility on incessant hardball among lawyers.[92] Hardball, according to Chicago lawyer Philip Corboy, "is when a lawyer, whether plaintiff's or defense, is personally antagonistic or insistent on all of the procedural rules being followed."[93] Defining "antagonistic or insistent," however, has never been easy. Given a lawyer's unquestioned duty to his or her client, characterizing "insistence" as a negative attribute is hardly a proposition that is universally accepted.[94]

The hardball approach, some assert, arises from the transition in the minds of many lawyers that lawyering is now as much a business as a profession. A bottom-line mentality of "win-at-any-cost" often exacerbates tensions in lawyer relationships.[95] But this so-called mindset change was not of recent origin. Rather, it has accompanied times of prior professionalism crises.[96]

VI. Were the Creeds Code or Aspiration?

While it has been said that the proliferation of creeds was a response to the "recent awareness of the civility crisis, or more appropriately, the shift in focus to the cure of the civility crisis,"[97] the rise in creed-need also paralleled the change in ABA model standard focus from aspiration to rule orientation.

The 1990s wave of creeds may have been little more than a natural evolutionary outgrowth of the change in tone of the ABA model ethics pronouncements. The change of ABA model ethics pronouncements and their adoption by the states over the 20th century may have made the rise of the modern creeds all but inevitable. As the codes became more law-like and less filled with aspiration, the profession lost

---

[92] *See* Stephanie B. Goldberg, *Playing Hardball*, A.B.A. J., July 1987, at 48, 51.

[93] *Id.* at 48; *see also* Daniel J. Lehmann, *Church Plays Legal Hardball*, CHI. SUN TIMES, Jan. 13, 1994, at 14 (describing Catholic Church litigation tactics); Carole Bass, *Playing Litigation Hardball*, CONN. L. TRIB., Jan. 2, 1995, at 1 (describing US Surgical's 200 hour deposition of opposing party); Randall Samborn, *Priest Playing Hardball to Battle Abuse Charges*, NAT'L L.J., July 4, 1994, at A1 (discussing priest's litigation tactics in sex abuse case); Stanley S. Arkin, *Blackmail and the Practice of Law*, N.Y. L.J., Feb. 7, 1995, at 3 (discussing use of blackmail as a legal tactic); MARK A. DOMBROFF, DOMBROFF ON UNFAIR TACTICS (2d ed. 1988) (discussing tactics for playing hardball in lawsuits).

[94] *See, e.g.,* Goldberg, *supra* note 91, at 52; MONROE H. FREEDMAN, UNDERSTANDING LAWYERS' ETHICS 6–10 (1990); ELLIOT E. CHEATHAM, CASES AND MATERIALS ON THE LEGAL PROFESSION 182–184 (2d ed. 1955).

[95] Thomas M. Reavley, *Rambo Litigators: Pitting Aggressive Tactics Against Legal Ethics*, 17 PEPP. L. REV. 637, 654 n.89 (1990).

[96] *See id.* at 639–642 (discussing the author's experiences with aggressive lawyers as a practicing attorney from 1948 through 1964, and from 1977 through 1979); *1906 AALS Porceedings*, *supra* note 7, at 10–11.

[97] Brent E. Dickson & Julia Bunton Jackson, *Professionalism in the Practice of Law*, 28 VAL. U. L. REV. 531, 537 n.49 (1994).

its ability to tout its own specialness: it had become just another regulated business. It needed the high-sounding tones of aspiration.

The profession may, in fact, need lawyer creeds to fill an aspirational niche. Aspirational pronouncements provide both a psychological[98] and a pragmatic, public relations benefit to the individual professional and to the profession. The desire for these benefits are in significant measure responsible for the rise of the modern lawyer creeds; they replaced the aspirational elements of the former organized bar ethics pronouncements when they were first trimmed from the Canons to the Model Code and then almost entirely eliminated from the Model Code to the Model Rules.[99]

According to a survey commissioned by the ABA, the 1990s public perception of lawyers was relatively unfavorable.[100] The survey suggested, for instance, "a disturbing pattern that the more a person knows about the legal profession and the more he or she is in direct personal contact with lawyers, the lower an individual's opinion of them."[101] When asked to volunteer in their own words changes that should be made in the legal profession, the largest segment of respondents—22 percent—suggested improvements in ethics, integrity, and accountability.[102] These responses suggest that lawyer creeds would be supported by the public, and that the profession would benefit by articulating properly framed and based aspirations and then fulfilling them. But history reminds us that the public has before blamed increases in litigiousness,[103] bad economic times,[104] and all manner of other social ills on lawyers rather than on the cultural and societal changes that have largely spawned the tumultuous times.[105]

In a broader view, the rise in creed-need coincided with a general rise in global competitiveness and social angst that produced such phenomena as road rage. And as always, when promoting this and other reforms, was the profession's fear that failure to reform would invite change from outside forces. As the "Blueprint for Professionalism" noted:

> It behooves the profession to act.... If such action is not taken, far more extensive and perhaps less-considered proposals may arise from governmental and quasi-governmental entities attempting to regulate the profession.[106]

---

[98] *See, e.g.,* SIBYLLE K. ESCANOLA, AN APPLICATION OF THE LEVEL OF ASPIRATION EXPERIMENT TO THE STUDY OF PERSONALITY 4–6 (1948); ARCHIBALD O. HALLER & IRWIN W. MILLER, THE OCCUPATIONAL ASPIRATION SCALE: THEORY, STRUCTURE AND CORRELATES 11 (1971).

[99] *See Blueprint, supra* note 2, at 257–259.

[100] See Gary A. Hengstler, *Vox Populi*, A.B.A. J., Sept. 1993, at 60, 60–61.

[101] *Id.* at 62.

[102] *See id.* at 64.

[103] *See* chapter 6.

[104] Debt collection after the Revolutionary War.

[105] *See* CHARLES WARREN, A HISTORY OF THE AMERICAN BAR 214–216 (William S. Hein & Co. 1990) (1911) (recounting the popular opinion regarding the sharp increase in debt collection following the American Revolution).

[106] *Blueprint, supra* note 2 at 305.

A. MISTAKEN ENFORCEMENT

Some courts mistakenly enforced the new creeds, though they were meant to be aspirational. Frustration with lawyer behavior was sufficiently widespread that these few courts felt a high level of moral righteousness in enforcing what were meant to be purely aspirational creeds. In the mission of restoring a lost golden age, unenforceable 19th-century principles of proper deportment and etiquette now found greater vitality and power in the late 20th.[107]

The creed most often cited in case law was the "Texas Lawyer's Creed—A Mandate for Professionalism," adopted in 1989.[108] Although the Creed's Order of Adoption states that the rules are "primarily aspirational," the Creed was used as a basis for penalties, such as sanctions, as some of the following cases illustrate.[109]

When a plaintiff filed a motion for sanctions and censure against the defendant's attorney, a federal district court sanctioned the attorney for intentionally misleading opposing counsel in order to obtain ex parte interviews with opposing party witnesses.[110] The *Horner* court cited both the Texas Lawyer's Creed and the section of the Texas Disciplinary Rule prohibiting dishonesty with another attorney.[111] Although the court referred only to the disciplinary rule as "mandatory and [having] the status of law,"[112] the court cited the Creed as a part of its reasoning toward the imposition of sanctions.[113] The sanctions were attorneys' fees and relevant expenses incurred by the plaintiff incident to the motion.[114]

The same court had previously threatened application of the Texas Lawyer's Creed as a sanctions rule in another case.[115] Ruling on various discovery motions filed in a patent infringement lawsuit, the court, after granting the defendant's motion to compel the completion of a deposition, stated,

> Counsel are admonished that their failure to comply with the Texas Lawyer's Creed—A Mandate for Professionalism promulgated by the Supreme Court of Texas and the Texas Court of Criminal Appeals and adopted by

---

[107] *See, e.g.,* Committee on Prof'l Ethics & Conduct of the Iowa State Bar Ass'n v. Durham, 279 N.W.2d 280, 285–286 (Iowa 1979).

[108] *See* Cook, *supra* note 73, at 674–675.

[109] *See, e.g.,* McLeod, Alexander, Powel & Apffel v. Quarles, 894 F.2d 1482 (5th Cir. 1990). In *McLeod,* the defendant, proceeding for part of the case pro se as a former client of the plaintiff-law firm, failed to respond, without good cause, to discovery requests by the plaintiff. *Id.* at 1483–1484. The appeals court, upholding the district court's adoption of a magistrate's order of default judgment against the defendant, cited the specific rule of the Federal Rules of Civil Procedure used by the magistrate—Rule 37—for default judgment. *Id.* at 1484–1486. The appeals court also cited a section of The Texas Lawyers' Creed—A Mandate for Professionalism, which requires attorneys to comply with reasonable discovery requests. *Id.* at 1486–1487.

[110] Horner v. Rowan Co., Inc., 153 F.R.D. 597, 598 (S.D. Tex. 1994).

[111] *Id.* at 603.

[112] *Id.*

[113] *See id.* (citing Texas Lawyer's Creed—A Mandate for Professionalism (1989)).

[114] *See id.*

[115] Exxon Chem. Patents, Inc. v. Lubrizol Corp., 131 F.R.D. 668 (S.D. Tex. 1990).

this court will result in monetary sanctions being imposed against counsel individually.[116]

The court's warning undoubtedly changed lawyer conduct by force of the court's power to execute on the warning, and was effectively an enforcement of the creed.

A pro se attorney seeking to recover damages and attorneys' fees from a former client was held to have acted unethically and to have violated the Texas Lawyer's Creed by seeking a default judgment against parties who had filed their answer under the wrong case number, and who the attorney knew were represented by legal counsel.[117] The court cited the Creed provision that states that a lawyer will "not take advantage, by causing any default or dismissal to be rendered, when [he or she knows] the identity of an opposing counsel, without first inquiring about that counsel's intention to proceed."[118]

The Dallas Bar Association Lawyer's Creed and Guidelines for Professional Courtesy, both adopted in 1987, were used as the basis of a federal district court's adoption of standards of litigation conduct in the *Dondi* case, referred to previously.[119] The standards, in 11 sections, were taken nearly verbatim from sections of the two Dallas Bar Association documents.[120]

The courtesy creed discussed and adopted as an enforceable, sanction-supporting code by the court was applied in a wrongful refusal to pay insurance claims case.[121] The insurance company's lawyers filed a late brief.[122] Not only was the brief filed late, but it was filed late without the lawyers either requesting consent for the late filing from the plaintiff or seeking leave of court to excuse the lateness.[123] The insurance company lawyers had "clearly violated" the filing and leave of court requirements of the civil procedure code.[124] The court was justifiably concerned about the company's lawyers' neglect and tardiness.[125] But when the plaintiff's lawyer moved to strike the late filing, as the court's rules explicitly and understandably authorized them to do,[126] the court indicated its inclination to sanction the *plaintiff's* lawyers under the courtesy creed.[127] Announcing its view that attorney conduct

---

[116] *Id.* at 674.

[117] Owens v. Neely, 866 S.W.2d 716, 720 (Tex. Ct. App. 1993).

[118] *Id.* at 720 n.2 (quoting Texas Lawyer's Creed—A Mandate for Professionalism).

[119] Dondi Properties Corp. v. Commerce Savings & Loan Ass'n, 121 F.R.D. 284, 287–88 (N.D. Tex. 1988).

[120] *See id.*

[121] *See id.* at 285.

[122] *See id.* at 286.

[123] *See id.* at 291.

[124] *Id.*

[125] *Id.*

[126] Naturally, as contemplated by the rules, in the first instance the option of complaining about party misconduct such as late filings should rest with the opposing party.

[127] *Dondi*, 121 F.R.D. at 287–289; *see also* Monroe Freedman, *In the Matter of Manners*, LEGAL TIMES, March 11, 1991, at 23 (recounting the Dondi court's stated intention to impose sanctions on lawyers who violate the courtesy creed).

had deteriorated, the court mentioned several possible causes: the increase in the size of the bar has decreased collegiality, the legal profession has become merely a business, and veteran attorneys have ceased to teach new lawyers proper standards of conduct.[128] Similar statements about reasons for deteriorating lawyer behavior could be found as the 20th century opened and immigrant lawyers trampled the profession's good name.

Unlike the Dallas Bar Association Lawyer's Creed and Guidelines for Professional Courtesy, which do not mention sanctions or other methods of enforcement, the district court in *Dondi* did discuss consequences of creed violations. Violations of these creeds will result in "an appropriate response from the court, including the range of sanctions the Fifth Circuit suggests in the Rule 11 context: 'a warm friendly discussion on the record, a hard-nosed reprimand in open court, compulsory legal education, monetary sanctions, or other measures appropriate to the circumstances.'"[129] The court had lost sight of the difference between a legislatively adopted, enforceable rule of civil procedure and a bar association-adopted aspirational statement about lawyer behavior.

Aspirational creeds were thus used to police lawyer conduct that complied with the language of procedural rules such as Rule 11 of the Federal Rules of Civil Procedure, default judgment rules, or filing deadlines enforcement rules. If a currently authorized practice, such as moving for default judgment when no answer has been timely filed or moving to strike a late-filed brief, ought rather to be prohibited, then the procedural rules should themselves be amended to reflect the measure of diligence with which lawyers should be expected to enforce violations. The lawyers sanctioned for violating the creeds were advancing client interests by using procedural devices authorized by the court rules. Courts and bar authorities want "higher" (that is, different) standards to prevail that would require counsel to excuse opposing counsel's errors. Rule 11 is itself the best example of amending a rule to reach a desired result: in 1993, it was amended to include a safe harbor provision, requiring notice to opposing counsel and an opportunity to cure a defect before proceeding to court enforcement of Rule 11's strictures.[130] If lawyers should be expected to notify opposing counsel that opposing counsel's brief or pleading is late before proceeding to seek default judgment or late filing sanctions, then the appropriate rules should be amended to reflect such a requirement. Lawyers ought to be expected to seek enforcement of the rules as those rules are written rather than be expected to be a gentleman to opposing counsel while compromising client interests.

This was not a new, uncivil way of thinking. In 1902, George Warvelle described the late 19th- and early 20th-century "general practice" as follows:

It is the client's right to have his cause tried at the time set; to have adverse pleadings filed within the time allowed; and to insist that his attorney shall

---

[128] *Dondi*, 121 F.R.D. at 286.

[129] *Id.* at 288 (citing Thomas v. Capital Sec. Servs., 836 F.2d 866, 878 (5th Cir. 1988)).

[130] *See* FED. R. CIV. P. 11 advisory committee's note to 1993 amendment.

take every legal advantage the case may afford, and this duty an attorney may not capriciously avoid nor is he at liberty to withdraw from the case merely because his client insists upon the strict observance of his rights. Whatever the feelings of counsel may be toward the counsel for the other side, and however much he may desire to accommodate him in matters of practice, he is yet under a paramount duty to follow his client's instructions in all matters pertaining to the legitimate conduct of the litigation.[131]

Inexplicably, the 1990s legal profession imagined a gentler 19th century to which it desired a return.

To the extent that the modern creed is a sought-for replacement for the former, now lost, ABA-sponsored aspirational statements of the Canons and Code, the modern creed drafter must attend to the goals of that aspirational activity, and courts and disciplinary bodies must refrain from enforcing the aspiration. Once enforced, an aspirational statement becomes a rule and the lost-aspiration cycle renews.

To the extent that the creeds became treated as if they were enforceable rules, their rationale, of course, became critical. As with any other legal rule, the rule is its rationale, and it may be expected that an *enforceable* lawyer rule will be appropriately ignored when its rationale fails to account for a particular proposed application of the rule. A particular error of some of the creeds was the tendency to base them in part on client interests.[132] Some creeds purport to rest in part on the rationale that, as a lawyer, one should not be uncivil with opponents because such conduct harms the client's interests.[133] Unfortunately, a creed based on such a rationale is doomed to fail. It may well be that uncivil, hardball conduct sometimes harms client interests, but lawyers who engage in such conduct do so largely because they believe that it furthers client interests.[134] When, as is almost inevitable, a lawyer

---

[131] WARVELLE, *supra* note 82, § 317, at 197; *see also* JOSEPH G. BALDWIN, THE BENCH AND THE BAR (1854) (stating that older lawyers in the 1830s took advantage of "quirks and quibbles" to prevail for their clients against those of younger lawyers), *reprinted in* DENNIS R. NOLAN, READINGS IN THE HISTORY OF THE AMERICAN LEGAL PROFESSION 113–115 (1980).

[132] "As a professional, I should always...recognize that uncivil conduct does not advance and may compromise the rights of my clients." The Virginia Bar Association Creed (1996) (on file with author). "I will act at all times to preserve the mutual feeling of camaraderie among lawyers...because without it my clients and I suffer." Pulaski County Bar Association Code of Professional Courtesy 23 (1986) (on file with author). "Excessive zeal may be detrimental to my client's interests...." ABA Torts and Insurance Practice Section Lawyer's Creed of Professionalism § C (1) (1988) (and numerous state and local bar creeds modeled after the ABA model) (on file with author). "For us, the idea that civility and candor stand in the way of desired results in fact inconsistent with the achievement of long term goals, including successful results for our clients." Los Angeles County Bar Association Litigation Guidelines pmbl. (1989) (on file with author).

[133] *See*, e.g., Texas Lawyer's Creed—A Mandate for Professionalism (1989) (stating that "abusive tactics" are harmful to clients).

[134] For a discussion of the pragmatic rationale of lawyers' uncivil conduct, see *supra* notes 139–142 and accompanying text.

believes that uncivil conduct will further client interest, lawyers who would normally apply the rule will appropriately ignore it. Even the ABA, and not merely the bad apples of the profession that the ABA has always complained of, staged seminars designed to introduce lawyers to the methods of "Killer Cross."[135] These are tactics that lawyers, including leaders of the organized bar, believe benefit their clients at least some of the time.

On example is the Virginia Lawyers' Creed that requires the lawyer to promise to "always recognize that uncivil conduct does not advance and may compromise the rights of my clients."[136] Lawyers who engage in uncivil conduct did not buy this pronouncement. Lawyers who engage in uncivil conduct do so primarily to further their clients'—and vicariously their own—interests: "Hardball is vigorous advocacy for your client."[137] "The tug between doing right by your client and [doing] justice" makes hardball a way of life for the lawyer.[138] "Anyone...[who] cannot fulfill the prescribed obligations of a professional [including the use of aggressive tactics for a client] should not undertake those obligations."[139] Lawyers treat litigation as "war" to impress clients, send a message to opposing parties, and prove that the best defense is a good offense.[140]

B. MUDDYING STANDARDS

Some of the provisions of the creeds were mere restatements of the enforceable law governing lawyers. Some of them expressed the profession's desire for lawyers to behave according to standards different from the enforceable law governing lawyers. Neither works. Restating enforceable law as a creed promise adds no value; suggesting a conflicting standard confuses.

The restatement of an existing standard within a creed does no good and some mischief. It is as if the creed drafters thought that saying the same thing as the enforceable code a second time would cause greater compliance with the enforceable norm. For example, some creeds included provisions like these from the Seventh Circuit's Standards: "In civil actions, we will stipulate to relevant matters if they are undisputed and if no good faith advocacy basis exists for not stipulating";[141] "We will base our discovery objections on a good faith belief in their merit and will not

---

[135] Killer Cross: A Look at New Techniques of Cross Examination and Impeachment in Criminal Cases, Conference sponsored by ABA Section on Criminal Justice (April 3–5, 1992) (brochure on file with author).

[136] Virginia Bar Association Creed (1996) (on file with author).

[137] Goldberg, *supra* note 91, at 49.

[138] *Id.* at 50.

[139] Charles Fried, *The Lawyer as Friend: The Moral Foundations of the Lawyer-Client Relationship*, 85 YALE L.J. 1060, 1065 (1976).

[140] Haig & Getman, *supra* note 5, at 26 (quoting a local bar president).

[141] SEVENTH CIRCUIT STANDARDS FOR PROFESSIONAL CONDUCT 9 (1997). Query: Under *Dondi*, would it be uncivil to file a motion for sanctions against a lawyer who would not so stipulate? For a discussion of *Dondi*, see *supra* notes 123–134 and accompanying text.

object solely for the purpose of withholding or delaying the disclosure of relevant information."[142] Both were mere restatements of the enforceable codes or other law governing lawyers. These do no good and some harm by diminishing the clarity of the enforceable norms that they paraphrase and by diminishing the force of the enforceable norms by commingling the enforceable with the aspirational nature of the creed's main focus. No good, save that of public relations, comes from requiring a lawyer to promise to do what the law already requires the lawyer to do.

More trouble still is caused when the creeds were at odds with the enforceable law. The *Dondi*[143] case is a prime example of the competition between the law's standards and those of civility. When the defendants failed to timely file their brief, the rule of procedure allowed the plaintiff's lawyers to move the court for sanctions.[144] When the plaintiff did so, the court threatened the plaintiff with sanctions for failing to accommodate the defendant's counsel, essentially implicating a Rule 11-like safe harbor provision on the ground that it would be more civil for plaintiff's lawyer to have asked defendants about their intentions before filing the permitted motion with the court.[145] All the plaintiff did in *Dondi* was what the law permitted. Even in the good old days, which the creeds seemed intent on re-creating, a client was permitted to insist that the lawyer take advantage of procedural defaults of an opposing party.[146] Imposing an aspirational goal as a mandatory rule that strikes a balance between competing duties can only alter the balance and create conflicting standards of conduct that cannot both be satisfied by a lawyer.

VII. The Creeds Sought a Happily Lost Past

The late 20th-century creeds were erroneously and dangerously based on a pragmatic, client-interest rationale and were reflective of a past era's false civility. They are, to too great an extent, a harkening back to a happily-lost homogeneity and common moral basis for the profession that, if it ever was, is no longer dominant. The moral basis for the 21st-century legal profession must be more inclusive and less elitist than the 19th-century basis sought by the creeds.

Much of the substance in the wave of creeds mirrored the 19th-century work of Hoffman and Sharswood, whose work was more creed than code. The irony of the Hoffman/Sharswood story is this: they wrote a description of the ideal 19th-century lawyer, to which lawyers should aspire; 50 years later, their work was used by the organized bar to form the basis of the profession's first uniform, mandatory

---

[142] SEVENTH CIRCUIT STANDARDS FOR PROFESSIONAL CONDUCT 9 (1997). These are rough paraphrases of Rules 3.1 and 3.4(d) of the MODEL RULES OF PROFESSIONAL RESPONSIBILITY (1995).

[143] Dondi Properties Corp. v. Commerce Savings & Loan Ass'n, 121 F.R.D. 284 (N.D. Tex. 1988).

[144] *See id.* at 285–286.

[145] *Id.* at 291–292.

[146] *See* WARVELLE, *supra* note 82, 310, at 197.

ethics pronouncements; throughout the 20th century, these ethics pronouncements in turn formed the basis for the profession's sets of enforceable rules; and traces of their work are now evident in the organized bar's effort to revitalize aspiration by way of the creeds. Back to the 19th century once again.

The move from 19th-century creed to late 20th-century code in the ABA models was in part a reflection of the slowly expanding pluralism of the profession. As the organized bar has lost full control over admission to the practice, it recognized in its models that the former moral understanding, sometimes real and sometimes imagined—the "take care of one another before all other interests" understanding that naturally results from the sort of in-breeding that once dominated the profession—needed to be replaced by rules. Calls for a more rule-like code of ethics following Watergate were partly induced by the sense that the bar had lost its homogeneity. And it had. The profession replaced the former moral common ground of the elite with rules, a code, to control the behavior of the lawyer outsiders. The Model Rules are not aspirational as were the Canons,[147] to some extent the Model Code,[148] and as are the 1990s creeds.

The calls for creeds persist in 2012[149] despite their ineffectiveness. The attempted reinvigoration of the former understanding has failed because that former moral understanding no longer prevails in the pluralist bar. The former moral understanding cannot be divided away from its sources. Too great a part of the former moral understanding was a devotion to one's segment of the profession before the client and before public service, easy enough for those lawyers who were members of a club that would not compete with one another for clients and who had no need of regularly attracting new clients through other than social means. The former moral common ground was to too great an extent wedded to the exclusivity of those who formed and announced it. It exists as no more than memories, some real and some imagined, of a golden age, not unlike every other golden age: it is meant to pass and be left behind when social advancements make it irrelevant to current affairs. Only aspiration that reflects a new moral understanding that is based not on in-breeding, but on openness in law school admissions, increasing openness in job placement, a pluralist profession, and acceptance of a variety of models of the "good lawyer," will find the support of the new profession. It must look forward rather than backward.

The profession that operated under the former moral understanding was one in which civility existed but was delivered only within one's own practice cohort. In particular, outsiders of a wide variety were the recipients not of civility but of scorn, ridicule, abuse, and exclusion. The story of the organized bar's discrimination against women, blacks, particular political groups, and religious and geographic

---

[147] *See id.* at 257.
[148] *See id.* at 258.
[149] G. M. Filisko, *Be Nice: More States Are Treating Incivility as a Possible Ethics Violation,* A.B.A. J., (Apr. 1, 2012, 3:20 AM), http://www.abajournal.com/magazine/article/be_nice_more_states_are_treating_incivility_as_a_possible_ethics_violation/

ethnic groups is well known by now.[150] The point, however, is that the form of civility lost from that earlier age is too closely associated with the bar's serious sins, and was not given to all. That form should not be sought. It was a form that encouraged taking care of one's own socioeconomic/practice cohort, and excluding from the practice cohort if not the practice itself those regarded as unworthy because of their skin color, gender, religion, or ethnicity.

From colonial times, outsiders were treated by more established fellow lawyers not with civility but with scorn and exclusion. The early Massachusetts bar, rabidly federalist, ostracized the handful of anti-federalist lawyers who attempted to practice in the state.[151] One target of the New York federalist's exclusion fought back. Thomas Addis Emmet, hated because he was Irish and because his brother was an Irish patriot, ascertained the league formed to exclude him, and "he did not wait for an attack. He proved the assailant. Whenever he met any of the league at the Bar, he assumed the attitude of professional war, and he lost nothing by contact."[152]

On the 19th-century Western frontier, older lawyers took whatever advantage of younger lawyers that their experience would allow. The older lawyers kept their experience "as a close monopoly," forcing younger lawyers to "run a gauntlet of technicalities" at a "considerable tuition fee to be paid by [the young lawyers'] clients."[153]

The blatant discrimination against the emerging plaintiffs' bar in the late 19th and early 20th centuries is well known and documented. With some conspicuous exceptions to the contrary, Jewish law review editors were excluded from partnerships in the prestigious corporate law firms until after World War II; blacks and women were outsiders until their token entry in the late 1960s and early 1970s.[154]

Although the organized bar's efforts at exclusion retarded the entry of outsiders into the profession, the eventual democratization and diversification of the profession remade the profession into a diverse, pluralistic entity that would be hardly recognizable to Hoffman, Sharswood, Baldwin, Drinker, Root, and the drafters of the 1908 Canons.[155] If the law is what the lawyers are, and the lawyers are what the law schools make them, then a profession is what its members are, and its moral common ground is that of its members. Backward-looking aspiration fails the contemporary profession in its modern incarnation.

---

[150] *See generally,* AUERBACH, *supra* note 86 (describing the bar's history of discrimination); WARREN, *supra* note 104, at 303–310.

[151] *See* WARREN, *supra* note 104, at 306.

[152] *Id.* at 303 (quoting CHARLES G. HAINES, MEMOIR OF THOMAS ADDISON EMMET (1829)).

[153] JOSEPH G. BALDWIN, THE FLUSH TIMES OF ALABAMA AND MISSISSIPPI: A SERIES OF SKETCHES (1854), *reprinted in* NOLAN, *supra* note 130, at 113–115.

[154] *Id.* at 29–30.

[155] *See Blueprint, supra* note 2, at 251–252; ABA Section of Legal Educ. and Admissions to the Bar, *Legal Education and Professional Development—An Educational Continuum,* 11–27 (1992) (commonly known as the MacCrate Report); Thomas D. Morgan, *Economic Reality Facing 21st Century Lawyers,* 69 WASH. L. REV. 625, 625–626 (1994); RICHARD L. ABEL, AMERICAN LAWYERS tbls. 26–30 (1989).

Thomas Shaffer was among the commentators who recognized the backward-looking view of the profession's 1980s and 1990s professionalism drive.

> The gentlemen's ethic, in and out of the legal profession, has always implied that lawyers are superior people. The ABA campaign, if it were to admit that what it is pushing is the old-fashioned American lawyer-gentlemen's ethic, would find itself involved in a latter-day defense of elitism—of a superiority the gentleman-lawyer has always taken for granted.[156]

Not only were the proposals backward looking, they were ill-founded, Shaffer said.

> [The ABA's report's] section on training in professionalism in law school proposes that law teachers instill the 'principles of the profession' in law students. The Report calls for examinations and investigations and for forcing law students to watch videotapes in which 'experienced lawyers' discuss moral issues in a 'Socratic' fashion. Socrates would be appalled. None of that is education. None of it is 'professional.' None of it is ethics. Ethics is talking about morals. Socrates did not set his students down and make them listen to him; he asked questions and listened to them... ethics does not instill principles. Ethics questions principles.[157]

Anthony Kronman was among the prominent academic sounders of alarm.[158] He was surely among the most past glorifying of the commentators during the period. He called for a return to the lawyer-statesman, most examples of which he chose from prior to the 20th century. This lawyer as statesman, Kronman said, acted in the public interest. But surprisingly, nearly all of the examples of lawyer-statesmen he chose were primarily government and not private practice lawyers. This led critics to say that Kronman discounted the historical value of lawyers for clients (whether individual or corporate) and only honored the public servant-lawyer.

> First, by using the label 'lawyer-statesman,' Kronman links the moral authority of the profession as a whole to the accomplishments of its most distinguished public servants. This link, however, is a double-edged sword. All of the lawyers Kronman singles out as exemplifying the lawyer-statesman ideal are respected primarily for their work as public officials or judges rather than for what they did while in private practice.[159] Lawyers can therefore venerate these heroes while at the same time discounting their example for their own

---

[156] Thomas L. Shaffer, *Inaugural Howard Lichtenstein Lecture in Legal Ethics: Lawyer Professionalism as a Moral Argument*, 26 Gonz. L. Rev. 393, 398 (1990).

[157] *Id.* at 410.

[158] Anthony T. Kronman The Lost Lawyer: Failing Ideals of the Legal Profession 3–4 (1993).

[159] David B. Wilkins, *Book Review, Practical Wisdom For Practicing Lawyers: Separating Ideals From Ideology In Legal Ethics*, 108 Harv. L. Rev. 458, 464 (1994).

day-to-day practices on the ground that the public-regarding ideals of lawyer-statesmen have little relevance to what Kronman describes as the 'mundane business of earning a living in the law.'[160]

VIII. Plural Bar

Although the ABA had already declared diversity victory in 1986 when women accounted for 15 percent of the bar, the profession had truly changed by the late 1990s and beyond. Although positions of power had not been widely distributed as yet, the now far more pluralistic profession was no longer of one mind. Now there were competing visions of what it meant to be a good lawyer. Even advertising was not universally seen as evil among powerful members of the bar. Now, instead, one creed articulating one vision could no longer apply. The Seventh Circuit's survey results were claimed to support the need for reform and promises of the good behavior of old. But in fact, according the survey, most lawyers and judges did not believe there was a civility problem in the first instance, hardly inspiring a mandate for reform.[161] But while frustrated judges and the bar elite could still force through creeds filled with old-fashioned values, the rank and file saw little or no need.

There has been a change in the moral common ground in the profession, most of which is for the better. Much of this change is the result of the inability of the bar to control entry and confine it as it once did to the very whitest males.[162] Where will the new moral common ground lie? There is, as yet, no certain answer; there are only signs pointing in particular directions. There are proposed models of the ideal, some of which show more forward-looking promise than others.[163]

For example, Anthony Kronman suggests a refreshing of the lawyer-statesman ideal;[164] David Luban might favor the "moral activist lawyer" as the ideal;[165] Monroe Freedman proposes an ideal of a more client-favoring lawyer who relies heavily on role morality and whose primary moral decision occurs when he or she agrees to represent a particular client.[166] William Simon suggests that lawyers engage in "the practice of justice."[167]

Our more plural profession had existed for barely 10 years during the onset of the civility crisis—hardly long enough to have expressed a change in moral common

---

[160] *Id.* at 465, quoting KRONMAN, *supra* note 163, at 12.

[161] *See* INTERIM REPORT, *supra* note 36.

[162] *See Blueprint*, *supra* note 2, at 251–252 (describing the increasing diversity of the American Bar).

[163] *See, e.g.,* Atkinson *supra* note 74, at 303–320 (identifying three models of the good lawyer and identifying the one favored by the current creeds).

[164] KRONMAN, *supra* note 163.

[165] DAVID LUBAN, LAWYERS AND JUSTICE: AN ETHICAL STUDY xxii (1988).

[166] MONROE H. FREEDMAN, LAWYERS' ETHICS IN AN ADVERSARY SYSTEM 4 (1975).

[167] WILLIAM SIMON, THE PRACTICE OF JUSTICE (2000).

ground in a manner that would be certain to stick and be dominant for the foreseeable future. It took some time for the business lawyer to emerge as the dominant form in the late 19th, early 20th century. The pluralist profession we now have may have to accept that there is no single model of the "good lawyer," unless it is that the good lawyer is the lawyer who is accepting of multiple models of good lawyering. Perhaps that will emerge as the common moral ground, acceptance of multiple models of what makes good lawyering rather than insistence on a single model that represents a description of the current professional elite.

One form of practical wisdom, not the form Kronman declared had been lost,[168] is the practical wisdom of searching for a satisfying middle ground on which to base decisions and moral consensus. It is this middle ground that has moved. The middle has moved because there is a more widely divergent range of views about what the profession is and ought to be represented by those who are of the profession. The wider range of views and experiences of life now form the full landscape of the profession's membership; and unlike past times, even some of the leadership and power in the profession comes from those who hold a broader view of the profession's mission. The search is for a new middle, and given the new diversity at the bar, there may be no true middle.

> Both the culture of law school and the bar's professional rhetoric promote the idea that the profession is unitary, with a single or dominant conception of what it means to be a good lawyer.... Professional rhetoric likewise supports the conception of a unitary profession.... In fact, the profession is not unitary in any meaningful sense. Lawyers do different kinds of work,...[they]work in different organizational settings,...in different geographic settings,...[and] represent different kinds of clients.[169]
>
> [C]omparing the professional ideologies of lawyers across work settings reveals most starkly that the vision of a unitary set of professional values invoked by leaders of the bar is a fiction. Workplace contexts develop widely varying and often mutually contradictory 'local versions' of professionalism. At least some of these are inconsistent with the professional ideals projected in the bar's official rhetoric.[170]

The profession of the new millennium is not our grandfather's legal profession. There is no single version of a good lawyer. And the organized profession lacks the power it once had to impose such a single version.

---

[168] KRONMAN, *supra* note 163, at 2–3.

[169] Eleanor W. Myers, *Simple Truths about Moral Education*, 45 AM. U. L. REV. 823, 839–840 (1996).

[170] ROBERT L. NELSON ET AL., LAWYERS' IDEALS/LAWYERS' PRACTICES: TRANSFORMATION IN THE AMERICAN LEGAL PROFESSION 199 (1992).

IX. Conclusion

For all of the energy and resources that were poured into them, the creeds had virtually no effect. Cries of bad behavior continue to the present. Threats and actions by state bars to enforce civility have continued. In 2012, enforcement of civility notions was on the rise. States are formally enforcing aspiration as if it were rule. ABA presidents were still chiding lawyers for uncivil behavior. "Civility used to be inherent in public discourse. Where did we go wrong?" said then-ABA President Stephen N. Zack in a speech during the 2011 ABA Annual Meeting in Toronto. "As lawyers, we must honor civility."[171] Despite its best efforts to make it so, the spirit of the profession has not been rekindled.

Writing in 1992, Nelson and Trubek saw the situation through clear eyes:

[T]he literature [of the organized bar] reflects this most recent wave of official concern with 'professionalism' and gives the impression that there is a major problem to which the organized bar has turned its attention. If the amount of time devoted to the issue, the prestige of the people involved, and the attention paid to it by leaders of the bar throughout the country are any indication, one would have to conclude that the organized bar is very disturbed by the possibility that professionalism is in decline, and that it is committed to doing something about this decline. If one analyzes the reports, editorials, and commentary on professionalism in some detail, however, the situation seems less clear-cut. First, it is hard to derive any precise or concrete notion of 'professionalism' from much of the literature. The definitions offered are vague; examples of 'unprofessional conduct' are rare. Second, although the rhetoric suggests a decline in professionalism, no clear or convincing account is given of why that might be occurring today and what forces might lie behind alleged lapses from professional norms. Third, although a number of 'remedies' are offered to curb the decline of professionalism, these are so diffuse in nature that they undermine the very idea that they deal with any coherent issue, and often seem to consist of cosmetic generalities or moralistic exhortations.[172]

The new profession, barely a generation old, has begun to exert its influence on the profession's moral ground. Where it will land is still an open question. But with certainty, it will not reflect the 19th-century values that the profession sought to demand all lawyers return to during the civility crisis. The creeds had no chance of affecting the developing lawyer culture. The new lawyer culture was a part of all that existed around it. Levels of competition were heightening in business, government, politics, and daily life. In the face of such change, the legal profession imagined it could exist apart, in a 19th-century world that the profession conjured from myths and fables and legends of a gentler golden age.

---

[171] Filisko, *supra* note162.
[172] Nelson & Trubek, *supra* note 10, at 177, 189.

8

The Fear of Sharing Power: MDPs and ABS

Beginning in the 1930s with the realization that their corporate clients might want to provide legal services to their customers, the profession has expressed its fear of sharing control over the provision of legal services in multiple ways. The fear and attendant refusal to adapt has continued to persistently manifest itself, through the "Fear of Sears" while the Kutak Commission proposals were before the ABA House of Delegates in the early 1980s, to the resistance to Multidisciplinary Practice (MDPs) and Alternative Business Structures (ABS). In 2012, the profession's almost violently negative reaction to the modest ABS proposals made by the Ethics 20/20 Commission continues the story. Rules dictating exclusive ownership of law firms by lawyers and prohibitions on lawyers sharing fees with non-lawyers execute the profession's desire to resist sharing power with others.[1]

Of course, MDPs and ABS are not precisely the same phenomenon, as the Ethics 20/20 Commission has tried to convince members of the House of Delegates.[2] In an MDP, lawyers would be cast as partners with other professionals, and they would share power as organizational equals. In an ABS setting, outside ownership of a law firm (or any organization that provides legal services) would have a superior organizational position to the lawyers. But in either setting, lawyers would be required to share power. More important from the profession's position, the profession itself would have to yield some measure of control over lawyer conduct. And this, it seems, the American legal profession simply cannot abide.

By prohibiting lawyers from sharing fees with non-lawyers, the profession prohibits partnerships with non-lawyers, or MDPs. The prohibition reaches so-called Wall Street and Main Street MDPs. Wall Street MDPs would partner lawyers with accountants, financial planners, lobbyists, and other business consultants, typically in urban environments. Main Street MDPs would partner lawyers with small-town occupations such as tow truck drivers, funeral home directors, and local versions of Wall Street professionals such as accountants or financial planners. The market has long wished to access MDPs, allowing a business to engage in one-stop professional services shopping and allowing individuals to do the same when planning

---

[1] MODEL RULES OF PROF'L CONDUCT R. 1.5(d), 5.4, 5.7 (2012).
[2] James Podgers, *Summer Job: Ethics 20/20 Commission Shelves Nonlawyer Ownership, Focuses on Other Proposals*, June 1, 2012 A.B.A. J. 12 (2012).

retirement and other ordinary passages of life that simultaneously involve legal and nonlegal issues. Lawyers and other professionals have found ways to edge close to forming MDPs without violating the legal profession's norms. "Strategic alliances" create close working relationships between law firms and other professionals without the prohibited sharing of fees.

The rules of the American legal profession also prohibit the market from owning shares in a law firm. Neither non-lawyer stockholders nor corporate ownership of law firms is permitted. Dubbed Alternative Business Structures (ABS) by the government-enacted reforms in the United Kingdom and Australia, the U.S. legal profession has thus far prohibited any such arrangements.[3] The ABS innovation in the United Kingdom is young and still developing, but so far, no untoward consequences have been felt in Australia, where the experiment has been ongoing for nearly a decade.

The profession has resisted sharing power over law firms on the claim that non-lawyers would not be sensitive to the ethical demands under which lawyers must function, and as part owners would undermine the high ethical standards of the profession. To be sure, each profession and business functions differently in ethical terms, owing to the nature of the particular profession or business. Doctors serve patients without the necessity of harming another's interests: when a doctor cures a patient's disease, there is no other individual who suffers a corresponding loss of health. Likewise, properly functioning accountants serve a client without harming others. Lawyers, by contrast, often serve a client by harming another. When a plaintiff wins a judgment, a defendant pays it. When a lawyer's client purchases property, the act excludes others who also wished to own the property. These fundamental differences among professions do drive different ethical norms per profession. Lawyers' conflict of interest concerns are fundamentally different from accountants' conflict of interest concerns, for example. These differences explain why accountants can serve business competitors without pause, while lawyers must always be cautious when doing so because the two clients' interests may be frequently at odds and require the lawyer to impermissibly choose sides, harming one client to serve another. Similarly, because lawyers represent their clients' interests to an outside world in the form of courts, legislatures, and administrative bodies, lawyers are far more likely to encounter clients with opposing interests than are accountants, who, in theory at least, serve each client in a sort of individual silo. The circumstances allowing a test of whether professions with varied ethical norms can function together have been rare. The aspects of the Enron defalcations that emerged from the collective interests of lawyers and accountants under the Arthur Andersen umbrella provide an exception. Otherwise, the legal profession's claim rests on the assertion that non-lawyers will demand lawyers in their charge or with whom they are partnered to behave in a way that offends lawyer norms. Whether that is so remains an untested proposition. The counterargument is that

---

[3] The minor exception, creating a very modest crack in the prohibition, is D.C. Bar Rule 5.5.

non-lawyer owners or partners of lawyers would want the lawyers to avoid ethical issues that would threaten the lawyers' licenses, produce malpractice liability, disqualify the lawyers from representation, and result in other highly unprofitable results of unethical conduct.

I. The Development of Fear

The 1908 Canons said nothing that would prohibit non-lawyer ownership of law firms or partnership with non-lawyers. Based as they were on Hoffman's 1834 work and Sharswood's 1853 work, as channeled through the 1887 Alabama Code of Ethics, it undoubtedly never occurred to anyone that a lawyer, a solo in that time frame, would or could be owned by anyone but himself. Lawyers had only recently begun partnering with one another.

Neither was there a clear and binding statement of the contours of the lawyer monopoly. The understanding of what constituted lawyer's work was informal. Early legislative efforts to define the practice of law, and thus the lawyer monopoly, spoke almost exclusively of appearance in court on behalf of another. But modern practice, especially corporate practice, fast outstripped that narrow definition. Concern about corporations practicing law appeared early in the 20th century but grew rapidly in the 1920s. By the late 1920s, a spate of banks, trust companies, title insurance companies, and others infringing on what the legal profession regarded as its turf caused an uproar of lawyer demand for adoption of unauthorized practice of law (UPL) statutes. Lawyer-dominated state legislatures obliged.[4] Late 1920s amendments to the ABA Canons[5] and eventually a 1961 ABA Formal Opinion[6] set the course for the language of the Model Code that was copied to become that of Model Rule 5.4 in 1983. Since then, the unwavering commitment of the organized bar has been to prohibit both non-lawyer ownership of the provision of legal services and partnerships between lawyers and non-lawyers.

Occasionally, when a creative enterprise has tried to provide access to legal services through a corporate-owned model, for example, Consolidated Legal Forms, Inc., in 1980 and LegalZoom in the 2010s, the profession's quick and stern response has been unauthorized practice allegations.[7] Consolidated Legal Forms did maintain

---

[4] Barlow F. Christensen, *The Unauthorized Practice of Law: Do Good Fences Really Make Good Neighbors—or Even Good Sense?*, 5 AM. B. FOUND. RES. J. 159, 189–197 (1980).

[5] Canons 33, 34 and 35 (1928).

[6] ABA Comm. on Ethics & Prof'l Responsibility, Formal Op. 303 (1961).

[7] 386 So. 2d 797 (Fla. 198) (ownership by non-lawyers of legal forms provider ruled unauthorized practice of law); LegalZoom has been identified as one of the most innovative new companies. *See* David Lidsky, *The World's 50 Most Innovative Companies*, Fast Company (Feb. 2012), http://www.fastcompany.com/most-innovative-companies/2012/legalzoom; LegalZoom has also been accused of unauthorized practice by various state bars. *See, e.g.,* Connecticut Bar Association Comm. on Unauthorized Practice of Law, Informal Op. 35 (2008), *available at* http://www1.ctbar.org/sectionsandcommittees/committees/UPL/08-01.pdf.

corporate restrictions on how its lawyers would represent clients, curtailing the length of a client interview, for example. But no comparable outcry has accompanied the far more detailed brand of limitation on lawyer representation that is routinely exercised by insurance carriers when lawyers represent their insureds.[8] The lucrative insurance defense practice is simply a necessary part of doing business for lawyers. And in recent years, numerous major corporate clients have imposed, as they can with no real bargaining in today's legal market, significant policy directives on their outside law firms. These "outside counsel" policies now sometimes direct law firms in their hiring, staffing, HR policies, environmental policies, and more.[9] But more open direction by corporate entities or non-lawyer professionals in the form of ABS and MDPs is too much for the profession to swallow.

Despite the strong stance, there have been periodic proposals for forward-looking reform, mostly driven by market desire and competition. The market seems never willing to let the idea rest for too long. Multidisciplinary practice is the nine-lived cat of the lawyer ethics world.

II. The Fear of Sears

In the process of reforming the Model Code into what would eventually become the Model Rules, the Kutak Commission considered the bar's prohibitions on multidisciplinary practice and corporate investment in law firms. The Commission saw both the difficulty of precisely defining the practice of law to exclude corporate-owned practice and the market demand for legal services to middle-income people that were not being effectively provided by the traditional lawyer or law firm. Venturing a forward-looking view, the Commission proposed that corporate ownership of law firms be permitted, provided safeguards would be in place to protect the lawyer's independent professional judgment.[10]

One question and its answer derailed any possibility of the MDP and corporate investment proposal during the House of Delegates debate on the package of Kutak Commission proposals: "Does this mean Sears can open a law firm?" Geoffrey Hazard, Reporter for the Commission said "Yes," and the debate ended with a resounding defeat of the proposal. The "fear of Sears," as it has come to be called, conjured images of major retailers selling not only insurance and financial advice through in-store affiliates, but legal services. The attractive possibility that ordinary Americans might be able to obtain simple legal services quickly and easily was of no matter. Also of no moment to the Delegates was the reality that the proposal

---

[8] *See, e.g.,* Pfeifer v. Sentry Ins., 745 F. Supp. 1434 (E.D. Wis. 1990).

[9] Christopher J. Whelan & Neta Ziv, *Privatizing Professionalism: Client Control of Lawyers' Ethics*, 80 FORDHAM L. REV. 2577 (2012).

[10] CENTER FOR PROFESSIONAL RESPONSIBILITY, AMERICAN BAR ASSOCIATION, A LEGISLATIVE HISTORY: THE DEVELOPMENT OF THE ABA MODEL RULES OF PROFESSIONAL CONDUCT, 1982–2005, 579–581 (Chicago 2006).

would allow law firms to raise capital to expand, to finance contingent fee cases, to add new technologies, to explore providing new services. Only the fear of competition from corporate interests and the fear of losing lawyer control over professional independence were of consequence that day.

The rationale expressed has always been protection of a lawyer's independent judgment, but often there is a curious reference that imagines lawyers as if they were still 17th-century British nobles doing legal representation as a rich man's hobby. The Model Rules' legislative history suggests that the profession cannot allow non-lawyer ownership interests because "a non-lawyer, motivated by a desire for profit, would be unable to appreciate the ethical considerations in representing a client."[11] By contrast, according to this reasoning, lawyers have no "desire for profit" and have had no difficulty maintaining focus on client interests before lawyer interests. In fact, the profession, when it is more convenient, has decried the fact that lawyers are so very profit driven since the earliest moments of the 20th century and before:

> [T]he evil [of lawyer contentiousness]...is not so much a professional as an American fault. It has its source in our inordinate love for the almighty dollar.[12]

It is not news that law is a business; it is not news that the profession continues to deny that it is so.

The profession shows a remarkable talent for deluding itself about its disconnection from business and profit, when in fact its motives are to forestall any sharing of its profit with non-lawyer investors. The multiple places in the legal press where one can review the "profits per partner" standings of the major law firms more accurately describes the "desire for profit" among lawyers than pious statements made to justify defeat of a business form that is so demanded by the market that it repeatedly rises from the dead.

The defeat of the Kutak Commission proposal effectively killed the idea of lawyer participation in MDPs for nearly two decades.

III. Rise of de facto MDPs

Meanwhile, as the profession slept, client demand instigated the rise of de facto MDPs. The Big Five accounting firms (PricewaterhouseCoopers, Deloitte Touche Tohmatsu, Ernst & Young, KPMG, and Arthur Andersen) became sizable legal employers during the 1990s.

By January 1998, Arthur Andersen had subsidiaries practicing law in England, France, Spain, and Australia. All told, the firm had more than 1,500 lawyers working in 27 different countries. Deloitte Touche Tohmatsu had 586 lawyers working

---

[11] *Id.*
[12] Proceedings of the Association of American Law Schools 11 (1906).

in 14 countries. In July 1999, KPMG's tax practice was growing rapidly, from 150 to 300 lawyers. KPMG had more than 650 employees with law degrees in its U.S. offices. By 1999, the Big Five employed more than 5,500 non-tax lawyers throughout the world. Only two law firms in the world employed more attorneys than PricewaterhouseCoopers, the largest accounting employer of attorneys.

These lawyers were not practicing law, or so said their employers. They were consulting, or "practicing tax." Had they been practicing law and openly admitted as much, they would be patently in violation of their lawyer ethics code. Whether they were engaged in the unauthorized practice of law was less clear, but utterly crucial to the legal profession.

Law firms were unhappy with these changes, believing the Big Five to be acting as prohibited MDPs. The bar ethics rules could only reach the conduct of the individual lawyers. To police the firms, the profession would have to turn to the uncertain world of unauthorized practice of law. Ill at ease about what courts would determine to be the scope of the lawyer monopoly, the organized profession did little except for an unsuccessful move against Arthur Andersen in Texas.

The states did respond in more tepid ways, asserting in resolution form their objections to MDPs and implicitly to the Big Five's unofficial MDPs. In June of 1999, the New York State Bar Association passed a resolution explaining that such organizations will "adversely and irreparably affect the independence and other fundamental principles of the legal profession" unless it could be shown that clients and society would not be harmed. Such resolutions shifted the burden of proof to the MDPs. As any litigator knows, when little evidence exists pointing one way or the other, the placement of the burden decides the controversy. Other states bars, such as the ones in Florida and Ohio, also expressed concern and requested that the matter be studied and debated before any decisions were made.[13]

Still, the Big Five continued to grow its legal business. "Accounting firms are expanding and providing more than just traditional accounting services. These firms [were] 'aggressively soliciting clients [and] offering services remarkably similar to those traditionally offered by law firms....'"[14] And the firms were not just limiting themselves to work in the United States but instead, were still expanding worldwide. The *American Lawyer* in 2000 reported that Ernst & Young had at least 850 lawyers in a total of 32 countries, and that more than 600 of those lawyers were providing services in Europe. The firms were also working on acquisitions abroad. Ernst & Young had connections in Canada and had acquired Donahue & Partners, a captive Toronto law firm. KPMG Peat Marwick had close to a thousand lawyers working for it worldwide, and around the turn of the century it acquired the largest

---

[13] Edward J. Cleary, *Multidisciplinary Practice: Minnesota Moves Forward*, BENCH & BAR OF MINNESOTA, Sept. 2001.

[14] Katherine L. Harrison, *Multidisciplinary Practices: Changing the Global View of the Legal Profession*, 21 U. PA. J. INT'L ECON. L. 879, 902 (2000) (quoting Commission on Multidisciplinary Practice to the ABA House of Delegates, Background Paper on Multidisciplinary Practice: Issues and Developments, Jan. 1999).

law firm in France, DPMG Fidal Peat International. In the United Kingdom, KPMG then created its own law firm, Klegal, anticipating that multidisciplinary partnerships would soon be approved in the United Kingdom. Around the same time, KPMG created an alliance with U.S. law firm Morrison & Foerster, marking the first major tie-up between a Big Five accounting firm and a U.S. law firm. By this time, PricewaterhouseCoopers was making the most extensive use of lawyers, with more than 1,600 lawyers in 39 countries, 350 of these in 17 different European countries. This firm also announced its intention to build the fifth largest law firm in the world by the year 2004, estimating that it would employ 3,000 lawyers and generate one billion dollars in revenue.[15]

Lawyers were out of step with the market. While lawyers scrambled to find strategies to fight the expanding de facto MDPs, the market wanted the MDP option. A *Financial Times* survey from September 1999 revealed that 75 percent of major American corporations would consider using the MDPs for work needed. Meanwhile, lawyers were busy reflecting on the history of the battle between law and business, and complaining that the Big Five were creating nontraditional global connections, offering an expansive array of specialties, and were corrupting the legal profession's legitimacy.[16] Because lawyers working for the Big Five denied that they were actually providing legal services, fear developed that similar claims could open the door to non-lawyers doing lawyers' work throughout the economy.

Law firms wanted the power to compete with the de facto MDPs on a level field. The organized profession preferred to put the accounting firms out of the "law-consulting" business.

IV. Multidisciplinary Practice Commission

In the years following the ABA rejection of the Kutak Commission proposal in 1983, the organized profession watched as de facto MDPs satisfied a market demand. U.S. law firms were paying more attention than their organizational representatives as their market shrank and began clamoring for equity in the marketplace. As a group, the Big Five had become the most significant employer of the law trained, and yet it was not "practicing law." The organized bar felt largely powerless to stop the trend because of the vague unauthorized practice standards, and because the market was four-square behind the MDP concept, even if the Big Five had to continue its illusion that it was not doing legal work. The market understood

---

[15] *Id.*

[16] Yves Dezalay & Bryant G. Garth, *The Confrontation between the Big Five and Big Law: Turf Battles and Ethical Debates as Contests for Professional Credibility*, 29 Law & Soc. Inquiry 615, 633–637 (2004). *See also* Yves Dezalay & Bryant G. Garth, The Big Five Versus Big Law: Confrontational Rhetoric in the Service of Legitimating Shifting Relationships between Business and Law (J. Drolshammer & M. Pfeifer eds., Kluwer Law Int'l 2001).

and registered its approval. In Europe, MDPs were gaining official ground. U.S. law firms felt the pinch both at home and abroad.

After years of being in denial about the rise of de facto MDPs, the ABA was jump-started into action by the reaction to an *ABA Journal* article called "Squeeze Play."[17] The article highlighted the competitive disadvantage of law firms as compared to the Big Five's seemingly endless freedom to expand its services and markets. Describing the competition from accounting firms for legal business, the article quoted lawyers who saw a "holy war" on the horizon. They characterized the competition not as a matter of competence or quality of service for the client, but as "a question of morality." Gibeaut alerted the legal profession that the "huge accounting firms are well-armed with billions of dollars in revenues, making even the largest law firms appear like specks in the marketplace." They were accomplishing all this with "consumer-directed, one-stop shopping for professional services," something U.S. law firms could not provide because of the profession's own constraints in the form of bar ethics rules.

Gibeaut warned that "the battle" was spreading with the entry of smaller accounting firms, banks, investment firms, and others straying into territory formerly held by law firms. Talk of "professionalism" was being scoffed at as medieval when offered as the legal profession's reason for opposing what the market was demanding.

The problem of accountant intrusion on legal markets was seen as being exacerbated by the possible role of the World Trade Organization (WTO) in administering trade treaties that purported to govern cross-border provision of professional services. The WTO had a history of hostility to "self-interested regulation," such as the American legal profession's.

And the worries were not confined to the Big Five and the major Wall Street law firms. Small city lawyers wondered why they were prohibited from forming partnerships with financial planners and counselors to serve their elderly clientele's financial needs. Some of these lawyers called the profession's position "bizarre." "They just want to circle the wagons and talk about professionalism."[18]

If talk of professionalism would not do the trick, what would? Lawrence Fox, who later played an instrumental role on the Ethics 2000 Commission in fending off proposals for a confidentiality exception for corporate frauds, confessed that the issue "hurts my head just to think about it.... If the profession doesn't get its act together, we're just going to get bulldozed." The Gibaeut article sent a wake-up call to the profession.

One answer was to attack the MDPs for claimed UPL violations. But the likelihood of success was highly questionable, especially to the extent they were engaged in tax consulting. The blurry line between authorized tax work, properly done by a wide range of non-lawyer entities and professionals, and the practice of law could

---

[17] John Gibeaut, *Squeeze Play*, 84 A.B.A. J. 42 (1998).
[18] *Id.*

not support UPL actions. Many federal agencies explicitly allow non-lawyers to engage their administrative processes on others' behalf, further distorting any distinctions to be drawn. The tax act reforms of the late 1990s afforded an evidentiary privilege between a client and an authorized tax consultant, further blending law advice with tax advice and advantaging the accounting firms in the marketplace. Despite all odds against, the Texas Bar, one of the most aggressive and well funded, did engage its UPL process against Arthur Andersen (AA), claiming that AA was "engaged in the unauthorized practice of law by offering 'attorney only' services," such as estate planning, drafting corporate and partnership documents, and "filing petitions in the Tax Court." Andersen responded with guns blazing and after 11 months, the Texas Bar withdrew its complaints, leaving the market open to tax advisors and their non-lawyer employers.

At least to the extent that a lawyer feared bar discipline, the profession's own rules gave it power to restrict lawyers themselves from partnering with non-lawyers or accepting corporate financing and ownership. But absent successful UPL enforcement, the profession was powerless to police entity conduct. It effectively had no control over the Big Five.

Without a robust, lawyer-favoring enforcement of the UPL laws and with more and more lawyers willing to work for accounting firms without fear of bar discipline, the profession seemed powerless to stem the wave of competition that was inundating the profession's beach property. One option was left in the eyes of some reform-minded lawyers: change the profession's rules to allow lawyers to compete on a level field with accountants and other professional encroachers.

Enter the ABA Multidisciplinary Practice Commission. The Commission heard about the rise of the Big Five and of the market's desire for MDPs' one-stop professional services shopping. To no one's surprise, corporate interests lined up to testify of their desire to have the MDP option. But so did small businesses[19] and representatives of ordinary consumers. For example, Affordable Consumer Services of Alabama testified that low income people need to make use of multiple professionals and would be benefited by having MDPs that include social workers, lawyers, financial counselors, and so on. Family law practitioners suggested that their clients could use the combination of talents available from lawyers, counselors, family planning experts, and others.[20] An AARP advocate testified about the MDP needs of senior citizens.[21] Testimony made clear that the long-standing debate about whether law is a profession or a business did not exist outside the legal profession itself. Law firms are businesses that provide legal services, pure and simple. The

---

[19] ABA Commission on Multidisciplinary Practice, *Statement of George Abbott, MDPs Hearings* (Feb. 12, 2000), *available at* http://www.abanet.org/cpr/abbott.html.

[20] ABA Commission on Multidisciplinary Practice, *Comments of Marna S. Tucker* (Apr. 7, 1999), *available at* http://www.abanet.org/cpr/tucker3.html.

[21] ABA Commission on Multidisciplinary Practice, *Testimony of Wayne Moore, Director of AARP Legal Advocacy Group* (July 27, 1999), available at www.abanet.org/cpr/aarp.html.

notion that they are unaffected by desire for profit and exist to protect client needs first and foremost is regarded as an idea that is no different from the customer-service, market-driven desire of other businesses to serve their clients well so that the business's profits will increase.

The Commission heard the testimony and made essentially a five-part proposal in its 1999 Report:

1. An MDP not controlled by lawyers could be formed only if it would provide the highest courts of the relevant states with "written undertakings" that the MDP would "establish and maintain procedures protecting the independent professional judgment" of its lawyers;
2. Annually, the managers of the MDP would certify to those courts that their procedures had been observed;
3. At any time, a court could initiate its own investigation to determine whether the MDP was complying with its undertakings;
4. The MDPs would bear the cost of administering this mechanism; and
5. Noncompliance by an MDP could result in the "withdrawal of its permission to deliver legal services or other appropriate remedial measures ordered by the court."

The Commission had been created in the second half of 1998 and submitted a proposal for consideration by the ABA House of Delegates at its annual meeting in the summer of 1999. The Commission moved quickly, perhaps too quickly. The one-year ABA presidential term may have pressed the Commission to somewhat hasty action, issuing its Report in time for 1999 ABA action. The Big Five urged the Commission to propose a form of MDP that would permit a Big Five firm to come out in the open and acknowledge its de facto blend of legal and other profession services. The Commission assured the legal profession that it was "particularly mindful" that "appropriate safeguards" would be needed to protect the "core values" of the legal profession in the context of MDPs. It identified three core values: "professional independence of judgment, the protection of confidential client information, and loyalty to the client through the avoidance of conflicts of interest."[22]

The Commission worked to make MDPs palatable to the legal profession. It built proposals that would place not only an MDP's lawyers, but the entire MDP under the legal profession's rules of professional ethics. In other words, if other professionals will behave as lawyers do, they may associate with lawyers.

Although the 1999 ABA Commission on Multidisciplinary Practice Report attempted to deal with questions of legal ethics that might arise if the practice of law by lawyers were integrated into an enterprise in which non-lawyers had a

---

[22] Sydney M. Cone, III, *Five Years Later: Reconsidering the Original ABA Report on MDP*, 29 Law & Soc. Inquiry 597 (Summer 2004).

significant degree of ultimate control, the Report failed to satisfy its many critics. For lawyers worried about giving up any control over lawyers' work, the proposed mechanism of self-certification of compliance with rules of legal ethics was not enough to allay fears. Neither did the Big Five welcome the 1999 Report. They were opposed to being required to observe the rules on conflicts of interest applicable to the legal profession, and they were also seeking the right to include legal services in the services offered by them to the general public without the legal profession's tradition of judicial supervision of those services. Perhaps both lawyers and the Big Five wanted too much. Both complained that the 1999 Report did too little for them.

Distracting attention from a direct debate over the merits of the 1999 Report, the New York Bar in July 1999 formed a special committee to consider the law governing firm structure and operation. This development caused some to think more time to study the issue was needed before any ABA action would be ripe. Meanwhile, state bar after state bar initiated studies to determine whether MDPs should be permitted. Some scholars supported the Report and the modest opening it created for MDPs to exist within the lawyer ethics rules.[23]

When the time came for the House of Delegates' consideration of the 1999 Report, the Report was about to be rejected outright when an alternative was proposed and passed by a 3-1 margin: the alternative said no change should be made without further study.[24]

Study further the Commission did, and it heard essentially the same messages about market demand from Wall Street and Main Street. Corporate clients wanted, and ordinary people needed, multifaceted professional services. As the Commission continued to hear of the need for MDPs, the writing was already on the House of Delegates' wall. There would be no approval of MDPs in the ABA. The Commission heard the world; the House of Delegates knew better.

The ABA finally put the Commission and its proposals out of their misery at the 2000 Annual Meeting. Still, the House did not speak for everyone when it disbanded the Commission. The Commission's Report was supported by many lawyers who embraced the regulated-MDP option, claiming that it would then bring uniformity of standards back to the profession.[25] And, of course, the ABA action to disband the Commission did nothing to stop the Big Five's rapid expansion into more and more markets for legal services. Other events would soon accomplish what the profession could not.

---

[23] *See, e.g.,* Laurel S. Terry, *A Primer on MDPs: Should The "No" Rule Become A New Rule?,* 72 TEMPLE L. REV. 869 (1999); Ronald Rotunda, *Multidisciplinary Practice: An Idea Whose Time Has Come,* 3 PROFESSIONAL RESPONSIBILITY, LEGAL ETHICS, AND LEGAL EDUCATION NEWS 3 (Federalist Society, No. 2, 1999).

[24] *ABA Refuses to Change Ethics Rules Unless Studies of MDPs Dispel Concerns,* 15 LAW. MAN. PROF. CONDUCT 396 (1999).

[25] Terry, *supra* note 22.

V. Enron and Sarbanes-Oxley to the Rescue.

The Enron and WorldCom defalcations changed everything in the MDP world and saved a bent-on-no-reform legal profession. Without Enron, without Sarbanes-Oxley (SOX), MDPs were eating the legal profession's proverbial lunch, and in time, would so severely have cut into the market share for legal services that had 20 years earlier been the exclusive province of law firms.

Suddenly, opponents of MDPs had their evidence: some aspects of the Enron frauds could be traced to the close financial relationship ties of the Andersen accountants and the Andersen lawyers who, of course, professed that they were not practicing law. Never mind the possible misconduct of Enron's outside counsel; never mind the possible misconduct of inside counsel. It was Arthur Andersen's consultant "counsel" that mattered to MDP critics. Almost overnight, MDPs were declared dead in the United States. Again.

The resultant government response was Sarbanes-Oxley, which effectively prohibited accounting firms from employing lawyers who pretended not to practice law.

In the House, SOX received 423 votes in favor with 8 abstaining, and in the Senate it received 99 votes in favor with 1 abstaining. The main purpose of the Act was to create stricter disclosure requirements, financial report certification requirements, and corporate governance rules in order to instill public confidence in economic exchanges. The Big Five were disadvantaged by the Act outlawing accounting firms from providing certain consulting services. If an accounting firm was hired to perform an audit, that firm was prohibited from also rendering valuation or appraisal services, legal or other expert services, actuarial services, or management services to that same client.

The Enron debacle followed by the adoption of SOX saved the legal profession from its feared competition. Prior to Enron and SOX, the MDPs associated with the Big Five accounting firms were an irresistible and rapidly growing force. Their sizes were comparable to global law firm giants Clifford Chance and Baker & McKenzie. Figures reported in May of 2000 gave Clifford Chance over 3,000 lawyers, including the then-recent merger with Rogers and Wells in New York; Baker & McKenzie, almost 2,800 lawyers; 2,860 for Andersen Legal; 1,500 for PricewaterhouseCoopers' Landwell; and 3,300 for KPMG's Klegal.

By 2003, Clifford Chance was reporting some 3,700 lawyers, and Baker & McKenzie 3,200, a collective increase of more than 16 percent. By contrast, Andersen Legal no longer existed, and Ernst and Young's legal network numbered 2,600 lawyers, Landwell 2,850, and KLegal some 2,000 (1,650 of whom were in Europe).[26] Landwell's growth

---

[26] Eric L. Martin, *Liberalization and Cravathism: How Liberalization Triggered the Reorganization of the Legal Profession in Germany and Japan,* 43 STAN. J. INT'L L. 184–191 (2007); Ben Jaaniste & Reena Sengupta, *Crowds Desert the One-Stop Shops,* FIN. TIMES (London), Mar. 24, 2003, at 16.

occurred when it absorbed some of Andersen's firms. The *Economist* reported that "lawyers tied to PwC are leaving in droves." K Legal group formally separated from KPMG, The *National Law Journal* reported that the changing landscape resulted from "market decisions, including the U.S. Sarbanes-Oxley Act—which restrict the provision of non-audit services to audit clients, particularly legal services."[27] In 2004, the *Economist* stated that "sobered by their experience... [since the late 1990s], the 'Big Four' accountants are retreating from the legal arena, with KPMG the first to the towel in altogether."[28] The de facto MDPs and their threat to the U.S. law firms were no more.

As well, within its purview, SOX and the resultant SEC regulations reformed lawyer ethics, despite outcries of foul from the profession. The diminution of the duty of confidentiality and increase in the duty to report client frauds occasioned by SOX was perhaps the most significant single lawyer ethics reform of the prior 50 years. Of course, the profession had its chances to implement its own such reforms but rejected them in the consideration of the Kutak Commission report in 1983,[29] again in 1991, this time from its ethics committee, and again when Ethics 2000 proposed such reforms in 2002.[30] Government imposed its will on the profession, albeit in a watered-down fashion after heavy professional lobbying.[31] The ABA's Ethics 2000 Commission had sent the academic proponent of the eventual SEC regulation "packing"[32] less than a year before Sarbanes-Oxley section 307 ("eerily captioned 'Rules of Professional Responsibility for Lawyers'" by profession opponent Lawrence Fox)[33] was passed, triggering the SEC to adopt its regulations.

The profession complained bitterly about the government intrusion on its claimed self-governance rights. But this time, the profession had ceded that responsibility by repeated failures to self-regulate effectively. And, although never officially acknowledged, the legislation had saved the profession from the greater threat of the Big Five.

The legal profession might claim that the legal profession itself resisted the professional and ethical challenge that was raised by the Big Five as they moved into legal services. But that is an empty claim. Without Enron, the rejection of the MDP Commission's proposals would have meant little or nothing to the Big Five. Their

---

[27] Bryant G. Garth, *"'From the Trenches and the Towers': MDPs after Enron/Andersen: Multidisciplinary Practice after Enron: Eliminating a Competitor but Not the Competition,"* 29 LAW & SOC. INQUIRY 591 (Summer 2004).

[28] *International Law Firms: Trying to Get the Right Balance,* ECONOMIST (Feb. 26, 2004), *available at* http://www.economist.com/node/2459364.

[29] CENTER FOR PROFESSIONAL RESPONSIBILITY, AMERICAN BAR ASSOCIATION, A LEGISLATIVE HISTORY: THE DEVELOPMENT OF THE ABA MODEL RULES OF PROFESSIONAL CONDUCT, 1982–2005 100 (Chicago, 2006).

[30] *Id.* at 117–129.

[31] *Id.* at 291–314.

[32] Lawrence J. Fox, *The Academics Have It Wrong: Hysteria Is No Substitute for Sound Public Policy Analysis* at 864, in Nancy Rapoport and Bala Dharan, ENRON CORPORATE FIASCOS AND THEIR IMPLICATIONS (Foundation Press 2004).

[33] *Id.* at 865.

market would likely have continued to expand to the detriment of professionally hamstrung U.S. law firms.

Further, the profession's argument is itself based on the abstract position that the lawyers working for accountants would be unable to resist the pressure to take ethical shortcuts. However, when Bryant Garth conducted a number of interviews in Europe in 1999 and 2000, he did not find evidence that these abuses in fact materialized. The negative assumption directed toward accountants is based in large part on a mistrust of accountants' ethics. But of course, the two professions are simply different in their relationships with clients and their clients' competitors, whether they be business or legal claim competitors. Neither is inherently more ethical than the other. They simply fill different roles. The legal profession's claim that lawyers, because they are lawyers, are not profit driven and can resist the temptation to put business above professional ethics has repeatedly been debunked.

Enron saved the legal profession's market for corporate legal services. Sarbanes-Oxley put the Big Five out of the legal services business. The legal profession's efforts during this period changed nothing.[34]

VI. And Yet Again

The MDP and ABS landscape during the decade of Enron was bleak for the reform minded. The MDP opponents had their proof in hand and MDPs were declared "dead."[35] Outside the United States, ABS advanced in the United Kingdom, Australia, and some Canadian provinces. MDPs reformed as strategic alliances and in some instances as ancillary businesses. But the movement in the American legal profession toward either MDPs or ABS was DOA. Still, the idea managed to reignite from a single cinder.

The economic downturn of 2008 has allowed the ideas of MDPs and ABS to emerge as the saviors of law firms.[36] The idea's rebirth was shocking to some and inevitable to others. As the large law firm business model collapsed and demonstrated its lack of long-term viability,[37] to the rescue came the many-times-declared-dead alternative business structure models. There is much to be said in support of Larry Ribstein's analysis, some of which begins with Richard Susskind's premises.[38] And why not? The concepts have proved remarkably resilient. Large American law firms, hoping to compete in international markets with their London competitors, want the same freedom to raise capital and partner with other professionals. Why?

---

[34] *See generally,* Garth, *supra* note 26; Cone, III, *supra* note 21.

[35] Lawrence J. Fox, *MDPs Done Gone: The Silver Lining in the Very Black. Enron Cloud,* 44 ARIZ. L. REV. 547 (2002); Jay S. Zimmerman & Matthew J. Kelly, *MDPs May Be Dead After Enron/Anderson, But Subsidiary Businesses Thrive,* 29 LAW & SOC. INQUIRY 639 (Summer 2004).

[36] Larry E. Ribstein, *The Death of Big Law,* 2010 WIS. L. REV. 749 (Aug. 1, 2010).

[37] *See* chapter 9.

[38] RICHARD SUSSKIND, THE END OF LAWYERS (Oxford 2010).

Because the market has spoken, and spoken, and spoken again. Legal problems, particularly the complex legal problems of global corporations, do not exist in isolation. The market has demanded the opportunity to attend to its problems with one set of associated professionals, commonly interested in the corporation's success. Only the American legal profession's restrictive, anachronistic rules have stood and continue to stand in the way of the market's satisfaction and the return to long-term health of law firms. If the market continues to desire MDPs, they will continue to exist in whatever form is possible.[39]

The profession, however, continues its almost pathological fear of sharing power with non-lawyers. Ethics 20/20[40] was formed in 2009 to "perform a thorough review of the ABA Model Rules of Professional Conduct and the U.S. system of lawyer regulation in the context of advances in technology and global legal practice developments."[41] This is a worthy enterprise to be sure. But its membership is entirely made up of lawyers, a highly unlikely group to appreciate the dramatic changes in technology and global economic forces that it was created to study,[42] and its stated mission is to preserve the status quo to the greatest extent possible. Despite the impetus for the Commission's creation ("radical" advances in globalization and new technologies), its fundamental principles sound a preservative, inward-looking note: "The principles guiding the Commission's work are protection of the public; preservation of core professional values; and maintenance of a strong, independent and self-regulated profession."[43] "Protection,...preservation,...and maintenance...." Its proposals through 2012 do no more than capitulate to some technological and globalization changes that have already occurred. Among its first decisive acts was to rule out of order any suggestion of following the Australian or U.K. ABS innovations of the prior decade.[44] As its work continued, proposals to create a modest opening for MDPs and ABS were considered. Eventually, the Commission determined to place before the House of Delegates the most modest proposal, one that went even less far than the DC Bar Rule 5.4, which had been in existence without untoward professional consequences since 1990. The proposal was to come before the House of Delegates in February 2013. But the Illinois Bar

---

[39] Zimmerman & Kelly, *supra* note 34.

[40] More on Ethics 20/20 in chapter 9.

[41] *About Us*, AMERICAN BAR ASSOCIATION (2012), http://www.americanbar.org/groups/professional_responsibility/aba_commission_on_ethics_20_20/about_us.html.

[42] *Id.*

[43] *ABA President Carolyn B. Lamm Creates Ethics Commission to Address Technology and Global Practice Challenges Facing U.S. Lawyers*, http://apps.americanbar.org/abanet/media/release/news_release.cfm?releaseid=730

[44] American Bar Association, *ABA Commission on Ethics 20/20 Working Group on Alternative Business Structures: For Comment: Issue Paper Concerning Alternative Business Structures*, (April 5, 2011). (Finding that "[a]t its February 2011 meeting in Atlanta, the Commission decided that two options for alternative business structures—passive equity investment in law firms and the public trading of shares in law firms—would not be appropriate to recommend for implementation in the United States at this time, though both have been adopted elsewhere since July 2000.").

interposed its own resolution, the essence of which would prohibit even the discussion of the Commission's unambitious proposal. Faced with such opposition and wanting to save face and credibility with the House, the Commission withdrew its proposal.[45] MDPs and ABS are so intensely feared that even their discussion is out of bounds in the present-day ABA.

VII. Conclusion

Among the profession's chief fears has been the fear of sharing power. It has held tight to its claims of self-regulation when those claims have long since become highly questionable. It has ignored market demand for multidisciplinary partnerships. It has held fast to its traditional model of fully lawyer-owned provision of legal services, while other models have been tried without adverse consequences elsewhere and promise to provide more services to more people. Its mantra has been that it must protect the core values of the legal profession. One value that it professes but does little to serve is to make legal services more broadly available. It should consider the needs of society for legal services as a core value. Without doing so, its monopoly on provision of legal services should not continue to exist.

Even more than fear of outsiders invading the bar's homogeneity or of new styles of lawyering, the fundamental fear of sharing power with non-lawyers has animated the profession's self-preservationist instincts. And yet sharing power is the greatest need of the legal profession going forward: creative non-lawyers are needed to help manage the regulation of the legal profession and the justice system.

---

[45] Podgers, *supra* note 2.

9

Multijurisdictional Practice, Globalization, Technology, and Economic Crisis

The first decade of the millennium had already seen dramatic change in technology and globalization, and then economic crisis struck. As a direct result, significant change has come to the ways in which law is practiced and legal services are delivered. Even more pronounced legal services delivery changes are in the wings. Multijurisdictional practice, now a "quotidian" part of the practice,[1] motivated extensive study and only modest change at the decade's beginning; globalization and technology trends have imposed enormous change on practice but no more than bare acknowledgment in lawyer regulation, even as of 2012. The economic crisis hastened fundamental changes in the way in which corporate legal services are purchased, while the organized profession has had little to say on the subject. The 2009 ABA president, writing at the depths of the economic crisis, encouraged members to use more of the Association's "programs, publications and other activities"... "during [the economic crisis]."[2]

This time the crisis is real, and it is rapidly washing over the profession's walls with fundamentally new ways of doing the business of law. It will not just pass as some previous crises have. It will not simply change the manner and intensity of lawyering. It will not simply add new perspectives of recent profession entrants. It will produce a new legal profession with fundamentally different monopoly boundaries, staffing practices, products, and delivery mechanisms. To emerge intact from this crisis, the legal profession cannot spend its energy trying to maintain its status quo. The status quo is changing so rapidly and so drastically this time, that a status quo legal profession left behind will be little more than a shell of its current self.

---

[1] In re Desilets, 291 F.3d 925 925 (2002); More traditional judges disagree: see Judge Merritt's dissent in Desilates. ("I did not know until I read Judge Boggs' opinion that for lawyers it is now a regular, everyday practice—part of the profession's 'quotidian forms of practice' to use the court's words—for lawyers to practice in the federal courts of State A...while living and being licensed in State B.")

[2] Tommy Wells, *Facing Challenges in Crisis Mode*, 95 A.B.A. J. 9 (2009).

I. A Technology and Globalization Revolution

In more ways than are imaginable, life has changed in the late 1990s and the first decade of the 21st century. Both business and personal matters are dramatically faster paced, and the simple capacity for *doing* has been astonishingly enlarged.

A. TECHNOLOGY

The Internet, e-mail, videoconferencing, instant communication, social networking, and file sharing are all second nature to 21st-century business and law practice. The pace at which these innovations have gone from drawing board to second nature has been startling. Between 1995 and 2012, there has been nothing short of a communication and information revolution.

Although the Internet was born in 1969 when the U.S. Government's Advanced Research Projects Agency connected four of its computers together through a 56k line known as Arpanet,[3] real and common usage did not occur until the last decade of the 20th century. Originally the Internet was restricted to research purposes only, but "[s]tarting in the early 1980's..., the Internet grew beyond its primarily research roots to include both a broad user community and increased commercial activity."[4]

The growth in Internet usage can be attributed to British scientist Tim Burners Lee and his creation of the World Wide Web (the Web).[5] Not to be confused with the Internet itself, the Web is a system of interlinked computer documents that are accessed via the Internet.[6] This innovation created a user-friendly system for sharing information across the Internet, revolutionizing the way we use computers and making the Internet more accessible to the general public.[7] On August 6, 1991, in a move consistent with the idealistic tech movement of the early 90s, Burners Lee gave the World Wide Web free to the public so it would continue to grow.[8]

The Web works, first, by entering a URL (Uniform Resource Locator), which points to a specific web page on a web server.[9] Next, routers direct the request

---

[3] *Imagining the Internet A History and Forecast*, ELON U. SCH. OF COMM., http://www.elon.edu/e-web/predictions/150/1960.xhtml (last visited July 27, 2012).

[4] Barry M. Leiner et al., *Brief History of the Internet*, INTERNET SOC'Y, http://www.internetsociety.org/internet/internet-51/history-internet/brief-history-internet/ (last visited July 27, 2012).

[5] *Tim Berners-Lee*, NNDB, http://www.nndb.com/people/573/000023504/ (last visited July 27, 2012).

[6] *Modern Marvels: 90's Tech* (The History Channel television broadcast July 20, 2012) *available at* http://www.amazon.com/gp/product/B0050WMWZO/ref=atv_purch_to_dp?ie=UTF8&ASINS=B0050WMWZO&a=B0050WMWZO&h=6f2c55229bc075106d1a6b0d83fb8cb7&o=B0050WMWZO&orderID=D01-8088446-9654314&t=1343054223000#ATV_PLAYER

[7] *Id.*

[8] *See August 6, 1991: The www debuts*, CNN (Mar. 10, 2003), http://articles.cnn.com/2003-03-10/us/sprj.80.1991.www_1_tim-berners-lee-web-page-hypertext?_s=PM:US.

[9] *How the Web Works*, LEARN THE NET, http://www.learnthenet.tv/learn-about/how-the-web-works/index.php (last updated Jan. 13, 2011).

from the requestor's computer across the network through the web server. The information is then sent back to the requestor's computer, and the webpage is displayed on the monitor.[10] Routers today can run at 92 terabits per second.[11] This represents a speed *two billion times* faster than the original 56k line used in 1969.[12] These improvements helped grow world Internet usage to 30.2 percent in 2010.[13]

That system worked only if the user knew the URL attached to the webpage that he or she wanted to access. With the Web growing exponentially, consumers needed a way to find relevant information quickly. Enter the first search engines in the mid-1990s and then Google; the popular search engine was launched in September of 1998 helping consumers locate relevant web addresses in less than a second.[14] Google works by sending out "spiders" to crawl the web scanning each web page.[15] Next, the information retrieved by the "spiders" is entered into an index.[16] Google software sifts through the index and ranks the matches returning results in order of relevance, and in some instances, commercial considerations.[17]

To provide this service to consumers, Google started with only 30 servers, but recent estimates now put that number somewhere around 450,000.[18] This increase can be attributed to the enormous growth in search queries. By the end of 1998, Google was servicing 10,000 search queries a day; just two years later that number had grown to 100 million.[19] By 2011, Google was conducting an astonishing 4,717,000,000 searches per day.[20]

E-mail capitalized on the development of the Internet. Barely heard of in 1990, by 1996 e-mail was poised to become the main source of communication in the United States, eclipsing the telephone and standard mail.[21] By 2007 over 170 billion e-mail messages were being sent every day.[22] That amounts to almost *2 million e-mails* sent every second. Unfortunately, 70 percent of e-mail is identified as spam or viruses.[23] Despite the high percentage of junk mail, e-mail volume grew to

---

[10] *Id.*

[11] *Modern Marvels: 90's Tech, supra* note 6.

[12] *Id.*

[13] *Internet users (per 100 people)*, THE WORLD BANK, http://data.worldbank.org/indicator/ IT.NET.USER.P2/countries/1W?display=graph (last visited July 27, 2012).

[14] *Our History in depth*, GOOGLE, http://www.google.com/about/company/history/ (last visited July 27, 2012).

[15] *See* Nancy Blachman et al., *How Google Works*, GOOGLE GUIDE, http://www.googleguide. com/google_works.html (last modified Feb. 2, 2007).

[16] *Id.*

[17] *Id.*

[18] *Modern Marvels: 90's Tech, supra* note 6.

[19] *Id.*

[20] *Google Annual Search Statistics*, STATISTIC BRAIN, http://www.statisticbrain.com/google-searches/ (last updated July 14, 2012).

[21] *Modern Marvels: 90's, supra* note 6.

[22] *Id.*

[23] *Id.*

an estimated 294 billion e-mails sent daily in 2010.[24] Despite all the spam, a 2012 study shows e-mail has become a fixture of American life, reporting that 90 million Americans access e-mail through a mobile device, with 64 percent doing so on a near-daily basis.[25] The business saturation of e-mail usage is far higher.

Popular e-mail providers include Hotmail, Gmail, and Yahoo mail. In 1996 one of the first web-based e-mail services, Hotmail, provided consumers with an easier and lightning-fast way of communicating online.[26] It was so popular that Microsoft bought the company for $400 million the next year.[27] In 2004 Google got in on the action and released Gmail service, which offered more memory and better user interface than both Hotmail and Yahoo mail. In response, Microsoft released Windows Live Hotmail, an enhanced e-mail system, which by 2009 had grown to nearly 300 million users.[28] Not finished, in August 2012, Microsoft announced it is moving subscribers from Hotmail to a new e-mail program, designed to "push the boundaries of email."[29]

As users began to dabble in e-mail, everyone seemed to have a life-changing "e-mail moment" to remember. Sending a message from a small town in Virginia to Bulgaria and having a reply come a few minutes later caused users to stop and contemplate all that had just changed in life. The possibilities that e-mail opened for long-distance collaborations and partnerships opened minds to new ventures.

Another popular form of communication made possible by the Internet is Instant Messaging (IM). Described by BBC reporter Jon Kelly as "more immediate than email, [and] less fiddly than texting," IM was once thought to be on track to surpass e-mail, but is now on the decline. BBC reported a 9 percent drop in time spent instant messaging between 2007–2010.[30]

In the 1990s IM was popular because there was no need to refresh the browser to check an e-mail account. Instead, it allowed for communication in real time.[31] It also offered employees a means of circumventing their employers' e-mail usage policy.[32] Business users on conference calls or video conferences found creative uses for IM. Negotiation partners could sit a thousand miles apart and "pass notes under the table" via IM without their negotiation opponents/counterparts seeing them.

---

[24] Heinz Tschabitscher, *How Many Emails Are Sent Every Day?*, About.com, http://email. about.com/od/emailtrivia/f/emails_per_day.htm (last visited July 27, 2012).

[25] *Id.*

[26] Prashant Sharma, *The "Hotmail" Evolution*, TechPluto (June 22, 2009), http://www.tech-pluto.com/hotmail-evolution/.

[27] *Id.*

[28] *Id.*

[29] David Goldman, *Microsoft Reinvents Hotmail as Outlook*, CNN Money (July 31, 2012, 12:01 PM), http://money.cnn.com/2012/07/31/technology/hotmail-outlook-overhaul/.

[30] Jon Kelly, *Instant messaging: This conversation is terminated*, BBC, http://news.bbc.co.uk/2/hi/uk_news/magazine/8698174.stm (last updated May 24, 2010).

[31] *Id.*

[32] *Id.*

Problems, however, slowed the growth of IMs.[33] For example, in the early days, IM systems were noncompatible so AIM (AOL Instant Messenger) users were unable to interact with Yahoo Messenger.[34] Moreover, the rise of Facebook and Twitter offered users more than IM servers could.[35] Some still argue that the principles of IM survive, but sites like Facebook and Twitter let users talk to a wider audience via a wider range of platforms.[36] While IM may be on the decline, social media sites like Facebook and Twitter are booming.

Founded in 2004, Facebook's mission is "to make the world more open and connected."[37] Facebook's website explains: "[p]eople use Facebook to stay connected with friends and family, to discover what's going on in the world, and to share and express what matters to them."[38] People accomplish this objective through a variety of features including creating friend lists, messaging on people's boards (2004), joining or creating groups (2004), uploading photos and video (2005), reading the News Feed (2006), or reviewing a user's activity log (2011).[39] The variety of features attracted users to the site, and by the end of March 2012, Facebook had 901 million monthly active users.[40]

A big draw to Facebook is the ability to post and comment on a friend's pictures. In 2005, Facebook became the first photo site with an unlimited quota for uploads.[41] By 2007, Facebook hosted the greatest number of monthly visitors to a photo site with 23.9 million.[42] In 2008, Facebook hit the milestone of hosting 10 billion pictures.[43] In 2009, 2.7 million photos were uploaded to Facebook every 20 minutes.[44] Facebook expected to have 100 billion photos uploaded by the end of summer 2011.[45]

Lawyers joined in, too. By 2009, an estimated 750,000 lawyers belonged to some social networking site, Facebook included.[46] And law firm after law firm, large and small, established their own Facebook pages.

---

[33] *Id.*

[34] *Id.*

[35] *Id.*

[36] Jon Kelly, *Instant messaging: This conversation is terminated*, BBC, http://news.bbc.co.uk/2/hi/uk_news/magazine/8698174.stm (last updated May 24, 2010).

[37] FACEBOOK, http://newsroom.fb.com/content/default.aspx?NewsAreaId=22 (last visited July 27, 2012).

[38] *Id.*

[39] *Id.*

[40] *Id.*

[41] Craig Kanalley, *A History of Facebook Photos (INFOGRAPHIC)*, THE HUFFINGTON POST, http://www.huffingtonpost.com/2011/08/02/facebook-photos-infographic_n_916225.html (last updated Oct. 2, 2011, 6:12 AM).

[42] *Id.*

[43] *Id.*

[44] *Id.*

[45] *Id.*

[46] *2009 Networks for Counsel Study: A Global Study of the Legal Industry's Adoption of Online Professional Networking, Preferences, Usage, and Future Predictions*, LEADER NETWORKS, 10 (2009), *available at* http://www.leadernetworks.com/documents/Networks_for_Counsel_2009.pdf.

The massive growth and use of Facebook has begun to generate new legal questions.[47] For example, a New York state court decision held that Facebook photos and content could be used as evidence in court.[48] Another court ruled that users do not need permission to tag other users in Facebook photos.[49] And a Florida judicial ethics commission ruled that judges are prohibited from being Facebook friends with lawyers who practice in the judge's court.[50]

Another popular social media site is Twitter. Twitter describes itself as "a real-time information network that connects you to the latest stories, ideas, opinions, and news about what you find interesting."[51] Twitter users communicate through small bursts of information called tweets. Each tweet is limited to 140 characters, but the service also allows a user to see photos, video and conversations.[52] Lady Gaga is the most followed Twitter account with 27,434,650 followers.[53] President Barack Obama comes in at number six with 17,777,509.[54]

Twitter is an amazing technological development in that it only took 3 years 2 months and 1 day to reach the 1 billionth tweet.[55] Now, 1 billion tweets are posted each week.[56] The average tweet per day increased from 50 million in March of 2010 to 140 million in February of 2011, an increase of 280 percent.[57]

In the latter portion of the 2000's decade, it became commonplace for television news programs to use quotes from blogs and tweets and Facebook posts as news. The reporting of events was supplemented and in some instances overtaken by the observations and opinions of Twitter users. During the 2012 Olympic Games in London, Twitter became a staple of network sports broadcasts. Tweets of athletes and their fans or detractors became an integral part of the event broadcasts.

Part of the reason for e-mail, Facebook, and Twitter's success is their ability to work on a mobile device. The development of the portable computer and the cell phone allowed consumers to take technology with them wherever they go. Portable computers date as far back as the early 1980s with the release of the Osborne 1. Released in 1981, the Osborne 1 cost about $1,800, and was described by one

---

[47] *Id.*

[48] Craig Kanalley, *A History of Facebook Photos (INFOGRAPHIC)*, THE HUFFINGTON POST, http://www.huffingtonpost.com/2011/08/02/facebook-photos-infographic_n_916225.html (last updated Oct. 2, 2011, 6:12 AM).

[49] *Id.*

[50] *See* Florida Judicial Ethics Advisory Comm. Op. 2010-06, Sixth Judicial Circuit of Florida (Mar. 26, 2010), http://www.jud6.org/LegalCommunity/LegalPractice/opinions/jeacopinions/2010/2010-06.html.

[51] TWITTER, https://twitter.com/about (last visited July 27, 2012).

[52] *Id.*

[53] TWITTER COUNTER, http://twittercounter.com/pages/100 (last visited July 27, 2012).

[54] *Id.*

[55] *Twitter Statistics*, KISSMETRICS, http://blog.kissmetrics.com/twitter-statistics/ (last visited July 27, 2012).

[56] *Id.*

[57] *Id.*

technology expert as "a 25 pound boat anchor."[58] Representing the very begin-ning of the portable computer, it was a far cry from the modern laptop computer, but for the first time consumers could take their computer with them.[59] By the early 1990s the technology for portable computers had developed significantly. For example, the PowerBook 170 was released in 1991 and sold for $4,600. It repre-sented "the defining embodiment of everything notebook..." with improved fea-tures including a slimmer, more contemporary look, a more effective screen, a track ball, and palm rests for typing.[60] In 2012, the market is saturated with hundreds of models and designs, selling for far less than their predecessors. Laptops, tablets, notebooks, and iPads have all made business computing more and more portable. Airport terminals and coffee shops, with their wireless Internet connections, are now as routine a workplace as an office. Lawyers carry computers to court, where judges allow them to do so.

The portable cell phone also got its start in the early 1980s. First marketed in 1983, the Motorola Dynatech 8000x was the first widely available cell phone.[61] It cost $3,995 and weighed about two pounds earning it the nickname "the Brick."[62] Like a modern cell phone, "the Brick" operated like a sophisticated radio system. When a user dials, the phone sends a message to a nearby radio tower. The tower sets up the call with two frequencies: one for the user's voice and one for the person called. This system can transmit on hundreds of radio frequencies so each tower can handle dozens of calls at once. If a phone is moving, its signal is transferred from one tower to the next spaced apart at appropriate intervals. Cell phones even-tually went from analog signal to digital, and as the decade progressed, cell phones got smaller, faster, and cheaper. The first smart phone, marrying the cell phone with the computer, was introduced in January of 1993.[63] The IBM Simon sold for $900 and was the precursor to the Blackberry.[64]

Yet another important piece of technology developed in the 90's was the Global Positioning System ("GPS"). The U.S. Department of Defense began developing GPS technology in 1972 to track troop movement and to improve the accuracy of weapons.[65] The 14 billion dollar GPS system reached full operational ability in July of 1995.[66] The 1990s consumer use of GPS was not as precise as its capabilities due to a government-imposed selective availability feature.[67] This restriction pro-duced an intentional error rate for nonauthorized users of about 100 meters of

---

[58] *Modern Marvels: 90's Tech*, *supra* note 6.

[59] *Id.*

[60] *Id.*

[61] *Modern Marvels: 80's Tech* (The History Channel television broadcast July 20, 2012) *available at* http://www.veoh.com/watch/v17089973Rs3gJneB.

[62] *Id.*

[63] *Modern Marvels: 90's Tech*, *supra* note 6.

[64] *Id.*

[65] *Id.*

[66] *Id.*

[67] *Id.*

your location.[68] In May of 2000, President Clinton turned the selective availability function off, and GPS can now identify a position within 10 feet.[69]

Video conferencing saw advancement and development in the 1990s due to many factors, including technical advances in Internet Protocol (IP) and also more efficient video compression technologies that were developed, permitting desktop or PC-based videoconferencing.[70] In 1991, IBM introduced the first PC-based video conferencing system, named PicTel.[71] Although it was a black and white system that was very inexpensive to use, costing only $30 per line, per hour, the system itself cost $20,000.[72]

By 2003, the cost of PCs and web cameras had come down, and broadband Internet access was available in nearly every region of the world.[73] As a result, the average person can now video conference the whole world over for as little as $12.00 a month and the price of a phone, while industry giants like Yahoo, Skype, and MSN have made laptop-based video conferencing virtually free.[74]

B. TRAVEL

For many people's experience, travel may seem not to have significantly changed during the past decade or so. But in fact, travel has changed in dramatic ways that have opened new markets and helped "flatten" the globe.

If one wanted to travel from Omaha to Chicago in 2013, the experience might not feel differently than it would have in 1995. O'Hare Airport has changed only modestly. The Boeing or Airbus or even the regional jet on which the flight would take place is not significantly different. The travel time would be about the same except for time spent on increased security since September 11, 2001. Perhaps the last significant changes to flights within the United States (aside from increased security after 9/11) occurred in the Reagan years of deregulation, when many small markets lost their flights entirely as deregulated airlines abandoned unprofitable routes, and regional airlines failed or were bought by major ones. The more recent loss of complimentary peanuts is a small sacrifice.

Roughly the same could be said for most flights within the United States and Canada, as well as those to and from Western Europe. The Concorde experiment promised much but delivered little and was discontinued. A few more departure cities exist for flights from the United States to Western Europe, but the flights are largely unchanged. Roughly eight hours from East Coast cities to Frankfurt,

---

[68] *Modern Marvels: 90's Tech, supra* note 6.

[69] *Id.*

[70] *Video Conferencing History*, NEFSIS, http://www.nefsis.com/Best-Video-Conferencing-Software/video-conferencing-history.html (last visited July 30, 2012).

[71] *Id.*

[72] *Id.*

[73] *Id.*

[74] *History of Video Confrencing*, VIDE, http://www.hometechanswers.com/streaming-video/history-of-video-conferencing.html (last visited July 30, 2012).

Munich, Paris, London, or Amsterdam. Fewer flights to Madrid, Rome, and a few other destinations. Not much different from 1995 to 2013. About the same can be said of U.S. flights to Asia. Mostly the same airlines (or their successor owners) going to mostly the same cities taking about the same time in the air.

But in ways that have dramatically affected global markets, and with them global legal markets, the travel situation *has* changed in the past 15 to 20 years.

A. EASTERN EUROPE

First, the opening of Eastern Europe has had profound effects on market expansion. And easier travel has played a role. Airports in places like Tbilisi, Georgia, as recently as 2006, were dark, dreadful, one-gate places, into which only the most determined of business travelers would venture. Now, that and many other airports in the Caucasus, former Yugoslavia, and formerly Soviet-dominated Eastern Bloc countries are modern, pleasant, and efficient. Airports in Zagreb and Ljubliana have had major improvements in the last decade, and those in Ukraine and Poland freshened up for Eurocup 2012. Business has followed, or seen another way, demanded, the improvements. Whether chicken or egg came first, travel to many Eastern European capitals is now an entirely palatable experience, and business has grown.

B. ASIA

More significantly still, air travel into significant Asian markets has opened. Despite recent dramatic growth, Singapore was Singapore as early as the early 1990s. Hong Kong was Hong Kong even earlier. But air travel to Bangkok and Jakarta and numerous other key cities has become far more comfortable and accessible. A seasoned traveler has no qualms whatever about travel to these major multimillion population cities today. Even more dramatic change has come to the secondary-market cities of China, Indonesia, and India.

Take Indonesia as the example, although these conditions are largely replicated in China and India. In the early to mid-1990s, and well into the decade of the 2000s, travel to and from Jakarta with its 20 million people, massive oil and gas reserves, and other market riches, was possible but unpleasant. Until 1985, there simply was no acceptable civilian airport. From 1985 until 1992, the airport operated with a single terminal and a capacity of 8 million passengers per year. The capacity was tripled in 1992 but remained largely unchanged until 2008 when a third terminal nearly doubling the 1992–2008 capacity came online. With the new terminal, the airport has been regularly rated among the worldwide top 10 in efficiency by *Forbes Traveler*.[75]

---

[75] *10 Most On-Time Airports*, FORBES TRAVELER.COM, http://web.archive.org/web/20080614002444/ http://www.forbestraveller.com/jets-planes/on-time-airports-slide-6.html. (last visited Aug. 11, 2012).

The airport has now passed Singapore's in traffic, and construction is nearly finished for another doubling of capacity.

But while travel to Jakarta may have been unpleasant, travel to and from other major Indonesian cities was next to impossible and conjured images of Indiana Jones scraping treetops in marginal aircraft. Flights to many significant cities were petrifying experiences.

Take Medan, Sumatra's largest city with 2.1 million people, as an example:

On 11 July 1979, a Fokker F28 of Garuda Indonesia Airways crashed into Mount Sibayak while on approach to Medan-Polonia airport. All 61 passengers and crew on board were killed;

On 4 April 1987, Garuda Indonesia Flight 035, crashed into power lines and a television aerial in bad weather as it attempted landing at Medan-Polonia. Twenty-two of the 45 passengers and crew on board were killed;

On 18 June 1988, Vickers Viscount PK-MVG of Merpati Nusantara Airlines was damaged beyond economic repair when it suffered a hydraulic system failure and departed the runway;

On 26 September 1997, another Garuda Indonesia Flight 152, an Airbus A300, crashed into woodlands 18 miles short of Medan-Polonia airport. All 235 passengers and crew on board were killed. Flight 152 is the worst aviation disaster in Indonesia history.

The new Medan airport is about to come online in 2012–13. Kuala Namu International Airport (also known as New Medan International Airport) will soon replace Polonia International Airport. Construction began on June 29, 2006, shortly before the first anniversary of the crash of Mandala Airlines Flight 091. Other major Indonesian cities have new airports replacing old ones with similarly dismal safety records. Makassar (Ujang Pandang) (new terminal in 2008, international flights began in mid-1990s), Banjarmasin (new expansion in 2004 to accommodate 767s), as well as Surabaya and Yogjakarta.

Medan, Makassar, Surabaya, Banjarmasin, and Yogjakarta are not small, backwater villages. Surabaya has a population of nearly 3 million (and 7–9 million in the metropolitan area). Its airport underwent a major expansion in 2006, and traffic has increased from 2 million to nearly 14 million passengers per year from 1999 to 2011. Medan is Sumatra's largest city with 2.1 million people; Makassar has 1.3 million people, is the "first-city" of Eastern Indonesia and now an air hub, an utterly unimaginable state of affairs prior to 2008; Banjarmin is 600,000 and home to major oil and gas industrial assets of Kalamentan; Yogyakarta, a historically significant city of 500,000 is a major tourist destination.

Until recently, Garuda Indonesia, the national airline and major carrier for the country's air travel system, tempted fate all too frequently. Its safety record was so poor that it was banned from flying in EU airspace for much of the late 2000s. The crashes piled up during the 1980s, 1990s, and early 2000s. Many hundreds of deaths resulted from crashes so frequent as to make accidents seem routine. Aircraft burst into flames and crashed into volcanoes and neighborhoods surrounding airports. The risk was too much for even intrepid businesspeople.

In 2013, although there continue to be marginal airlines with questionable safety records flying in Indonesia, the important Indonesian cities and many, many others are served safely by both Garuda and by recent market entrant (2000) Lion Air. Both have nearly new fleets that rival those of any airline worldwide. In 2009, Garuda embarked on its "Quantum Leap" strategy, resulting in dramatically improved safety and passenger comfort conditions; Lion purchased 60 of Boeing's new generation of 737s in 2005, which continue to be regularly delivered. Such a purchase would have been unthinkable in the 1990s: the new planes would have had nowhere to land outside Jakarta and, of course, Bali, a longtime favorite international tourist destination with an international flight terminal to match.[76]

The Indonesian economy boomed in the 1990s, although it suffered mightily during the Asian financial crisis in 1998. Annual real gross domestic product (GDP) growth averaged nearly 7 percent from 1987–97, and most analysts recognized Indonesia as a newly industrializing economy and emerging major market.[77] The economy has sustained consistent, impressive growth in the decade of the 2000s, even as the European and U.S. economies faltered and were bailed out by government. The advances in travel ease came alongside the economic growth, each fueling the other. But without the dramatic advances in air travel safety of the past 15 years, one wonders how the economic growth could have been sustained. There was business that could be done in places that very few would venture before the upgrades in airline travel, and even in the Internet world, some measure of business still gets done face to face.

Indonesia weathered the recent global financial crisis relatively smoothly. Increasing investment by both local and foreign investors has supported solid growth. Although the economy slowed to 4.6 percent growth in 2009 from the 6 percent-plus growth rate recorded in 2007 and 2008, by 2010, growth returned to a 6 percent rate and remained there in 2011. During the recession, Indonesia outperformed most of its regional neighbors.[78]

Indonesia has been the third-fastest growing G-20 member, trailing only China and India. Indonesia's improving growth prospects and sound macroeconomic policy have many analysts suggesting that it will become the newest member of the "BRIC" grouping of leading emerging markets. In December 2011, Fitch Ratings

---

[76] Currently, Garuda Indonesia Airline consists of: 8 Airbus A330–200, 6 Airbus A330-300, 10 Boeing 737-300, 10 Boeing 737-400, 5 Boeing 737-500, 56 Boeing 737-800 and 3 Boeing 747-400. Currently, Lion Air fleet consists of the following aircraft: 2 Boeing 737–300, 7 Boeing 737-400, 60 Boeing 737-900ER, 2 Boeing 747-400, 1 McDonnell Douglas MD-82, 3 McDonnell Douglas MD-90-30.

[77] Bureau of E. Asian & Pac. Affairs, *U.S. Relations with Indonesia*, U.S. Dep't St. (July 31, 2012), http://www.state.gov/r/pa/ei/bgn/2748.htm.

[78] *Indonesia Economy 2012*, http://www.theodora.com/wfbcurrent/indonesia/indonesia_economy.html (last modified Mar. 6, 2012).

upgraded Indonesia's sovereign debt rating to investment grade. A similar upgrade to investment grade is expected from Standard and Poor's and Moody's.[79]

Without advances in travel, the markets, including legal markets, in Indonesia, China, India, Thailand, and so on, simply would not have developed into the powerhouses that they are.

What has changed for business has changed for the practicing lawyer and law firm. The concept of sending a letter to opposing counsel or a client is now reserved for only the most formal of communications. Land-line telephones ring rarely. E-mail has replaced almost all other communication needs. Lawyers can meet in virtual workrooms with the clients and collaborating lawyers in nearly every corner of the world. U.S. and London lawyers represent their international business clients in collaboration with lawyers from Prague and Bratislava, Jakarta and Bangkok, sometimes in person, but more often by e-mail and Skype. No longer need they wait for the arrival of a letter as transactions are documented with an e-mail and attached portable document format (PDF) with an electronic signature.

Lawyers' clients need not be global businesses for their work to routinely cross state and national boundaries. Far more than clients of prior generations of lawyers, today's clients move from one state to another, making their domestic relations issues national and international matters. Immigration implications attend even the most routine and local criminal matters. And businesses as small as a local jewelry artisan advertise their wares on the Internet, embroiling them and their lawyers in far-reaching disputed transactions. •

Combined, changes in communications, travel, and information sharing have fundamentally changed global markets for goods and services. They have advanced the distribution of knowledge. They have changed life. Even those of us who lived most of our lives before the Internet and e-mail struggle to imagine life without them.

II. The Economic Crisis

Today's American legal profession, already wracked with uncertainty because of the late 1990s rise of unofficial MDPs and the Enron debacle, found itself a victim of the mid-to-late 2000s economic crisis. Early-decade calls for abolition of state-by-state licensure resulted in the modest changes eventually adopted to the multijurisdictional practice restrictions.[80] Enron and the resulting SEC reforms temporarily quelled the call for MDP approval.[81] Then the economic crisis, even as Australia and

---

[79] http://www.gmanetwork.com/news/story/278775/economy/finance/s-p-progress-needed-for-indonesia-phl-to-make-investment-grade.

[80] American Bar Association, Commission on Multijurisdictional Practice, Report (2002).; MODEL RULE OF PROF'L CONDUCT 5.5.

[81] Sarbanes–Oxley Act of 2002, Pub. L. No. 107–204, 116 Stat 745. *See also* Robert R. Keatinge, *Multidimensional Practice in a World of Invincible Ignorance: MDB, MJP, and Ancillary Business after Enron*, 44 ARIZ. L. REV. 717 (2002).

the United Kingdom were adopting major reforms allowing alternative business structures and outside investment on law firms.[82] It had been a jarring decade.

A. GLOBAL FINANCIAL CRISIS

The global economy declined in the latter half of the 2000s. The origins of this crisis can be traced back to the burst of the tech bubble in the late 1990s.[83] The decline in the stock market beginning in 2000 and subsequent recession in 2001 led to the Federal Reserve dramatically lowering interest rates.[84] Lower interest rates led to greater demand for homes, which in turn increased prices.[85] Many homeowners also refinanced their homes, taking advantage of lower interest rates and taking out significant portions of their equity generated by rising home prices.[86] As the housing market experienced growth, banks increasingly made subprime loans, high-risk loans given to homeowners with poor credit histories.[87] These high-risk loans, along with other assets, were packaged together to create collateralized debt obligations, which were then sold to global investors.[88]

Rising interest rates from 1 percent to 5.32 percent from 2004 to 2006 triggered a slowdown in the housing market.[89] Homeowners began to default on their adjustable rate mortgages, as many could barely afford the payments when interest rates were low.[90] The defaults on subprime loans affected banks worldwide. In June 2007, Bear Stearns announced the collapse of two hedge funds it owned. These funds had been heavily invested in the subprime market.[91] Liquidity in the credit market dried up, and the rate at which banks would lend to each other increased sharply.[92] In September 2007, Northern Rock, a British bank, asked for emergency financial support from the Bank of England, as the lack of liquidity in the credit markets dried up its funding. The day after this announcement, depositors withdrew large sums of money, creating the largest run on a British bank for over a century. The next month, several other investment banks, including UBS, Citigroup,

---

[82] *Legal Profession Act 2004*, NEW S. WALES CONSOLIDATED ACTS, http://www.austlii.edu.au/au/legis/nsw/consol_act/lpa2004179/ (last visited Aug. 11, 2012).; *Legal Profession Regulation 2005*, NEW S. WALES CONSOLIDATED ACTS, http://www.austlii.edu.au/au/legis/nsw/consol_reg/lpr2005270/ (last visited Aug. 11, 2012).

[83] *Credit Crisis: the Essentials*, N.Y. TIMES (Jan. 11, 2011), http://topics.nytimes.com/top/reference/timestopics/subjects/c/credit_crisis/index.html.

[84] *Id.*

[85] *Id.*

[86] *Id.*

[87] *Timeline: Credit crunch to downturn*, BBC NEWS, http://news.bbc.co.uk/2/hi/business/7521250.stm#table (last updated Aug. 7, 2009).

[88] *Id.*

[89] *Id.*

[90] *Credit Crisis, supra* note 83.

[91] *Id.*

[92] *Credit Crunch, supra* note 87.

and Merrill Lynch, all announced billions of dollars in losses related to subprime investments.[93]

The Federal Reserve took several steps to help the situation on Wall Street.[94] In March 2008, the Fed assumed $30 billion in Bear Stearns liabilities and helped engineer a sale of the investment bank to JP Morgan Chase to prevent its bankruptcy.[95] However, losses on Wall Street continued, with the subprime crisis spreading to other sectors, including commercial property, consumer debt, and company debt.[96] Concerns over the sliding stock prices of Fannie Mae and Freddie Mac, the United States' largest lenders, led to government takeover of these entities on September 7, 2008.[97] A few days later, government and finance officials gathered to discuss the fate of investment bank Lehman Brothers, which was facing bankruptcy.[98] This time, the U.S. government failed to intervene, and Lehman collapsed, the first major bank to do so since the beginning of the credit crisis. Merrill Lynch, in order to avoid the fate of Lehman, sold itself to Bank of America that month. AIG, the United States' largest insurance company, was then bailed out by the government with an $85 billion rescue package.[99]

On September 18, Treasury Secretary Henry Paulson announced a $700 billion government proposal to bail out the United States' largest banks by buying toxic assets from major banking institutions.[100] This plan was designed to increase confidence in the U.S. markets and improve the banks' balance sheets. The bailout plan was the largest U.S. government intervention into the financial markets since the Great Depression.[101] Days after Congress approved the bailout package, European countries also followed suit with bailouts for Hypo Real Estate, a large German lender; and Fortis, a major European financial company.[102]

In November, stocks fell to their lowest levels in a decade, while unemployment reached its highest level in 15 years.[103] Home prices fell, and retailers suffered major losses, with stores such as Sharper Image, Circuit City, and Linens 'n Things filing for bankruptcy.[104] The Fed cut its benchmark interest rate to an unprecedented rate of nearly zero percent in December, while other nations cut interest rates as well.[105]

In the beginning of 2009, Congress passed a $787 billion stimulus package to revive the U.S. economy. By the summer of 2009, it seemed that a total financial

---

[93] *Id.*

[94] *Credit Crisis, supra* note 83.

[95] *Id.*

[96] *Credit Crunch, supra* note 87.

[97] *Credit Crisis, supra* note 83.

[98] *Id.*

[99] *Id.*

[100] *Id.*

[101] *Credit Crunch, supra* note 87.

[102] *Id.*

[103] *Credit Crisis, supra* note 83.

[104] *Id.*

[105] *Id.*

meltdown had been avoided, and by the end of the year major banks reported large profits and were in the process of repaying the bailout money they had received from the U.S. government. However, despite the increased stability in the financial markets, throughout 2009, unemployment levels rose to the highest seen in a generation.[106] The U.S. unemployment rate rose from 5.0 percent in December 2007 to 9.9 percent in December 2009.[107]

B. IMPACT ON U.S. LEGAL MARKET

The decline in the U.S. economy had a major impact on the legal market. Law firms had hired more employees during the early economic boom of the 2000s, with an emphasis on adding attorneys to corporate law practice groups.[108] With the downturn in the financial sector, however, firms had to drastically reduce the number of attorneys in these practice groups.[109] Firms shifted attorneys in corporate practice areas, such as real estate and securitization practice groups, into other areas, such as bankruptcy.[110]

Instead of merely shifting practice groups, other law firms reacted to the economic downturn with large attorney layoffs. In 2009, law firms laid off 12,259 attorneys and staff, often in large numbers at once. In early February 2009, six major law firms—Bryan Cave, Dechert, DLA Piper, Faegre & Benson, Goodwin Procter, and Holland & Knight—reported large attorney and staff layoffs.[111] On one day alone in late February 2009, Latham and Watkins laid off 440 employees, a total of 190 attorneys and 250 staff.[112] During a two-week period that March, law firm layoffs totaled nearly 2,700.[113] While not as massive, an additional 234 lawyers and 511 staffers, a total of 745 law firm employees, were laid off in 2010.[114] Even more drastic than layoffs, several firms ceased to exist in light of the poor economic

---

[106] *Id.*

[107] *Labor Force Statistics from the Current Population Survey*, BUREAU OF LAB. STAT., http://data.bls.gov/timeseries/LNS14000000 (last updated Aug. 11 2012).

[108] Michael J. de la Merced, *The Legal Profession Feels the Pain of Recession*, N.Y. TIMES, March 26, 2009, at SPG2.

[109] *Id.*

[110] *Id.*

[111] Martha Neil, *Bloody Thursday: Six Major Law Firms Ax Attorneys*, A.B.A. J. (Feb. 12, 2009), http://www.abajournal.com/news/article/bloody_thursday_4_major_law_firms_ax_attorneys_more_layoffs_at_others/.

[112] Ashby Jones, *Law Firm Layoff Watch: Latham Cuts 190 Lawyers, 250 Staff*, WALL ST. J. L. BLOG (Feb. 27, 2009), http://blogs.wsj.com/law/2009/02/27/law-firm-layoff-watch-latham-cuts-190-lawyers-250-staff/.

[113] Martha Neil, *March Mayhem: Law Firm Layoffs in 1 Week Total Nearly 1,500*, A.B.A. J. (Mar. 4, 2009), http://www.abajournal.com/news/article/march_mayhem_law_firm_layoffs_top_500_today_over_1200_since_friday/.

[114] Debra Cassens Weiss, *2010 Sees a Huge Dropoff in BigLaw Layoffs; Fewer than 800 Job Losses Chronicled*, A.B.A. J. (Jan. 25, 2011), http://www.abajournal.com/news/article/2010_sees_a_huge_dropoff_in_biglaw_layoffs_fewer_than_800_job_losses_chroni/.

conditions. Wolf Block of Philadelphia and Thelen and Heller Ehrman of San Francisco dissolved, leaving many attorneys without employment.[115]

As the availability of legal jobs decreased, the number of newly minted lawyers wanting employment increased. The increase has been in both the number of law schools and law degrees awarded. ABA statistics show that in 2006, 43,883 juris doctor degrees were awarded, an increase of 15 percent from only four years prior in 2002, when 37,909 were awarded.[116] There was also an 11 percent increase in the number of ABA-accredited law schools since 1995, with the 2010 total at 196 and rising.[117] Many universities see value in adding law schools in terms of prestige and financial benefits. Law schools are often money makers for universities, as costs per student are low compared to other graduate schools.[118]

Along with the number of juris doctor degrees awarded, the amount charged in tuition has also rapidly increased in recent years. Tuition has almost tripled the rate of inflation during the past 20 years. As the recession deepened in 2006, graduates of public law schools borrowed an average of $54,509; and graduates of private law schools borrowed an average of $83,181, up 17 percent and 18.6 percent from the same figures in 2002.[119]

The economic downturn, unsurprisingly, has had a major effect on employment for recent law school graduates. The Association for Legal Career Professionals' (NALP) report on the law school graduating class of 2009 revealed an overall employment rate of 88.3 percent of graduates for whom employment status was known.[120] This rate has decreased for two years in a row, decreasing 3.6 percent from the 91.9 percent for the class of 2007.[121] The employment figure for the class of 2009 is the lowest employment rate reported since the mid-1990s.[122]

And even these steadily decreasing numbers are regarded as an inflated estimate of the likelihood of postgraduation employment.[123] The actual employment realities for law school graduates in 2009 were bleaker still. Nearly 25 percent of all employment for law school graduates was reported as temporary.[124] This includes reports that 41 percent of all of the public interest jobs were temporary, 30 percent of all business jobs were temporary, and even 8 percent of the private practice jobs

---

[115] de la Merced, *supra* note 108.

[116] Amir Efrati, *Hard Case: Job Market Wanes for U.S. Lawyers*, WALL ST. J., Sept. 24, 2007, at A1.

[117] *Id.*

[118] *Id.*

[119] *Id.*

[120] *Class of 2009 Faced New Challenges with Recession: Overall Employment Rate Masks Job Market Weakness*, NALP (May 20, 2010), http://www.nalp.org/2009selectedfindingsrelease.

[121] *Id.*

[122] *Id.*

[123] David Segal, *Is Law School a Losing Game?*, N.Y. TIMES (Jan. 8, 2011), http://www.nytimes.com/2011/01/09/business/09law.html?_r=1&pagewanted=all.

[124] *Id.*

were temporary in nature.[125] Many of these temporary jobs are positions as contract attorneys, often conducting document review for $20 per hour with no benefits.[126]

Controversy has surrounded the manner in which law schools report their employment data. Law schools blame the ABA's system for collecting such data and the competition engendered by the *US News* rankings system. In 2011 and 2012, at least 15 law schools were sued by their graduates who claim that they were misled by the law schools rosier-than-true employment statistics.[127] In August 2011, the ABA passed a resolution encouraging law schools to report accurate data and make it available to prospective students.[128]

The 88.3 percent NALP employment rate was also inflated by the practice of many law schools providing recent graduates with short-term employment to improve their employment statistics. Law schools have increasingly provided recent graduates with employment through fellowships, grant programs for public interest work, and on-campus jobs.[129] These programs provided an estimated 2 percent of employment for the class of 2009, over 800 jobs in total.[130]

Law school graduates are also increasingly accepting employment that is part time or nonlegal in nature. More than 10 percent of all employment for the law school graduates in 2009 was recorded as part time, up 6 percent from the previous year.[131] The percentage of law school graduates employed as practicing attorneys has decreased. In 2009, 70.8 percent of law school graduates were employed in jobs that required a juris doctor, compared with 74.7 percent of the graduates in the previous year.[132]

Along with the decrease in employment numbers for law school graduates, the economic downturn also changed the nature of law firm hiring and recruitment. Summer associate programs, once the breeding grounds for associate jobs at law firms, have either been totally cut or shortened at many firms.[133] The number of students receiving employment as a summer associate has also sharply decreased. In 2010, a survey reported that large law firms reduced their summer associate classes by an average of 44 percent.[134]

Many law school graduates who *did* receive an offer for employment postgraduation at a law firm, saw these offers deferred for a period of time. These deferrals

---

[125] *Id.*

[126] Efrati, *supra* note 116.

[127] *Breaking: 12 more law schools facing class actions*, L. Sch. Transparency (Feb. 1, 2012, 10:15 AM), http://www.lawschooltransparency.com/2012/02/breaking-12-more-law-schools-facing-class-actions/.

[128] ABA Res. 111b, 2011 H. of Del., (2011) *available at* http://www.abanow.org/wordpress/wp-content/files_flutter/13105754842011_hod_annual_meeting_summary_of_resolutions.auth-checkdam.pdf.

[129] NALP Report, *supra* note 120.

[130] *Id.*

[131] *Id.*

[132] *Id.*

[133] de la Merced, *supra* note 108,

[134] Nicole Hong, *Summer Hiring Survey: 44 Percent Down in 2010*, Am. L. Daily (July 21, 2010), http://amlawdaily.typepad.com/amlawdaily/2010/07/summer-associates.html.

lasted up to a year or longer.[135] Some law firms provided stipends for their deferral period or provided an opportunity to work in pro bono fellowships.[136] Other deferred associates were not as fortunate and had to find other employment while waiting for their start dates at firms.[137] Most law firms did eventually employ their deferred associates, although some firms rescinded their employment offers entirely during the deferral period.[138]

The general economic woes' effect on law practice resulted in part as corporate clients became highly sensitive to the long-standing practice of staffing low-level lawyer tasks to beginning law firm associates. Instead, corporate clients began using in-house, salaried lawyers to do the work formerly done by outside counsel's associates. Both clients and law firms began to outsource work to lower cost service providers in India and Pakistan, as well as contract lawyers present at the firm for task-specific duration.

These changes, especially the staffing up of General Counsel offices to avoid paying the hourly rates of law firm junior associates, had been slowly in progress for perhaps 20 years. But the economic downturn accelerated the pace of change. The adjustments seem unlikely of reversal. To be sure, an upturn in economic activity will produce more legal work. But it is hard to imagine corporate clients deciding to return to higher spending for legal services once they have established the means to avoid those costs.

The changes in GC offices and corporate spending habits for legal services have had effects that ripple through the systems for provision of legal services. Corporate clients now use their procurement staff to consider how and when to spend money on legal services in the manner they decide how and when to purchase paper clips. Major law firms have adjusted in several ways. First, not only corporate clients, but law firms, have explored ways of outsourcing low-level legal tasks, allowing firms to compete for the business of their clients. Second, law firms have trimmed low-level staff and made the road to partner longer and less likely of success. Third, key partners from major firms have spun off into smaller firms, leaner in their own low-level staffing as well as location (and therefore rent and other overhead) and other expense factors. These changes, too, seem unlikely of reversal.

Further down the pecking order of legal services providers, the competition for the consumer legal services dollar has intensified. LegalZoom, virtual law firms, and others have begun to compete for nearly commoditized products, and lawyer-less dispute resolution products exist in the form of such web-based businesses as Legalfaceoff.com. The organized bar has lashed out at these low-cost, tech-savvy

---

[135] Dana Mattioli, *First Task for Law-Firm Hires: Finding an Interim Job First*, WALL ST. J. (Oct. 6, 2009),http://online.wsj.com/article/SB125478012114565787.html.

[136] *Id.*

[137] *Id.*

[138] Debra Cassens Weiss, *Some Deferred Start Dates May Become Withdrawn Job Offers*, A.B.A. J. (May 12, 2009), http://www.abajournal.com/weekly/warning_possible_associate_pile-up_ahead_and_some_will_crash_and_burn.

providers, often on the claim that they are engaged in unauthorized practice in particular jurisdictions.[139]

Law school employment numbers plummeted, although by some measures it was hardly noticeable. Plummet, they did, however, and law schools struggled with reform efforts and realignments. At the same time, new pressures were being brought to bear on law schools. The law firm training of associates, most often done through the assignment of low-level corporate work had dried up. In essence, clients stopped paying for beginning associates to be trained on the job. Frequent career changes also discouraged law firms from lavish spending on associate training. All eyes turned to law schools and their deficient professional training. Both applicants and employers of graduates began to demand better preparation for practice.

The roots of the law schools' troubles date from the late 19th century when both legal and medical education underwent reform and "scientification." For many reasons, the two were reformed in different ways and headed in opposite directions. Medical education decided that its mission would be to create doctors; legal education decided that its mission would be to create law professors. Law departments at major universities resembled philosophy or social science departments, with theory and scholarship the main products. Langdell famously said that for law, the "library is the laboratory," and that there was no use in having students engage with courts or practitioners, except for the study of appellate court opinions reported in the library stacks. Meanwhile, medical education began its move toward practice education, clinical work, and residencies for fledgling doctors. Legal education and the legal profession still pay the price for that choice.

The recent demand that law schools attend to practice teaching was a 180-degree change from the 1970s and before. Major law firms preferred to teach new associates in their own ways and were happy enough for law schools to refrain from teaching practice habits that the law firms would have to reteach. But by bits, all that had changed until the mid-2000s, when the tide had fully turned.[140]

By 2009, the profession was in the deepest throes of economic trouble. Every corner of the profession had suffered some form of economic hardship, and every corner was contemplating what would be the ways in which practice forms would need to adjust, not only to economic pressure but to technological and global developments. Presaging the appointment of the Ethics 20/20 Commission by his successor, ABA President H. Thomas Wells announced that it was crisis time. In his President's Page, Facing Challenges in Crisis Mode,[141] he spoke of the economic crisis:

---

[139] See 28 Law. Man. Prof. Conduct 312 (2012) (identifying multiple lawsuits pending against LegalZoom for unauthorized practice, many of which are listed on Legal Zoom's IPO Prospectus). See LegalZoom.com, Inc., Registration Statement (Form S-1) (May 10, 2012) (showing the Prospectus filed with SEC) available at http://www.sec.gov/Archives/edgar/data/1286139/000104746912005763/a2209299zs-1.htm.

[140] More on needed legal education reforms in chapter 10.

[141] H. Thomas Wells Jr., Facing Challenges in Crisis Mode Extraordinary Times Require Extraordinary Efforts from Lawyers, 95 A.B.A. J. 9 (2009).

These times promise a sea of change for government, private industry and the legal profession. The economic crisis is affecting every business and line of work, and lawyers have been hit relatively early and hard.

His suggestion: "It's during times like these that our members can take excellent advantage of association resources, [such as] programs, publications and other activities." Magazines. CLE. Seminars.

III. Multijurisdictional Practice

Business and lawyers in the 1990s and beyond changed what they thought of as their location. Technological advances and ease of travel made borders, especially state borders in the United States seem less relevant. States' laws became more and more uniform. Businesses did not slow down when they crossed from Ohio into Pennsylvania, nor from New Jersey into New Mexico. Law firms, and not only major ones, began to routinely represent clients whose interests paid no attention whatsoever to state borders.

Dynamic change "over the last century" in the nature of law practice, especially its increasingly cross-border nature, inspired the ABA to establish the Multijurisdictional Practice Commission in 2000.[142] It engaged in a wide gathering of information for its lawyer membership to consider. When it issued its final report, the tone appeared to foretell major recommendations for change. It recited considerable evidence that would support major change, including the abolition of the anachronistic, outdated state-by-state licensing system. But after the bold-sounding build-up, its first recommendation was to preserve the state-by-state licensing system in the United States.

The Report recites the history of UPL restrictions, noting that they mattered little when practice was local and client's business interests were largely confined by state lines. It notes that the 1960s brought change to these state-bounded law practices, and that knowledge of federal, state, and international law was now commonplace for lawyers whose clients stretched beyond state lines that had little to do with their business interests. It described changes in transportation and communications technology that enabled lawyers and their clients to routinely expand their horizons such that the most important acts of lawyers now involved the laws of multiple jurisdictions. It explained that the regulation of lawyers, licensing systems, and UPL restrictions had failed to adjust to these changes in transportation, communications, and business culture. The Report acknowledged that the profession's rules do not "enable the lawyer to serve the legal needs of clients in a national and global economy."

---

[142] American Bar Association, Commission on Multijurisdictional Practice, Report (2002).

After reciting all of the evidence pointing toward the need for major reform from the Commission's extensive study, its first listed recommendation was that "The ABA affirm its support for the principle of state judicial regulation of the practice of law."[143]

The evidence recited and the contrary conclusion reached remind me of a Fifth Circuit Judge bent on humor, who, after reading a district judge's opinion, scrawled in the margin, "For substantially the reasons stated by the district judge, Reversed." The Commission understood modern law practice and business conditions. Political realities within the structure of the ABA and state bars made the Commission pause. Bold change, no matter how much conditions might call for it, simply was beyond the pale.

The institution of the bar exam and state-by-state admissions form the basis for the jurisdictional restrictions. Before there were formal bar exams and admission was largely a court-by-court affair, and before interstate travel and commerce were commonplace, little need was seen for territorial unauthorized practice restrictions. The earliest formal UPL statutes were adopted in the 1800s although the 1920s and 1930s saw their most dramatic expansion. But they were meant almost exclusively to fend off non-lawyer competitors rather than out-of-state lawyers.

The practice by non-lawyers remains the major focus of unauthorized practice enforcement, to be sure. The UPL enforcement against lawyers from other states has always been sporadic and idiosyncratic. Violation of the cross-border restriction and its sporadic enforcement has given rise to characterizations of cross-border unauthorized practice as "sneaking around."[144] The idiosyncratic enforcement and widespread violations draw comparison to Soviet-style law enforcement: rules exist that are violated routinely, and enforcement comes only when an authority is particularly motivated to prosecute one among many violators. In a JonesDay "Commentary," meant to educate firm counsel and clients about risks, two cases of cross-border unauthorized practice enforcement are referred to as "lightning bolts from the sky."[145]

One of those examples involved Atlanta lawyers who gave advice to a private university in North Carolina, Gardner-Webb University. Retained by the university's trustees to opine on the activities of the university president's special handling of a grade issue for a star basketball player, the firm investigated and wrote a report. The work might well have gone under the radar, as the vast majority of such cross-border services do, except that a local lawyer took offense at the "threatening tone of" letters sent by the law firm to some figures in the controversy. The offended

---

[143] ABA, *supra* note 142.

[144] Charles Wolfram, *Sneaking Around in the Legal Profession: Inter-jurisdictional Unauthorized Practice by Transactional Lawyers*, 36 S. TEX. L. REV. 665 (1995).

[145] Jones Day, Commentary, *Bar License Requirements For In-House Counsel*, (2006) *available at* http://www.jonesday.com/files/Publication/89eb9ef7-e976-45e1-bef3-00a7fafe75f3/Presentation/PublicationAttachment/fdf33929-cb77-4d5f-8eb4-0582dc035fb4/Bar%20License.pdf.

local lawyer's name was O. Max Gardner III (as in Gardner-Webb University), and he brought the initial complaint against the law firm through the North Carolina Bar. Eventually the lawyers and their Atlanta firm were indicted by action initiated by the local prosecutor.[146] The cross-border practice rule seems to be: go ahead with safety, provided you do not offend a powerful local lawyer or prosecutor.

Starting with New Hampshire in 1880, states began to create state bar examination boards.[147] By 1898, only 12 states had established state boards, and it was not until 1931 that all states but 1 (Indiana) had a state board.[148] Between 1870 to 1900, the number of law schools increased from 28 to 100.[149] The state boards created written examinations, the first one taking place in California in 1919.[150] Still, oral examinations continued well into the 20th century in more rural jurisdictions.[151] The state-by-state bar exam was a necessary component of the state-by-state licensing system.

Despite the ABA Section on Legal Education's early efforts to reform the bar admission standards, the chairman of this Section did not create a committee to work on the bar exam itself until 1931. The result was the establishment of the National Conference of Bar Examiners (NCBE) that year.[152] The court-by-court, then state-by-state licensing system, began in the first century of the nation's existence when virtually all practice was local and court based, continued into the 20th century despite changing practices of business and communications, and further continued in the 21st century long after it had become an anachronism. Its continued existence stifles sensible approaches to law practice and frustrates clients.

IV. Ethics 20/20

Like the committee charged with drafting the Canons in 1905[153] and the Kutak Commission during the 1970s, in to cure the current professional malaise came the 2009 Ethics 20/20 Commission, formed to "perform a thorough review of the ABA Model Rules of Professional Conduct and the U.S. system of lawyer regulation in the context of advances in technology and global legal practice

---

[146] Alan Ford, *GWU lawyers, firm indicted for practicing without N.C. license*, SHELBYSTAR.COM (Mar. 19, 2004, 12:00 AM), https://www.accessnorthga.com/detail.php?n=173606&c=2.

[147] Margo Melli, *Passing the Bar: A Brief History of Bar Exam Standards*, 21 THE GARGOYLE 3, 3 (Univ. of Wisc. Law School) *available at* http://law.wisc.edu/alumni/gargoyle/archive/21_1/gargoyle_21_1_2.pdf.

[148] *Id.*

[149] Michael J. Thomas, *The American Lawyer's Next Hurdle: The State-Based Bar Examination System*, 24 J. LEGAL PROF. 235 (2000), *available at* http://heinonline.org.

[150] *California Bar Examination: Information and History*, The State Bar of California, http://admissions.calbar.ca.gov/Portals/4/documents/Bar-Exam-Info-History.pdf (last visited May 16, 2012).

[151] MELLI, *supra* note 148, at 4.

[152] *Id.*

[153] *See* Transactions of the Twenty-Eighth Annual Meeting of the American Bar Association, 28 A.B.A. Rep. 3, 132 (1905).

developments."[154] This is a worthy enterprise to be sure. But as with most ABA commissions, its membership is entirely made up of lawyers.[155] Despite the impetus for the Commission's creation ("radical" advances in globalization and new technologies), its fundamental principles sound a preservative, inward-looking note: "The principles guiding the Commission's work are protection of the public; preservation of core professional values; and maintenance of a strong, independent and self-regulated profession."[156] "Protection,... preservation,... and maintenance...." Among its first decisive acts was to rule out of order any suggestion of following the Australian or UK alternative business model innovations of the prior decade.[157] Once again, we learn that "hindsight is 20/20." This time the lesson has been delivered by the ABA's Ethics 20/20 Commission.

A. WAVE 1

In its first wave of action, the Commission's recommendations were modest and could be characterized as a combination of housekeeping, reorganizing, and modest updating to include references to more current technological advances. Aside from ruling out any consideration of the British and Australian alternative business models innovations, the Commission's main early proposals were the following:

  1. *Incoming Foreign Lawyers report, proposed amendments to MR 5.5, May 2, 2011*[158]

Essentially maintained status quo from 2002 but recommends moving the temporary practice authorization for foreign lawyers into MR 5.5 rather than have it in a separate model rule. This may have the positive effect of having more states adopt the temporary foreign authorization, but it suggests no substantive change in ABA policy. The proposal maintained the status quo's narrower range for temporary practice by foreign lawyers.

  2. *In-house counsel registration May 2, 2011 recommendation*[159]

---

[154] *About*, A.B.A. COMMISSION ON ETHICS 20/20; http://www.americanbar.org/groups/professional_responsibility/aba_commission_on_ethics_20_20/about_us.html (last visited Aug. 11, 2012).

[155] *Id.*

[156] *ABA President Carolyn B. Lamm Creates Ethics Commission to Address Technology and Global Practice Challenges Facing U.S. Lawyers*, A.B.A., http://apps.americanbar.org/abanet/media/release/news_release.cfm?releaseid=730 (last visited Aug. 11, 2012).

[157] American Bar Association, *ABA Commission on Ethics 20/20 Working Group on Alternative Business Structures: For Comment: Issue Paper Concerning Alternative Business Structures*, (April 5, 2011). (Finding that "[a]t its February 2011 meeting in Atlanta, the Commission decided that two options for alternative business structures—passive equity investment in law firms and the public trading of shares in law firms—would not be appropriate to recommend for implementation in the United States at this time, though both have been adopted elsewhere since July 2000.").

[158] ABA Comm. on Ethics 20/20, Initial Draft Proposal—Model Rule 5.5 (2011).

[159] ABA Comm. on Ethics 20/20, Initial Draft Proposal—In-House Counsel Registration (May 2, 2011).

The Report suggests amending the in-house counsel registration rule to include foreign lawyers, as has been done in seven states.

3. *Outsourcing May 5, 2011*[160]

The Report says no changes to black letter rules are required but recommends additions to comments to Model Rules 1.1, 5.3, 5.5, none of which would change current law.

4. *Technology and Confidentiality May 2, 2011*[161]

This Recommendation includes numerous housekeeping edits to Model Rules, most of which restate the fairly obvious. It also adds MR 1.6(c), which articulates a duty to take reasonable care with client information, not a surprising proposition.

5. *Pro Hac Vice recommendations May 2, 2011*[162]

This Recommendation would add foreign lawyers to the scope of the rule's application, following the lead of 13 states, and add more formalities to the application process for pro hac vice admission, making the application process somewhat more onerous.

6. *Use of Technology recommendations June 29, 2011*[163]

This Recommendation updates the nature of electronic client getting in the Model Rule Comments. It changes the nature of prospective client determination in 1.18 to exclude from the category of "prospective client" one who "communicates with a lawyer for the primary purpose of disqualifying the lawyer from handling a materially adverse representation on the same or a substantially related matter..."

At most, these early proposed changes would help catch up to actual changes in technology and globalization that have occurred between the last major amendments to the Model Rules in 2002 and the present. Every technology reference in the proposed recommendations simply adds a word here or there in the Model Rules with which all have become familiar: "e-mail," "electronic document." The proposed changes do not change. They articulate what change technology has already made.

Some of the recommendations simply reorganize provisions (such as the inclusion of foreign lawyer temporary practice in Model Rule 5.5 rather than elsewhere). None is especially forward looking. None modified policies in the major areas of

---

[160] ABA Comm. on Ethics 20/20, Initial Draft Proposal-Outsourcing (May 2, 2011).

[161] ABA Comm. on Ethics 20/20, Initial Draft Proposals—Technology and Confidentiality (May 2, 2011).

[162] ABA Comm. on Ethics 20/20, Initial Draft Proposal-Pro Hac Vice (May 2, 2011).

[163] ABA Comm. On Ethics 20/20, Initial Draft Proposals on Lawyers' Use of Technology and Client Development (June 29, 2011).

change: alternative business models and multidisciplinary practice. Some of the recommended changes to multijurisdictional practice would catch the ABA up to state-adopted changes. Many appear motivated to enhance monitoring of foreign lawyer involvement in the United States, involvement that has become a foregone conclusion and can no longer be prevented as some might wish. The most dramatic changes possible—alternative business practices reforms—were largely ruled out of order near the beginning of the reform process. Once again, change, if any, will have little effect on the bar's elite.

B. PROPOSALS TO THE HOUSE OF DELEGATES, 2012

In its group of proposals to the House of Delegates, formally considered at the August 2012 Annual Meeting, the Commission ensures by its mildness that nothing will happen that has not already happened by virtue of already-changed technology and global trends. Once again, the American legal profession is changing as little as possible, and then only by capitulating to events that have already taken hold.

The Commission acknowledged the fact of modern lawyer life, true for at least 20 years, that lawyers move from state to state more frequently than in the past. But instead of making any proposals that would fundamentally change the state-by-state license system or even change admission on motion to a system more fitting to 21st-century lawyer life, the Commission merely proposed changes to the admission-by-motion model rule requiring practice in five of the immediately preceding seven years to three of the immediately preceding five years, something already in place in many states. Additionally, the Commission proposed that a lawyer be permitted a temporary period of practice in a new state pending his or her application for admission on motion. Neither proposal changes the landscape significantly, nor catches the rules up with current practice let alone looks forward.

The Commission also proposed a useful change in the confidentiality rule, allowing a lawyer to reveal confidential information to the extent necessary to detect and resolve conflicts. While useful, this proposal has little to do with the Commission's charge to examine the rules in light of the dramatic changes in technology and globalization.

In a nod to the past decade or so, the Commission proposed adding the words "e-mail address" and "website" to the Comments to Model Rules relating to advertising media. Adding these words will not embolden lawyers to use websites and e-mail addresses. That happened in the late 1990s. The Commission proposed that the ABA strike as passé language regarding "autodialed" telephone calls. Recognizing that there are new ways of communicating electronically, the Commission proposed changing the word "e-mail" to "electronic communications." Again, changes not likely to affect practice.

Further on its effort to catch the Model Rules' language up with the last decade or so of changes to technology, the Commission proposed adding the words "or electronically stored information" to the rule regarding inadvertent disclosures. Along similar lines, the Commission proposed new language to the definition of "screen" for purposes of imputed conflict analysis that would require a screened lawyer to be kept away from electronic information as well as tangible documents. Finally on this topic, the Commission acknowledged that outsourcing of legal work is occurring and proposed adding Comment language suggesting that lawyers should be competent in making relationships with those outside the firm. Lawyers who outsource work will not be surprised to learn that they should be competent in doing so.

In perhaps its most constructive proposal, the Commission does explicitly propose adding a suggestion that lawyers be competent with respect to technology. Even this adds no new duty for lawyers, but at least creates some attention on the topic of tech competence.

Also without creating any new duty, the Commission does use the word "metadata" in the proposed Comments to the Model Rule regarding inadvertent disclosures. The profession must start somewhere: expanding its vocabulary cannot hurt, but is unlikely to lend itself to forward thinking.

In August 2012, the House of Delegates considered this first wave of Ethics 20/20 Commission proposals. The proposition was proved once again: if a study commission wants House of Delegates' approval, it must keep the proposals modest. With slight adjustments, the House approved all of the Commission's modest proposals. Little, if any, real reform occurred.

On the most controversial topics, even when an ultra-modest change has been proposed by the Commission, it has been pre-stymied by the House of Delegates and cautious state bar associations. Following its preemptive ruling out of ABS changes on the scale of those in place in the United Kingdom and Australia, the Commission continued to consider more modest changes. The District of Columbia is the only U.S. jurisdiction to permit any non-lawyer ownership of law firms. Its form of permission is very modest, very controlled, and very restrictive. So restrictive, in fact, that it is also very little used. No untoward consequences of this crack in permission for non-lawyer ownership has been noticed in the 10 years of its limited DC existence. The Commission concluded that it would propose a change in the ABA rules that would be a *still more modest* crack than that adopted and successfully implemented in DC. That proposal would have been debated at the February 2013 ABA meeting. But in an April 2012 preemptive strike, the Illinois Bar, in conjunction with the ABA Senior Lawyers Division, interposed a resolution that, if adopted, would prohibit even the discussion of the more-modest-than-DC reform. From the Report supporting the Resolution:

Substantial media attention has been placed on the Commission's activities. Among other things, this attention may have created the perception that the ABA is going to change its Model Rules to permit fee splitting and non-lawyer ownership of law firms.... The American Bar Association should wait no longer to make it clear to the public that this is not going to happen.[164]

As the days passed, the Illinois proposal gained more and more momentum. When Illinois State Bar President John Thies briefed his association on the progress of their proposal, a number of states had already indicated their support for the ISBA/Senior Lawyers Division resolution, including Arizona, Indiana, Maryland, Mississippi, North Carolina, and Tennessee:

[T]his is about defending the core values of our profession against the encroachment of non-lawyers—to the detriment of clients. It's gratifying that so many other states are lining up behind us, and I expect this to continue as we approach the ABA meeting in August.[165]

Faced with a contentious fight before getting to the merits, the Commission withdrew its proposed amendment.[166] Once before the House of Delegates in August 2012, after briefer than expected debate, the Illinois Resolution was postponed indefinitely. Although the Illinois resolution was postponed rather than adopted, the ABA characterization of the event was that the ABA "Reaffirms Policy on Sharing Legal Fees with Non-Lawyers."[167] The 2000 rejection of MDPs was reaffirmed in 2012: there is to be no sharing of power with non-lawyers in the American legal profession.

This failure of various commission reform proposals is a regularly occurring pattern. When the Kutak Commission proposed fraud-prevention exceptions in the original Model Rules, the House of Delegates rejected them. Revivals of the same proposals were rejected in 1991. Essentially the same proposals were shelved by the Ethics 2000 Commission in the shadow of likely rejection by the House of Delegates. Those reforms, three times rejected, were all but forced on a resistant profession by Sarbanes-Oxley and the subsequent SEC action. In 2002, the Multijurisdictional Practice Commission, appearing to have teed up significant reforms in cross-border practice, backed off the major reforms and settled for efforts that were largely articulations and adoptions of common practice. Useful,

[164] Debra Cassens Weiss, *ABA House Postpones Resolution Reaffirming Opposition to Nonlawyer Ownership of Law Firms*, A.B.A. J. (Aug. 6, 2012, 11:26 AM), http://www.abajournal.com/news/article/resolution_confirms_aba_stance_against_nonlawyer_ownership_of_law_firms/.

[165] Chris Bonjean, *ISBA submits resolution regarding ABA's Ethics 20/20*, ILLINOIS STATE B. Ass'N (Jun. 20, 2012) http://iln.isba.org/blog/2012/06/20/isba-submits-resolution-regarding-abas-ethics-2020.

[166] James Podgers, *Summer Job: Ethics 20/20 Commission Shelves Nonlawyer Ownership*, A.B.A. J. (June 1, 2012, 2:50 AM) http://www.abajournal.com/mobile/article/summer_job_ethics_20_20_commission_shelves_nonlawyer_ownership.

[167] *Reaffirms Policy on Sharing Legal Fees with Non-Lawyers*, ABA NOW, http://www.abanow.org/2012/06/2012am10a/ (last visited Aug. 11, 2012).

to be sure, but not reforms. At roughly the same time, the Multidisciplinary Practice Commission proposed major reforms in 1999 and 2000, only to be first sent back to further deliberate and second, rejected outright by the House of Delegates. Now, when the sledding in the House of Delegates appears it will be rough, Ethics 20/20 has backed off even modest reforms on controversial subjects and settled for little more than housekeeping and tinkering.

The lesson is clear but not its implications. ABA commissions that remain modest with proposals will pass through the House of Delegates' gauntlet; ABA commissions that propose actual reform will fail. One might argue that if the successful commissions (MJP and Ethics 20/20) gauge *exactly* what the House would tolerate in the way of change, they at least have accomplished that amount of change. And likewise, those commissions that fail on reform proposals (Kutak and MDP) have accomplished nothing by their willingness to propose more ambitious reform.

There are problems with this analysis, however, making it less clear that getting proposals past the House of Delegates equates with success.

First, what if the successful commissions guessed wrong and were too mild in their proposals? If so, they will have left some reform capacity on the table, and the immediate opportunity will have passed. It could be, as some ideologues have suggested, that a game-advancing 5–4 Supreme Court decision is preferable to a watered-down unanimous one.

Second, what if the change that the House is willing to approve is no real change at all? If so, then what can really be said about the enormous personal resources spent by commission members and staff? Did passage of proposals amount to enough to warrant the cost? Even if the modest changes are just that, baby steps in times of rapid technological and social change just cannot keep up.

Third, what if the ABA is not the end of the reform game? The Kutak Commission fraud revelation proposals were defeated by the House of Delegates. But 20 years later, they were adopted almost verbatim by an ABA that was forced to act by Congress and the SEC following the Enron debacle. The Kutak Commission proposals may have had no connection to the later action whatsoever. But they may have laid groundwork for it. Indeed, so many states adopted the Kutak fraud revelation proposals that by the time the ABA was forced to act 20 years later, the ABA and the states were out of step with social need.

Ethics 20/20 has succeeded in getting its proposals adopted by the House of Delegates. But did it succeed at reform? One good way to determine the Commission's success at reform is to ask what has actually changed in the law governing lawyers as a result of its work. Examining the nature of the adopted proposals makes plain that little has changed. There will be little or no work for treatise and casebook authors in their next editions based on the proposals adopted. One new section of the confidentiality rule that adds no new duty and multiple changes to Model Rule Comments that articulate what has already happened as a result of technology and lawyer mobility. The casebook and treatise writers can make the Ethics 20/20 induced changes to their next editions in 30 minutes or less.

The success of Ethics 20/20 in August 2012 was success in achieving its mission statement: It "protect[ed] the public; preserv[ed] core professional values; and maint[ained] a strong, independent and self-regulated profession."[168] It did not, however, take serious account of rapid change in technology and globalization. It succeeded in making as little change as possible.

V. A Crisis with Genuine Consequences

Of all the crises faced by the legal profession, this one is unique and most genuine. Unlike some prior crises, now there is no "other" to exclude from the club. Unlike the Watergate crisis, this one is not primarily a public relations issue. Unlike the civil rights movement or the civility crisis, the changes feared are not primarily a new style of aggressive lawyering. The current crisis most closely strikes at the heart of the system of legal services delivery. It promises the shortest-term, most thorough change ever wrought by a crisis in the American legal profession.

Law firms will not be what they have been for the last 100 years; legal services will be distributed by means that make a mockery of the state-by-state licensing model. Technology and globalization have won in blitzkrieg fashion, rapidly overrunning the profession's defenses. No prior crises brought such rapid change to the profession's core function of delivering legal services. The turn-of-the-20th-century immigrants entered and changed the demographics if not the fundamental values of the profession over the first 50 years of their presence. Women and minority lawyers entered beginning with the civil rights movement and did the same in still more significant ways over a period of 40 years. Communism came and went. The reality and impact of the litigation boom remain topics for debate, as does the loss of civility. Neither has fundamentally changed the character of legal services delivery and the ethos of the profession. But of the current crisis it must be said that the essence of the profession and legal services delivery are truly at stake. It promises the most significant change since the corporate lawyer supplanted the country lawyer as the professional model of excellence.

Individual lawyers and firms do innovate to deal with changes happening around them, but the profession as an entity does not. For example, not long ago there were but two kinds of lawyers at law firms: partners and associates. Now there are 8 or perhaps 10: contract lawyers, part-time associates, associates, permanent associates, equity partners, non-equity partners, and equity partners in the management committee circle, not to mention outsourced work recipient lawyers. These employment-category developments have all been responses to market conditions, aimed at permitting firms to thrive as change occurs. But of course, not all law firms are forward looking either. Chairman of an innovative, international firm, Seyfarth Shaw warns: "Never underestimate the resistance to change from lawyers. Even

---

[168] Lamm, *supra* n. 157.

more likely, never underestimate the ability of lawyers to describe virtual status quo efforts as revolutionary change."[169]

Implicit in the multiplying ways to describe lawyers at law firms is the reality that there are multiplying ways of using a JD degree. No longer is the degree a ticket to a paycheck, let alone a six-figure one. More law graduates have to be entrepreneurs, and fewer are cashing a check written to them by an employer. Scholars have suggested that accreditation standards should not demand a one-size-fits-all legal education, but rather allow for variable law-related degrees with varying levels of qualification to practice.[170] The suggestions are more sophisticated versions of the Carnegie-commissioned Reed Report recommendations that were roundly rejected by the organized bar in the 1920s.[171] So far, the modern versions of these ideas have gained little traction with the profession or its legal education segment.

Instant global communications and data transfer, e-mail, document-sharing programs, Twitter, and Internet-based legal services marketing have not waited for the legal profession's blessing and approval. They all happened before the Multijurisdictional Practice Commission and Ethics 20/20 began their work of resisting their impact or making after-the-fact cosmetic changes. In fairness to both commissions, the looming presence of the House of Delegates promised rejection of more significant reforms.

These technological and globalization changes have made significant outsourcing possible when it was not before. They have made possible and far more effective the inroads of LegalZoom and other Internet-based providers of legal services when they were not before possible. They have made plausible the still-unrealized demands by staffed-up GC offices to provide legal services to their corporation's customers and clients. They have reinvigorated the push for MDPs, thought dead earlier in the decade, and fostered the image of the "legal services aisle" at Target or Walmart with staff lawyers in kiosks waiting to customize purchased wills, LLCs, name changes, and divorces-in-a-box.

A. LAW AND THE PROFESSION'S TECHNOLOGICAL INEPTITUDE

Neither law nor the legal profession can hope to cope with technological advance without the guidance of expert non-lawyers. Tech change is simply too nimble and pervasive for law to deal with it. Common law, bar ethics opinions, bar commissions,

---

[169] Stephen Poor, *Re-Engineering the Business of Law*, DEALB%K (May 7, 2012), http://dealbook.nytimes.com/2012/05/07/re-engineering-the-business-of-law/.

[170] DEBORAH L. RHODE, IN THE INTERESTS OF JUSTICE: REFORMING THE LEGAL PROFESSION at 185–90 (2000); *See generally* THOMAS MORGAN, THE VANISHING AMERICAN LAWYER (2009).

[171] ALFRED Z. REED, TRAINING FOR THE PUBLIC PROFESSION OF THE LAW (1921); ROBERT STEVENS, LAW SCHOOL: LEGAL EDUCATION IN AMERICA FROM THE 1850S TO THE 1980S (1983); Special Committee, Section of Legal Education and Admissions to the Bar, American Bar Association, *Report of the Special Committee to the Section of Legal Education and Admissions to the Bar of the American Bar Association*, 46 ANN. REP. A.B.A. 679 (1921).

legislatures,... none can keep pace. By the time a new rule is drafted and adopted, by the time courts do their work, by the time bar associations study and declare policy, the technology they studied and purport to govern has changed. The U.S. federal civil justice system has been called the "Conestoga Wagon on the information highway."[172]

Early bar ethics rulings regarding e-mail confidentiality held that without encryption or client consent, sending client information via e-mail violated the duty of confidentiality. South Carolina was the first state to address the confidentiality of lawyer-client e-mail. In 1994, the state bar's Ethics Advisory Committee issued an opinion that a lawyer's use of e-mail to communicate with a client, "absent an express waiver by the client," would violate the ethical duty to maintain client confidences. Analogizing e-mail to cellular phones, the committee explained, "[T]he very nature of on-line services is such that the system operators of the on-line service may gain access to all communications that occur on the on-line service."[173]

Soon thereafter, Iowa authorities dealt with the issue. In 1995, its Supreme Court's Board of Professional Ethics ruled that a lawyer using e-mail to communicate "sensitive material" with a client must encrypt the message to avoid violation of disciplinary and ethical rules.[174] A year later, Iowa revisited the issue. This time it went even further, saying that to communicate with a client via e-mail, not only must a lawyer use encryption, but the lawyer must first obtain the client's written consent, including the client's acknowledgment of the security risk.[175]

The rulings did not hold sway for long. In 1997, various bar authorities began issuing opinions that better understood the technology and the legal business's need for it. But as late as 2011, the ABA was still fixated on e-mail communication interception, ruling that lawyers have a duty to warn clients about the risk of interception when, for example, clients or lawyers use networks that share space with hotels, family, and the like.[176]

Next, predictably, will be controversy over lawyer use of "cloud" computing and document storage.[177] Lawyers' use of technology will not wait the many years needed to gain the profession's blessing. Instead, change in practice will happen, and a decade or so on, the profession will spend years studying and making the modest changes necessary to temporarily catch up to practice.

---

[172] KOURLIS & OLIN, REBUILDING JUSTICE 109 (2011) (quoting federal judge John Kane of Colorado).

[173] South Carolina Bar Ethics Advisory Opinion 94-27.

[174] The Iowa State Bar Association Committee on Ethics and Practice Guidelines Opinion 95-30.

[175] The Iowa State Bar Association Committee on Ethics and Practice Guidelines Opinion 96-1.

[176] ABA Formal Op. 11-495.

[177] Nicole Black, *Cloud Computing and the Encryption Red Herring*, SUI GENERIS (Apr. 18, 2011), http://nylawblog.typepad.com/suigeneris/2011/04/cloud-computing-and-the-encryption-red-herring.html.

One example of the profession's technological ineptitude, as it applies to the regulation of lawyers: metadata. Metadata is "data about data," essentially the information that exists behind the page of a word processing or other document. It can tell an interested and tech-savvy observer who wrote a document, when it was first created, who edited it, when and in what manner. In short, it can reveal information that would normally be protected by confidentiality rules and the privilege. The sender of a document that has not been stripped of its metadata has in fact revealed such information, perhaps unwittingly, or in the language of this topic, "inadvertently." It is fairly uncontroversial to say that the sending lawyer has in all likelihood breached confidentiality duties. Ethics 20/20 proposed cosmetic language that will include "tech competence" in the Comments to Model Rule 1.1 and 1.6, a modestly helpful clarification of what already is true. But the recipient lawyer is another story. As of early 2012, 11 state bars and the ABA had issued opinions regarding the ethical propriety of the recipient lawyer searching for the metadata in a received document. The bar opinions run in opposite directions, with some 180 degrees opposed. Pennsylvania and Maryland, for example, permit metadata mining while New York and Florida prohibit it.[178] The New York opinion is among the earliest treating the issue (2001) while the Pennsylvania opinion is among the more recent (2009).

How can the bars get so crossed on an issue? First, judges and lawyers are not among the top tier of the tech savvy. This absence of sophistication seems not to prevent judges and lawyers from weighing in on tech issues. In Florida, a judge is prohibited by the judicial ethics machinery from having lawyers who practice in the judge's court as Facebook friends. The decision makers in this instance clearly fail to understand that Facebook friends are by and large not real friends, but rather more commonly are acquaintances at best. Judges have more significant relationships with lawyers in their community, in church or synagogue, country club or social group. The misconception of the tech version of casual acquaintance drove a mistaken decision. The first bar ethics opinions to treat confidentiality of e-mail prohibited its use without full encryption on a similar misunderstanding and fear of technology. Within two years, e-mail use was so ubiquitous that any effort to regulate it would have been like spitting into the technological wind.

More important, technology changes more quickly than the justice machinery moves. A decision from a state supreme court can be several years apart from the framing of the dispute by the trial court pleadings. And the trial court pleadings are sometimes years removed from the events that gave rise to the claim. Each and every precedential decision is therefore functioning on years-old information framed by the parties' original claims. Decisions of two authorities from different states, whether courts or bar authorities, a mere two years apart dealing with essentially the

---

[178] Florida Bar Prof'l Ethics Comm., Advisory Op. No. 06-2 (September 15, 2006); Maryland State Bar Opinion 2007-09 Ethics of Viewing and/or using Metadata (2006). N.Y. State Bar Ass'n Comm. on Prof'l Ethics, Op. No. 749 (Dec. 14, 2001); Pennsylvania Bar Ass'n Comm. On Legal Ethics and Professional Responsibility, Formal Op.2009-100 (2009).

same topic can come to correctly different conclusions because of the intervening changes in technology or changes in the understanding of its import. Legislatures are little better. The process of getting Federal Rules of Evidence 502, dealing in part with the consequences of inadvertent disclosures, took four and a-half years from Advisory Committee discussion to presidential signature. Technology does not stand still that long. Law's current efforts to deal with technology with ordinary common law analysis and legislative and administrative rule creation look foolish and stuck in legal-process mud. The profession's efforts to police lawyers' use of technology is similarly perpetually behind the times.

B. ONE BAR

Reading the introduction to the Multijurisdictional Practice Report issued in 2002, the reader could not help but anticipate a recommendation to form a single, U.S. bar, abandoning the anachronisms of the state-by-state license system. At minimum, the reader might have anticipated a recommendation that admission-by-motion restrictions be reduced to mere formality levels. Practicing law in this millennium is a multistate, not to mention, international affair.

Corporate work has for some time been so and law firms of any size have had to find workarounds for the restrictions of the state-by-state licensing system: organizing offices in multiple states with lawyers licensed to practice in still additional states; routine use of pro hac admission; routinely turning a blind-eye to possible unauthorized practice charges when attending mediations and arbitrations once the *Condon & Frank* case sent shockwaves through the multistate bar; and strategic alliances with strategically placed regular cocounsel outside the firm's states of authorized practice. With one bar, or greatly reduced admission on motion standards, of course, none of these artifices would be necessary. Together they are wasted effort and a drag on productivity and client service.

But now the multistate practice has spread far beyond corporate and business practice. Even what has been traditionally local work has greater cross-border implications. Criminal defense lawyers are obliged to advise their clients regarding collateral immigration law consequences of guilty pleas.[179] Mobility has made child custody and divorce practice subject to the likely application of various uniform statutes and international treaties on the subject.[180] Small, previously local businesses advertise on their websites, accessible across virtually all borders with corresponding multijurisdictional implications for the governing legal rules, personal jurisdiction, and the practice of the small business lawyer outside her home state.

---

[179] Padilla v. Kentucky, 130 S. Ct. 1473 (2010).
[180] *See* Uniform Child Custody Jurisdiction and Enforcement Act, (1997), *available at* http://www.familylaw.org/uccja.htm

The amendments to Model Rule 5.5 in 2002 were the profession's typical approach of making changes that merely acknowledge what had already occurred outside its walls. The amendments explicitly allowed the sort of intermittent cross-border practice outside of court that was already routinely taking place in the practice. What did not change was the system of 51 jurisdictions wastefully running their own bar exams, guarding their borders from elsewhere-licensed intruders making inroads on their monopoly market, and issuing their own licenses the power of which ends at their state lines. The system conjures images of *Pennoyer v. Neff*, the 19th-century personal jurisdiction case limiting state courts' jurisdictional powers to state borders.[181] And *Pennoyer*, in turn, has always conjured images of the classic Western movies, in which the posse pursues the evildoers until, reaching the state border, law enforcement must rein in their horses and hope that their quarry will one day return to within the reach of their power, all set to dramatic chase music. The evildoers, of course, cross lines as they please; the law cannot.

Under the state-by-state system, odd cases like *Ranta v. McCarney* occur.[182] A competent and sought-after Minnesota lawyer served a handful of business clients in North Dakota much to the clients' satisfaction, until one such client died and his estate hoped to avoid paying the lawyer's bill. The North Dakota courts ruled that the fee contract was connected to unauthorized practice and would not be enforced because of the strong public policy of protecting North Dakota residents from the dreaded threat posed by non-North Dakota lawyers. Never mind that the Minnesota lawyer had served the North Dakota client's interests well and effectively for several years and been paid without controversy by the North Dakota client during his lifetime; never mind that the Minnesota lawyer was the one chosen by the North Dakota client, perhaps the most competent lawyer available within a reasonable distance to handle the tax and business representation involved. The Minnesota lawyer simply was not a *North Dakota* lawyer. The modest multijurisdictional practice reforms in Model Rule 5.5 do not change the result in cases like *Ranta*.

Under the state-by-state system, state bars clung to residency and citizenship requirements to keep others away until the Supreme Court at long last ruled those practices unconstitutional.[183]

In modest ways, even the bar exam, among the most intransigent of legal institutions, has adjusted. The adjustments, if taken to their logical conclusion, make state-by-state bar examination wholly unnecessary.

The NCBE, along with the ABA and the Association of American Law Schools, created the Code of Recommended Standards for Bar Examiners in

---

[181] 95 U.S. 714 (1878).
[182] Ranta v. McCarney, 391 N.W. 2d 161 (N.D. 1986).
[183] Sup. Ct.of N.H. v. Piper, 470 U.S. 274 (1985); In re Griffiths, 413 U.S. 717 (1973).

1958.[184] These standards pushed for states to conduct written examinations in essay format.[185]

About a decade later, in the 1970s, the NCBE blended these guidelines into one exam—the Multistate Bar Exam (MBE).[186] It created the exam through a grant that it had received from the ABA, and in part the exam was a result of discussions since the 1940s to have a national bar exam, something that had never materialized because of the fear of usurping states' power.[187] Thus, when the MBE was created, control over whether to use the test, and what the passing grade would be, was left to the states.[188] The creation of the MBE resulted in part because of the states' struggle to keep up with the admission process—applications had risen from 16,000 in 1960 to 58,000 in 1980. A uniform exam and multiple choice questions make the grading process more far more efficient and effective.[189] Days and weeks of inevitably inconsistent graders' reading essay answers could be reduced to a moment's application of computer grading of scannable answer sheets.

In the aftermath of Watergate, the NCBE created the Multistate Professional Responsibility Exam (MPRE) in 1980.[190] It has allowed for a national exam of professional responsibility matters, again with states determining the passing score, as if some states require their lawyers to be more ethically knowledgeable than others. Nonetheless, on the same date, multiple times each year, every prospective new lawyer takes the same exam with the same questions and test conditions.

Addressing the states' continuing desire for essay exams, the Multistate Essay Exam (MEE) was created as an attempt at consistency and quality-control for the essay portion of the bar exams.[191] For the MEE, the NCBE provides the jurisdictions with nine 30-minute questions, and each jurisdiction can choose which essay questions it wants to use.[192] Three of the questions are drawn from the MBE topics, while six are drawn from the broader list of MEE topics, which are "Business Associations, Conflict of Laws, Family Law, Federal Civil Procedure, Trusts and Estates, and Uniform Commercial Code."[193]

The NCBE has also created an examination called the Multistate Performance Test (MPT).[194] The NCBE offers two 90-minute prompts, and, like the MEE, jurisdictions can choose to administer one or the other, or both.[195] Each of these prompts includes a "File," which is a compilation of documents such as memos, contracts,

---

[184] Melli, *supra* note 148, at 4.

[185] *Id.*

[186] *Id.*

[187] *Id.*

[188] *Id.*

[189] *Id.*

[190] *Id.* at 5.

[191] *Id.*

[192] *Multistate Essay Examination (MEE)*, NATIONAL CONFERENCE OF BAR EXAMINERS (2012) http://www.ncbex.org/multistate-tests/mee/.

[193] *Id.*

[194] *Id.*

[195] *Id.*

police reports, the lawyer's notes, and other paperwork.[196] The prompt also includes a "Library," which contains "cases, statutes, regulations, or rules," some of which may not be relevant, and a memo from a supervising attorney with the specific task the test taker is supposed to perform.[197] This task could be writing a memo, a brief, a discovery plan, part of a contract, and various other services.[198].

Finally, the NCBE has also created the Uniform Bar Examination (UBE),[199] the first administration of which was in 2011 in Missouri, North Dakota, and Alabama.[200] The UBE is a compilation of the MBE, MEE, and MPT, with the MBE given a weight of 50 percent of the score, the MEE 30 percent, and the MPT as 20 percent.[201] Still concerned with the balance of power between the states and the NCBE, the latter lists on its website all of the ways that the jurisdictions can still have control after adopting the UBE, such as still being able to make character and fitness determinations and deciding who can take the exam.[202]

All of these national exams are in use, but not all have been used equally. According to the NCBE,[203] the MBE is used in 46 jurisdictions,[204] the MEE in 22 jurisdictions, 27 jurisdictions use or will soon use the MPT,[205] 53 jurisdictions use or will soon use the MPRE,[206] and 9 jurisdictions use or plan to use the UBE.[207] According to the ABA, the most common testing arrangement is a two-day bar examination, in which the MBE is taken one day, and on the second day, the testers work on "locally crafted essays from a broader range of subject matters [than the MBE]."[208]

The state of the art in design for bar exams has changed dramatically since 1975. Lincoln's time, when judges examined applicants in casual settings has long since passed, but the stultifying ramifications of state-by-state licensing have not.

---

[196] *Id.*

[197] *Id.*

[198] *Multistate Essay Examination (MEE)*, NATIONAL CONFERENCE OF BAR EXAMINERS (2012) http://www.ncbex.org/multistate-tests/mee/.

[199] *The Uniform Bar Examination (UBE)*, NAT'L CONF. OF B. EXAMINERS, http://www.ncbex.org/multistate-tests/ube/ (last visited Aug. 11, 2012).

[200] *UBE Jurisdictions*, NAT'L CONF. OF B. EXAMINERS, http://www.ncbex.org/multistate-tests/ube/ube-jurisdictions/ (last visited Aug. 11, 2012).

[201] *The Uniform Bar Examination (UBE)*, NAT'L CONF. OF B. EXAMINERS, http://www.ncbex.org/multistate-tests/ube/ (last visited Aug. 11, 2012).

[202] *Id.*

[203] *NCBE Testing Services*, NAT'L CONF. OF B. EXAMINERS (Feb. 29, 2012), http://www.ncbex.org/assets/media_files/Multistate-Tests/2012NCBETesting-Services-including-UBE-jurisdictions022912.jpg.

[204] The NCBE's statistics include all of the U.S. jurisdictions that use its services, and therefore, the statistics include information for all 50 states, plus the District of Columbia, the Northern Mariana Islands, Puerto Rico, Palau, and the Virgin Islands.

[205] Connecticut is adding the MPT in July 2014.

[206] Washington will have the MPRE in July 2013.

[207] Montana, Nebraska, and Washington are soon adopting the UBE.

[208] *Bar Admissions Basic Overview*, A.B.A., http://www.americanbar.org/groups/legal_education/resources/bar_admissions/basic_overview.html (last visited Aug. 11, 2012).

Fifty-one jurisdictions staff up to administer and grade 51 exams, different from one another only by the state essay portion, which is itself beginning to fade in usage. The tools exist for a single bar exam, administered nationally. Only parochial state bar associations and their economic protectionism stand in the way.

VI. Conclusion

The organized legal profession cannot and will not find its own way out of this current, and most genuine of crises. On its own, it cannot deal effectively with technology. It does not understand the implications of global market changes. It cannot deal effectively with its own political power structure of the 51 territorial, parochial bars. Its only way out will be through the expertise and intercession of others, non-lawyers with the technological or business expertise and mindset to see forward. It cannot break free from its golden age recidivist reflexes to deal effectively with changes in technology and globalization that simply will not wait for the profession's ponderous ways of analysis. Without the expertise of non-lawyers, as with multiple prior crises, change will come and overwhelm an unprepared profession. But this time, the change will be more fundamental and will leave behind a legal profession unrecognizable by today's norms.

{ 10 }

Changing the Change-Game

The history of the legal profession's self-regulation during self-identified crisis times (such as the present) is not a happy one. The profession has resisted change. When it did institute change, it was directed not at the existing members of the profession, but at new entrants. Changes made have been in service of the status quo. Mostly, change that has come has been forced by influences of society, culture, technology, economics, and globalization, and not by the profession itself. Watergate, communist infiltration, arrival of waves of immigrants, the litigation explosion, the civility crisis, and the current economic crisis that blends with dramatic changes in technology and communications and globalization. In every instance, the profession held fast to its history and its ways, long after those ways became anachronistic. The profession seems to repeat the same question in response to every crisis: how can we stay even more "the same" than we already are?

I. Protect, Preserve, and Maintain

In short, the legal profession is ponderous, backward looking, and self-preservationist. The ABA's currently functioning Ethics 20/20 Commission was established because of the dramatic changes in economics of law practice, globalization, and technology. Yet its mission statement sets the tone for its work: "The principles guiding the Commission's work are protection of the public; preservation of core professional values; and maintenance of a strong, independent and self-regulated profession." Protect, preserve, and maintain. This most recent "reform" mission statement is strikingly similar to that of the first bar associations, born in the 1870s of "crisis" and formed for their profession's "protect[ion], pur[ifaction] and preserv[ation]."[1] I recommend a more forward-looking approach, one that welcomes the views and even control of non-lawyers, innovators in business, and other enterprises. My hope is that the legal profession going forward can be more like Apple and IBM and Western Union, and less like Kodak.

---

[1] *Professional Organizations*, 6 ALBANY L. J. 233 (1873); Walter B. Hill, *Bar Associations*, 5 GA. BAR ASSOC. REPORTS, 75 (1888).

Albert Einstein taught us, "You cannot solve a problem from the same consciousness that created it. You must learn to see the world anew."[2] The American legal profession tries to solve problems with the same thinking that created them. It clings to the past and precedent. It "protects..., preserves...and maintains...."[3] It acts as if preserving the status quo will solve all, when in fact it will solve nothing. This backward thinking, the same thinking that preceded the crisis, exacerbates the impact of the crisis. More than anything else, the legal profession would benefit from the thinking patterns of innovative non-lawyers.

Time after time, the profession has resisted change when it cannot prevent it. The profession's efforts to keep out immigrants failed to reflect the true spirit of the changes that were happening to America all around it: the country was growing stronger by the cultural contributions and diversity of viewpoint that was the true baggage being unloaded from boats full of immigrants. The profession's efforts to prevent the new kind of lawyering that accompanied the civil rights movement failed because the newest entrants to the profession were already steeped in the notion that activism could cure social ills. The profession's efforts to stem the tide of competitive juices that fueled what the profession deemed incivility failed because the lawyers of the time were also people of the time, and the world had become a more competitive place.

When change comes to the legal profession, it is effected by forces outside the profession. The turn of the 20th-century immigrants eventually integrated themselves into the bar notwithstanding the bar's efforts to diminish and exclude them. Other changes in demographics and culture, leading to the entry of women and blacks into the profession, have been inevitable, even if resisted by the profession at various times. Communism came and went on its own without being affected by the bar's efforts to stem the tide of its professional infiltration. The so-called civility crisis of the 1990s came into the profession as the world was becoming a more competitive place, and road rage reflected one external symptom of an anxious society. The profession's decades-long, repeated efforts to protect confidentiality even in the face of corporate frauds finally collapsed in the post-Enron era when change in the Model Rules was largely driven by Securities and Exchange Commission (SEC) regulations adopted over the profession's objections. Economic changes in the 2000s are what they are. The legal market, domestic and global, will be what it will be, and the bar's reaction to these changes will not stay their effects. Instead of

---

[2] Other versions of this quote, usually credited to Einstein but unconfirmed, include, "We can't solve problems by using the same kind of thinking we used when we created them."

[3] *See* ABA Comm. on Ethics 20/20, Working Group on Alternative Business Structures, *For Comment: Issues Paper Concerning Alternative Business Structures* (Apr. 5, 2011). (Stating that "[t]he American Bar Association Commission on Ethics 20/20 is examining the impact of globalization and technology on the legal profession. The principles guiding the Commission's work are protection of the public; preservation of core professional values; and maintenance of a strong, independent and self-regulated profession."), *available at* http://www.americanbar.org/content/dam/aba/administrative/ethics_2020/abs_issues_paper.authcheckdam.pdf

resisting change, the profession should become more attuned to events and trends outside its walls. The profession should adjust and become a player in how change is assimilated into established ways, and how outmoded-but-established ways are replaced by more effective ones.

What change is occasionally[4] wrought at the hands of the organized bar seems designed to leave the lives of the bar's elite as-is to the greatest extent possible. The major changes that followed in Watergate's wake raised entry barriers (the MPRE and required ethics courses in law school), but had barely a wisp of effect on the already admitted.[5]

The legal profession and the society it claims to serve would be better off if regulation of the legal profession were more open and viewpoint inclusive. No entity, whether motivated by profit, altruism, or a mixture of the two, can manage itself without an eye to the future. Successful businesses and institutions engage in forward-looking strategic planning. Successful businesses and institutions examine society's trends to predict future markets and to modify their own ways to be well positioned to succeed in whatever happens to be the business or institution's place and goal set.

In contrast, the American legal profession regulates primarily in response to crisis. And when it does regulate, it makes as little change as possible. Much of the "change" actually made is done in the service of preserving the status quo. The 1908 Canons were almost entirely copied from materials published in 1834, 1854, and the 1880s; and the only new material prohibiting advertising was meant to thwart the effectiveness and market penetration of the emerging plaintiffs' lawyer class, mainly of immigrant stock; the scramble of change in the late 1970s was meant primarily to quell the furor over Watergate; and the Ethics 20/20 proposed changes to date do little more than formally capitulate to the irresistible forces of technology and global changes that have already happened. This is management by looking backward and inward, management in service of the status quo.

Change should be studied and embraced rather than resisted. For the legal profession to do so, it must change its manner of regulation in a fundamental way. It must welcome the views of non-lawyers not merely to mollify the public but because lawyers are not all knowing. It must view change for its benefit rather than its detriment. Open meetings must be open in spirit and not merely in form. In its current mode of regulation, the legal profession necessarily fails to take advantage

---

[4] The ABA Canons were in force for 62 years (1908 to 1970) when at long last they were replaced by the Model Code. The ink on the Model Code barely dried when Watergate sent the profession scrambling for public relations cover in 1976 in the form of the Model Rules. The major Model Rules' amendments between 1983 and 2012 have been driven by forces outside the profession, such as the post-Enron amendments to MR 1.6 and 1.13 and the currently proposed Ethics 20/20 amendments that largely reflect changes in technology that have already occurred. Otherwise, the amendments to the Model Rules have been more like tinkering than reform.

[5] The change from Model Code to Model Rules, as adopted rather than as proposed, was more repackaging than concept or lawyer-obligation changing.

of trends and movements in society. To be effective, it must begin to see outside itself with open eyes rather than suspicious ones.

II. Why Non-Lawyers?

To open itself to forward-looking regulation, the legal profession needs the help of non-lawyers. Why non-lawyers? Lawyers by nature, training, and practice are not aggressively forward-looking organizational planners. Litigators work to minimize the harm or maximize the gain from past events. Their work is, by its nature, backward looking.

Even transactional lawyers, while focused on the future plans of their clients, do their work with a goal of avoiding controversy for their clients. They seek in their drafting and negotiating work to avoid future conflict for their business clients, while the business clients themselves look to the future of their business, anticipating new markets and positioning their businesses to take advantage of what they believe the future may hold. The business clients do this work by being sensitive to trends and changes in culture and society. They do this work by seeing opportunity and growth, rather than by seeing and avoiding controversy.

I am not diminishing the importance of lawyers' work: without the lawyer's sensitivity to conflict avoidance, a business client may fall into life's traps and be swallowed up by dangerous future liabilities. But the lawyer does not seek to grow a client's business. A lawyer relies on precedents and on hard statements of current legislation and regulation to do her work. Lawyers are tied to the past and bound by habit and training to overvalue the past. Drafting of documents itself provides such an indication: lawyers choose the words that have always worked, even when those words have lost their meaning in modern language. Lawyers "give, devise and bequeath" when "give" would do just as well. The reliance on ancient words, formalisms, and coupled synonyms is well-documented evidence of lawyers' tendency to be conservative, reliant on the past, and even insecure.[6] Lawyer regulation needs the talents of those who can see the road ahead. Such people are more likely to be non-lawyers than lawyers, to be more like Steve Jobs than John W. Davis. Successful lawyers look backward.

Certainly there are exceptions, but the most forward-thinking lawyers are not likely to be the leaders of the profession. Richard Susskind, for example, a forward thinker and lawyer, is an unlikely candidate for chairman of the UK Bar Council. Certainly, were he an American, he would not likely rise to president of the ABA. He simply has not followed the historical path to that position. With few exceptions, the path to organized bar leadership runs through successful practice in a large firm, where the values of precedent, history, and tradition are strongest, and where the interest in modest if any change is most likely to preserve current competitive

---

[6] *See generally* David Mellinkoff, The Language of the Law (Res. Publ'ns 2004).

advantages earned by years of steady, conservative management. The path to high leadership in the ABA and the profession is well marked. Of the 11 ABA presidents from 2001 to 2012,[7] one came from a firm of less than 100. Most came from firms of 150 to 800. Several came from firms of 2,000 lawyers. All had long leadership records with ABA, ALI, or state bars. First bar licensing for each was in the 1970s or before. Interestingly, unlike earlier generations of ABA presidents, most did not graduate from elite law schools. At least for this generation, an elite law school diploma is not a prerequisite to professional success. "Lawyers tend to look backward, and bar leaders who have been financially successful under the current system have little incentive to face squarely the world as it is likely to become."[8] By contrast, successful businesspeople, scientists, and others who lead successful institutions *do* face squarely the world as it is likely to become. They must. And so must innovative individual lawyers face the world as it is likely to become. But as of yet, they are as unlikely to be bar leaders as are businesspeople or scientists. This, too, needs to change for the future health of the profession.

When the Dotcom Revolution occurred, major existing businesses were faced with a choice: hold tight to traditional ways and try to ride out this revolution until it passed, or look forward and blend what they did well with new forms and devices. Jack Welch at GE, for example, first wondered how the dotcoms might destroy his business, but quickly turned that analysis into ways to grow GE's business, asking how the successful dotcoms' innovations could be used to make GE more effective.[9]

Watson, the IBM computer technology, provides an example of non-lawyer thinking used to solve a problem. Rather than continue with the tried and true method of endlessly packing more and more information inside a computer's memory, the IBM scientists pursued an entirely new form of computing: create a computer capable of analyzing unstructured data, in natural language.[10] Not more volumes of information; better computing.

III. Be Western Union, Not Kodak

Two household-name corporations, founded in the same era as the legal profession organized, provide a lesson in contrasting management from which the legal profession could learn.

---

[7] Wm. T. (Bill) Robinson III, (2011–2012); Stephen Zach, Immediate Past President (2010–2011); Carolyn Lamm (2009–2010); H. Thomas Wells, Jr. (2008–2009); William H. Neukom (2007–2008); Karen Mathis (2006–2007); Michael S. Greco (2005–2006); Robert S. Grey (2004–2005); Dennis Archer (2003–2004); Alfred P. Carleton Jr. (2002–2003); Robert E. Hishon (2001–2002).

[8] Thomas Morgan, *Toward Abandoning Organized Professionalism*, 30 Hofstra L. Rev. 947, 975 (2002).

[9] Richard Susskind, The End of Lawyers 4 (Oxford Univ. Press, paperback ed. 2010).

[10] IBM, http://www-03.ibm.com/innovation/us/watson/watson-for-a-smarter-planet/watson-schematic.html (last visited Aug. 11, 2012).

In the late 19th century, at about the same time that the legal profession cre-
ated undoubtedly its most lasting product innovation, the corporate form, George
Eastman was founding Kodak, an American icon known for technology innovation of cameras, film, and processing. Kodak was once one of the top brands in
America, at its peak owning 90 percent of the U.S. film market. For over 120 years,
Kodak looked inward for problem solving and innovation. In fact, at one time
they raised their own cattle for the bones needed to produce photographic gelatin.
Market dominance reinforced the belief that the company had the right business
model and management structure to continue to succeed.

By 1975, Kodak knew digital photography was coming and understood the
threat to its core business. It developed the first digital camera and had a sense of
the future of photographic technology. But the profits from its established product,
film, were so enormous that they feared a rapid decline in film sales once digital technology was broadly available. Kodak was so fearful of the future of image
making that for 25 years, while the image market changed dramatically, Kodak
stayed largely out of the digital market. Within five years of its late entry in 2000, it
became a leader in that market, but by then the number of competitors and changes
in the way images were being created and used had largely commoditized the digital
camera market, and profit margins were exceedingly thin.[11]

> Immensely successful companies can become myopic and product oriented
> instead of focusing on consumers' needs. Kodak's story of failing has its
> roots in its success, which made it resistant to change. Its insular corporate
> culture believed that its strength was in its brand and marketing, and it under-
> estimated the threat of digital.[12]

Kodak's insular corporate culture and resistance to change caused them to miss
the shift of how consumers "consumed" photography. The market became one in
which it did not matter what technology was used to create the image (camera,
phone, laptop). Kodak did not foresee the shift from a product market to an electronic services-based one. They recognized the problem too late and were too slow
to react. Nancy West, a University of Missouri professor who wrote a history of
Kodak's early years, commented:

> When (George Eastman) died,... Kodak immediately became bound up in
> nostalgia. Nostalgia's lovely, but it doesn't allow people to move forward.[13]
>
> The seeds of the problems of today go back several decades.... Kodak
> was very Rochester-centric and never really developed a presence in centers

---

[11] Avi Dan, *Kodak Failed By Asking the Wrong Marketing Question*, Forbes, (Jan. 23, 2012,
9:59 AM), http://www.forbes.com/sites/avidan/2012/01/23/kodak-failed-by-asking-the-wrong-
marketing-question/.

[12] *Id.*

[13] *Kodak: What led to bankruptcy*, Hindustan Times (Jan. 22, 2012), http://www.hindustan
times.com/technology/IndustryTrends/Kodak-What-led-to-bankruptcy/SP-Article1-800633.
aspx.

of the world that were developing new technologies. It's like they're living in a museum.[14]

Kodak filed for bankruptcy protection in January 2012, with a business plan to sell its patents, a marker of a business's final capitulation.

Had Kodak looked outside itself, it might have behaved more like Western Union. Founded in the same era as Kodak and the organized form of the American legal profession, Western Union adjusted to each change in society's development. It handled the first transcontinental telegram in 1861 and started the business of transferring money by wire 10 years later. Like Kodak, it executed a series of firsts: a city-to-city facsimile service, a microwave communications system, a commercial satellite network, and online money transfer.[15]

Why has Western Union been able to adapt to severe disruptions and survive over so many years? It never confused the *business* it was in with the *way* it conducted its business. (emphasis added.) At its core, Western Union was about facilitating person-to-person communications and money transfers—whether via telegraph, wireless networks, phone, or the Internet. "We always saw ourselves as a communications company."[16]

Founded in 1851 as a telegraph company, Western Union's early company history is one of growth by expansion to create a coast-to-coast U.S. network. It was successful in acquiring most of its competitors (but declined to buy patents from Alexander Graham Bell for telephone technology), and created a monopoly. In 1869, it developed the first stock ticker and in 1871 introduced money transfers. Western Union was one of the first 11 companies on the Dow Jones Average.

In the United States, Western Union offered the first consumer charge card, the first singing telegram, the first city-to-city fax service, had the first commercial satellite, and sold the first prepaid disposable phone card. They owned a large physical infrastructure of pre-Internet communications. The age of the Internet changed the game. Profits had already dropped after World War II as the phone became more prevalent than the telegraph. By the early 1980s, Western Union had mounting debt and divested itself from some of its telecommunications-based assets. At the same time, deregulation offered the opportunity for them to expand their money transfer services outside the United States; Western Union saw the opportunity and took it.[17]

---

[14] *Id.* (quoting Rosabeth Kanter, the Arbuckle professor of business administration at Harvard Business School).

[15] Steve Hamm & William C. Symonds, *Mistakes Made On the Road To Innovation*, BLOOMBERG BUSINESSWEEK MAGAZINE (Nov. 26, 2006), http://www.businessweek.com/stories/2006-11-26/mistakes-made-on-the-road-to-innovation.

[16] *Id.* (quoting Chistina Gold, Western Union president).

[17] FUNDINGUNIVERSE, http://www.fundinguniverse.com/company-histories/New-Valley-Corporation-Company-History.html (last visited Aug. 8, 2012); WESTERN UNION, http://corporate.westernunion.com/history.html (last visited Aug. 8, 2012).

By 1987, the company went through a massive restructuring just prior to being forced into Chapter 11 protection. In the next several years, they transformed from an asset-based company into an electronic services-based company with international money transfers at its core. Unlike Kodak's clinging relationship to film, the Western Union telegraph was laid to rest in 2006. But the electronic money transfer service they started in 1871 is today in 200 countries. "At its core, Western Union was about facilitating person-to-person communications and money transfers— whether via telegraph, wireless networks, phone, or the Internet."[18]

The legal profession behaves more like Kodak, whose own success in the film market blinded it to the reality that it was in the image business. From its first half-century of existence, the legal profession saw its conservative ideologies being rejected by the American sociopolitical consensus, and expended much of its energy trying to restore a lost American past.[19]

IV. Law Firms But Not the Profession

The legal profession needs the consultation of non-lawyers to guide its future regulation. Non-lawyers will have none of the legal profession's self-interest and will more likely have the abilities and temperament conducive to forward-looking planning. Law *firms*, of course, have done just this, but they are not the institutional legal profession. The non-lawyers hired by law firms to manage business interests and personnel issues within law firms are not owners of the firms, but they do occupy positions with significant decision-making power and influence.

The phenomenon is escalating at a more and more rapid pace. Where, even 10 years ago, the notion of non-lawyer law firm managers was met with discomfort if not scorn, today it is highly prevalent and normal. The job descriptions and duties of non-lawyers who hold managerial positions in law firms are widely available.

A number of high-level, non-lawyer jobs exist in law firms today. All non-lawyer managers (executive directors, administrators, and chief operating officers) hold key responsibilities.[20] Non-lawyer chief financial officers direct and oversee the financial aspects of the firm including accounting, forecasting, financial planning and analysis, budgeting, and financial reporting.[21] Law firm administrators, executive directors, chief managing officers, and chief operating officers[22] all manage the business side of legal practice through such roles as hiring, branding, marketing,

---

[18] Hamm, *supra* note 15.

[19] John Matzko, The Early Years of the American Bar Association, 1878–1928 at 518 (1984) (unpublished dissertation, University of Virginia) (on file with author).

[20] 07–5 Law Off. Mgmt. & Admin. Rep. 2.

[21] Sally Kane, *Legal Jobs—Part II: Non-Lawyer Careers in a Law Firm*, About.com, http:// legalcareers.about.com/od/legalcareerbasics/a/Legal-Jobs-Part-Ii-Non-Lawyer-Careers-In-A-Law-Firm.htm (last visited Aug. 8, 2012).

[22] *Id.*

human resources, compensation, benefits, business development, and technology, to name just a few.[23] This principal administrator typically reports directly to the managing partner or executive committee.[24] The Human Resources Manager has overall responsibility for all personnel matters regarding support staff, which includes hiring, assignments, supervision, orientation and training, evaluation, personnel records, and benefits administration.[25] A marketing coordinator is responsible for implementing the various individual, departmental, and firm-wide marketing plans, projects, and strategies.[26] Non-lawyers are managing the business of law firms and the lawyers who work in them.

The practice of employing high-level business people to manage law firms had become sufficiently prevalent that in May of 2005, George Washington University first began to offer a course within its College of Professional Studies in Formal Law Firm Management Instruction.[27] At many large law firms, lawyers regularly work alongside non-lawyer professionals who help guide business decisions.[28] Many of those professionals sit in on partnership meetings and are compensated by a bonus system that mimics profit sharing.[29]

About 10 years ago, a controversial statement appeared in an *ABA Journal* publication. Robert W. Denney wrote: "The practice of law is a profession, but a law firm is a business and must be managed like a business."[30] That statement produced indignant replies from lawyers saying emphatically that a law firm is *not* a business and castigating him for saying it is.[31] The same statements about law having become a business have distressed lawyers for a century or more. But the profession persists in denying that the statement is the truth. D.L.A. Piper recently took a highly unusual approach to senior management.[32] Instead of electing one of its partners as cochair, the firm recruited an outsider for the position.[33] That individual had most recently held two top-level corporate management positions and, prior to that, for

---

[23] *Id.*; *See also How Many Non-Lawyers Does It Take to Run a Law Firm?*, Freedman Consulting, http://www.pa-lawfirmconsulting.com/pdfs/hr/HOW_MANY_NON_LAWYERS_DOES_IT_TAKE_TO_RUN_A_LAW_FIRM.pdf (last visited Aug. 8, 2012).

[24] *How Many Non-Lawyers Does It Take to Run a Law Firm?*, Freedman Consulting, http://www.pa-lawfirmconsulting.com/pdfs/hr/HOW_MANY_NON_LAWYERS_DOES_IT_TAKE_TO_RUN_A_LAW_FIRM.pdf (last visited Aug. 8, 2012).

[25] *Id.*

[26] *Id.*

[27] *New Academic Course in Law Firm Management Seems Worth the Tuition*, Of Counsel, May 2005, *available* at http://cps.gwu.edu/master-professional-studies-and-graduate-certificate-law-firm-management.

[28] *Id.*

[29] *Id.*

[30] Robert W. Denney, *Managing the Firm as a Business*, A.B.A., http://www.americanbar.org/publications/law_practice_magazine/2012/march_april/trends-report.html (last visited Aug. 8, 2012).

[31] *Id.*

[32] *Id.*

[33] *Id.*

nine years had been firm-wide managing director of Linklaters.[34] Major law firms understand their need for non-lawyer managers.

Although not bringing them into management positions, some other firms—both large and midsized—are involving outside business executives in management, some of whom might be non-lawyer industry experts or top legal consultants.[35] For instance, several years ago, national insurance law firm Nelson Levine de Luca & Horst formed an executive board of retired executives from the insurance industry to advise it on operations and strategy.[36] So, while the term has not been used in this context, the "new normal" in law firm management is business-style management with non-lawyers prominently featured.[37]

Non-lawyers and their special skills matter in the management and planning for a law firm. The profession as an entity, however, has yet to make serious use of the talents of non-lawyers. History demonstrates that lawyers are inept at being their own profession's exclusive regulators. Lawyers tend to look backward to precedent and sideways to existing articulations of law. When lawyers do look forward, their primary task is to predict and guard against risk. It is not in lawyers' nature to be forward-looking planners, sensitive to cultural trends. These conservative ways of managing have caused the legal profession to manage in reaction to crisis. And even then, to seek preservation of the status quo for as long as possible, until cultural and economic events impose their own unwanted change on the legal profession.

Change happens. The American legal profession resists change until the change dictates its own terms with the profession. As a result, the legal profession is a passive member of society. The profession itself fails to play a serious role in social change, even when some of its forward-looking members are doing so. Its failure of vision seriously limits its flexibility to change. It seems to have eyes in the back of its head. But not on its face.

The unwelcome cure is to enlist non-lawyers in the regulation of the legal profession: planners and evaluators of cultural trends. The profession needs people who can participate in lawyer regulation without the self-interest of the established members of the bar, people who have a wider view, people who can see the path ahead and not merely the ground already trod.

V. Other Impediments to Reform

The profession has struggled with its capacity for reform. But some discrete aspects of the profession have done their part to make reform more difficult than it would

---

[34] *Id.*

[35] *Id.*

[36] Robert W. Denney, *Managing the Firm as a Business*, A.B.A., http://www.americanbar.org/publications/law_practice_magazine/2012/march_april/trends-report.html (last visited Aug. 8, 2012).

[37] *Id.*

otherwise be. Two of the key stages to gaining entry to the profession—legal education and the bar exam—have handicapped reform in the profession as a whole. Each has its own power structure. Each, to be sure, has close ABA ties, but each exists as a land unto itself.

A. LEGAL EDUCATION'S RECALCITRANCE TO REFORM

Legal education has not been much better than the profession itself at innovation. Legal education's last transformative reform occurred in the late 19th century when Christopher Columbus Langdell and James Barr Ames invented the case method, the casebook and the basic curriculum that remains the staple of nearly every U.S. law school now, 130 years later. (Certainly, changes in legal education have occurred during those 130 years, but the core of that reform remains the core of today's legal education.) The Harvard-led reform of Langdell and Ames was part of a larger move toward scientification. Higher education was becoming more scientific, and unless a discipline could be described as a serious science, it was doomed to lower-class status within the academic community. So the legal education reforms, meant to make law feel like Biology (Biology's taxonomic ranks and classification "trees" look not unlike the West Key Number System for classifying decided cases[38]) and like Geometry (in terms of "proofs" based on certain axioms) made sense. But a fateful choice was made: medical education, reformed at the same time, decided its mission would be to generate doctors; legal education decided its mission would be to create law professors. There was resistance to the professional separation strategy of Langdell and Ames. In an 1883 letter from Harvard Law Dean Ephraim Gurney to Harvard President Charles W. Eliot, he lamented:

> Langdell's ideal is to breed professors of Law, not practitioners; erring, as it seems to me, on the other side from the other schools, which would make only practitioners. Now to my mind it will be a dark day for the School when either of these views is able to dominate the other, and the more dangerous success of the two would be the doctrinaire because it would starve the School. In my judgment, . . . if . . . the School commits itself to the theory of breeding within itself its Corps of instructors and thus severs itself from the great current of legal life which flows through the courts and the bar, it commits the gravest error of policy which it could adopt. . . . Another feature to my mind of the same tendency is the extreme unwillingness to have anything furnished by the School except the pure science of the law. It seems to a layman that when the School exacts a year more than any other of study for its degree, it might concede something, at least at the start, of their time to such practical training as might be given successfully in such a school. I have never been able to

---

[38] First described by John B. West in 1909, John B. West, *A Multiplicity of Reporters*, 2 Law Libr. J. 4 (1909).

see why this should be thought belittling to the School or its instructors.... If you[r] LLB at the end of his three years did not feel as helpless on entering an office on the practical side as he is admirably trained on the theoretical, I think he would begrudge his third year less.[39]

Legal education intentionally disconnected from the legal profession, much to the dismay of some old standard law professors.[40] The legal profession is still recovering from that choice.

Periodically, legal education has been criticized as disconnected from the profession, by the profession. Among those critiques was Harry Edwards in his 1992 *Michigan Law Review* article. The Edwards's critique received plenty of attention,[41] but little reform resulted.

Now, legal education is in the crosshairs of multiple shooters: law firms and other legal employers; law firms' clients (GCs and business people alike); prospective students; *The New York Times*. And so on. At the 2011 Fourth Circuit Court of Appeals Annual Conference, Chief Justice John G. Roberts, Jr. expressed the same sentiment as Harry Edwards had in 1992. Unlike the former professor, Judge Edwards, Justice Roberts made his remarks at a judicial conference rather than in print for a law journal. As had Edwards, Roberts suggested that the disconnect between the academy and the profession produces very little scholarship that is either helpful to the practicing bar or judges or influential on the development of law.[42] Indeed, Roberts stated he could not remember the last law review article he read.[43] Similarly, *The New York Times* critiqued law schools for producing cryptic, unhelpful, and, often, unread faculty scholarship despite the millions of dollars devoted to such work in law school budgets.[44] In the shadow of this outlay, law students often leave law school with little or no practical training.[45]

---

[39] Letter from Ephraim Gurney, Dean, Harvard University, to Charles Elliot, President, Harvard University *in* ARTHUR E. SUTHERLAND, THE LAW AT HARVARD: A HISTORY OF IDEAS AND MEN, 1817–1967, at 188–189 (1967) (alteration in original).

[40] Moliterno, *Legal Education, Experiential Education and Professional Responsibility*, 38, WILLIAM & MARY L. REV. 71, at 82–90 (1996).

[41] Harry T. Edwards, *The Growing Disjunction Between Legal Education and the Legal Profession*, 91 MICH. L. REV. 34 (1992); Harry T. Edwards, *The Growing Disjunction Between Legal Education and the Legal Profession: A Postscript*, 91 MICH. L. REV. 2191 (1993) (recounting the immediate "extraordinary" response).

[42] Chief Justice John G. Roberts, Jr., Remarks at Fourth Circuit Court of Appeals 77th Annual Conference at 30:30 (June 25, 2011), http://www.c-span.org/Events/Annual-Fourth-Circuit-Court-of-Appeals-Conference/10737422476-1/.

[43] *Id.* Roberts was, however, the only Justice who had not cited a law review article during the prior term. Kenneth Jost, *Roberts' Ill-Informed Attack on Legal Scholarship*, JOST ON JUSTICE (July 19, 2011, 10:56 AM), http://jostonjustice.blogspot.com/2011/07/roberts-ill-informed-attack-on-legal.html

[44] David Segal, *What They Don't Teach Law Students: Lawyering,* N.Y. TIMES, Nov. 19, 2011, at A1, *available at* http://www.nytimes.com/2011/11/20/business/after-law-school-associates-learn-to-be-lawyers.html.

[45] *Id.*

The economy that today's students face is highly discouraging. Everyone, except older lawyers opposing change for opposition's sake, and a majority of law professors who have a stake in the status quo, is demanding law schools do better. If ever there were a time for innovation in legal education, it is now.

One set of reforms taking hold addresses the market for legal education: increased transparency regarding employment prospects, varied accreditation standards, and less availability of government-guaranteed student loans. Will these measures cause some law schools to fail? Probably so. Some law schools are likely to fail as prospective students become less willing to pay $120,000 while foregoing income for an uncertain future. As the ABA belatedly unmasks deceptive employment statistics, all created in compliance with the ABA's former regime of reporting, prospective students will be less willing to mortgage their future to attend marginal law schools that offer little hope of remunerative employment upon graduation. When the Japanese installed U.S.-style graduate legal education in 2003, 80-plus new law schools sprang up. But the bar pass rate, always exceedingly low in Japan, did not increase anywhere near the proportion of the new law schools' output. Many law schools found themselves graduating entire classes of students, *none of whom* passed the bar. Thirty-plus of those 80-plus have closed. Not all of the remaining 50 or so are stable. In the United States, the difference between poor job prospects and supply of graduates is not as stark as the Japanese example, but when transparency comes, the public will learn that some law schools have single digit full-time employment rates at graduation. Some measure of failure will likely occur.

Some law schools are responding to the challenge and finding ways to tap private bar resources to help pay for the increased costs associated with smaller classes and more hands-on teaching methods.[46] Recruiting expert practitioners to teach practice-oriented courses at little or no cost to the law school can form a partnership between the practicing and teaching branches of the profession. Expert lawyers-functioning-as-teachers from significant law firms can, by this device, share the training once provided to their own beginning lawyers with all students who register for their course.

The future law graduate faces a world we did not envision in the 1980s, 1990s, and even the first half of the prior decade. But now, changes in the market for legal services have come, despite the organized profession's futile clinging to old forms. UPL restrictions must and will fall, especially but not exclusively as they relate to cross-border practice. Competition will be the driver of reform that the organized bar resists: competition from commoditization of law products, competition from UK firms armed with new corporate financing for global dominance. In such a new legal services market, fewer graduates will find high-figure paychecks being cut by employers. More graduates will be entrepreneurs.

---

[46] *Washington and Lee's New Third Year Reform*, Washington & Lee University School of Law, http://law.wlu.edu/thirdyear/ (last visited Aug. 8, 2012).

Law schools must reform, at long last, to generate law graduates better able to contribute to clients of law firms and to clients of their solo or small-firm entrepreneurial endeavors. Teaching one skill, legal analysis, as was done from the 1880s until the 1980s, is no longer enough, even for elite law schools that will be more delayed in reacting to change because of their market strength. Teaching the laundry basket of skills of the 1980s and 1990s (interviewing, negotiating, advocacy, writing), as critical as they are as a base, is no longer enough. Law schools must prepare students to contribute. To be positive members of teams. To understand how projects are managed. To be creative in their view not only of legal analysis but also of business, markets, needs of clients. Law schools must prepare some students to engage in sophisticated practice for higher paying clients, and others who will devise creative legal services delivery mechanisms for less-high-paying clients. To do so, students need to acquire the sensibilities of successful lawyers. They need to take ownership of client problems, be willing to be "out there" and not merely answer posed questions, and be able to solve problems with ingenuity and creativity.

There are those who would abolish the third year of the JD degree, and if it remained a mere extension of the first and second years, that might be wise. But rather than abandon the opportunity to education in the third year, legal education must produce value in the third year.

The most advantageous answer for this kind of education is sophisticated experiential education. For a century from the Harvard-led reforms of the 1880s, legal education taught one skill (or lawyer experience), that of formal analysis of law in the form of appellate decisions. The teaching of that necessary skill, largely through the magic that attends the first year of the JD curriculum, has and should be continued. With the dawn of clinics in the 1970s and 1980s, an attendant light was cast on the teaching of a basket of basic lawyer skills[47]: writing, interviewing and counseling clients, negotiation, advocacy. These skills, too, are necessary and must continue to be the staple of legal education they have become in the past 30 years. But more, far more, is needed in the range of skills and attributes provided by legal education. Adding to experiential education means more clinics, to be sure, and more now-traditional skills courses (legal writing, trial ad, negotiation etc.), but it means far more. The "far more" should come in the form of sophisticated, practice-setting sensitive simulation courses taught by a mixture of professors and expert practitioners. In these courses, students are urged to make the transition from student to lawyer. Students continue to learn law, but now do so as lawyers do, with a client's need as the driver, rather than as students do, with a three-hour exam as the driver. In such circumstances, students transition to the thought processes of lawyer-problem-solver and away from learning for no more reason than acquiring knowledge. This kind of third year can be a year with one foot in the academy and one in the practice. Far from exclusively skills courses, these courses develop habits

---

[47] The term "skills education" should be abandoned because its usual meaning has become too narrow and too pejorative in some circles.

of the lawyer's mind that are not developed in the traditional courses aimed at appellate legal analysis. This third year can be a kind of "mental pathways' transition time."

An economic transfer is taking place. Law firms formerly trained beginning lawyers in their specific firm ways, mainly by billing their hours to corporate clients. That system no longer exists. Now, law firms are demanding that law schools undertake more practical preparation.[48] Ironically, 30 or more years ago, major law firms preferred that law schools not so engage, fearing that law faculty would ruin otherwise trainable new associates. But the transfer is now taking place from corporate client/law firm expenditures to law school expenditures aimed at more expensive clinical and skills courses. The only way for this transfer to function well is for it to be incomplete: law schools must engage the low-cost, part-time faculty resources that are available to teach practice preparation. At some schools, this has long been the case for courses in, for example, trial advocacy and mediation skills. More effective still, would be elaborate simulation courses focused on particular practice settings and specialties. So, for example, courses like "The Lawyer for Failed Businesses" might replace or supplement a "Bankruptcy" course; a course called "Corporate Counsel" or "The Defense Lawyer" might do the same for courses in Corporate Law and Criminal Procedure. Depending on how the new courses were structured, they might replace the former course or add a layer of application to it. Attracting and welcoming this no- or low-cost contribution of excellent lawyers (often alumni) not only ameliorates cost but represents a more altruistic contribution of the practicing branch to the education enterprise. Rather than exclusively teaching their particular firm's newest members, they will be providing their expertise to any students who enroll in their course.[49]

B. REFORM INHIBITION CAUSED BY THE BAR EXAM

The bar exam has, in turn, made needed reforms in legal education more difficult. Each state tests a myriad of subjects beyond the core subjects tested on the Multistate Bar Exam and the Multistate Professional Responsibility Exam. Beyond restraining standard, modern practices with outmoded restrictions on cross-border practice, the standard form of the bar exam has also inhibited reforms in legal education. A typical law school requires 84 credits during the students' 3 academic years. Courses average 3 credits each, so a typical student takes about 28 courses. Some state bar exams test just as many subjects.

---

[48] *See, e.g.,* Massachusetts Bar Association Report, April 2012.

[49] This is no pipe dream as it is precisely what has occurred at Washington & Lee University School of Law. About 30 such new courses exist, half of which are taught by part-time faculty members who have, for practical measures, donated their time and are doing excellent work instructing their courses.

Virginia[50]	New York[51]	California[52]	Illinois[53]	Texas[54]	Pennsylvania[55]	Michigan[56]
Agency	Business Relationships including Agency, Business Corporations, Limited Liability Companies, Partnerships and Joint Ventures	Civil Procedure	Business Associations	Business associations, including agency, corporations, partnerships, limited liability companies and professional associations	Business Organizations (including corporations, partnerships, limited liability companies and professional corporations)	Real and Personal Property
Conflict of Laws		Community Property	Agency and Partnership			Wills and Trusts
Constitutional Law	Civil Practice and Procedure (New York, except as noted)	Constitutional Law	Corporations and Limited Liability Companies	Trusts and guardianships	Employment Discrimination (limited to Title VII, ADA and ADEA)	Contracts
Contracts		Contracts	Conflict of Laws	Wills and administration		Constitutional Law
Corporations	Conflict of Laws	Criminal Law and Procedure	Constitutional Law	Family law	Professional Responsibility	Criminal Law and Procedure
Creditor's Rights	New York and Federal Constitutional Law	Evidence	Contracts	Uniform Commercial Code	Civil Procedure (Pennsylvania and federal)	Corporations, Partnerships, and Agency
Criminal Law		Professional Responsibility	Criminal Law and Procedure	Consumer rights, including DTPA and insurance	Evidence (Pennsylvania and federal)	Evidence
Criminal Procedure	Contracts and Contract Remedies	Real Property	Evidence	Real property, including oil and gas	Real Property	Creditor's Rights, including mortgages, garnishments, and attachments
Domestic Relations		Remedies	Family Law	(2) Texas Real Property	Criminal Law (including related Pennsylvania and federal constitutional issues and DUI)	Practice and Procedure, trial and appellate, state and federal
Equity		Torts	Federal Civil Procedure	Oil and Gas		
Evidence		Trusts	Real Property	(2) Business Associations	Family Law	
Fed Practice & Procedure		Wills and Succession	Torts	(2) UCC	Torts	
Local Government Law				Articles 2 & 2A (Sales & Leases)		
Partnerships						
Personal Property						
Professional Responsibility						
Real Property						
Sales						
Suretyship						
Taxation						

Virginia[50]	New York[51]	California[52]		Texas[54]	Pennsylvania[55]	Michigan[56]
Torts	Criminal Law and Procedure	Trusts and Estates	Articles 3 & 4 (Payment Systems)	Conflict of Laws		Equity
Trusts	Evidence	Decedents' Estates	Article 9 (Secured Transactions)	Federal Constitutional Law		Torts (including no-fault)
Uniform Commercial Code	Matrimonial and Family Law	Trusts and Future Interests	(2) Family Law	U.C.C., Art. II—Sales		The sales, negotiable instruments, and secured transactions articles of the Uniform Commercial Code
VA Pleading, Practice & Procedure in Law & equity (including appellate practice)	Professional Responsibility	Uniform Commercial Code	(2) Wills & Estates	Contracts		
Wills & Estate Administration	Real Property	Negotiable Instruments and Bank Deposits and Collections	(1) Trusts or Guardianship	Federal Income Taxes (personal only and limited to taxable and non-taxable income, deductions, proprietorships and capital transactions)		Michigan Rules of Professional Conduct
	Torts and Tort Damages	Secured Transactions	(1) Consumer Law	Wills, Trusts and Decedents' Estates (including related fiduciary responsibilities)		Domestic Relations
	Trusts, Wills and Estates; and		Crossover Topics			Conflicts of Laws
	UCC Articles 2, 3 and 9		Bankruptcy			Worker's Compensation
			Federal Income Tax			

50 http://www.vbbe.state.va.us/pdf/VBBERules.pdf

51 www.nybarexam.org/Docs/CONTENT%20%28revised%20May%202010%%29.pdf

52 http://admissions.calbar.ca.gov/Portals/4/documents/gbx/Scopeoutlines.pdf

53 http://www.ncbex.org/assets/media_files/Information-Booklets/SMOs-from-MEEIB2012.pdf

54 http://www.ble.state.tx.us/Rules/NewRules/appendixA.htm; https://law.txwes.edu/CurrentStudents/PlanningYourCourseofStudy/AppendixAOverviewoftheTexasBarExam/tabid/1700/Default.aspx

55 http://www.pabarexam.org/bar_exam_information/testsubjects.htm

56 http://www.multistateedge.com/michigan-bar-exam.shtml

Other states follow these patterns. Insecure students have invested upwards of $150,000 in their legal education and will invest thousands more in bar prep courses. They understandably fear facing the bar exam without having taken as many of the tested subjects as possible during their three years of law school. This fear exists in inverse proportion to the status of the law school attended and the qualifications of the students. The further down the pecking order the law school, the more insecure are the students about facing the bar exam. So while elitism impedes reform at the highest ranked schools, fear of the bar exam impedes reform at the lowest ranked schools. (To be sure, other factors play significant roles as well, such as the ranking system itself and the inflexibility of the accreditation standards, both of which motivate all law schools to look as much as possible like Yale.) By pressuring students to be prepared for a dizzying number of subjects, the bar exam impedes reforms that would assist students in being prepared to practice law. Courses, or activities within courses, on writing, problem solving, project management, teamwork, business savvy, financial knowledge, and the like are not tested on the bar exam. So the official message sent is that they are not a concern of the organized bar. They simply do not play a role in the gatekeeping function. Instead the gate bears little relationship to what is beyond the gate. To the extent that it is impossible to adequately test this range of necessary lawyer attributes on a limited time exam, the bar exam itself should at least be structured so that legal education can afford to teach in these realms without penalizing students trying to pass an anachronistic bar exam. In that way, the law degree would signify some achievement in these critical areas.

Often justified for its "gatekeeper" function, protecting the public from incompetent lawyers, the profession has lost sight of the function of a gatekeeper. To be a rational gatekeeper, passage through the gate must be related to what is on the other side of the gate—in this instance, the practice of law. A macramé-skills exam would also keep many from passing through the gate, but there would be no confidence that those who passed could practice law. Purely testing knowledge of a wide array of topics fails to assure competence as well. The current typical bar exam tests too much and too little. The sheer number of substantive subjects tested and the absence of serious testing of the skills of law practice combine to make the bar exam a counterproductive exercise.

No lawyer knows all the law that would be useful to know. Lawyers should have a baseline level of knowledge of the core of legal subjects. Beyond that, every lawyer must know how to learn what is needed to serve his or her clients. I have met lots of lawyers in my 32 years since law school. So far I have never had a lawyer say that she solved a client's problem solely based on what she learned during a particular Tuesday afternoon session of the Torts or Contracts class. Client problems are more complex than that and almost always require some measure of synthesis of topics. No matter how many subjects we test, we will never ensure that every beginning lawyer knows all the law that would be useful to know. There is too much law, and it is too complex. The current bar exam is aimed at an unrealistic and unnecessary goal.

Aiming to meet an unnecessary and unattainable goal of instruction in all potentially useful subjects acts as a deterrent to law school reform. Simply no positive reason exists for the wide range of subjects. When law schools require more writing courses, more practice-oriented courses, more ethics courses, students and alums rationally ask: "But how will they pass the twenty-seven subjects tested on the Bar exam?" Students, depending on their level of insecurity, feel a need to fill up their schedules with as many bar courses as possible. Law schools feel a corresponding obligation to offer as many bar courses as possible. Ten subjects, including the MBE subjects, ethics, and state-specific procedure, would be more than sufficient to satisfy desires to make the exam a difficult, character-building rite of passage. Every subject tested beyond those incrementally diminishes the ability of law schools to reform their curricula to pay more attention to all the attributes law students should have when they undertake law practice.

In the justifiable clamor for law schools to require more courses that demand that students write, solve problems, learn business sense, project management and so on, the profession maintains a bar exam that frightens students into enrolling in as many of the 25+ bar subjects of the 28 courses they might typically take to earn their JD.

VI. If Not from Forward-looking Leadership, from Where Will Change Come?

Two other obvious sources of regulation and forced change outside the profession present themselves: government and competition. The former is especially resisted in the U.S. context while the latter has and will continue to force changes and regulatory reform on an unwelcoming profession.

Government has been the source of reform in the United Kingdom.[57] The so-called Tesco law, permitting non-lawyer ownership of law firms, was not initiated by the legal profession but by Parliamentary studies and action.[58] In the United States, arguably the most significant, single substantive change in the law governing lawyers of the past century was forced by government action.[59] The early 21st-century reduction in the scope of the duty of confidentiality that was signaled by

---

[57] For an excellent account of these reforms, *see* Christopher Whelan, *The Paradox of Professionalism: Global Law Practice Means Business*, 27 Penn St. Int. L. Rev. 465, 472–482 (2008).

[58] The Clementi Report; Legal Services Act of 2007.

[59] The only competitor for most significant single change came from the courts applying First Amendment principles, striking down the organized bar's near-blanket prohibitions on advertising. Bates v. Arizona Bar, 433 U.S. 350 (1977) (striking down near-blanket prohibitions on advertising); Goldfarb v. Virginia State Bar, 421 U.S. 773 (1975) (holding minimum fee schedules to be unlawful); Supreme Court of New Hampshire v. Piper, 470 U.S. 274 (1985) (striking down residency requirements); *In re* Griffiths, 413 U.S. 717 (1973) (striking down citizenship requiremenets).

amendments to Model Rules 1.6 and 1.13 was born not of professional preference or reform, but of the fallout and government action following the Enron defalcations. Nearly the same language, finally adopted by the ABA in 2003, was rejected in the 1980s during ABA consideration of the Kutak Commission proposals[60] and again in the Ethics 2000 proposals in 2002. When the reduction in duty of confidentiality was finally adopted in 2003, it was merely the play-out of a fait accompli set in motion by the Sarbanes-Oxley Act and the resultant SEC regulations. True, the SEC regulations governed only lawyers representing publicly traded corporations, but the government attention to what it regarded as a demonstrably flawed duty of confidentiality that allowed Enron's lawyers to keep secret their client's frauds essentially dictated the ABA action.[61] Even in this instance of regulation coming from government action, the ABA used a "saturation bombing attack" to stave off the originally proposed version of the SEC regulations that would have increased the obligations of lawyers to report up the ladder.[62]

Despite this major instance of government regulation forcing reform of the law governing lawyers, the mood for such regulation is far different in the United States from, for example, the United Kingdom, and certainly from typical civil law jurisdictions. The independence of the legal profession from government power, as is true for judicial independence as well, is far more pronounced in the United States than elsewhere. In most civil law jurisdictions, the legal profession is explicitly subject to a ministry of justice or its equivalent.[63] In the U.K., the legal profession

---

[60] CTR. FOR PROF'L RESPONSIBILITY, ABA, A LEGISLATIVE HISTORY: THE DEVELOPMENT OF THE ABA MODEL RULES OF PROFESSIONAL CONDUCT, 1982–2005 at 101 (2006).

[61] Thomas D. Morgan, *Toward Abandoning Organized Professionalism*, 30 HOFSTRA L. REV. 970 (2002) ("[T]he effect of competition on clients will have an inevitable impact on lawyers."). Morgan argues that ABA pronouncements are of decreased importance because policy justifications for a lawyer monopoly are losing their persuasiveness. Morgan argues lawyers have no unique claim to core lawyer values. Furthermore, lawyers' attempts to limit who clients may consult are doomed to fail due to market forces; CTR. FOR PROF'L RESPONSIBILITY, ABA, A LEGISLATIVE HISTORY: THE DEVELOPMENT OF THE ABA MODEL RULES OF PROFESSIONAL CONDUCT, 1982–2005 101, 118–119, 133–137, 291, 308 (ABA Center for Professional Responsibility, 2006).

[62] Robert W. Gordon, *A New Role for Lawyers?: The Corporate Counselor After Enron*, 35 CONN. L. REV. 1185 (2003), *reprinted in* ENRON CORPORATE FIASCOS AND THEIR IMPLICATIONS 571–623 (Nancy B. Rapoport & Bala G. Dharan eds., 2004). ("Prior to Sarbanes-Oxley, the corporate bar had long strenuously resisted adding an 'up the ladder' reporting requirement to its ethics rules; although, in the wake of the Enron scandal, and seeing the writing on the wall, and ABA Task Force actually did recommend this modest but important reform in 2002," p. 767. In December 2002, the SEC proposed rules that would put teeth into up-the-ladder reporting by requiring lawyers whose client's boards failed to take any action to make a "noisy withdrawal" from representing that client—that is, to inform the SEC that they were withdrawing for professional reasons," p. 767. "The ABA and many other bar organizations and law firms conducted a saturation bombing attack on the proposed rules and have succeeded, at least for the present, in getting the SEC to suspend the 'noisy withdrawal' rule, pending more comments.").

[63] *Justice in France*, MINISTERE DE LA JUSTICE (Apr. 26, 2011), http://www.justice.gouv.fr/multilinguisme-12198/english-12200/justice-in-france-22126.html. In France, the Civil Affairs and Seals Directorate, a subdivision of the Ministry of Justice, supervises the legal professions including lawyers.

has long been treated far more like any other business by the government.[64] In the United States, professional resistance to being treated like other businesses subject to government regulation is much more powerful.

> The very idea of the Senate of the United States enacting or directing others to enact rules of professional responsibility for lawyers should be enough to cause collective professional indigestion and indignation. A foundation of our independent profession is that our rules of professional conduct are promulgated by the states. Time and again, we have quite correctly resisted efforts to have the federal government usurp... the traditional role of regulating lawyers through the respective state Supreme Courts.... [T]here is no greater threat to lawyer independence than having anyone other than courts establish the lawyer rules for practice.[65]

In *Hishon v. King & Spaulding*,[66] an Issue Statement in the Supreme Court brief of King and Spaulding makes clear that one of its chief arguments against the applicability of race, religion, and gender discrimination laws to law firms was the fact that these laws are administered by a government agency, the EEOC:

> Whether Congress intended through Title VII of the Civil Rights Act of 1964 to give the Equal Employment Opportunity Commission, a politically appointed advocacy agency engaged in litigation, jurisdiction over invitations to join law firm partnerships.

When the Federal Trade Commission (FTC) preliminarily decided that lawyers should be covered by its regulations pursuant to the Gramm-Leach-Bliley Act of 1999,[67] the ABA responded quickly, requesting a lawyer exemption from the privacy-policy regulations.[68] Despite support from select members of Congress, the FTC declined to make the lawyer exemption. Lest the legal profession be regulated by a federal agency on this narrow topic, the ABA and the New York State Bar Association filed lawsuits in federal district court seeking to have the application of the FTC regulations to lawyers enjoined. Nineteen state and local bar associations

---

[64] *Welcome to the Legal Services Board*, LEGAL SERVICES BOARD, http://www.legalservices-board.org.uk/ (last visited Aug. 11, 2012). The new independent body responsible for overseeing the regulation of lawyers in England and Wales. Shares regulatory objectives with the Approved Regulators.*See, e.g.,* Legal Aid and Advice Act of 1949. This Act's propriety and wisdom was debated by U.S. lawyers on the pages of the ABA JOURNAL. Robert G. Storey, *The Legal Profession versus Regimentation: A Program to Counter Socialization*, 37 A.B.A. J. 100 (1951); Warren Freedman, *The Legal Profession and Socialization: A Reply to Dean Robert G. Storey*, 37 A.B.A. J. 333 (1951).

[65] LAWRENCE J. FOX, *The Academics Have It Wrong: Hysteria Is No Substitute for Sound Public Policy Analysis*, IN ENRON CORPORATE FIASCOES AND THEIR IMPLICATIONS 851, 866 (Nancy Rapoport & Bala Dharan eds., 2004).

[66] 467 U.S. 69 (1984).

[67] Pub. L. No. 106-102 (1999).

[68] *Govermental & Legislative Work*, ABA, Abanet.org/poladv/letters/privacy071001.html (last visited Aug. 18 2012).

filed amicus briefs with the court. The litigation succeeded, and lawyers were effectively exempted from the privacy obligations of the regulations.[69]

Similar protestations occurred as the SEC was drafting its regulations pursuant to the Sarbanes-Oxley Act.[70] As a government "opponent" in litigation, the SEC was seen as a biased, outside force in its efforts to generate lawyer regulation reform. Of course, the profession had its chances to implement its own such reforms but rejected them in the consideration of the Kutak Commission report in 1983[71] and again when Ethics 2000 proposed such reforms in 2002.[72] Government imposed its will on the profession, albeit in a watered-down fashion after heavy professional lobbying, regarding corporate counsel confidentiality only after repeated rejection of such reforms by the profession over a two-decade period.[73] The ABA's Ethics 2000 Commission had very recently sent the academic proponent of the eventual SEC regulation "packing"[74] less than a year before Sarbanes-Oxley section 307 ("eerily captioned 'Rules of Professional Responsibility for Lawyers'" as described by profession-opponent Fox)[75] was passed, triggering the SEC to adopt its regulations.

Beyond the independence shield to government regulation, lawyers have dominated legislative bodies to a far greater extent in the United States than elsewhere. In the late 1950s, two-thirds of the Senate seats and 56 percent of House seats were occupied by lawyers.[76] The lawyer-dominance in legislatures is on the decline but retains significance. In the early 1970s, 51 percent of Senate members were lawyers, compared to 37 percent in 2012. In the 1960s, 43 percent of U.S. House members were lawyers, compared to 24 percent in 2012.[77] This reality alone makes significant reform at the hands of government less likely and confined to narrow issues that present real electoral fallout for candidates, such as the Enron disaster.

In all likelihood, reform of the legal profession and the law governing lawyers in specific areas will continue to be the result of government imposition. But just as likely, in the United States, wide-ranging reforms like those represented by the United Kingdom. ABS innovations will be stymied by lawyer-dominated legislatures and well-organized professional resistance.

---

[69] New York State Bar Assoc. v. FTC, 276 F. Supp.2d 110 (S.D.N.Y. 2003).

[70] Fox, *supra* note 63.

[71] Ctr. for Prof'l Responsibility, ABA, A Legislative History: The Development of the ABA Model Rules of Professional Conduct, 1982–2005 100 (2006).

[72] *Id.* at 117–129.

[73] *Id.* at 291–314.

[74] Fox, *supra* note 63 at 864.

[75] *Id.* at 865.

[76] Ross Malone, *The Lawyer's Role in Promoting the Rule of Law*, 45 Marq. L. Rev. 3 (1959).

[77] Debra Cassens Weiss, *Fewer Prelaw Students Interested in Political Careers; Is Money the Reason?*, ABA Journal (Apr. 9, 2012, 6:00 AM), http://www.abajournal.com/news/article/fewer_prelaw_students_interested_in_political_careers_is_money_the_reason/.

Of course, all the assertions of self-governance and the relative silence of legislatures mask a reality about who or what actually governs lawyer's behavior.[78] Bar ethics rules and disciplinary processes are but one form, and likely not the most important form, of lawyer regulation "on the ground." In a lawyer's day-to-day life, he or she is more likely to be governed by a dizzying array of forces and factors. Malpractice liability, a creature of state law, governs lawyer conduct. Procedure and evidence rules, in the main adopted by courts, sometimes with an assist and influence by Congress or a state legislature, govern lawyer conduct.[79] Decisional law regulating prosecutorial misconduct governs some lawyers' conduct. Courts, state and federal, in the form of rulings on motions to disqualify, in the main now have responsibility for policing conflicts of interests. Even outside the realm of publicly made law, the private law of malpractice insurance carriers governs lawyer conduct. Malpractice carriers direct lawyers in their adoption of office procedures to ferret out conflicts of interest, to protect confidentiality, to supervision of non-lawyer staff, and many other matters. All of these and more lawyer control devices have advantages over bar discipline as a motivator of lawyer behavior. Malpractice liability is more attractive for claimants because they receive compensation. Violations of evidence and procedural law can have direct monetary consequences for the governed lawyer. Malpractice insurance carriers have a virtual monopoly on a necessary commodity for lawyers, and the carriers are powerfully motivated to regulate lawyer conduct to control their own level of risk.

Finally, of course, the market governs lawyer conduct and regulation as well. Competition is playing a greater role in reforming the legal profession than ever before. In the international sphere, UK law firms now have the prospect of tapping capital markets for expansion, especially into emerging global markets. U.S. law firms were slower than their UK counterparts to recognize and chase foreign markets for legal services. But that is changing and as it does, the need to compete will drive U.S. law firms to lobby the ABA and Congress for the opportunity to compete more effectively in global markets. Clearly, the organized profession will not on its own adopt U.K. or Australia-like ABS models. In one of its first actions, ABA Ethics 20/20 preemptively rejected any such changes taking place during its examination of "radical" changes of technology and globalization.[80]

Other sources of competition are forcing reforms in the delivery of legal services. Some of these reforms will force change in lawyer regulation as web-based providers cross borders and staffed-up GC offices clamor for the right to sell their services to their own corporate customers.

---

[78] David Wilkins, *Who Should Govern Lawyers*, 105 HARV. L. REV. 801 (1991); Fred. C. Zacharias, *The Myth of Self-Regulation*, 93 MINN. L. REV. 1147 (2009).

[79] Examples include the evidentiary privilege, mainly a creature of the common law with modest procedural rule modifications F.R.E. 501, 502, and frivolous claims rules such as F.R.C.P. 11 and its state law counterparts.

[80] ABA Commission on Ethics 20/20, Working Group on Alternative Business Structures, *For Comment: Issues Paper Concerning Alternative Business Structures* (April 5, 2011).

General Council offices are staffing up and changing their way of doing business with law firms.[81] Corporate procurement offices now manage the purchase of
legal services much as they have managed the purchase of paper clips, or in the
UK as they manage the purchase of "loo rolls."[82] Outsourcing of low-level legal
tasks has continued to grow, being utilized by both corporate clients and law firms
alike.[83] Large firm lawyers have moved out to form their own, leaner, small firms,
sometimes moving to the suburbs or to smaller markets to save rent and overhead
expenses, allowing them to compete for the corporate business against urban firms.[84]
Legalzoom[85] and other online providers including virtual law firms have entered the
market for service provision to small businesses and individuals. Private judging
websites such as legalfaceoff.com promote the opportunity to skip both lawyers and
courts when resolving modest-value disputes.

In a dramatically different form, the legal profession is being influenced and
changed by non-lawyers, in the form of corporate clients. Through their GCs, corporate clients are imposing behavior guidelines on their outside counsel in the form
of Outside Counsel Procedures.[86] These documents come in all sizes and shapes,
some quite modestly requiring outside counsel to behave ethically and others dictating employee policies at outside counsel, including diversity hiring, task-staffing
policies, and establishment of work/life balance and flextime policies. "Behaving
ethically" in this context itself means more than merely abiding by professional
norms. It includes maintaining whistleblower protection, engagement in the community, and other distinctively non-lawyer professional norms.[87]

---

[81] Jennifer Smith, *Law Firms Keep Squeezing Associates*, WALL ST. J. L.J. (Jan. 30, 2012) http://
online.wsj.com/article/SB10001424052970203363504577186913589594038.html.

[82] Christopher J. Whelan & Neta Ziv, *Privatizing Professionalism: Client Control of Lawyers'
Ethics*, 80 FORDHAM L. REV. 2577, 2586 (2012).

[83] Christopher J. Whelan & Neta Ziv, *Privatizing Professionalism: Client Control of Lawyers' Ethics*,
80 FORDHAM L. REV. 2577 (2012); Debra Cassens Weiss, *Nixon Peabody Isn't Shy About Its Hiring of
an Outsourcing Company*, ABA JOURNAL (Jan. 31, 2012, 9:20 AM), http://www.abajournal.com/news/
article/nixon_peabody_isnt_shy_about_its_hiring_of_an_outsourcing_company/.

[84] Clark Baird Smith LLP, Press Release of September 1, 2010 (on file with author).

[85] LEGALZOOM, http://www.legalzoom.com/ (last visited Aug. 11, 2012). Identified as one of
the most innovative new companies. *See* David Lidsky, *For Bringing Tech and Accessibility to the
Hidebound Legal Industry*, FASTCOMPANY, http://www.fastcompany.com/most-innovative-compa-
nies/2012/legalzoom (last visited Aug. 11, 2012). And they were accused of unauthorized practice
by various state bars *See* http://www1.ctbar.org/sectionsandcommittees/committees/UPL/08-01.
pdf; http://greatestamericanlawyer.typepad.com/ncapccd4.pdf; Nathan Koppel, *Seller of Online
Legal Forms Settles Unauthorized Practice of Law Suit*, WSJ BLOGS (Aug. 23, 2011, 11:47 AM),
http://blogs.wsj.com/law/2011/08/23/seller-of-online-legal-forms-settles-unauthorized-practiced-
of-law-suit/. And, among others, patent lawyers. *See* Gene Quinn, *LegalZoom Sued in Class
Action for Unauthorized Law Practice*, IPWATCHDOG, http://www.ipwatchdog.com/2010/02/09/
legalzoom-sued-in-class-action-for-unauthorized-law-practice/id=8816/ (last visited Aug. 11,
2012). Also fought over by states wishing to bring in LegalZoom staff jobs. *See* Press Release,
Gov. Perry, LegalZoom to Move Up To 600 Jobs to Austin, TX, IPWATCHDOG (Feb. 19, 2010,
3:11 PM), http://www.ipwatchdog.com/2010/02/19/legalzoom-to-move-600-jobs-to-tx/id=9176/.

[86] *See generally*, Christopher J. Whelan & Neta Ziv, *Privatizing Professionalism: Client Control
of Lawyers' Ethics*, 80 FORDHAM L. REV. 2577 (2012).

[87] *Id.* at 2589 (citing Apple Outside Counsel policy).

This private reform of the legal profession is simply driven by contract, although at present, the legal services buyer's market dictates that corporate clients need do little if any negotiating over the terms of their outside counsel ("OC") policies. A turn in economic times could alter the bargaining positions of major law firms vis-à-vis their corporate clients, but the OC policies are here to stay, even if they become somewhat modified by future economic realities.

A rather twisted explanation of the OC policy phenomenon could claim it to be self-governance in a new form. After all, the drafters and main enforcers of the OC policy are lawyers, GCs. Not bar authorities to be sure, but lawyers nonetheless. Courts are not bar associations either, but they are essentially lawyers governing lawyers, and court regulation has been the core of the profession's claim of self-governance. But of course this argument is twisted: the GCs are not lawyers governing lawyers. They are doing their corporate employers' bidding and not attempting to impose professional norms on their outside counsel brothers and sisters. This is private ordering, pure and simple, and cannot be characterized as self-regulation.

In a fashion, this phenomenon is like the practice of insurance carriers providing guidelines for counsel engaged to represent their insured.[88] But the OC policy phenomenon is much more: both endeavor to influence counsel's staffing, use of electronic resources, and other expenses. But the OC policies go far beyond imposing internal policies on outside law firms, employment policies, environmental policies, and community engagement policies. And OC policies are imposed by the client. Insurance carrier guidelines, though heavily influential on insurance defense lawyers, must always remain in the form of "guidelines" because they come not from the insured client but from a third party paying for the legal services.

OC policies even go so far as to create new norms in traditional areas of professional regulation. Conflict "rules," as imposed on retained outside counsel expand to preclude engagements with other clients at the preference of the client. Coke, for example, might require its outside counsel to refrain from representing Pepsi, when the bar ethics rules would have nothing to say about it.[89]

VII. In the End, Change Comes. Always.

In the end, change always comes. At the same time as the profession was trying to turn back the civil rights clock, John Kennedy was looking ahead: "[T]ime and the world do not stand still. Change is the law of life. And those who look only to the past or present are certain to miss the future."[90] The legal profession has no choice

---

[88] *See* Pfeiffer v. Sentry Insurance, 745 F.Supp. 1434 (E.D. Wis. 1990).

[89] Whelan, *supra* note 84 at 2591.

[90] The full quote is as follows: "And our liberty, too, is endangered if we pause for the passing moment, if we rest on our achievements, if we resist the pace of progress. For time and the world do not stand still. Change is the law of life. And those who look only to the past or the present are certain to miss the future." (Address in the Assembly Hall at Paulskirche in Frankfurt. June 25, 1963).

about whether change will come or not. The legal profession's choice is whether or not to be engaged in the process of change or to have change imposed by forces of competition, government, technology, culture, and economics. Turning to creative non-lawyers presents the most advantageous way for the legal profession to grow and change on its own terms. Creative non-lawyers can predict and manage change that is likely to result from competitive forces. In the United States, changes made by the profession itself are highly likely to dampen pressure for change dictated by government. In the absence of self-reform, change will be effected either by government or the forces of competition.

A future of claimed self-regulation without the input of creative non-lawyers will be no self-regulation at all. Instead it will be regulation that results from competitive forces and government. The American legal profession can no longer stand on its claims to special status among businesses and pseudo-self-regulation. It can no longer act as if the world will somehow return to the late 19th century.

The need for non-lawyers is now critical. For one, fleeting moment of admirable humility and clear vision in 1989, the profession flirted with the notion of needing outsiders to help solve its problems. "The legal profession alone cannot solve its own problems, the problems of the justice system or those of the communities it serves."[91] The moment was fleeting, as little action followed realization. So there is hope, however small, that the legal profession has the capacity, somewhere, to see outside itself.

But if it cannot humble itself to look outside its walls for help, it will find itself as whatever change created by technology, competition, globalization, and government leave behind. It will have lost, finally, whatever vestige and claim of self-governance remains.

I, for one, do not lament the prospect of a future legal profession that would be absent lawyers exclusively regulating lawyers. Some would say it has never actually been so. Certainly it has not been so since forces of governance for lawyers beyond bar discipline have been recognized. To the extent it has ever been genuine self-regulation, the profession has failed repeatedly. No time remains for exclusively looking inward and backward. Change has come and will again. Unless the profession changes its change-game, it will do as it has always done and be washed over and passed by with every major development.

---

[91] *ABA Taskforce on Outreach to the Public*, 1988–89, 114 Ann. Rep. A.B.A. at 88.

{ INDEX }